"A really excellent introduction to philosophy does the following: meets the student at their level, then takes them up a notch, and approaches traditional topics in unique and interesting ways. This book does those things."

Fred Adams, *University of Delaware, USA*

Core Questions in Philosophy

Writing in an engaging lecture-style format, Elliott Sober shows students how philosophy is best used to evaluate many different kinds of arguments and to construct sound theories. Well-known historical texts are discussed, not as a means to honor the dead or merely to discuss what various philosophers have thought, but to engage with, criticize, and even improve ideas from the past. In addition—because philosophy cannot function apart from its engagement with the wider society—traditional and contemporary philosophical problems are brought into dialogue with the physical, biological, and social sciences. Text boxes highlight key concepts, and review questions, discussion questions, and a glossary of terms are also included.

Core Questions in Philosophy has served as a premier introductory textbook for more than two decades, with updates to each new edition. New improvements to this seventh edition include a lower price and a new Routledge companion website that includes:

- Updated supplementary readings, with the inclusion of more work from female philosophers
- New videos and podcasts, organized by their relevance to each chapter in the book.

Visit the companion website at: www.routledge.com/cw/sober

Elliott Sober is Hans Reichenbach Professor and William F. Vilas Research Professor in the Philosophy Department at the University of Wisconsin–Madison, USA. His most recent book is *The Design Argument* (2018).

Core Questions in Philosophy

Seventh Edition

Elliott Sober

Routledge
Taylor & Francis Group

NEW YORK AND LONDON

Seventh edition published 2020
by Routledge
52 Vanderbilt Avenue, New York, NY 10017

and by Routledge
2 Park Square, Milton Park, Abingdon, Oxon, OX14 4RN

Routledge is an imprint of the Taylor & Francis Group, an informa business

First edition published by Prentice Hall 1991

Sixth edition published by Pearson Education Inc. 2013

Library of Congress Cataloging-in-Publication Data
A catalog record has been requested for this book

ISBN: 978-1-138-48735-2 (hbk)
ISBN: 978-1-138-48733-8 (pbk)
ISBN: 978-1-351-04340-3 (ebk)

Typeset in Bembo
by Wearset Ltd, Boldon, Tyne and Wear

Visit the companion website: www.routledge.com/cw/sober

For Aaron

Contents

5 The Design Argument   54

6 Evolution and Creationism   62

21 Methodological Behaviorism   192

22 The Mind/Brain Identity Theory   200

23 Functionalism   206

30 Observation and Explanation in Ethics   266

31 Conventionalist Theories   275

Boxes

Preface

The philosophical problems investigated in this book concern fundamental facts about our place in the universe. Many of us were brought up to believe that God exists, that there is a real difference between right and wrong, that we can freely choose what sort of lives to lead, and that it is possible for us to gain knowledge of the world we inhabit. A major goal of philosophy is to discover whether these opinions can be rationally defended or are just comfortable illusions.

Core Questions in Philosophy emphasizes the idea that philosophy is a subject devoted to *evaluating arguments* and *constructing theories*. This is not the same as describing the history of what various philosophers have thought. Although I discuss historical texts, I do so because they are rich sources of ideas pertinent to answering philosophical questions. The point is not to say solemn and respectful words about worthy figures now dead, but to engage them in dialogue—to grapple with the theories they have proposed, to criticize these theories, even to improve upon them.

Besides proposing answers to philosophical questions, I also try to make clear which questions I have *not* answered. I hope that the reader will approach what I say the way I have approached the philosophical texts I discuss. This is a book to argue with, to dissect. It isn't my goal to have the reader accept without question the conclusions I reach.

The chapters are intended to flow together, so that the main areas covered—philosophy of religion, epistemology, philosophy of mind, and ethics—are connected to each other to make a coherent whole. The chapters I wrote are intended to be *launching pads* from which readers can pursue issues on their own. I believe students are best able to think about philosophy if they are first provided with some basic tools and concepts. It is the purpose of the chapters to provide these *core ideas*.

Each chapter is followed by review questions and problems for further thought. These should help readers to consolidate their understanding of what I have said, and to think creatively about related problems. The chapters often contain material in boxes; these boxes provide, in a nutshell, a restatement of an important idea or a brief discussion of a related matter that may interest the reader. A list of the boxes immediately follows the table of contents. Each main part of the book includes suggestions for further reading. There is also a glossary at the end of the book that provides simple definitions of the main concepts used.

Besides discussing a number of traditional topics, this book also takes up some contemporary theories and problems, both from philosophy and from other disciplines. Creationism and evolutionary theory are hotly debated now. The issues they raise are continuous with a tradition of argument in philosophy of religion that goes back (at least) to Aquinas, Hume, and Paley. The relation of mind and body is a philosophical problem of long standing, but the ideas of Freud and Skinner get a hearing along with those of Descartes. In ethics, there has long been a debate as to whether ethical truths are discovered or created.

Plato and Sartre are separated by more than two thousand years, but both speak to this issue. The problem of free will raises the question of whether every event is caused. Here, the contribution of modern physics must be brought into contact with a perennial problem of philosophy. Philosophy isn't the same as biology, psychology, or physics, but the problems of philosophy cannot be isolated from the sciences. One aim of this book is to connect philosophical problems with ideas derived from a wider culture.

The etymology of the word *philosopher* is *lover of wisdom*. This doesn't guarantee that all philosophers are wise, nor even that each individual philosopher is devoted to the attainment of wisdom. Philosophers *should* strive for wisdom; whether they do so, and whether they attain it, are separate questions. Wisdom involves understanding—seeing how things fit together. When the pieces of a puzzle are fitted together, one attains a sense of wholeness. Current philosophy is embedded in a historical tradition of philosophical discourse. It also is connected to problems in the sciences, the other humanities, and the arts. This book aims to give the reader a sense of these multiple connections.

Elliott Sober
University of Wisconsin–Madison

Acknowledgments

My debts to colleagues in philosophy at University of Wisconsin, Madison, are enormous. A fixed point in my work week has been discussions of the ideas and techniques that go into presenting central problems of philosophy to new students. My philosophical outlook, as well as the view I have of teaching, have been shaped by these conversations.

It is a pleasure to thank Michael Byrd, Claudia Card, Fred Dretske, Ellery Eells, Berent Enç, Malcolm Forster, Martha Gibson, Paula Gottlieb, Daniel Hausman, Andy Levine, Steve Nadler, Terry Penner, Mark Singer, Dennis Stampe, Daniel Wikler, and Keith Yandell. They were generous enough to suffer my trespasses onto philosophical terrain that belonged more to them than to me. Some read parts of this book and gave me comments; others listened patiently while I tried out what I thought was a new angle.

The first six editions of *Core Questions in Philosophy* elicited a steady stream of correspondence and phone calls from teachers of philosophy and their students. These took a variety of forms; there was praise and blame, suggestions on how to do better, and even a few not-so-gentle suggestions that I should turn my attention to other projects. On the whole, though, I was happy with what I heard, though this didn't mean that I felt that I should leave the book unchanged. I thank everyone who took the trouble to let me know what they thought. Most (but not all) will find evidence that I listened to what they said in the way this edition differs from the ones before.

Deserving of special mention are Richard Behling, Keith Butler, John Carpenter, William R. Carter, Paul Christopher, Hayley Clatterbuck, Robert Cummins, Katie Deaven, Stewart Eskew, Doug Frame, Phil Gasper, Ronald Glass, Richard Hanley, Casey Hart, John Hines, Burton Hurdle, Paul Kelly, Charles Kielkopf, John Koolage, Gregory Mougin, Bradley Monton, Margaret Moore, William Russell Payne, Howard Prospersel, David Ring, Roy Sorensen, Reuben Stern, Naftali Weinberger, Whilhelm S. Wurzer, Stephen Wykstra, and Joel Velasco. The help they provided was extremely valuable. I also must thank the anonymous readers of previous editions of this textbook for their valuable suggestions. I thank Sera Schwartz for her excellent work expanding the review questions found at the end of each chapter and updating the recommendations for supplementary readings, video, and audio, found on the companion website.

Writing an introduction to philosophy is a challenge. The challenge is to reconstruct what a problem or idea would sound like to someone who hasn't studied the subject before. The project requires that one return to the beginning—to the fundamentals of the subject. I hope what I found by beginning again will be useful to those who are beginning for the first time.

Routledge Companion Website

Provided with this text is a Routledge companion website.

Please visit at: www.routledge.com/cw/sober

Features available include:

- **Reading recommendations:** Reading suggestions for each chapter, comprising books, journal articles, encyclopedias, and blogs. These readings allow students to gain further understanding of the topics discussed in each chapter. Many of the readings are available to read for free online.
- **Recommended listening suggestions:** Links to free-to-listen podcasts and other audio recordings for most chapters, supporting learning.
- **Recommended watching suggestions:** Links to free-to-watch videos for most chapters, supporting learning.
- **Flashcard bank:** A collection of interactive flashcards to support the learning of key terminology.

Part I

Introduction

Chapter 1

What Is Philosophy?

When asked "do you have a philosophy?" most people say "yes," but what do they mean? They usually have in mind a set of beliefs that they admit are difficult to prove are true, but that nonetheless are important to the way they think of themselves and the world they inhabit. Sometimes people describe their philosophies by saying what they think makes an action right or wrong. The statement "it's part of my philosophy that people should help each other" might be an example. A person's philosophy might include the fundamental ethical principles he or she believes. But people often have more than *ethics* in mind when they talk about their philosophies. A religious person might say that it is part of his or her philosophy that God exists; an atheist might say that it is part of his or her philosophy that there is no God and that there is no life after death. These propositions are important to the people who believe them. They describe what exists; philosophers would say that they are part of *metaphysics*, not ethics. Metaphysics is the part of philosophy that attempts to describe, in very general terms, what there is.

If everyday people think of their philosophies as the important beliefs they have that are difficult to prove, how does this idea of philosophy relate to how philosophers understand their own subject? Sometimes a term is used in ordinary talk in a way that differs dramatically from the way it is used by specialists. People sometimes say that tomatoes are vegetables, but a botanist will tell you that tomatoes are fruits. Every day people say they are concerned about "ecology," but biologists understand "ecology" in a very different way. Perhaps philosophers use the term "philosophy" in a way that departs fundamentally from what ordinary people mean when they say that they have a philosophy.

To gain a better purchase on what philosophy is, I'm going to discuss the question of what is distinctive about philosophy from two angles. First, I'll sketch some of the main philosophical problems that I'll examine in this book. That is, I'll describe some *examples* of philosophy. But giving examples doesn't really answer the question of what philosophy is. If you asked, "What is a mammal?" and I showed you a human being, a hippo, and a cat, these examples might give you a *hint* about what a mammal is. However, citing examples isn't the same as saying what it is to be a mammal. That is why there will be a second stage to my discussion of what philosophy is. After giving some examples of philosophical problems, I'll present some theories about what philosophy is. I believe these theories have merit, though I admit none is entirely adequate.

Examples

The first philosophical problem we'll consider in this book is whether God exists. Some philosophers have constructed arguments that attempt to establish that God exists, others have tried to show there is no God, and still others think that the question can't really be answered. I'll evaluate some of the more influential arguments and try to see whether they work.

The second problem we will consider concerns knowledge. It is pretty clear that belief and knowledge are different. Long ago some people thought that the earth is flat. They *believed* this, but they didn't know it, since it isn't true. Of course, they *thought* they knew it, but that's different. It is also pretty clear that true belief isn't the same as knowledge. If you believe something for no reason at all, but happen to be right by accident, you have true belief but not knowledge. For example, think of a gullible gambler at a racetrack who believes for no good reason that the first horse in every race will win. Occasionally this person will be right—he will have a true belief. But it isn't plausible to say that he knew, on those races about which he turned out to be right, which horse would win. So having knowledge involves something more than having a true belief.

The philosophical problem about knowledge will split into two parts. First, there are the questions: What is knowledge? What makes knowledge different from true belief? Second, there is the question: Do human beings ever know anything? One philosophical position we will consider answers this last question in the negative. Sure, we have beliefs. And granted, some of our beliefs turn out to be true. Knowledge, however, we never have. We don't even know those things that we take to be most obvious. This position is called *philosophical skepticism*. We will consider arguments for skepticism and arguments that attempt to refute it.

The third philosophical subject that will be addressed in this book consists of a collection of topics from the philosophy of mind. The first of these is the so-called mind/body problem. You have a mind; you also have a brain. What is the relationship between these items? One possible answer is that they are identical. Although "mind" and "brain" are different words, they name the same thing, just like the names "Superman" and "Clark Kent." An alternative position in this area is called *dualism*; it says that the mind and the brain are different things. We will consider other theories that have been advanced about the mind/body problem as well.

Another topic from the philosophy of mind that we'll address concerns human freedom. Each of us has the personalities we have because we inherited a set of genes from our parents and then grew up in a sequence of environments. Genes plus environments make us the sorts of people we are. We didn't choose the genes we have, nor did we choose the environments we experienced in early life. These were thrust upon us from the outside. Each of us performs certain actions and abstains from performing others. This pattern of what we do and don't do results from the personalities we have. Can we be said to perform actions freely? Is it really in our control to perform some actions and abstain from others? Perhaps the fact that our actions are the results of factors outside our control (our genes and our early environment) shows that it is a mistake to say that we freely choose what we do.

Of course, we talk in everyday life about people doing things "of their own free will." We also think of ourselves as facing real choices, as exercising control over what we do. However, the philosophical problem of freedom asks whether this common way of thinking is really defensible. Maybe freedom is just an illusion. Perhaps we tell ourselves a fairy tale about our own freedom because we can't face the fact that we aren't free. The philosophical problem will be to see whether we can be free agents if our personalities are the results of factors outside our control.

The last problem area we will address is ethics. In everyday life, we frequently think that some actions are right and others are wrong. The philosophical problem about this familiar attitude divides into two parts. First, we'll consider whether there really are such things as ethical facts. Maybe talk about ethics, like talk about freedom, is just an elaborate illusion. Consider a parallel question about science. In every science, there are questions that are controversial. For example, physicists have different opinions about how the solar system began. But most of us think that there is something else to physics besides opinions. There are facts about what the world is really like.

Clashes of opinion occur in what I'll call the *subjective realm*. Here we find one human mind disagreeing with another. But facts about physics exist in the *objective realm*. Those facts exist independently of anybody's thinking about them. They are out there, and science aims to discover what they are. In science, there are both subjective opinions and objective facts—people have beliefs, but there also exists, independently of what anyone believes, a set of facts concerning the way the world really is. The question about ethics is whether both these realms (subjective and objective) exist in ethics, or only one of them does. We know that people have different ethical opinions. The question is whether, in addition to those opinions, there are ethical facts. In other words, does ethics parallel the description I've just given of science, or is there a fundamental difference here? The accompanying two-by-two table illustrates this question. *Ethical subjectivism* is the philosophical thesis that there are no ethical facts, only ethical opinions. According to this position, the claim that "murder is always wrong" and the claim that "murder is sometimes permissible" are *both* misguided—there are no facts about the ethics of murder for us to have opinions about. We'll consider arguments supporting and criticizing this position.

	Subjective Realm	*Objective Realm*
Science	Scientific opinions	Scientific facts
Ethics	Ethical opinions	Ethical facts?

The second question that arises in ethics is this: If there are ethical facts, what are they? Here we assume a positive answer to the first question and then press for more details. One theory we'll consider is *utilitarianism*, which says that the action you should perform in a given situation is the one that will produce the greatest happiness for the greatest number of individuals. This may sound like common sense, but I'll argue that there are some serious problems with this ethical theory.

Three Theories about What Philosophy Is

I've just described a menu of four central philosophical problems: God, knowledge, mind, and ethics. What makes them all *philosophical* problems? Instead of giving examples, can we say something more general and complete about what distinguishes philosophy from other areas of inquiry? I'll offer three theories about what is characteristic of at least some philosophical problems.

Several of the problems just described involve *fundamental questions of justification*. There are many things that we believe without hesitation or reflection. These beliefs that are second nature to us are sometimes called "common sense." Common sense says that the sense experiences we have (via sight, hearing, touch, taste, and smell) provide each of us with knowledge of the world we inhabit. Common sense also says that people often act "of their own free will," and common sense holds that some actions are right while others are wrong. Philosophy examines the fundamental assumptions we make about ourselves and the world we inhabit and tries to determine whether those assumptions are rationally defensible.

Another characteristic of many philosophical questions is that they are very *general*; often they're more general than the questions investigated in specific sciences. Physicists have asked whether there are electrons; biologists have investigated whether genes exist; geologists have sought to find out whether the continents rest on movable plates. However, none of these sciences really bother with the question of why we should think that physical objects exist. The various sciences simply *assume* that there are things outside the mind; they then focus on more specific questions about what those things are like. In contrast, it is a characteristically philosophical question to ask why you should believe that there is anything at all outside your mind. The idea that your mind is the only thing that exists is called *solipsism*. Philosophers have addressed the question of whether solipsism is true. This is a far more general question than the question of whether electrons, genes, or continental plates exist.

The third view of what philosophy is says that philosophy is the enterprise of *clarifying concepts*. Consider some characteristic philosophical questions: What is knowledge? What is freedom? What is justice? Each of these concepts applies to some things but not to others. What do the things falling under a concept have in common, and how do they differ from the things to which the concept does not apply?

We must be careful here, since many questions that aren't especially philosophical sound like the examples just given. Consider some characteristic scientific questions: What is photosynthesis? What is acidity? What is an electron? How does the first batch of questions differ from these? One difference between these questions concerns the ways in which *reason* and *observation* help answer them. You probably are aware that philosophy courses don't include laboratory sections. Philosophers usually don't perform experiments as part of their inquiries. Yet, in many sciences (though not in all), laboratory observation is central. This doesn't mean that observation plays no role in philosophy. Many of the philosophical arguments we will consider begin by making an observation. For example, in Chapter 5, I'll consider an argument for the existence of God that begins with the following assertion: Organisms are complicated things that are remarkably well adapted to the environments they inhabit. The thing to notice here is that this fact is something we know by observation. So philosophers, as well as scientists, do rely on observations.

Nonetheless, there is something distinctive about how observations figure in a philosophical inquiry. Usually the observations that are used in a philosophical theory are familiar and obvious to everyone. A philosopher will try to show by reasoning that those observations lead to some rather surprising conclusions. That is, although philosophy involves both observation and reasoning, it is the latter that in some sense does more of the work. As you will see in what follows, philosophical disputes often involve disagreements about reasoning; rarely are such disputes decidable by making an observation.

Each of these ways of understanding what philosophy is should be taken with a grain of salt (or perhaps with two). I think there is something to be said for each, even though each is somewhat simplified and distorting.

The Nature of Philosophy Has Changed Historically

One thing that makes it difficult to define "what philosophy is" is that the subject has been around at least since the ancient Greeks and has changed a great deal. There are many problems that are just as central to philosophy now as they were to the ancient Greeks, but there are other problems that have broken away from philosophy and now are thought of as purely scientific.

For example, ancient Greek philosophers discussed what the basic constituents of physical things are. Thales (who lived around 580 B.C.E.) thought that everything is made of water; many other theories were discussed as well. Now such questions are thought to be part of physics, not philosophy. Similarly, until the end of the nineteenth century, universities put philosophy and psychology together in the same academic department. It is only recently that the two subjects have been thought of as separate. Scientists in the seventeenth century—for example, Isaac Newton—used the term "natural philosophy" to refer to what we now think of as science. The term "scientist" was invented in the nineteenth century by the British philosopher William Whewell. The idea that philosophy and science are separate subjects may seem clear to us now, but the separation we now find natural was not so obvious in the past. Many of the problems that we now regard as philosophical are problems that have not broken away from philosophy and found their way into the sciences. Perhaps there are problems now taken to be philosophical that future generations won't regard as such. The shifting historical nature of what counts as philosophy makes it difficult to say anything very precise about what that subject is.

Philosophical Method

Having tried to say something about what philosophy is, I now want to say something about what philosophy is *not* (at least not in this book). You may have the impression that doing philosophy involves lying under a tree, staring up at the sky, and making deep and mysterious pronouncements off the top of your head that sound very important but that are hard to make sense of when you try to think about them clearly. I'll call this the *mystical guru model* of philosophy. Your experience reading this book won't correspond to this impression.

There is, however, another experience you've probably had that comes closer. If you took a high school geometry course, you'll remember proving theorems from axioms. If your geometry course was like the one I had, the axioms were given to you with very little explanation of why you should believe them. Maybe they looked pretty obvious to you, and so you didn't wonder very much about their plausibility. Anyhow, the main task was to use the axioms to prove theorems. You started with the axioms as assumptions and then showed that if they are true, other statements must be true as well.

Philosophers tend to talk about "arguments" rather than "proofs." The goal is to try to reach answers to important philosophical questions by reasoning correctly from assumptions that are plausible. For example, in Chapter 4, I'll examine some attempts to prove that God exists. The idea here is to start with assumptions that practically anybody would grant are true and then show that these assumptions lead to the conclusion that there is a God. This resembles what you may have done in geometry: Starting with simple and supposedly obvious assumptions, you were able to establish something less obvious and more complex—for example, that the sum of the angles of a triangle equals two right angles (180°).

Sometimes the philosophical questions we'll consider will strike you as difficult, deep, even mysterious. I won't shy away from such questions. I'll try, however, to address them with clarity and precision. The goal is to take hard questions and deal with them clearly, which, I emphasize, should never involve trying to pull the wool over someone's eyes by making deep-sounding pronouncements that mean who-knows-what.

Summary

I began this chapter by describing how every day people use the term "philosophy." In fact, their usage is not so distant from what philosophers mean by the term. Philosophy *does* address the most fundamental beliefs we have about ourselves and the world we inhabit. Precisely because these assumptions are so central to the way we think and act, it is difficult to step back for a moment from these assumptions and examine them critically. The French have an expression: "the most difficult thing for a fish to see is water." Some assumptions are so natural and seemingly obvious that it is hard to see that we are making assumptions at all. Philosophy is the effort to help us identify these assumptions and evaluate them. Each of us *does* have a philosophy. What divides some people from others is their willingness to ask probing questions about what they believe and why. This is what philosophy as a discipline tries to add to the philosophies that each of us carries with us through our lives.

Review Questions

1   What is the difference between objective and subjective?
2   If you want to say what philosophy is, why isn't it enough to list some examples of philosophical problems?
3   What is the difference, if any, between "having a philosophy" and "doing philosophy"?
4   How do disagreements in reasoning differ from disagreements about observations? How do you think such disagreements are typically resolved?

A Problem for Further Thought

Which of the ideas presented here about what philosophy is also apply to mathematics? Which do not?

Recommended Readings, Video, and Audio

Visit the companion website at www.routledge.com/cw/sober for suggestions of readings, video, and audio, for this chapter.

Chapter 2

Deductive Arguments

Philosophy involves constructing and evaluating arguments. In this respect, philosophy is no different from any other rational activity—mathematicians do this, as do economists, physicists, and people in everyday life. The distinctive thing about philosophy isn't that philosophers construct and evaluate arguments; what is distinctive is the kinds of questions those arguments aim to answer. In the previous chapter, I talked about what makes a question philosophical. The goal in this chapter is to develop some techniques that can be used to tell whether an argument is good or bad.

Arguments

An argument divides into two parts: the premises and the conclusion. The premises and the conclusion are statements; each is expressed by a declarative sentence. Each is either true or false. When people argue that a given statement is true, they try to provide reasons for thinking this. The reasons are the premises of their argument; premises are assumptions. The statement to be established is the argument's conclusion.

In high school geometry, you talked about axioms and theorems. Axioms are assumptions (premises); the theorem (the conclusion) is what is supposed to follow from those assumptions. In geometry you may have spent little or no time asking whether the axioms are true. Not so for the philosophical arguments I discuss in this book. We'll want to see whether the premises are plausible. We'll also want to see whether the premises, if they were true, would provide a reason for thinking the conclusion is true as well. I'll pose these two questions again and again.

Good Arguments

I now want to talk about different kinds of "good arguments." What does "good" mean? A good argument is *rationally persuasive*; it gives you a substantial reason to think the conclusion is true. Advertisers and politicians sometimes use arguments that trick people into believing what they say. These arguments sometimes persuade people, but they don't always provide *good* reasons.

A good argument should have true premises; if the premises are false, how could they give you good reasons to believe the conclusion? But more is required than this. In the following argument, the premise is true, but it doesn't provide you a good reason to think that the conclusion is true:

> Grass is green
> ——————————
> Roses are red

What is wrong here is that the premises are irrelevant to the conclusion. A good argument should contain true premises, but it should also cite premises that are related in the right way to the conclusion. The truth of the premises should give you a reason to think that the conclusion is true. The three types of "good argument" that I'll now describe differ in what relationship their premises and conclusions have to each other.

Good arguments can be divided into two categories, and one of those categories can be divided into two more:

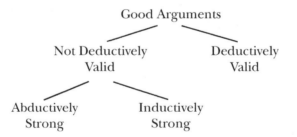

I'll treat the three categories (deductively valid, inductively strong, and abductively strong) as *mutually exclusive*. If an argument belongs to one category, it can't belong to any of the others. At the end of Chapter 3, I'll modify this classification slightly.

You may have heard some of this terminology before. Deduction is what you do in a mathematical proof. Induction involves sampling from a population to decide what its characteristics are. "Abduction" may be a less familiar term. It has nothing to do with kidnapping. The word was invented by the great nineteenth-century American philosopher Charles Sanders Peirce. Philosophers sometimes use the longer label "inference to the best explanation" to describe what Peirce meant by abduction.

I'll consider deduction in this chapter, induction and abduction in the next. The goal in each case is to describe some of the considerations that are relevant to deciding whether an argument is good or bad.

Deductive Validity Defined

The first type of good argument consists of ones that are "deductively valid." Here are two examples of this type of argument:

All fish swim.   All particles have mass.
All sharks are fish.   All electrons are particles.
_____   _____

All sharks swim.   All electrons have mass.

In these arguments, the premises are the statements above the horizontal line; the conclusion is the statement below. These arguments say that the premises are true and that, therefore, the conclusion also is true.

Here is what deductive validity means:

> *A deductively valid argument* is an argument that has the following property: *IF* its premises were true, its conclusion would have to be true.

I've capitalized the word *IF*. I'd print it in bright colors if I could because it is important not to forget this two-letter word. *A valid argument need not have true premises.* What is required is that the conclusion would have to be true *IF* the premises were true. Take a minute to look at these two arguments. Convince yourself that they are deductively valid.

"Validity" Is a Technical Term

What philosophers and logicians mean by "valid" doesn't have much in common with what we mean by "valid" in ordinary English. In everyday life, we say that a statement is "valid" if it is plausible or true. The technical use of the term that I just explained differs from ordinary usage in two ways. First, we never say that a *statement* or an *idea* is valid or invalid. Validity is a property of *arguments* and of arguments only. Second, an argument can be valid even if the statements it contains are wildly implausible. A valid argument can have false premises and a false conclusion.

Here is an example:

All plants have minds.
All ladders are plants.
_____

All ladders have minds.

Logical Form

What makes an argument deductively valid? The three example arguments described so far have different subject matters. The first is about fish, the second is about particles, and the third is about plants. Although they are about different things, they have the same structure. The structural property that they have in common is called their "logical form." Think of each argument as the result of substituting terms into the following skeleton:

All *B*s are *C*s
All *A*s are *B*s
_____

All *A*s are *C*s

This is the logical form of the three arguments given. You can think of *A*, *B*, and *C* as blanks into which terms may be substituted. Take a minute to see how the arguments just stated can be obtained from the above skeleton by substitution—by "filling in the blanks."

An argument is valid or invalid solely because of the logical form it has. The subject matter of the argument is irrelevant. Since the three example arguments have the same logical form, they are all valid or all invalid. They have the same logical form, so they are in the same boat. As already mentioned, they are valid. Indeed, each and every one of the millions of arguments you can construct by substitution into the above skeleton is valid as well.

Invalidity

The definition of validity tells you what a deductively *invalid* argument will be like. If there is even the smallest possibility that the conclusion could be false when the premises are true, then the argument is deductively invalid.

The ladder argument is valid, although all the statements it contains are false. Is the reverse situation possible? Can an argument be *invalid*, even though all the statements it contains are true? The answer is *yes*. Here's an example:

Emeralds are green.

Lemons are yellow.

The premise is true, and so is the conclusion. So why isn't the argument deductively valid? The definition of validity says that the premises in a valid argument must provide an *absolute guarantee* that the conclusion is true. But the fact that emeralds are green doesn't guarantee that lemons must be yellow. The color of lemons isn't entailed by the fact that emeralds are green. Validity concerns the *relationship* of premises to conclusion, not the question of whether the premises and the conclusion each happen to be true.

Sometimes it isn't so obvious that an argument is invalid. The above example is pretty blatant—the premise has nothing to do with the conclusion. But what do you think of the following argument? Is it valid or not?

If Jones stands in the heavy rain without an umbrella, then Jones will get wet.

Jones is wet.

Jones was standing in the heavy rain without an umbrella.

Imagine that all three of the statements in this argument are true. Imagine that Jones is now standing before you soaking wet and that Jones just came in from the rain.

Even if all the statements in this argument are true, this argument is still invalid. It is just like the argument about emeralds and lemons. Although the premises and the conclusion happen to be true, the premises don't *guarantee* that the conclusion must be true.

How can we see this more clearly? I said before that all arguments that have the same logical form are in the same boat. This means that if the argument about Jones is invalid, so is each and every argument that has the same form. Let's begin by isolating the argument's logical form. Here it is:

If P, then Q
Q

P

What do P and Q stand for in this argument skeleton? You can substitute any statement (declarative sentence) you please for these letters to obtain an argument with this logical form. Notice that the letters in this skeleton differ in their function from the letters in the previous skeleton. There, *A, B,* and *C* are blanks into which terms denoting kinds of things ("fish," "electrons," etc.) can be substituted. Anyhow, we now have the logical form of the argument about Jones. If it is invalid, so are *all* arguments that have the same logical form. This means that if there is even one argument that has this logical form in which the premises are true and the conclusion false, then the argument form is invalid. This will mean that the initial argument about Jones is invalid as well.

Here is an argument that has the same logical form as the argument about Jones that settles the question:

> If Sam lives in Wisconsin, then Sam lives in the United States.
> Sam lives in the United States.
>
> _____
>
> Sam lives in Wisconsin.

The premises of this argument are true, but the conclusion, I assure you, is false. The Sam I'm talking about lives in Georgia.

Testing for Invalidity

So here's a strategy to use if you want to know whether an argument is invalid: First, ignore the argument's subject matter and isolate the logical form (the "skeleton") of the argument. Second, see if you can invent an argument that has this logical form in which the premises are true and the conclusion is false. If you can find even one rotten apple of this type, you are finished. If there is even one argument with this property, then *every* argument of that form is invalid.

When an argument has true premises and a false conclusion, it is quite obvious that the truth of the premises doesn't *guarantee* that the conclusion must be true. The premises can't be guaranteeing this, as the conclusion is false. But this tells you something general. It tells you that each and every argument of this form will be such that the premises don't guarantee the truth of the conclusion.

So far, I've presented some examples of arguments. I've explained that a valid argument needn't have true statements in it and that an argument composed solely of true statements needn't be valid. This should make you wonder whether there is any connection at all between the question of whether an argument is valid and the question of whether the premises and conclusion are true.

There *is* a connection. It is illustrated by the following table. If an argument is valid, it can exhibit three of the four following combinations in which the premises are either all true or not all true and the conclusion is either true or false:

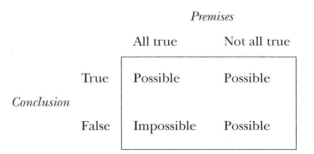

		Premises	
		All true	Not all true
Conclusion	True	Possible	Possible
	False	Impossible	Possible

This table indicates that a valid argument can't have true premises and a false conclusion. However, the fact that an argument is valid leaves open which of the other three cells the argument occupies.

What can be said of an *in*valid argument? If an argument is invalid, are any of the four combinations impossible? I leave this to you to figure out by consulting the definition of validity.

When you find an invalid argument, you may want to ask if the argument can be repaired. Is there anything that can be done to an invalid argument to turn it into an argument that is valid? There is. By adding premises, you can turn a deductively invalid argument into a valid one. Consider the following argument:

Smith lives in the United States.
_____

Smith lives in Wisconsin.

This is invalid, but it can be made valid by adding a premise:

Smith lives in the United States.
Everyone who lives in the United States lives in Wisconsin.
_____

Smith lives in Wisconsin.

Notice that the conclusion now follows from the premises. The trouble is that the second premise is false.

In the preceding pair of arguments, fixing the defect of invalidity just substitutes one problem for another; instead of having to criticize an argument for being invalid, you now have to criticize an argument for having a premise that isn't true. The following argument pair is different. Here you can repair the defect of invalidity and obtain a perfectly fine argument. Notice first that the following argument isn't deductively valid:

Smith lives in Wisconsin.
_____

Smith lives in the United States.

The argument can be repaired, however, by adding a premise:

Smith lives in Wisconsin.
Everyone who lives in Wisconsin lives in the United States.
_____

Smith lives in the United States.

This argument is valid and has true premises as well. You can see from these two pairs of arguments that invalidity is easy to fix. Just add premises. What is harder is to add premises that not only make the argument valid, but that are true as well.

This idea will come up repeatedly when I discuss various philosophical arguments. I will sometimes claim an argument is invalid. When this happens, you should ask yourself whether the argument can be repaired. Often the price of making the argument valid (by adding a premise) is that you have to supply a new premise that you think is false. In making this addition, you are trading one defect (invalidity) for another (false premises). If you can't repair the argument so that it is both valid and has all true premises, then you should consider the possibility that there is something fundamentally flawed about the whole line of argument. On the other hand, sometimes an invalid argument can be replaced by a valid one merely by supplying a true premise that maybe you neglected to mention because it is so obvious. In this case, the defect in the original argument isn't fundamental.

So far I've emphasized two questions that we will want to ask about arguments:

1   Is the argument deductively valid?
2   Are all the premises true?

If the answer to both questions is *yes*, the conclusion of the argument must be true.

Arguments are tools. We use them to do things. When the goal is rational persuasion, a good argument will provide a good reason to think that the conclusion is true. If an argument is deductively valid and has true premises, is that sufficient to make the argument good? To see why validity and true premises aren't enough, consider the following argument:

> Lemons are yellow.
> _____
> Lemons are yellow.

Here the conclusion merely repeats what the premise asserts. This argument is valid and the premise is true. But there is something defective about this argument. What is it?

I Conditionals

If/then statements are called conditionals. Conditional statements have other statements as components. For example, the statement "If pigs fly, then grass is green" is a statement of the form "If *P*, then *Q*," where *P* and *Q* are themselves statements.

In the statement "If *P*, then *Q*," *P* is called the *antecedent* and *Q* is called the *consequent*. A conditional doesn't say that its antecedent is true; the statement "If Joe drinks arsenic, then Joe will die" does not say that Joe drinks arsenic. And a conditional doesn't say that its consequent is true; "If there is a nuclear war, then Washington will be attacked" doesn't say that Washington will be attacked.

Conditionals can be rewritten without changing what they say. Consider the statement "If you live in Wisconsin, then you live in the United States." This is equivalent in meaning to "If you don't live in the United States, then you don't live in Wisconsin." The conditional "If *P*, then *Q*" is equivalent to "If not-*Q*, then not-*P*," no matter what *P* and *Q* happen to be. Here's a piece of terminology: The statement "If not-*Q*, then not-*P*" is the *contrapositive* of the conditional "If *P*, then *Q*." A conditional and its contrapositive are equivalent.

Consider the following two conditionals: "If *P*, then *Q*" and "If *Q*, then *P*." Are they equivalent? That is, do they mean the same thing? The answer is *no*. "If you live in Wisconsin, then you live in the United States" is true, but "If you live in the United States, then you live in Wisconsin" is false. These two if/then statements can't mean the same thing, because one is true while the other is false. "If *Q*, then *P*" is termed the *converse* of the conditional "If *P*, then *Q*." A conditional and its converse are not equivalent.

Circularity, or Begging the Question

The previous argument is *circular*; it *begs the question*. Suppose you didn't already have an opinion as to whether lemons are yellow. The above argument wouldn't help you resolve your uncertainty. The argument would be useless in this regard.

Good arguments are tools that help answer questions about whether their conclusions are true. A good argument should give you a reason to accept the conclusion if you don't already believe the conclusion is true. So besides checking to see if an argument is deductively valid and has true premises, you should also see if the argument begs the question.

You'll notice in what I've just said that I am using the expression "begging the question" to name a defect in an argument. Unfortunately, the phrase is often used now to simply mean that a question is being asked. You'll hear this usage on the evening news—"the recession has not improved. This begs the question of whether government action can make things better." As with the term "validity," the term "begging the question" is used by philosophers with a special, technical meaning, one that doesn't coincide with ordinary usage.

Truth

One other idea needs clearing up before I leave the topic of deductive validity. You'll notice that the definition of validity makes use of the concept of truth. What is truth?

There are deep philosophical questions here, most of which I'll skirt. My goal is to describe the concept of truth I use in this book. It is beyond the scope of this book to defend this choice or to fully develop its implications. To begin with, whether a statement is true is an entirely different question from whether you or anybody happens to believe it. Whether someone believes the statement "The Rocky Mountains are in North America" is a psychological question. If beings with minds had never populated the earth, no one would have thought about the location of this mountain range. But this doesn't affect the question of whether the statement is true. There can be truths that no one believes. Symmetrically, there can be propositions that everyone thinks are true, but that aren't. There can be beliefs that aren't true.

---

2 Begging the Question

To understand what makes an argument question-begging, it is useful to examine some examples.

Suppose you were trying to convince someone that God exists. The argument you give for thinking that this is true is that the Bible says that there is a God. Would this argument convince someone who didn't already believe that there is a God? Probably not. Anyone who doubts that there is a God probably doesn't think that everything the Bible says is true.

Here's a second example. Someone is very suspicious about the reliability of consumer magazines. You try to convince him that *Consumer Reports* is reliable by pointing out that *Consumer Reports* ranks itself very highly in an article evaluating the reliability of consumer magazines. Probably your argument will fail to convince.

In these two examples, identify the premises and conclusion in each argument. Then describe what it is about the argument that makes it question-begging.

When I say that a certain sentence has the property of being true, what am I saying? For example, when I say that the English sentence "The Rocky Mountains are in North America" is true, am I attributing some mysterious property to the sentence? Not really.

All I'm saying is that the world is the way the sentence says it is. When I say that the sentence is true, all I'm saying is that the Rocky Mountains are in North America. So in a way, the concept of truth is often "redundant." Sometimes when I use the concept of truth, I could say the same thing without using that concept.

In high school English, your teacher might have told you to avoid redundancy. If you hand in an essay containing the sentence "Oscar is an unmarried bachelor," the essay might come back with "unmarried" crossed out and the marginal comment "avoid redundancy." The word "unmarried" is redundant because "Oscar is an unmarried bachelor" means exactly the same thing as "Oscar is a bachelor." Adding the word "unmarried" is to spill useless ink. The Redundancy Theory of Truth claims that the word "true" is redundant in just this sense. "It is true that the Rockies are in North America" says exactly what the sentence "The Rockies are in North America" asserts. This helps show why truth isn't a mysterious property. If you believe a statement *P*, you also believe that *P* is true. So, if you have any beliefs about the world at all, you should be quite comfortable applying the concept of truth to those beliefs.

"True for Me"

You'll see from these remarks that the expression "It is true for me" can be dangerously misleading. Sometimes saying that a statement is true "for you" just means that you believe it. If that is what you want to say, just use the word "belief" and leave truth out of it. However, there is a more controversial idea that might be involved here. Sometimes people use the expression "true for me" to express the idea that each of us makes our own reality and that the beliefs we have constitute that reality. I'll assume this is a mistake. My concept of truth assumes a fundamental division between the way things really are and the way they may seem to be to this or that individual. This is what I meant in Chapter 1 by distinguishing the objective realm and the subjective realm.

Wishful Thinking

Closely related to this distinction between objective and subjective is a piece of advice: *We should avoid wishful thinking*. Most of the things we believe aren't made true by our believing them. That the Rockies are in North America is a fact that is independent of our thought and language. We don't bring this geographic fact into being by thinking or talking in the way we do.

Self-Fulfilling Prophesies

In saying this, I'm not denying that the thoughts we have often affect the world outside the mind. If I think to myself, "I can't hit a baseball," this may have the effect that I do badly in the batter's box; here my believing something has the effect that the belief is made true. This is the idea of a "self-fulfilling prophesy." Notice how this causal chain works:

Thought	**Action**	**Truth**
I believe that I won't hit the baseball. $\longrightarrow$	I swing too high. $\longrightarrow$	I don't hit the baseball.

My believing a proposition causes an action, which has the effect of making the proposition true.

I have no problem with the idea that various statements may be caused to be true by individuals thinking thoughts to themselves. What I deny is that the mere act of thinking, unconnected with action or some other causal pathway, can make statements true in the world outside the mind. I'm rejecting the idea that the world is arranged so that it spontaneously conforms to the ideas we happen to entertain.

Later in this book, I'll investigate whether there are any exceptions to this principle that says that we should avoid wishful thinking. Maybe there are some statements that become true just because we think they are. Here are some philosophical claims we'll consider:

- Mathematical statements and definitions are made true by our regarding them as such; for example, "2 + 3 = 5" is true just because we choose to define our terminology ("2," "+," etc.) in the way we do (Chapter 4).
- Some statements about the contents of my own mind (for example, "I am in pain") are made true just by my believing they are true (Chapter 13).
- Ethical statements are true just because God, society, or some individual agent thinks they are (Chapter 31).

I'm mentioning these philosophical claims here without tipping my hand as to whether I think any of them is plausible. If any of them were correct, they would be exceptions to the pattern I've just described. For the moment, though, I'm merely noting that belief and truth are generally very separate questions.

Review Questions

1   When is a statement or idea valid? (a trick question)
2   Define what it means to say that an argument is deductively valid.
3   Invent an example of a valid argument that has false premises and a true conclusion. Invent an example of an invalid argument that has true premises and a true conclusion.
4   Can a statement be a premise in one argument and a conclusion in another? If you think so, give an example.
5   Which of the following argument forms is valid? Which is invalid? For each of the invalid ones, construct an example of an argument with that form in which the premises are true and the conclusion false:

(a)
$$\frac{\text{If } P, \text{ then } Q}{Q}$$
P

(b)
$$\frac{\text{If } P, \text{ then } Q}{P}$$
Q

(c)
$$\frac{\text{If } P, \text{ then } Q}{\text{Not-}Q}$$
Not-P

(d)
$$\frac{\text{If } P, \text{ then } Q}{\text{Not-}P}$$
Not-Q

For the argument forms you think are fallacious, invent names for these fallacies by using the vocabulary about conditionals presented in the box on page 18.

6   A sign on a store says, "No shoes, no service." Does this mean that if you wear shoes, then you will be served?

7   What does it mean to say that an argument is "circular," that it "begs the question"? Construct an example of an argument of this type different from the ones presented in this chapter.

8   What does it mean to say that truth is objective, not subjective?

9   What is the logical difference between the statements "I believe that *p*" and "*p* is true"? (Hint: Can you imagine a situation in which the latter, but not the former, is true? A situation in which the latter, but not the former, is false?)

10   Can an argument be "partially" or "somewhat" valid? Can a premise or conclusion be "partially" or "somewhat" true? Why or why not?

11   What does it mean to say that the premises of an argument support its conclusion?

12   Why do philosophers distinguish between considerations of "validity" and "truth"? (Do all valid arguments yield true conclusions? Do all true conclusions follow from valid arguments?)

Problems for Further Thought

1   The Redundancy Theory of Truth may seem plausible as an account of what the following sentence means:

   It is true that the Rockies are in North America.

Does it work as well as an explanation of what the following sentence means?

   Some statements that are true have not been formulated yet.

2   Consider the following argument:

   I release an otherwise unsupported apple from my hand a few feet from the earth's surface.

   _____

   The apple falls to earth.

Is this argument deductively valid? What is the logical form of this argument?

3   (Here is a problem that was drawn to my attention by Richard Behling.) In this chapter, I said that each argument has a *single* logical form. This is the skeleton into which terms can be substituted to obtain the argument. What I said is an oversimplification. A given argument can be obtained from *many* logical forms. For example, consider the following argument:

   Fred lives in California.
   If Fred lives in California, then Fred lives in the United States.

   _____

   Fred lives in the United States.

This argument can be obtained from *both* of the following skeletons by substitution:

        X R
        If X, then Y S
   (a) ——   (b) ——
        Y T

Argument form (a) is valid, but (b) is *in*valid. The argument about Fred is valid.

Here's the problem: Use the concept of logical form to define when an argument is valid, and when it is invalid, without falling into the trap of thinking that each argument has *exactly one* logical form.

4   In this chapter, I claimed that there are "objective truths." Do you agree? Construct an argument in which you try to demonstrate that such things exist, or that they do not.

Recommended Readings, Video, and Audio

Visit the companion website at www.routledge.com/cw/sober for suggestions of readings, video, and audio, for this chapter.

Chapter 3

Inductive and Abductive Arguments

In Chapter 2, I explained the idea of deductive validity. In a deductively valid argument, the premises provide an *absolute guarantee* that the conclusion is true: If the premises are true, there is no way in the world that the conclusion can be false.

Deductive Validity Is a Limitation

This feature of deductive arguments may sound like a virtue. It is a good thing when an argument provides this sort of strong guarantee. This virtue, however, can also represent a kind of limitation. Granted, a deductively valid argument that has true premises can't have a false conclusion; but it is also a property of such arguments that the conclusion can't say anything that wasn't already contained in the premises.

To see what this means, consider what you could validly deduce from the result of an opinion survey. Suppose you were interested in finding out what percentage of registered voters in a county are Democrats. You don't feel like contacting each of them and asking, so you open the phone book and make, let's say, one thousand telephone calls.

Suppose the result of your survey is that 60 percent of the people called say they are Democrats. What you want to know is the percentage of Democrats in the whole county. Could you construct a deductively valid argument here? Can you deduce that (approximately) 60 percent of the voters in the county are Democrats from a premise that describes the result of your survey? The answer is *no*, for two reasons. The fact that 60 percent of the people called *said* they are Democrats doesn't deductively guarantee that any of them are. And even if 60 percent of the people called are Democrats, you can't validly deduce from this that (approximately) 60 percent of the voters in the county are Democrats. That is, neither of the following arguments is deductively valid:

> 60 percent of the people called said they are Democrats.
> _____
> 60 percent of the people called are Democrats.

> 60 percent of the people called are Democrats.
> _____
> Approximately 60 percent of the voters in the county are Democrats.

Why can't you validly deduce these conclusions? The reason is that in a deductively valid argument, it is impossible for the conclusion to be false if the premises are true. But it *is* possible that everyone you called in your survey lied. In addition, it is possible that the percentage of Democrats in the whole county is only 25 percent, even if nobody lied in your phone survey. In saying this, I'm not saying that the people you called actually lied, and I'm not saying that the real percentage in the whole county is only 25 percent. I'm just saying that these are *possible*, given the result of your phone calls. The result of your telephone survey doesn't absolutely rule out these possibilities; this means that you can't *deduce* the percentage of Democrats in the whole county from what the one thousand people said on the phone.

So the absolute guarantee that a deductively valid argument provides has this limitation: Insisting that an argument be deductively valid prohibits you from reaching conclusions that go beyond the information given in the premises.

It would make sense to insist that an argument be deductively valid if you wanted to avoid even the smallest risk of having a false conclusion with true premises. However, we are often willing to gamble. For example, we might think that the result of the phone survey does provide information about the composition of the county. We might think that the survey provides a pretty good reason for concluding that about 60 percent of the county voters are Democrats. However, the "good reason" isn't a deductively valid one.

Nondeductive Inference—A Weaker Guarantee

We have here a fundamental characteristic of nondeductive inference. Suppose we conclude that about 60 percent of the voters in the county are Democrats, based on the premise that 60 percent of the people called said they were Democrats. In this case, the premise doesn't provide an absolute guarantee that the conclusion is true. However, there is a lesser kind of guarantee that this premise may provide. If the argument is a strong one, the premise makes the conclusion *probable*; it provides a *good reason* for thinking the conclusion is true; it makes the conclusion *plausible*. Instead of an absolute guarantee, we have here a weaker guarantee. You are running a risk of being wrong about your conclusion, even if your premise is true. But this risk might be a reasonable one to take. The conclusion might be a good bet, given that the premise is true.

Two Gambling Strategies

The language in the previous paragraph suggests that you can think about the difference between deductive and nondeductive arguments in terms of ideas about gambling. Consider two sorts of gamblers. The first I'll call the *extreme conservative*. This individual refuses to wager unless winning is a sure thing. The second individual I'll call the *thoughtful risk taker*. This individual at times enters into risky gambles hoping to win. Each strategy has its virtue and its limitation. The virtue of the conservative strategy is that you'll never lose a gamble. Its limitation is that there are gambles you will decline to take that you could have won. The limitation of thoughtful risk taking is that you can lose money. Its virtue is that it can lead you to win wagers by taking risks.

Limiting yourself to deductively valid arguments is a conservative strategy. You avoid the risk of reaching false conclusions from true premises. The limitation is that you decline to say anything that goes beyond the evidence. Nondeductive arguments are riskier. The gain is that you can reach true conclusions that go beyond what the premises say; the risk is that you may reach a false conclusion from true premises.

In science as well as in everyday life, we make nondeductive inferences all the time. We are often prepared to take risks. Each of us has beliefs about the future. These, however, aren't deduced from the observations we made in the present and past.

Universal Laws

Science is a risky business in another way. Scientists often try to reach conclusions about *universal laws*. An example is Isaac Newton's (1642–1727) universal law of gravitation, which you may have studied in high school. This law says that the gravitational attraction between two bodies is proportional to the products of their masses and is inversely proportional to the square of the distance between them. This law describes how much gravitational attraction there is between any two objects, no matter where those objects are located and no matter when those objects exist. Newton's law is *universal* in scope—it describes what is true at any time and place. This isn't an isolated example. In lots of sciences, there are universal statements that scientists think are well supported by evidence.

Could Newton have deduced his law from the observations he made and the experiments he conducted? *No.* His law is universal in scope. His observations, however, were conducted in a rather narrowly limited range of places and times. Newton didn't go backward in time to check if his law held true 3 million years ago. Nor did he send a spaceship to a distant galaxy to do the required measurements. When scientists conclude that a universal law is true or probably true, based on premises that describe the observations they have made, they aren't making deductively valid arguments.

Science is an ambitious enterprise. Science ventures beyond what is strictly observed in the here and now, just as the conclusion in a nondeductive argument ventures beyond the information strictly contained in the premises.

Detective Work

I said before that nondeductive arguments are constantly used both in science and in everyday life. Newton was my scientific example. Let me describe the calculations of Sherlock Holmes as my everyday one.

Holmes was constantly telling Watson that he figures out detective problems by "deduction." Although Holmes was a very good detective, I doubt that he solved his puzzles by strictly deductive methods. Holmes didn't observe the crimes he was later called upon to investigate. What he observed were *clues*. For example, suppose Holmes is trying to solve a murder. He wonders whether Moriarty is the murderer. The clues Holmes gathers include a gun, a cigar butt, and a fresh footprint, all found at the scene of the crime. Suppose the gun has an "M" carved in the handle, the cigar is Moriarty's favorite brand, and the footprint is the size that would be produced by Moriarty's ample foot. Can Holmes deduce from these clues that Moriarty is the murderer? No. Although the information may make that conclusion plausible or probable, it doesn't absolutely rule out the possibility that someone else did the dirty deed.

I've been emphasizing that in a strong nondeductive inference, the premises make the conclusion plausible or probable; they don't absolutely guarantee that the conclusion must be true. I now want to talk about the difference between two sorts of nondeductive inference—inductive and abductive.

Induction

Inductive inference involves taking a description of some sample and extending that description to items outside the sample. The voter survey discussed before provides an example:

60 percent of the county voters called are Democrats.

Approximately 60 percent of the county voters are Democrats.

Notice that in this example the vocabulary present in the argument's conclusion is already used in the premise. Although the conclusion goes beyond what the premise asserts (which is what makes the argument nondeductive), no new concepts are introduced in the conclusion.

Two Factors Influence Inductive Strength

In the case of deduction, I said that an inference is either deductively valid or it isn't. Validity is a yes/no affair. It is like pregnancy. Inductive strength, however, isn't a yes/no matter; inductive arguments are either stronger or weaker. Inductive strength is a matter of degree.

Two factors affect how strong or weak an inductive argument is. The first is sample size. If you called one thousand individuals in your phone survey, that would make your conclusion stronger than if you had called only one hundred. The second factor is the representativeness or unbiasedness of the sample. If you called one thousand individuals drawn at random from a list of voters, that would make the resulting inference stronger than if you had called one thousand members of labor unions. The percentage of Democrats in labor unions may be higher than that found in the population as a whole. If so, you are biasing your sample by drawing it exclusively from a union membership list.

By making a telephone survey, you are failing to contact people who don't have phones. Is this a problem? That depends. If the percentage of Democrats with phones is approximately equal to the percentage of Democrats among registered voters, no bias is introduced. On the other hand, if people with phones are disproportionately Democrats or disproportionately Republicans, your phone survey will have introduced a bias.

How do you avoid having a biased sample? Sometimes this is done by "randomization." If you have a list of all the county voters, drawing names "at random" means that each name has the same chance of being selected. However, this process of selecting at random can fail to ensure an unbiased sample. For example, suppose you draw names at random, but all the people you contact happen to be women. If women are disproportionately Democrats or disproportionately Republicans, your sample is biased. I don't say that random draws from the voter list will *probably* result in this sort of bias. My point is just that randomizing doesn't absolutely guarantee that your sample is unbiased. I won't say more here about how you can avoid having a biased sample. This fine point aside, the basic idea is this: Inductive arguments are stronger or weaker according to (1) the sample size and (2) the unbiasedness of the sample.

Abduction

I now move to abduction—inference to the best explanation. I'll begin with an example of an abductive inference that was important in the history of science. After saying what is distinctive about this form of inference, I'll describe two principles that are relevant to deciding whether an abductive inference is strong or weak.

Inferring What Isn't Observed

Gregor Mendel (1822–1884) was an experimental biologist who worked in a monastery in Moravia. He is credited with having discovered genes, the particles in living things that allow parents to transmit characteristics to offspring in reproduction.

The first thing to note about Mendel's discovery is that he never actually saw a gene (or an "element," as Mendel called them). Although more powerful microscopes made this possible later, Mendel never saw even one of them. Rather, Mendel reasoned that the observations he made could be explained if genes existed and had the characteristics he specified.

Mendel ran breeding experiments in the monastery's garden. He crossed tall pea plants with short ones and noted the proportion of tall and short plants among the offspring. Similarly, he crossed plants that had wrinkled peas with plants that had smooth peas, and he noted the mix of wrinkled and smooth plants among the progeny. He then crossed some of those offspring with each other, and he saw the proportion of various characteristics found in the next generation.

Mendel observed that when plants of certain sorts are crossed, their offspring exhibit characteristics in very definite proportions. Mendel asked himself a question that never figured in my discussion of induction. He asked *why* the crosses produced offspring with characteristics distributed into such proportions.

This why-question led Mendel to invent a story. He said, suppose each plant contains particles (genes) that control the observed characteristics of tall and short, wrinkled and smooth, in certain specific ways. He conjectured that each parent contributes half its genes to the offspring and that this process occurs in accordance with definite rules. The whole invented story had this property: If the story were true, that would explain why the breeding experiments had the results that Mendel observed them to have.

It should be quite clear that Mendel's theory of the gene went beyond the observations then available to him. He never saw a gene, but his theory postulates the existence of such things. I noted before that it is a general feature of nondeductive inference, whether inductive or abductive, that the conclusion goes beyond the premises. We see here, however, a respect in which abduction differs from induction.

Abduction Differs from Induction

If Mendel had made an inductive inference, he simply would have claimed that the observed results of the experiments he ran in his garden would also occur elsewhere. His experiment was made in Europe at the end of the nineteenth century. An inductive extension of the description of his experiment might conclude that the same results would occur in twentieth-century North America as well. Had Mendel limited himself to this suggestion, no one would remember him now as the father of genetics. His important inference was abductive, not inductive. He didn't simply claim that the experiment could be replicated. Rather, he formulated a theoretical explanation of *why* the results occurred. Mendel's inference drew a conclusion concerning something he did *not* see (genes), based on premises that described what he *did* see (the results of the experimental crossings).

Can You Deduce the Explanation from the Observations?

Let's attend to Mendel's inference more carefully. The following is *not* a deductively valid argument:

> Experimental crosses in the pea plants were observed to exhibit such-and-such results.
> _____
> There are genes, and they obey laws *L*.

Remember: You can't validly deduce a theory from a set of observations.

Why can't you do this? Basically, the last argument attempts to infer a theory about the cause from the observation of its effects. There are, however, lots of possible causes that might have been responsible for the observed effects. The argument is deductively invalid for the same reason the following argument is also invalid:

> A pistol with an "M" on the handle, an El Supremo cigar butt, and a size 12 footprint were found next to the murder victim's body.
> _____
> Moriarty is the murderer.

Although Moriarty may be the most plausible suspect, the clues, in themselves, don't absolutely guarantee that he must have done the deed. Mendel and Holmes were making an inference about what is *probably* true, given the observations. They weren't inferring what is *absolutely guaranteed* to be true by the observations.

Deducing Observational Predictions from a Theory

If a set of observations doesn't deductively imply a theory, then perhaps the reverse is true: Maybe a theory deductively implies some observations. This corresponds more closely to what Mendel did. He saw that his theory of the gene implies that certain experimental results ought to occur. He then saw that those predictions came true. He concluded that the truth of the predictions was evidence that the theory is true.

When the Prediction Comes True

So a better representation of Mendel's inference might go like this. The theory entailed a prediction. The prediction came true. Hence, the theory is probably true. What we now need to see is that the following form of argument is not deductively valid:

> If there are genes and they obey laws *L*, then experimental crosses in the pea plants should exhibit such-and-such results.
> Experimental crosses in the pea plants were observed to exhibit such-and-such results.
> _____
> There are genes and they obey laws *L*.

This is deductively invalid for the same reason that the following argument is too:

> If Jones lives in Wisconsin, then Jones lives in the United States.
> Jones lives in the United States.
> _____
> Jones lives in Wisconsin.

Note that these two arguments have the same logical form.

Scientists often test their theories by seeing whether the predictions made by the theories come true. There is nothing wrong with doing this. The point, however, is that the truth of the theory doesn't follow deductively from the truth of the prediction. Scientists are reasoning *non*deductively when they decide that a theory is plausible because its predictions have come true. *Successful prediction isn't absolutely conclusive proof that the theory is true.*

When the Prediction Turns Out to Be False

On the other hand, if the predictions entailed by Mendel's theory had come out false, that would have allowed him to deduce that the theory is mistaken. That is, the following argument *is* deductively valid:

> If there are genes and they obey laws *L*, then experimental crosses in the pea plants should exhibit such-and-such results.
> Experimental crosses in the pea plants did not exhibit such-and-such results.
> _____
> It is false that there are genes and they obey laws *L*.

In other words, *a failed prediction is conclusive proof that the theory implying the prediction is false.*

How True Predictions and False Predictions Are Interpreted

Let's generalize these points. Let *T* be a theory and *P* a prediction the theory makes. If the prediction comes out true, we can't deduce that the theory is true. If, however, the prediction comes out false, we can deduce the theory is false:

Invalid	*Valid*
If *T*, then *P*	If *T*, then *P*
P	Not-*P*
_____	_____
T	Not-*T*

---

3 Deducing that a Theory is true

Recall from Chapter 2 that a deductively invalid argument can be turned into a valid one by adding premises. I will now exploit this fact to show how the truth of a theory can be deduced from the fact that it makes a successful prediction, *if certain further assumptions are made.*

Suppose we wish to design an experiment that tests two theories. Here the problem isn't one of evaluating a single theory, but of seeing which of two theories is more plausible. To test one theory (T_1) against another (T_2), we want to find a prediction over which they disagree. Suppose T_1 predicts that P will be true, while T_2 predicts that P will be false. If we assume that one or the other theory is true, we can find out whether P comes true and then deduce which theory is true. For example, if P turns out to be true, we can reason as follows:

T_1 or T_2
If T_1, then P.
If T_2, then not-P.
P

T_1

Notice that this argument is deductively valid. Also note that if P had turned out to be false, we could have deduced that T_2 is correct.

The difference between these two arguments—one deductively valid, the other not—suggests there is an important difference between the way scientists argue that theories are true and the way they argue that theories are false. It is possible to reject a theory just on the basis of the false predictions it makes, using a deductively valid argument; but it isn't possible to accept a theory just on the basis of the true predictions it makes, using a deductively valid argument. I will discuss this difference again in Chapter 8.

So far I've explained how a deductively valid argument can lead a scientist to reject a suggested explanation. But how do scientists ever interpret observations as providing strong evidence in favor of the explanations they consider? This must involve a nondeductive inference. But what are the rules that govern such inferences? I now present two ideas that are relevant to evaluating abductive arguments. I call these the *Surprise Principle* and the *Only Game in Town Fallacy.*

The Surprise Principle: When Does Successful Prediction Provide Strong Evidence?

I've argued that you can't validly deduce that a theory is true just from the fact that some prediction it makes comes true. But maybe only a small modification of this idea is needed. Perhaps all we need to say is that a theory is made highly probable or plausible when a prediction it makes comes true. I now want to explain why this reformulation is also mistaken.

An unconscious patient is brought into the emergency room of a hospital. What is wrong? What would explain the fact that the patient is unconscious? The doctor on duty considers the hypothesis that the patient is having a heart attack. How should the doctor test whether this hypothesis is true? Well, the hypothesis predicts that the patient will have a heart (after all, if someone is having a heart attack, he or she must have a heart). The doctor verifies that this prediction is correct—the patient, indeed, does have a heart. Has the doctor thereby obtained strong evidence that the patient is having a heart attack? Clearly not. This is an example in which you don't obtain serious support for a hypothesis just by showing that one of its predictions is correct.

You go to the gym, and someone tells you he is an Olympic weight lifter. You reason that if he is an Olympic weight lifter, he should be able to pick up the hat you are wearing. You offer him your hat; he lifts it without difficulty. Have you thereby obtained strong evidence that he is an Olympic weight lifter? Clearly not. Once again, the hypothesis under test isn't strongly supported by the fact that one of its predictions turns out to be correct.

What has gone wrong in these two cases? In the first example, the presence of a heart isn't strong evidence that the patient is having a heart attack. The reason is that you would expect the individual to have a heart even if he weren't having a heart attack. In the second example, the man's lifting the hat isn't strong evidence that he is an Olympic weight lifter. The reason is that you would expect him to be able to do this even if he weren't an Olympic lifter.

What should you look for if you want to test the hypothesis that the patient has had a heart attack? What you want to find is a symptom that you would expect to find if the patient were having a heart attack, *but would expect not to be present if the patient were not having a heart attack.* Suppose an erratic electrocardiogram (EKG) almost always occurs when there is a heart attack but rarely occurs when there is no heart attack. This means that the presence of an erratic EKG would be strong evidence that the patient is suffering a heart attack.

What sort of test should you use if you want to see if the man in the gym really is an Olympic weight lifter? Suppose Olympic weight lifters (of this man's weight) can almost always lift four hundred pounds, but people who aren't Olympic lifters can rarely do this. This means that his managing to lift four hundred pounds would be strong evidence that he is an Olympic weight lifter.

Think of the unconscious patient and the weight lifter as posing *discrimination problems*. The problem is to find evidence that strongly discriminates between two hypotheses. In the first example, the competing hypotheses are as follows:

H_1: The patient is having a heart attack.
H_2: The patient isn't having a heart attack.

An erratic EKG strongly favors H_1 over H_2; the mere fact that the patient has a heart does not.

The same holds true for the second example. The problem is to find evidence that discriminates between the following two hypotheses:

H_1: This man is an Olympic weight lifter.
H_2: This man isn't an Olympic weight lifter.

The fact that the man can lift four hundred pounds strongly favors H_1 over H_2; the fact that he can lift a hat does not.

The Surprise Principle describes what it takes for an observation to strongly favor one hypothesis over another:

The Surprise Principle: An observation O strongly supports hypothesis H_1 over hypothesis H_2 if both the following conditions are satisfied, but not otherwise: (1) if H_1 were true, O is to be expected; and (2) if H_2 were true, O would have been unexpected.

Let's apply this principle to the first example. Consider the observation that the patient has an erratic EKG. If the patient were having a heart attack (H_1), we would expect him to have an erratic EKG. And if the patient weren't having a heart attack (H_2), we would expect him not to have an erratic EKG. This explains why the erratic EKG is strong evidence of a heart attack—the EKG strongly favors H_1 over H_2. Now consider the observation that the patient has a heart. If the patient were having a heart attack, we would expect him to have a heart. But we would expect him to have a heart even if he weren't having a heart attack. This explains why the presence of a heart isn't strong evidence that the patient is having a heart attack—the observation doesn't strongly favor H_1 over H_2. We were looking for an explanation of why the erratic EKG provides telling evidence, whereas the presence of a heart does not. The key is in condition 2 of the Surprise Principle.

---

4 No Surprise/Surprise

The Surprise Principle involves two requirements. It would be more descriptive, though more verbose, to call the idea the No Surprise/Surprise Principle.

The Surprise Principle describes when an observation O strongly favors one hypothesis (H_1) over another (H_2). There are two requirements:

(1) If H_1 were true, you would expect O to be true.
(2) If H_2 were true, you would expect O to be false.

That is, (1) if H_1 were true, O would be unsurprising; (2) if H_2 were true, O would be surprising.

The question to focus on is *not* whether the hypotheses (H_1 or H_2) would be surprising. The Surprise Principle has nothing to do with this. To apply the Surprise Principle, you must get clearly in mind what the hypotheses are and what the observation is.

Take a few minutes to apply the Surprise Principle to the example of the weight lifter. Make sure you see how the principle explains why being able to lift a hat isn't strong evidence, whereas being able to lift four hundred pounds is.

Evidence May Discriminate between Some Hypotheses While Failing to Discriminate between Others

In the examples of the heart attack and the weight lifter, H_2 says only that H_1 is false. In other abductions, however, H_2 may say more than this. Suppose you see someone crossing campus carrying several philosophy books. You wonder whether the person is a philosophy major. Here are two hypotheses you might consider:

H_1: The person is a philosophy major.
H_2: The person is an engineering major.

According to the Surprise Principle, the observation you have made favors H_1 over H_2. But now consider the following third hypothesis:

H_3: The person isn't a student, but is in the business of buying and selling philosophy books.

Although your observation discriminates between H_1 and H_2, it does not discriminate between H_1 and H_3.

This brings out an important fact about how the Surprise Principle applies to abductive inferences. *If you want to know whether an observation strongly supports a hypothesis, ask yourself what the alternative hypotheses are.* For an observation to strongly support a hypothesis is for it to strongly favor that hypothesis over the others with which it competes.

True Prediction Isn't Enough

The point of the examples about the unconscious patient and the weight lifter was to show why successful prediction doesn't automatically provide strong evidence. If someone is having a heart attack, that predicts that he will have a heart; but the presence of a heart isn't strong evidence the person is having a heart attack. If someone is an Olympic weight lifter, that predicts that he will be able to lift a hat; but lifting a hat isn't strong evidence the person is an Olympic weight lifter.

There is a scene in the Monty Python movie *The Life of Brian* that illustrates this idea. The setting is a marketplace. Around the perimeter of the market are assorted prophets and soothsayers. The camera pans from one to the other. We see that in each case, the prophet holds a crowd of people in rapt attention. The first prophet predicts that tomorrow a purple monster will rise out of the desert and devour three villages. The crowd is amazed at these predictions and no doubt will conclude that the prophet has special powers to foresee the future if the predictions come true. After showing us a few prophets of this sort, the camera comes to an individual who very calmly makes the following predictions: Tomorrow, many people will get up early. Others will sleep longer. Some people will decide to have break-fast, while others will postpone eating until later in the day. And so on. The joke is that the crowd that is looking at this guy is just as awestruck as the crowds that were in front of the more outlandish prophets.

There is a lesson here. How would you test the hypothesis that someone has special powers to foresee the future? If he predicts events that people without special powers can easily predict, it isn't very impressive that his predictions come true. If, however, he predicts events that normal people aren't able to foresee, and then these predictions come true, we are more impressed. The Surprise Principle explains why the success of "safe" predictions provides less compelling evidence than the success of "risky" predictions.

Here's a related example of the Surprise Principle in action. Many people thought that the astrologer Jeanne Dixon had special powers to predict the future. After all, she predicted the assassination of President John F. Kennedy and several other events that no one could have guessed were going to happen. If Jeanne Dixon played it safe and only predicted events that everybody knew were going to happen, we wouldn't be impressed. But aren't we being sensible in reasoning that she probably did have special powers, since this and other daring predictions came true?

Although this reasoning may seem to conform to the Surprise Principle, it doesn't. The thing people sometimes forget is that Jeanne Dixon made thousands of predictions and most of them turned out false. It isn't surprising at all that some handful of these should have come true. Although Jeanne Dixon predicted the Kennedy assassination, which surprised (practically) everyone when it happened, it isn't at all surprising that someone with no special powers should be lucky a few times every thousand tries. The Surprise Principle, properly understood, tells us why we shouldn't take Jeanne Dixon's few successes as strong evidence that she had special powers.

Modest Favoring

The Surprise Principle shows when an observation *strongly* favors one hypothesis over another. However, sometimes our observations are not so telling and unequivocal. Sometimes the observations (O) favor one hypothesis (H_1) over another (H_2), but only modestly. This will be true when H_1 confers on O a higher probability than H_2 does, but the difference is modest. What the Surprise Principle and this idea about O's modestly favoring H_1 over H_2 have in common is this: both make use of the idea that an observation favors one hypothesis (H_1) over another (H_2). This will be true when the probability of O, according to H_1, exceeds the probability of O, according to H_2.

The Surprise Principle Summarized

In summary, the Surprise Principle gives advice on what a hypothesis must do if it is to be strongly supported by the predictions it makes. First, the hypothesis shouldn't make false predictions. Second, among the true predictions the hypothesis makes, there should be predictions we would expect not to come true if the hypothesis were false.

When we ask whether an observation O strongly supports some hypothesis H_1, the Surprise Principle requires that we specify what the alternative hypotheses are against which H_1 competes. It may turn out that O strongly favors H_1 over H_2, but that O doesn't strongly favor H_1 over H_3. The example of the person carrying philosophy books across campus illustrates this point.

The Only Game in Town Fallacy

I now turn to a second principle for evaluating abductive inferences. Suppose you and I are sitting in a cabin in the woods. We hear a strange rumbling sound in the attic. You ask, "I wonder what that could be?" I reply, "That is the sound of gremlins bowling in the attic." You, being a sensible person, reply, "I really don't think there are gremlins in the attic." I then challenge you to produce a more plausible explanation of the noises. You reply, "Gosh, I really don't have any idea why those noises occurred. I just think your story is implausible." To this humble admission on your part, I make the following rejoinder: "Look, my story, if true, would explain why we just heard those strange noises. If you don't want to accept my explanation, you must produce a more plausible explanation of your own. If you can't, you have to accept my explanation of the noises."

---

5 An Investment Swindle

Suppose you received a letter every month for a year from an investment firm. In each letter, a prediction is made as to whether "the stock of the month" will increase or decline in value during the next thirty days. You keep track of what happens to the stocks described each month. Each prediction comes true. Would you conclude from this that the investment firm has a method for reliably predicting stock market events?

Some years ago an "investment firm" sent out such letters, but the mailing was a swindle. The firm began with a list of 10,000 investors. In the first month, 5,000 investors received letters predicting that stock A would go up; the other 5,000 received letters saying that stock A would go down. The firm then waited to see which prediction came true. During the second month, the firm sent letters to the 5,000 people who had received a true prediction during the first month. In the second month, 2,500 investors received letters predicting that stock B would go up; the other 2,500 received letters saying that B would go down. The process was repeated, so that by the end of ten months, a small number of investors had received ten letters, each containing a successful prediction.

The company then wrote to those people, asking each to invest a large sum of money. Most did so. The company then absconded with the funds. (This story is from Daniel Dennett's *Brainstorms: Philosophical Essays on Mind and Psychology*, Cambridge, MA, MIT Press, 1978.)

The investors who were swindled thought they were making a reasonable abductive inference on the basis of the company's track record. Describe the premise, the conclusion, and the reasoning that led the investors to think the conclusion was highly plausible. Were the investors making a strong inference?

What I just did was commit an abductive fallacy (mistake in reasoning), which I'll call the *Only Game in Town Fallacy*. The fact that you can't think of a more plausible explanation of the noises doesn't oblige you to accept the story I constructed. There is an alternative, which is simply to admit that the noises are something you don't know how to explain.

Abduction is sometimes described loosely as follows: If a theory explains some observation, and if no rival account is available that can do a better job of explaining it, then you should accept the theory. Although this description of abduction is roughly correct, it makes the mistake of sanctioning the Only Game in Town Fallacy. The fact that no rival account is better than the explanation I construct doesn't show my explanation is even minimally plausible. My gremlin theory is pretty silly, although maybe there is nothing now available that is clearly superior to it.

I won't at this point try to fine-tune the idea of abductive inference any further, even though there is a lot more to be said about it. We now have before us the basic idea of inference to the best explanation. We've seen that it is an important part of the scientific method. And I've described two principles that help guide us in evaluating whether an abductive inference is strong or weak.

Review Questions

1   What is the difference between deductive validity and inductive strength?
2   What is the difference between induction and abduction?
3   What factors affect how strong an inductive argument is?
4   Suppose a given observation discriminates between two hypotheses, but a second observation fails to do this. Construct an example, different from the ones presented in this chapter, illustrating the point. Show how the Surprise Principle applies to your example.
5   An observation can succeed in discriminating between hypotheses H_1 and H_2 but fail to discriminate between H_1 and H_3. Construct an example that illustrates this point that is different from the ones presented in this chapter. Show how the Surprise Principle applies to your example.
6   What is the Only Game in Town Fallacy? What does it mean to call it a "fallacy"?
7   Do all successful predictions provide strong evidence for the hypothesis or hypotheses guiding them? Why or why not?
8   Does the Surprise Principle commit us to viewing all successful and risky predictions as providing strong evidence for the hypothesis or hypotheses guiding them?
9   Are inductive and abductive arguments evaluated in the same way, or by means of the same considerations, as deductive arguments? If not, why not?

Problems for Further Thought

1 Suppose you wanted to find out what percentage of the adults in your county are vegetarians. You obtain a list of unmarried adults in the county and contact them to do a survey. Is this sample a biased one? Why or why not?

2 Although induction and abduction were described in this chapter as separate kinds of inference, they have a good deal in common. The Surprise Principle was introduced as applying to abduction, but it applies to induction as well. Suppose an urn is filled with one thousand balls, each of them either red or green. You reach into the urn, sampling at random, and bring out one hundred balls. Your sample contains fifty-one red balls and forty-nine green ones. Here are some hypotheses to consider:

   H_1: All the balls in the urn are green.
   H_2: 75 percent of the balls are green.
   H_3: 50 percent of the balls are green.
   H_4: 25 percent of the balls are green.

Suppose you think that H_1 and H_2 are the only possibilities. Does the observation strongly support one over the other? If so, which? How does the Surprise Principle apply to this question? Suppose, instead, that you think that H_2 and H_3 are the only possibilities. Does the sample strongly support one over the other? If so, which? Suppose, finally, that you think that H_2 and H_4 are the only possibilities. Which is best supported? Why?

3 Why think that any of the beliefs you have about the world outside your own mind are true? For example, why are you now entitled to think there is a printed page in front of you? Presumably you believe this on the basis of sense experience (sight, touch, etc.). Construct an abductive argument whose conclusion is that there is a printed page in front of you. Make sure your inference obeys the Surprise Principle. Does this abductive argument prove there is a printed page in front of you? Explain.

4 At the beginning of Chapter 2, I presented deductive validity, inductive strength, and abductive strength as mutually exclusive categories. This means that if an argument belongs to one category, it doesn't belong to any of the others. This is generally correct, but not always. Here is an inductive argument that isn't deductively valid:

   I've observed one thousand emeralds and all have been green.

   ――――――――――――

   All emeralds are green.

However, by adding a premise, I can produce a deductively valid argument:

   I've observed one thousand emeralds and all have been green.
   If there are over five hundred emeralds in the universe, they will all have the same color.

   ――――――――――――

   All emeralds are green.

Both of these arguments are inductive in the sense that both involve drawing a sample from a population and reaching a conclusion about that population. If so, some inductively strong arguments are also deductively valid.

   The same point holds for abductively strong arguments. Usually they aren't deductively valid, but sometimes they are. Construct a strong abductive argument that obeys the Surprise Principle. Show how it can be made deductively valid by adding or modifying a premise.

5   There is a difference between *not expecting* O and *expecting not-O*. A person who never considers whether O is true does not expect O, but it would be wrong to say that she expects not-O. Of course, if someone expects not-O, it will also be true that she does not expect O. Thus, "S expects not-O" implies "S does not expect O," but the reverse is not true. With this logical point in mind, explain why condition 2 of the Surprise Principle is formulated by saying "H_2 leads you to expect not-O," rather than saying that "H_2 does not lead you to expect O."

Recommended Readings, Video, and Audio

Visit the companion website at www.routledge.com/cw/sober for suggestions of readings, video, and audio, for this chapter.

Part II

Philosophy of Religion

Chapter 4

Aquinas's First Four Ways

Thomas Aquinas (ca. 1224–1274) was an enormously accomplished theologian and philosopher. In his masterwork, the *Summa Theologiae*, he presents five proofs that God exists (Aquinas called them "the five ways"). I'll discuss the first four now and the fifth in the next chapter.

Each of Aquinas's arguments begins with a simple observation that is supposed to be obvious to everyone. For example, the first argument begins with the observation that physical objects are in motion. Each argument then proceeds through various other premises to the conclusion that there is a God. Aquinas intends each of his proofs to be deductively valid.

In Chapter 3, I stressed that most of the hypotheses that scientists are interested in testing can't be deduced from observations. For example, Mendel couldn't deduce the existence and characteristics of genes from the observations he made on his pea plants. The same is true in Aquinas's arguments, as he fully realizes: You can't deduce the existence and characteristics of God just from the simple observations with which his arguments begin. The existence of motion doesn't, all by itself, deductively imply the existence of God. Aquinas's arguments always include additional premises. It is these further premises that are supposed to link the starting observation with the conclusion that God exists.

The Concept of God

Before describing Aquinas's arguments, I need to say something about what he means by "God" and how I'll use that term. Aquinas took God to be a person—one who is all-powerful (omnipotent), all-knowing (omniscient), and entirely good (omnibenevolent)—all-PKG, for short. This conception of God is a familiar one in the traditions of Judaism, Christianity, and Islam (though there is room to debate, in these traditions, whether God is properly described in this way and other religions have other views about what characteristics God has). I'll assume provisionally that God, if such a being exists, has the three characteristics just mentioned. If we don't start with some preliminary picture of what God is, we won't know what we are talking about when we ask whether God exists. However, it is important to bear in mind that this conception of God is not the only one that is possible. Indeed, in Chapter 11, I'll consider an argument that suggests that God, if there is such a being, can't be all-PKG. The definition of God as an all-PKG being is a useful place to begin discussion, but it is only a point of departure.

Another caveat I should mention is that my versions of Aquinas's arguments won't be accurate in all respects. It is often a subtle historical question what this or that philosopher had in mind in a given text. In this case and later in this book, when I discuss the ideas of other philosophers, I will often examine somewhat simplified versions of the arguments they constructed. This may lead you to ask: Why is it worthwhile studying simplified versions of a great philosopher's arguments? Admittedly, there is a loss, but there is also a gain. The main point to be made here, at the beginning of an introductory text, is that it is useful to evaluate these simpler arguments before more subtle arguments are addressed. At any rate, there is ample philosophical material to think about in the arguments I'll describe, even if these arguments don't capture the thoughts of various great thinkers with total accuracy and completeness.

The First Two Arguments: Motion and Causality

Aquinas's first argument for the existence of God is the argument from motion. Here it is, formulated as a deductive argument:

(I) (1) In the natural world, there are objects that are in motion.
     (2) In the natural world, objects that are in motion are always caused to move by objects other than themselves.
     (3) In the natural world, causes must precede their effects.
     (4) In the natural world, there are no infinite cause/effect chains.

(5) Hence there is an entity outside of the natural world (a supernatural being), which causes the motion of the first moving object that exists in the natural world.

(6) Hence, God exists.

Aquinas's second argument generalizes the ideas found in the first. Whereas the first argument is about motion in particular, the second argument is about causality in general:

(II) (1) The natural world includes events.
    (2) In the natural world, every event has a cause, and no event causes itself.
    (3) In the natural world, causes must precede their effects.
    (4) In the natural world, there are no infinite cause/effect chains.

    (5) Hence there is an entity outside of nature (a supernatural being), which causes the first event that occurs in the natural world.

    (6) Hence, God exists.

In both these arguments, I've drawn two horizontal lines to indicate that (5) is supposed to follow from premises (1)–(4) and that (6) is supposed to follow from (5).

What do premises (2) and (3) mean in these two arguments? Let's begin with an object (O_1) that is in motion now. Since it is in motion, there must be an earlier object—call it O_2—that sent O_1 into motion. If O_2 was itself in motion, O_2 must trace back to a previous mover, O_3, and so on. In the second argument, the subject is causality, not motion, but the idea is basically the same.

Premise (4) says that there can't be a cause/effect chain that extends infinitely far back into the past. The idea is that cause/effect chains (or mover/movee chains) leading from the present back into the past have a finite number of links. The arrow in the following diagram represents the relationship of causality:

$$O_f \longrightarrow \cdots \longrightarrow O_3 \longrightarrow O_2 \longrightarrow O_1 \longrightarrow \cdots$$

Past   Present   Future

Although Aquinas's argument focuses on chains that extend from the present back into the past, his principle (4) also has implications about chains that extend from the present forward into the future. These also must have a finite number of links. Cause/effect chains must be finite in both directions.

I'll begin with a criticism aimed just at argument I; after that, I'll lump the two arguments together and formulate some objections that apply to both.

Aquinas on the Cause of Motion

Aquinas thinks (premises 1–2) that if an object is in motion, it must be caused to move by something outside itself. Aquinas got this idea from Aristotle's physics. Aristotle (384–322 B.C.) held that if an object continues to move, its motion must be sustained by a force that keeps it in motion. If you remove the force, the object stops moving.

This idea didn't survive into modern physics. You may remember from your high school physics course that Newton, in the seventeenth century, held that an object remains in constant uniform motion unless acted on by a force. Recall that one of Newton's laws of motion is $F = ma$. This means that if an object of mass m is acted on by a force of value F, then it will accelerate to degree a. This Newtonian law says that an object that isn't acted on by a force won't accelerate, which means it will remain at rest *or in uniform motion*. Newton's laws say that an object can remain in motion forever without there being any force that sustains its motion.

Newton's laws do not exclude the following possibility: The universe contains exactly one physical object, which always moves in uniform motion without any forces ever acting on it. Of course, Newton's laws don't say that the universe we live in is like this. Our universe obviously contains more than one material object. My point, though, is that Newton's theory of motion was different from Aristotle's and so was different from Aquinas's. Aristotle and Aquinas thought that motion requires an outside force; Newton and more modern physical theories hold that it is acceleration, not simply change in position, that requires a force.

It is not difficult to rescue Aquinas's first argument from this Newtonian objection. Just replace his talk of motion with the concept of acceleration. If objects accelerate, there must be a force that causes them to do so. Then Aquinas' line of reasoning will lead us to the conclusion that there must exist a supernatural entity that causes the first accelerating object in nature to accelerate.

God Is a Person, Not Just a Cause That Exists Outside of Nature

I now turn to some problems that the two arguments share. First, it is important to see that proposition (5)—that there is an entity outside of nature that causes the first moving object in nature to move, or that causes the first event in nature to occur—does not guarantee the existence of God, where God is understood to mean a person with something like the three properties of omnipotence, omniscience, and omnibenevolence (an all-PKG being). As Aquinas himself realized, conclusion (6) does not follow from proposition (5), in either argument.

The Birthday Fallacy

Another problem arises when we ask whether the argument shows that there is *precisely one* first cause, or instead shows only that there is *at least one*. Suppose we grant that each causal chain in nature has a first member. According to Aquinas, each of these first members must be caused by some event outside of nature. However, it does not follow that there is exactly one such event outside of nature that set all causal chains in the natural world in motion. Here it is important to see the difference between the following two propositions; the first is different from and does not deductively imply the second:

- Every event in the natural world traces back to an event that occurs outside nature.
- There is a single event outside of the natural world to which each event in nature traces back.

The difference here parallels the logical difference between the following two propositions, the first of which is true and the second false:

- Every person has a birthday—a day on which he or she was born.
- There is a single day that is everybody's birthday.

I want to give a name to the mistaken idea that the second proposition follows from the first. I'll call this mistake the *Birthday Fallacy*.

So one problem with arguments I and II is that they don't show that there is exactly one first cause or unmoved mover; at best, they show that there is at least one. To think otherwise is to commit the Birthday Fallacy.

Why Can't Nature Be Infinitely Old?

Another objection to Aquinas's first two arguments is his claim that cause/effect chains cannot extend infinitely far into the past. Why is this impossible? If the natural world were infinitely old, each event could be caused by an earlier event. Every event that occurs in nature could have a cause that also existed in nature, so there would be no reason to infer that something outside of nature must exist as the cause of what occurs inside.

Aquinas thinks he has an answer to this question. He doesn't simply *assume* that causal chains extending into the past must be finite in length; he has an *argument* that he thinks shows why this is so. Here is his argument, which I'll reconstruct in terms of an example of a present event—you are reading this page now:

> You are reading this page now.
> A causal chain that extends from this present event infinitely into the past, by definition, lacks a first member.
> If a causal chain lacked a first member, then all subsequent events in the chain could not occur.
>
> _____
>
> Hence, the causal chain leading up to your now reading this page must be finitely old.

The third premise is where this argument goes wrong. Even if we assume that no event in nature can happen without its having a cause, it does not follow that there has to be a first natural event.

Many traditional theists will agree that the world could have an infinite future—that it could go on forever. However, if an infinite future is possible, why is an infinite past ruled out? If there doesn't have to be a last event in the history of the natural world, why must there be a first? Why accept Aquinas's claim that causal chains can't extend infinitely into the past? Here Aquinas gets some help from modern physics, which views the universe as finitely old. Although it is conceivable that the universe is infinitely old, apparently there are scientific reasons to think that this isn't so.

Why Must Every Event in Nature Have a Cause?

This brings me to my last objection to Aquinas's first two arguments for the existence of God. Even if the natural world is only finitely old, why must there be an explanation of the first event that occurs in nature? That is, why must *every* event that occurs in nature have a cause?

Do scientists assume that every event has a cause? Well, it is true that scientists often try to discover the causes of events that they observe. However, this activity of searching does not require that one actually *believe* that every event has a cause. Perhaps there are exceptions to this generalization. Scientists try to find causal explanations for the events they observe for a very simple reason: If you don't look, you won't discover the cause if there is one. Better to look and fail to find than never to look at all.

The Third Argument: Contingency

Aquinas's third argument for the existence of God, like the first two, begins with an observation that everybody would agree is true. The observation is put in language that may be unfamiliar, but once explained, it seems clear enough. The observation is that contingent things exist. What does it mean to say that a thing is contingent? The opposite of contingency is necessity. What makes an object contingent or necessary?

Necessary and Contingent Beings

You, I, the Washington Monument, the human race, the earth, the solar system, and the Milky Way are all examples of contingent things. Although all of us exist, we needn't have existed. The world could have failed to include any of us. If the particular sperm and egg that produced you hadn't encountered each other, you wouldn't have come into existence. Your parents would have had other children or no children at all. Likewise for the human race; although the world obviously includes human beings, it needn't have. Contingent things depend for their existence on something or other happening. In contrast, a necessary being is something that must exist no matter what. It doesn't depend for its existence on anything.

Possible Worlds

I want to represent the concepts of necessity and contingency by introducing a new idea. Consider the totality of things that have existed, now exist, or will exist at any place in the universe. This totality comprises a giant object that I'll call "the actual world." Imagine a census of the objects in the actual world. We might display this census on a very long time line, in which the durations of various objects are represented:

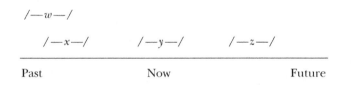

Past	Now	Future

Notice that the life spans, or durations, of objects w and x overlap. Objects w and x existed in the past and now are no more. Object y came into existence in the past, exists now, and will continue to exist until some future date, when it will cease to be. Object z hasn't yet come into being, but it will. Of course, this is a dreadfully incomplete inventory of everything that was, is, or will be. Never mind. You get the idea: The actual world consists of everything that has existed, exists now, or will exist, anywhere in the universe.

We know the world needn't have had precisely the census it does. Some of the objects in this census might have failed to exist. Other objects, which don't actually exist, might have done so. Let's call each possible way the world might have been a "possible world." There are many of these.

We may now say that an object is contingent if it exists in some but not all possible worlds. And an object is necessary if it exists in all possible worlds. Suppose the following are the censuses found in several possible worlds. As before, the horizontal line represents time within a possible world:

wx	y	z	Actual world
ab	y	z	Possible world 1
ac	d	z	Possible world 2

Past	Present	Future

Notice that w exists in the actual world, but not in the two alternative possible worlds represented. On the other hand, y exists in the actual world and in the first possible world, but not in the second. Object z is different—it exists in all the possible worlds depicted. Of course, there are more than three possible worlds, as there are more than two alternative ways the actual world might have been (the actual world, of course, is one of the possible worlds). Would z continue to appear if we listed not just a few possible worlds, but all of them? That is the question of whether z is a necessary being.

I cited some examples of contingent things—you, the Washington Monument, the earth, and a few others. These examples might strike you as typical of everything that exists. That is, you might find plausible the following philosophical conjecture: Everything that exists is contingent. Familiar objects clearly have this property. But is *everything* contingent? Aquinas argues in his third proof of the existence of God that not everything is contingent. There is at least one necessary being—namely, God.

Here is how his proof goes:

(III) (1) Contingent things now exist.
    (2) Each contingent thing has a time at which it fails to exist (contingent things are not omnipresent).

    (3) So if everything were contingent, there would be a time at which nothing exists (call this an "empty time").
    (4) That empty time would have been in the past.
    (5) If the world were empty at one time, it would be empty forever after (a conservation principle).

    (6) So if everything were contingent, nothing would exist now.
    (7) But clearly, the world is now not empty (see premise 1).

    (8) So there exists a being who is not contingent.

    Hence, God exists.

Aquinas's argument has two stages. First, there is his defense of proposition (6), which is contained in premises (1)–(5). Second, there is his use of proposition (6) to establish the existence of God. Before considering why Aquinas thinks (6) is correct, I want to focus on his use of (6) and (7) to infer proposition (8).

Reductio Ad Absurdum

Aquinas's proof of (8) from (6) and (7) has a distinctive logical form. His proof is a *reductio ad absurdum* argument (a "reductio," for short).

When I talked about deductive validity in Chapter 2, I emphasized that the word "valid" in logic and philosophy doesn't mean what it means in everyday life. The same holds for the idea of reducing something to absurdity. In ordinary speech, this means something like "making a mockery of an idea." In logic, however, *reductio* arguments are perfectly good arguments—they are deductively valid.

Here's how a *reductio* argument works. You want to prove a proposition *P*. To do this, you argue that if *P* were false, some proposition *A* would have to be true. But you construct the argument so that *A* is obviously false (it's an "absurdity"). From this, you may validly conclude that *P* is true. *Reductio* arguments, in other words, have the following valid logical form:

> If *P* is false, then *A* is true.
> *A* is false.
> ———————————
> *P* is true.

Aquinas tries to establish the existence of a necessary being by *reductio*. He argues that if only contingent beings existed, the world would now be empty. But it is obviously false that the world is now empty. Hence, not everything is contingent—there must exist at least one necessary being.

Let's now examine Aquinas's defense of proposition (6). Why should we think that the world would now be empty if there were no necessary beings? Aquinas's reasons for thinking this are contained in premises (1)–(5).

Contingency and Eternity

I'll begin by registering an objection to premise (2). Contrary to Aquinas, I submit that a contingent thing can be eternal; the fact that an object is contingent doesn't mean that there must be a time at which it fails to exist. I'll grant that familiar contingent objects aren't eternal. You are an example. You might have failed to exist; in addition, there was a time before you were born and there will be a time after you die. But this is just an example. We want to know whether *all* contingent beings must fail to be eternal.

Notice first that the considerations affecting contingency differ from those affecting the question of eternity. How can you tell whether an object is contingent in a diagram like the one given before showing the actual world and two possible worlds? You look *down* the list of possible worlds, checking to see if the object in question is present in each one. In that diagram, we might say that contingency is represented "vertically." Eternality is different. To see whether an object present in a given possible world is eternal, you look *across* the representation of that possible world, checking to see if it exists at all times in that world. So eternality is represented "horizontally."

Could an object exist in only some possible worlds and still exist at all times in the actual world? That is, could an object be both contingent and eternal? Aquinas says no. Here is a consideration that suggests he may be wrong.

The idea that material objects are made of very small indivisible particles has had a long history, going back at least to the ancient Greeks. Of course, we no longer think of atoms as indivisible particles—we have long since learned to talk about subatomic particles. However, suppose for the moment that the word "atom" names such indivisible particles. These particles are the basic building blocks of all material things.

One idea that has been put forward in atomistic theories is that atoms (fundamental particles) can't be created or destroyed. Large objects made of atoms can be created and destroyed by assembling and disassembling collections of atoms. But the basic particles themselves can't be destroyed, because you can't break them into pieces. Again, I'm not saying that this is true of the objects we now regard as the smallest material particles. I mention it only to describe a possible view of atoms.

Atoms, on the view I'm describing, are eternal. If a given atom exists now, it has always existed, and it will always exist. Let's call one of the atoms that populate the actual world by the name "Charlie." Charlie is eternal. Does it follow that Charlie is a necessary being—that the world couldn't have failed to include him? I would say not. The world could have contained more atoms than it does, or fewer. Indeed, it doesn't seem impossible that the world might have been entirely empty of matter. So Charlie, like all the atoms that happen to actually exist, is a contingent being. If this is right, then Aquinas's premise (2) is mistaken. Charlie, I've claimed, is a contingent being, but he is eternal. So contingent things needn't have a time at which they fail to exist.

The argument I've just given against premise (2) depends on a particular theory about the nature of atoms. If atoms really are indestructible, I can claim to have refuted Aquinas's premise. But are they, in fact, indestructible? Again, remember I'm discussing the smallest units of matter here. This is how I'm using the word "atom."

Conservation Laws in Physics

Current physics doesn't support the view that atoms are indestructible. Before Einstein, physics upheld a principle that said that the quantity of mass in the universe is constant. Einstein replaced this classical conservation law with another one. Mass isn't conserved; rather, a quantity that Einstein called "mass-energy" is conserved. This principle says that mass can be destroyed; it may be converted into energy. Modern physics, therefore, doesn't seem to allow me to tell my story about Charlie, the indestructible atom. So matter *can* be destroyed, according to current theory. But this doesn't mean that every contingently existing particle WILL be destroyed, sooner or later. It is the latter claim that Aquinas advances in premise (2). I don't know of any good reason to think this is so, although I'll leave the question open.

My conclusion thus far is that premise (2) is mistaken; a contingent thing doesn't have to have a time at which it fails to exist. Let's move on.

The Birthday Fallacy (Again)

The transition from premise (2) to statement (3) involves a fallacy. Even if we grant that every contingent entity has a time at which it fails to exist, we can't conclude that there is an empty time. The fallacy here is the same one discussed concerning Aquinas's first two arguments. Recall the point about birthdays; "Everybody has a birthday" does not deductively imply that there is a day that is everyone's birthday.

To make this point graphic, consider the following possible world, in which no object is eternal, and yet there is no empty time:

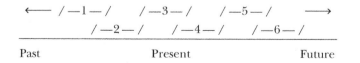

The arrows at the beginning and end indicate that the pattern should be repeated indefinitely into the past and into the future. So the supposition that everything is contingent doesn't imply an empty time. But there is an additional unjustified step. Even if there does have to be an empty time, why must it have been in the past? I see no reason to assume this.

Necessary Beings other than God

I've noted some problems in Aquinas's attempted *reductio* proof that not everything is contingent. Suppose, however, that Aquinas could show that there is at least one necessary being. Could he conclude from this that God exists? I want to argue that this, too, doesn't follow. In discussing Aquinas's first two arguments, I claimed that the existence of God doesn't follow from the existence of a first cause. I now want to suggest that the existence of God doesn't follow from the existence of a necessary being.

To explain why this is so, I need to develop an idea from the philosophy of mathematics. Until now I've described necessity and contingency as properties of entities. You and I are contingent beings, for example. Now, however, I want to discuss the idea that contingency and necessity are properties of propositions. Propositions, or statements, are true or false. They also have the properties of necessity and contingency.

Necessary and Contingent Propositions

Necessity and contingency as properties of propositions are definable in a way that parallels the way this distinction applies to entities like you and me. A proposition is necessarily true if it is true in all possible worlds. A proposition is necessarily false if it is false in all possible worlds. Contingent propositions are true in some possible worlds and false in others. A true statement is contingent if it is true in the actual world, though false in some possible world.

It is easy to cite examples of contingent propositions. Consider the fact that the United States is a country in North America. This is true, though only contingently so. Consider the following contingent falsehood: the Rocky Mountains are no higher than six thousand feet above sea level. This is false, but there are possible worlds in which it is true.

Mathematical Truths

Are there any necessary truths? Many philosophers have held that mathematical truths are necessarily true. Consider the fact that $7 + 3 = 10$. It isn't just that this happens to be true in the actual world. There is no possible world in which it is false. The sum of 7 and 3 could not fail to equal 10.

To see why this is at least a plausible view of mathematical propositions, you've got to be clear on what the proposition says. The proposition doesn't say that if you put seven rabbits together with three others, there will be ten bunnies forever after. Rabbits reproduce, but this doesn't contradict any fact of arithmetic. Take another example: If you pour three cups of sugar into seven cups of water, you will not obtain ten cups of liquid. But, again, this doesn't contradict the fact that $7 + 3 = 10$. Arithmetic is unaffected by this result; it just so happens that liquids and solids don't always combine additively.

Names Differ from the Things Named

Here is a somewhat more subtle point to notice. The proposition that $7 + 3 = 10$ doesn't say anything about the language we use in expressing that fact to ourselves. It is a contingent fact that human beings use the numeral "7" to refer to the number 7. We might have called that number by another name—we might have used the numeral "2" to denote the number 7. Similarly, it is a contingent fact that we use the symbol "=" to represent the relation of equality. So it is a contingent fact that the sentence "7 + 3 = 10" expresses what it does, and it is a contingent fact that the sentence expresses a true proposition rather than a false one. But this doesn't show that 7 + 3 might not have equaled 10. The fact couldn't have been otherwise, even though we might have used our terminology differently.

The distinction I'm drawing here is very obvious in some contexts, though it is easy to lose sight of it in others. Few things are more different than a thing and its name. You are a person, but your name isn't. Your name contains a certain number of letters, but you don't. Your name is a linguistic entity, but you aren't.

We mark this difference by using quotation marks. If we want to talk about a thing, we use its name. If we want to talk about the name of a thing, we put the name in quotation marks. So if I want to talk about a big mountain in western North America, I might say that the Rocky Mountains are tall. But if I want to talk about the mountain range's name, I'd say that the phrase "the Rocky Mountains" contains seventeen letters.

Numbers Aren't Numerals

This is obvious when you think about it. When it comes to mathematics, however, we tend to confuse these ideas. Numerals are names of numbers. But the number and its name are different, just as the phrase "the Rocky Mountains" differs from the mountains themselves. I grant that it is a contingent matter that the sentence "7 + 3 = 10" expresses a truth. I deny, however, that 7 + 3 might have failed to equal 10. The proposition is necessarily true, even though it is a contingent fact that the sentence expresses the proposition it does. Just as your name is part of a language, though you aren't, so the sentence "7 + 3 = 10" is part of a language, though the proposition it expresses is not.

Sets

So what does the proposition that 7 + 3 = 10 actually mean? It doesn't say anything about rabbit reproduction or about the way sugar and water combine when poured together. Nor does it say anything about the language we use. You can think of this statement as describing a basic property of mathematical objects called *sets*.

First, I need a bit of terminology. The *union* of two sets is the set that includes all the members of the first and all the members of the second, and no others. A set is any collection of objects. So the set {Groucho Marx, Napoleon, the Eiffel Tower} is a three-member set, and the set {Napoleon, the Rocky Mountains, the French Revolution} is also a three-member set. The items in a set needn't have anything special in common with each other. There are sets of similar things, but there are also sets of dissimilar things. The union of the two sets just mentioned is this set: {Groucho Marx, Napoleon, the Eiffel Tower, the Rocky Mountains, the French Revolution}.

The proposition that 7 + 3 = 10 can be understood to say the following: Consider any two sets where the first contains exactly seven objects and the second contains exactly three. If these sets have no common members, then the union of these two sets will have precisely ten members. Notice that the arithmetic proposition doesn't say that the Rocky Mountains exist, or that there are at least seven material things in the universe. The arithmetic fact doesn't rule out the possibility that the world contains no material objects at all. It simply describes a basic property of the operation of set-theoretic union.

Necessity and Certainty Are Different

I need to add a final clarification of the thesis that mathematical truths are necessary. In saying that it is a necessary truth that $7 + 3 = 10$, I'm not saying that I know that the proposition is true with absolute certainty. Nor am I saying that I'll never change my mind on the question of whether $7 + 3 = 10$.

This is a rather subtle point, because we sometimes express our lack of certainty about a proposition by saying that maybe the proposition isn't so. If I think there will be rain tomorrow, but entertain some small doubt that this will be so, I may express this by saying, "Possibly it won't rain tomorrow." But my certainty or uncertainty is a fact about *me*. It is a fact in the *subjective* realm. I want to distinguish this question from the question of whether a given proposition has the property of necessity or contingency. The latter question doesn't have anything special to do with me. Necessity and contingency are *objective*.

Here is a nonmathematical example that may make this clearer. Could there be perpetual motion machines? A machine of this sort wouldn't require any energy input to keep running, but it would provide a constant output of energy. Scientists for many hundreds of years tried to design such a machine. They always failed. Finally, in the nineteenth century, physicists working in the area called thermodynamics proved that perpetual motion machines are impossible.

Consider the proposition that there are or will be perpetual motion machines. This is, we now believe, a falsehood. Is it a necessary falsehood? I would say yes. It isn't just that no one will bother to build one; the point is that it is impossible to build one. This is what science tells us.

Now I'll ask an entirely separate question: Am I absolutely certain that no such machine will ever exist? I guess I'm not absolutely certain. After all, science has been wrong before, and so maybe it now is wrong when it says that such machines are impossible. Opinion has changed through history on the question of whether such machines could be built. Before the nineteenth century, many serious scientists thought such machines are possible. Later, *opinion* changed. Maybe it will change again.

So the certainty that a single scientist or a community of scientists may have about the issue may change. But there is something that doesn't change. Either it is possible for such things to exist or it isn't. This should convince you that *certainty* and *necessity* are different. People may change their degree of certainty about a proposition; they may even think at one time that the proposition is true, but later on think that it is false. However, the proposition itself doesn't change from true to false. Nor does a proposition cease to be necessary just because people stop believing it. So, to say that arithmetic truths are necessary isn't to say that people are certain about arithmetic. Nor is it to say that people have never changed their minds about arithmetic propositions. Again, these are questions about our attitudes toward the propositions. But whether a proposition is necessary or not has nothing to do with our attitudes. In this respect, necessity is like truth—both are objective issues, independent of what people happen to believe.

To sum up, I've described a prominent view in the philosophy of mathematics. It holds that arithmetic truths are necessary. I haven't provided that view with a complete defense, but I hope you can see what it asserts. I also hope you find it at least somewhat plausible, even if it is not entirely convincing.

What has this material about mathematics to do with the conclusion of Aquinas's third proof? Recall that Aquinas reasons that if there is a necessary being, then God must exist. Part of my point in talking about mathematical necessity here is that I want to describe a necessary being that no one would think is God.

Numbers Are Necessary Beings

Consider the fact that arithmetic includes various existence statements. Besides asserting that $7 + 3 = 10$, arithmetic also asserts that there is a prime number immediately after 10. Furthermore, if arithmetic truths are necessary, then it is a necessary truth that there exists a prime number immediately after 10. To put it bluntly, the philosophy of mathematics I've described holds that the number 11 is a necessary being. It exists in all possible worlds. This follows from the thesis that arithmetic truths are necessary and from the fact that arithmetic contains existence claims.

The conclusion that there is a God doesn't follow from the assertion that not everything is contingent. A philosopher of mathematics might claim that the number 11 is a necessary being, but this wouldn't entail that God exists. This is my last criticism of Aquinas's third argument.

Aquinas's Fourth Argument: Properties That Come in Degrees

I won't spend much time on Aquinas's fourth proof of the existence of God. It is rooted in an Aristotelian view of causality that seems radically implausible now. Here's the argument:

(IV)(1) Objects have properties to greater or lesser extents.
　(2) If an object has a property to a lesser extent, then there exists some other object that has that property to the maximum possible degree (call this a maximum exemplar of the property).
　(3) So, there is an entity that has all properties to the maximum possible degree.
　————————————
　Hence, God exists.

The argument begins with an observation that is obviously true: Some things are more powerful and some less; some are more intelligent and others less, and so on. The second premise, however, seems entirely implausible. The fact that Charlie Chaplin is less than maximally funny doesn't mean that there must exist a maximally funny comedian. And the fact that we are somewhat intelligent, though not perfectly so, doesn't seem to require that there exists a perfectly intelligent being.

The Aristotelian idea that Aquinas is using here is roughly as follows. Aristotle thought that fire is the maximally hot substance. When other objects are hot to some lesser degree, this is because fire is mixed in them to some extent. The property of heat can occur to a less than maximal degree in human beings, for example, only because there exists this substance, fire, which is hot to the maximum possible degree. Fire is the maximum exemplar of heat, from which lesser degrees of heat derive.

There are other problems with the argument. If each property has a maximum exemplar, it doesn't follow that there is an entity that is a maximum exemplar of all properties. Recall the Birthday Fallacy: The fact that everyone has a birthday doesn't imply that there is a single day on which everyone was born. So even if there is a maximum exemplar of intelligence, a maximum exemplar of power, and a maximum exemplar of moral goodness, it doesn't follow that there is a single entity who is all-knowing, all-powerful, and all-good.

Finally, there is the problem of contradiction. If intelligence has its maximum exemplar, then stupidity would have to have its maximum exemplar as well. By Aquinas's argument, this leads us to say that there is a single being who is both maximally intelligent and maximally stupid. But this is impossible. That concludes what I want to say about Aquinas's fourth argument for the existence of God.

Criticizing an Argument versus Showing the Argument's Conclusion Is False

None of the four arguments I've discussed here is successful. Does this mean there is no God? It means no such thing. There may be other arguments for the existence of God that are convincing. That the four arguments discussed here don't work doesn't mean that no argument will work. Not one word has been said here that shows that atheism is true. All we have seen is that some arguments for theism are flawed. In the next chapter, I'll consider Aquinas's fifth argument for the existence of God. Maybe it will fare better.

Review Questions

1   What objections are there to the first cause argument?
2   What is the Birthday Fallacy? How does it figure in the discussion of Aquinas's arguments?
3   Explain what it means for an object to be necessary or contingent. What is a "possible world"?
4   How are necessity and eternality related? How does this bear on Aquinas's third argument?
5   What is a reductio argument? Give an example.
6   What is the difference between necessity and certainty? What is meant by saying that necessity is "objective"?
7   What would it mean for something to be a first cause without being God? What would it mean for something to necessarily exist without being God
8   Aquinas seems to commit the Birthday Fallacy when he argues that, if every natural event has a cause, then there must be one "first cause." Why is this line of reasoning fallacious? Can you think of another example of the Birthday Fallacy?
9   Why does Aquinas think that it is "inconceivable" that the world is infinitely old? Do you think his argument is plausible? Why or why not?
10   Why, if at all, do you think it might be helpful to reflect on unsuccessful arguments for the existence of God? Explain your answer.
11   Which of the four arguments discussed above do you find most convincing? Why?

Problems for Further Thought

1   I formulated Aquinas's proofs by having him talk about objects that exist in "nature" (in "the natural world"). What does "nature" include? Does it include just the things we can see or hear or touch or taste or smell?
2   In discussing Aquinas's third proof, I talked about Charlie the atom as an example of a thing that is both eternal and contingent. Could something exist that is both necessary and noneternal? It would exist at *some* time in each possible world, though it would not exist at *all* times in the actual world. Can you give an example of such a thing?
3   I criticized Aquinas's third argument by discussing numbers, which I claimed exist necessarily. Can the argument be reformulated so that this objection no longer applies?

4   I criticized Aquinas's fourth argument by discussing "maximum stupidity." Can Aquinas reply to this objection by claiming that stupidity is just the absence of intelligence?

Recommended Readings, Video, and Audio

Visit the companion website at www.routledge.com/cw/sober for suggestions of readings, video, and audio, for this chapter.

Chapter 5

The Design Argument

There are three main traditional arguments for the existence of God—the cosmological argument, the design argument, and the ontological argument. Aquinas's first, second, and third ways, surveyed in the previous chapter, are cosmological arguments. Cosmological arguments take different forms; each cites a general feature of the whole universe as evidence that there is a God. The second type of traditional argument, the design argument, is the one we'll consider in the present chapter. The ontological argument will occupy our attention in Chapter 8.

Aquinas's fifth argument for the existence of God is an instance of what has come to be called the Argument from Design. The design argument has a variety of forms, some of which I'll describe. To start things off, here is a formulation that is close to the one Aquinas uses:

(1) Among objects that act for an end, some have minds whereas others do not.
(2) An object that acts for an end, but does not itself have a mind, must have been designed by a being that has a mind.
(3) Hence, there exists a being with a mind who designed all mindless objects that act for an end.

Hence, God exists.

Note as a preliminary point that the transition from (2) to (3) commits the Birthday Fallacy described in Chapter 4. If each mindless object that acts for an end has a designer, it doesn't follow that there is a *single* designer of all the mindless objects that act for an end.

Goal-Directed Systems

What does Aquinas mean by "act for an end"? This phrase corresponds to the modern idea of a goal-directed system. Human beings act for an end because they have desires; these desires represent the ends or purposes or goals to which behaviors are directed. Human beings are capable of goal-directed behavior because they have minds. Consider, however, a different example: a guided missile. It is a goal-directed system. Its goal or function is to reach and destroy its target. If the target veers off to the side, the missile can adjust its behavior so that it will achieve its purpose. Guided missiles are goal-directed systems, but they don't have minds. How is this possible? The answer is consistent with what Aquinas says in premise (2). Guided missiles are *artifacts*. They are devices built by creatures with minds—namely, human beings. This is how missiles obtained the machinery that allows them to engage in goal-directed behavior.

Are there other examples of goal-directed systems besides human beings and artifacts? Nonhuman organisms provide a third category. Even bacteria, which evidently don't have beliefs and desires, seek out nutrients and avoid poisonous chemicals. Because of this, it seems plausible to describe them as having the goal of surviving and reproducing. They are able to modify their behavior to achieve these ends.

Does the list stop with human beings, artifacts, and nonhuman organisms? Aquinas followed Aristotle in thinking that even inanimate objects such as rocks and comets have goals. This idea went out of fashion with the Scientific Revolution in the seventeenth century. It now seems implausible to describe a rock as being hard "in order to resist destruction." It also seems strange to say that rocks fall toward the center of the Earth when they are released "in order to attain the location that it is in their nature to seek." But this is how Aristotle thought about rocks, and Aquinas followed him here. Both thought that everything, whether living or not, should be understood *teleologically*—that is, as a goal-directed system. (This will be discussed further in Chapter 34.) I won't take issue with this general teleological picture, except to note that it is far more encompassing than the one provided by modern science. However, this point does not affect the design argument as I have formulated it. What is required is just that *some* mindless objects are goal directed.

Two Kinds of Design Argument

It will be useful to distinguish two kinds of design argument. Aquinas would have been willing to endorse them both. David Hume (1711–1776), who examined various design arguments in his *Dialogues Concerning Natural Religion* (1779), discusses both sorts. I'll call these two sorts of arguments *global* and *local* design arguments.

A global design argument cites some general features of the whole universe and argues that this feature should be explained by the hypothesis that it is the product of intelligent design. An example would be the argument that proposes to explain why the laws of nature are simple. Newton himself argued that the simplicity of natural laws is evidence that there exists an intelligent and perfect God who was their author.

A local design argument focuses on a more specific feature that one or more object in the universe has and claims that the hypothesis that God exists is the best or the only plausible explanation of that fact. The example I'll consider here concerns features of the organisms we observe on Earth. They are goal-directed systems; they are complex systems equipped with the ability to modify their behavior so that they can survive and reproduce. In this chapter, I'll focus on the local argument, which claims that special features of living things (including ourselves) are said to require explanation. In Chapter 7, I'll return to design arguments that are global.

Paley's Watch

During the eighteenth century and the early nineteenth century in Great Britain, design arguments were the rage. Numerous books were published arguing that the existence of God was required to explain this or that feature of the world we observe. One of the most influential works of this sort was produced by William Paley (1743–1805). Whereas Aquinas formulated his version of the design argument as a deductively valid argument, I'm going to interpret Paley's argument as an abductive argument, an inference to the best explanation.

Paley's striking formulation of the design argument goes like this: Suppose you are walking on a beach (actually, Paley talks about walking on a "heath") and find a watch lying on the sand. Opening it up, you see it is a complex and intricate piece of machinery. You also see that the parts of the watch work together to allow the hands to measure out equal intervals of time with considerable precision. What could explain the existence and characteristics of this object?

One hypothesis to consider I will call the *Random Hypothesis*. By the random action of the waves on the sand, a watch was accidentally produced. Even if you think that this explanation is possible, I bet you agree that it isn't very plausible. The idea that waves beating on sand could produce a useful object of such intricacy doesn't make a lot of sense. It is about as plausible as suggesting that a monkey randomly pounding on a typewriter will write out the complete works of Shakespeare. A far more plausible explanation is the *Design Hypothesis*. The intricacy and usefulness of the watch suggest that it is the product of intelligence. This hypothesis says that the watch exists because there was a watchmaker who produced it.

Why do we think the Design Hypothesis is more plausible than the Random Hypothesis? If there were a designer at work, then it wouldn't be surprising that the watch is complex and well suited to the task of measuring temporal intervals. If, however, the only process at work were waves pounding on sand, then it would be enormously surprising that the watch has these characteristics. The observed features of the watch are possible according to each hypothesis. But they are highly probable according to one and vastly improbable according to the other. In preferring the Design Hypothesis, we prefer the hypothesis that strains our credulity less.

I hope you see that Paley's argument uses the Surprise Principle described in Chapter 3. You've made some observations (call them O) and are considering whether O strongly favors one hypothesis (H_2) over another (H_1). The Surprise Principle says that O strongly favors H_2 over H_1 if H_2 says that O is very probable while H_1 says that O is quite improbable. O would be unsurprising if H_2 were true, but O would be very surprising if H_1 were true.

Not only do we infer the existence of a watchmaker from the watch we found, we can also infer something about the watchmaker's characteristics. We can say that the designer must have been fairly intelligent to produce an object of such intricacy. Chimps are somewhat intelligent, but the idea that a chimp could have made the watch is dubious. Rather, what we naturally infer is that the watchmaker must have had an intelligence at least on the order of human intelligence, given the features of the watch that we observe.

The Analogy

So far in this argument, Paley is simply describing what common sense would say about the watch on the beach. Paley then suggests an analogy. Look around the living world. Notice that it is filled with organisms that are extremely intricate and well adapted to living in the environments they inhabit. In fact, organisms are far more complicated than watches.

And as well suited as a watch is to the task of measuring time, organisms are even better suited to the tasks of surviving and reproducing.

How can we explain the fact that organisms are so amazingly intricate and well adapted? One possibility is the Random Hypothesis—that by a process akin to waves pounding on sand, orchids, crocodiles, and people came into existence. The other alternative is the Design Hypothesis—that an organism maker made the impressive pieces of machinery we call living things. Which explanation is more plausible? If the Random Hypothesis says that the existence of the watch is very improbable, then the Random Hypothesis must also say that the existence of these intricate and adapted organisms is very improbable. So if inferring the existence of a watchmaker is plausible in the first case, then inferring the existence of a designer of all life is plausible in the second.

Finally, we may ask how intelligent this maker of organisms must be, given the intricacy and fineness of adaptation that organisms exhibit. From what watches are like, we can infer that watchmakers must be pretty smart. By the same reasoning, we infer that the maker of organisms must be very, very intelligent—far more intelligent than human beings are. Paley's design argument concludes that the intricacy and adaptedness of organisms are best explained by postulating the existence of an *extremely* intelligent designer.

Abductive Arguments Often Postulate Unobserved Entities

There is a point that pertains to all of Aquinas's arguments that should be emphasized here. The design argument claims that there is something we observe—the complexity and adaptedness of living things—that is best explained by the hypothesis that there is a God. The conclusion of the argument concerns the existence of something we have not directly observed. Although there may be defects in this argument, the fact that it reaches a conclusion about a being we have not observed isn't one of them. Recall from Chapter 3 that abductive arguments frequently have this characteristic. It would cripple science to limit theorizing to a description of what scientists have actually observed. So my view of Paley's argument is that it is an abductive argument:

Organisms are intricate and well suited to the tasks of survival and reproduction.
=====================
Hence, organisms were created by an intelligent designer.

I've drawn a double line here to indicate that the argument does not aim at being deductively valid.

To show this is a strong abductive argument, Paley argues that it is analogous to a second inference to the best explanation:

The watch is intricate and well suited to the task of measuring time.
=====================
Hence, the watch was created by an intelligent designer.

Paley claims that if you grant that the watch argument is convincing, you should grant that the organism argument is convincing as well.

Hume's Criticisms of the Design Argument

Hume's *Dialogues on Natural Religion* contain several criticisms of the design argument. Sometimes he is talking about global design arguments—ones that argue that the entire universe must be the product of intelligent design. At other times, Hume addresses local arguments—ones that focus on the adaptedness and intricacy of organisms.

I've claimed that design arguments are abductive. Hume paints a very different picture. He represents the arguments as being *inductive arguments* or *arguments from analogy*. This may not look like a very important difference, as all of these formulations involve a nondeductive inference. But you will see in what follows that two of Hume's criticisms of design arguments aren't very convincing if we think of the design argument as an inference to the best explanation.

Is the Design Argument a Weak Argument from Analogy?

In this section, I'll discuss a criticism of the argument from design that Hume develops in Part II of his *Dialogues* (see the paragraph beginning "What I chiefly scruple ...").

To see what Hume has in mind when he talks about arguments from analogy, consider the following example of an analogy argument:

> Human beings circulate their blood.
> ===============
> Dogs circulate their blood.

I've drawn a double line between the premise and the conclusion, again to indicate that the argument isn't supposed to be deductively valid. In this argument, let's call human beings the *analogs* and dogs the *targets*. I say that dogs are the targets here because they are the items about which the argument aims to reach a conclusion. Hume suggests, with some plausibility, that such arguments are stronger or weaker depending on how similar the analogs are to the targets. To see what he means here, compare the above argument with the following one:

> Human beings circulate their blood.
> ===============
> Plants circulate their blood.

This argument is pretty weak because human beings and plants aren't very similar.

We can formulate Hume's point by saying that an analogy argument has the following logical form:

> Object A has property P.
> Object A and object T are similar to degree n.
> $n[$ ===============
> T has property P.

A is the analog and T is the target. The number n measures the degree of similarity between A and T. It goes from a minimum value of 0 (meaning that A and T aren't similar at all) to a maximum value of 1 (meaning that they share 100 percent of their characteristics). This number also represents a probability—that is why "n" is next to the double line separating premises from conclusion. A high value of n means that A and T are very similar and that the premises make the conclusion very probable. This expresses Hume's idea that the more similar A and T are, the more probable it is that the target object T has the property that is found in the analog A.

Hume uses this idea about analogy arguments to criticize the design argument. He thinks the design argument has the following form:

Watches are products of intelligent design.
$n[$ ===================
The universe is a product of intelligent design.

This is a very weak argument, Hume says, as the analog is really not very similar to the target. Watches resemble the universe as a whole in some ways, but fail to do so in a great many others. So n has a low value.

Here Hume is criticizing what I've called a global design argument—an argument that focuses on some large-scale features of the entire universe. Hume's point, however, also applies to local design arguments—to arguments that focus on organisms and their characteristics:

Watches are products of intelligent design.
$n[$ ===================
Organisms are products of intelligent design.

Hume's criticism is that organisms are really not very similar to watches. Watches are made of metal, but organisms aren't. Kangaroos hop around, but watches don't. Organisms reproduce and obtain nutrition from their environment, but watches don't. And so on. As analog and target are so dissimilar, the analogy argument is a very weak one; n is low here as well.

Hume's idea is that the strength or weakness of an analogy argument depends on the *overall similarity* of target and analog. You look at all the known characteristics of target and analog and try to say how similar they are overall. I grant that if you did this, you would conclude that watches and kangaroos aren't very similar. My view, however, is that this doesn't undermine the design argument at all when that argument is taken to be abductive. It is entirely irrelevant whether watches and kangaroos both have fur, or whether both hop around, or whether both reproduce. The design argument focuses on *a single pair of features* of each of these and asks how it should be explained. A watch's intricacy, as well as its being well suited to the task of measuring time, requires that we think of it as the product of intelligent design. Paley's claim is that an organism's intricacy, as well as its being well suited to the tasks of survival and reproduction, ought to be explained in the same way. It doesn't matter that the one is made of metal while the other isn't. *Overall* similarity is irrelevant.

The fundamental idea of Paley's argument is that the Surprise Principle tells us that the Design Hypothesis is better supported than the Random Hypothesis, given the observations we have made about living things. This argument stands on its own. To use the Surprise Principle in this case, it doesn't matter whether organisms are similar to watches or to anything else. I conclude that Hume is mistaken to criticize the design argument as a weak argument from analogy.

Is the Design Argument a Weak Induction?

A second criticism that Hume levels at the design argument rests on his assuming that the argument must be inductive if it is to make sense. (Here I have in mind the paragraph in Part II of the *Dialogues* that begins "And can you blame me …"; see especially the passage that begins "When two species of objects …")

Recall from Chapter 2 that inductive arguments involve observing a sample and extrapolating from it to some claim about one or more objects not in the sample. For example, suppose I call a large number of voters registered in a county and find that most of them are Democrats. This seems to license the inference that the next voter I call will probably be a Democrat. Hume observes, again with some plausibility, that the strength of an inductive inference is influenced by sample size. In particular, if my sample had included only five individuals, I would be on rather shaky ground if I used this as my basis for predicting what the next voter called would be like. My inference would be on even shakier ground if I ventured a guess about the next telephone call having never sampled even a single voter. A sample size of zero is just plain silly; an inductive argument can't be weaker than that.

Hume claims that if we are to have a reason for thinking that the universe we inhabit is the product of intelligent design, we must base this conclusion on induction. What would this involve? We would have to examine a large number of other universes and see that most or all of them were the result of intelligent design. If our sample size were sufficiently large, that would justify a conclusion about the universe that we inhabit. But how big *is* our sample size? How many universes have we observed being made by an intelligent designer? The answer is *zero*. The only universe we have ever experienced is the one we inhabit. We have not seen our universe being made by an intelligent designer, nor have we seen an intelligent designer make the organisms that exist in our universe. So no inductive argument can be constructed here.

My view is that this is true, but irrelevant. Small sample size does weaken an inductive argument. However, the design argument isn't an inductive argument. Hume assumed that the only sorts of inferences worth taking seriously are inductive and deductive. I think this is a mistake. There is abduction as well. Mendel didn't have to observe that lots of different organisms have genes before he could conclude that his pea plants have genes. Mendel never saw a single gene, but that didn't prevent him from inferring their existence. His inference was abductive, not inductive.

I've reviewed two of Hume's criticisms of the design argument. They don't work. Of course, this doesn't mean that the argument has no flaws, only that we have yet to uncover one. The design argument that Paley formulated considers two competing hypotheses—the hypothesis of intelligent design and the hypothesis of random physical processes. In the mid-nineteenth century, a new hypothesis was formulated that we now need to consider as a third alternative—this is Darwin's theory of evolution by natural selection. In the next chapter, I'll describe what this hypothesis asserts and discuss how it compares with the hypothesis of intelligent design.

Review Questions

1   What does it mean to say that the design argument is an abductive argument?
2   What is the difference between a global design argument and a local design argument?
3   How does Paley's argument about the watch use the Surprise Principle?
4   Hume formulated a principle that states how the strength of an analogy argument may be measured. What is it?

5   What two criticisms did Hume make of the design argument? Are these good criticisms if the argument is understood to be abductive in character?

6   In what respect can "mindless" objects, such as watches and walls, be said to "act for an end"? Can all mindless objects be characterized in the same way? Why or why not?

7   Aristotle and Aquinas believed that even natural objects like rocks and comets could be characterized as "goal-directed systems." Do you agree? If not, why not? What, if anything, do you think distinguishes these objects from things like bacteria, flowers, beatles, or foxes?

8   How do you think Hume would respond to my critique of his reconstruction of Paley's argument as an argument from analogy? as an inductive argument?

9   Suppose that Hume mischaracterized the logical structure of Paley's argument. Do you think that either of the two lines of critique he pursued on this basis (about the general dissimilarity of watches and organisms; about the lack of an independent sample) can be saved? What, if anything, can they still contribute to the debate?

Problems for Further Thought

1   It might be suggested that one difference between Paley's argument about the watch and his argument about organisms is that we have seen watchmakers, but have never directly observed God. Does this point of difference undermine the force of Paley's design argument?

2   I mentioned in passing that modern science no longer takes seriously the idea that *all* things are goal-directed systems. Consider the following pair of propositions. Can you think of a reason that the first of them might be true, whereas the second might be rejected?

The function of the heart is to pump blood.
The function of rain is to provide farm crops with water.
What does it mean to attribute a "function" to something?

3   In addition to the two criticisms that Hume makes of the design argument that are described in this chapter, Hume presents a third. He says that even if the design argument succeeds in showing that a designer made the universe (or the organisms in it), it does not succeed in establishing what characteristics that designer has. For this reason, the argument does not show that God exists. Is Hume's claim correct? How seriously does this undermine the design argument?

Recommended Readings, Video, and Audio

Visit the companion website at www.routledge.com/cw/sober for suggestions of readings, video, and audio, for this chapter.

Chapter 6

Evolution and Creationism

Aquinas and Paley maintained that the intricacy and adaptedness of organisms can be explained only by viewing them as the product of intelligent design, but they were not able to consider an alternative theory that Charles Darwin (1809–1882) put on the table in 1859 when he published his book *The Origin of Species*. Modern-day creationists do consider what their predecessors could not; they reject Darwin's theory and maintain that the old design argument is still correct. My goal in this chapter is to give a sample of the kinds of arguments that one needs to consider in thinking about the evolution versus creation debate. As I promised at the end of Chapter 3, I'll here introduce a new principle that is important to abductive inference, which will supplement the Surprise Principle and the Only Game in Town Fallacy. Unfortunately, I won't have time to provide a full treatment of the philosophical issues, and there are lots of biological details that are important here that I won't be able to discuss.

Creationism

Creationists (sometimes calling themselves "scientific creationists" or "intelligent design theorists") are present-day defenders of the design argument. Although they agree among themselves that intelligent design is needed to explain some features of the living world, they disagree with each other about various points of detail. Some hold that the earth is young (around 10,000 years old), whereas others concede that it is ancient—about 4.5 billion years old, according to current geology. Some creationists maintain that each species (or basic "kind" of organism) was separately created by an intelligent designer, whereas others concede that biologists are right when they assert, as Darwin did, that all life on Earth traces back to a common ancestor.

To clarify what creationism asserts, let's consider three possible relationships that might obtain among God (G), mindless evolutionary processes (E), and the complex adaptations that organisms are observed to have (O):

$$(\text{Theistic evolutionism}) \qquad G \longrightarrow E \longrightarrow O$$
$$(\text{Atheistic evolutionism}) \qquad E \longrightarrow O$$
$$(\text{Creationism}) \qquad G \longrightarrow E \nrightarrow O$$

Theistic evolutionism says that God set mindless evolutionary processes in motion; these processes, once underway, suffice to explain the complex adaptations we observe organisms to have. Atheistic evolutionism denies that there is a God, but otherwise agrees with theistic evolutionism that mindless evolutionary processes are responsible for complex adaptations. Creationism disagrees with both theistic evolutionism and atheistic evolutionism. It maintains that mindless evolutionary processes are incapable of giving rise to complex adaptations and that God directly intervenes in nature to bring these about. Creationism does not deny that evolution is responsible for some of the features we observe in nature; creationists concede that quantitative changes in a feature found in a species might be due to natural selection (an example of this sort of change will be described below). However, the emergence of genuinely novel, complex adaptive features is, for creationists, another story entirely.

You can see from these three options that belief in evolutionary theory is not the same as atheism. In my opinion, current evolutionary theory is neutral on the question of whether there is a God. Evolutionary theory can be supplemented with a claim, either *pro* or *con*, concerning whether God exists. It is also consistent with agnosticism, which is the view that we don't know whether there is a God. Evolutionary theory, however, is not consistent with creationism. It holds that mindless evolutionary processes (including the process of natural selection) are responsible for the complex adaptations we observe; creationism denies this.

Some Creationist Arguments

Some of the most frequently repeated creationist arguments contain mistakes and confusions. For example, some creationists have argued that evolutionary theory is on shaky ground because hypotheses about the distant past can't be proven with absolute certainty. They are right that evolutionary theory isn't absolutely certain, but then nothing in science is absolutely certain; recall the remarks in Chapter 3 about gambling. What one legitimately strives for in science is powerful evidence showing that one explanation is far more plausible than its competitors. Biologists now think that the hypothesis of evolution is about as certain as any hypothesis about the prehistoric past could be. Naturally, no scientist was on the scene some 3.8 billion years ago. However, it is nonetheless possible to have strong evidence about matters that one can't directly observe, as I hope my previous discussion of abduction has made clear.

Another example of an error that some creationists make is in their discussion of the Second Law of Thermodynamics. They claim that this law shows that it is impossible for order to arise from disorder by natural processes. Natural processes can lead an automobile to disintegrate into a junk heap, but creationists think the Second Law of Thermodynamics says that no natural process can cause a pile of junk to assemble itself into a functioning car. Here creationists are arguing that physics is inconsistent with the claim that life evolved from nonlife. What the Second Law actually says is that a *closed system* will (with high probability) move from states of greater order to states of lesser order. But if the system isn't closed, the law says nothing about what will happen. So if the earth were a closed system, its overall level of disorder would have to increase. But, of course, the earth is no such thing—energy from the sun is a constant input. If the universe as a whole is a closed system, then thermodynamics does entail that disorder will increase overall. But this overall trend doesn't prohibit pockets of order from arising and being maintained. The Second Law of Thermodynamics offers no basis for thinking that life couldn't have evolved from nonlife.

A full treatment of the evolution versus creationism debate would require me to describe the positive explanations that creationists have advanced. If you want to compare evolutionary theory and creationism, you can't just focus on the criticisms that creationists make of evolutionary ideas. You also should look carefully at what the alternative is. Doing this produces lots of difficulties for creationism. The reason is that creationists have either been woefully silent on the details of the explanation they want to defend, or they have produced detailed stories that can't withstand scientific scrutiny. For example, young earth creationists, as I mentioned, maintain that the earth is only a few thousand years old. This claim conflicts with a variety of very solid scientific findings from geology and physics. It isn't just evolutionary theory that you have to reject if you buy into this version of creationism, but a good deal of the rest of science as well.

As I have also indicated, there are many different versions of creationism. Creationism is not a single theory, but a cluster of similar theories. In the present chapter, I will focus on only a few of the options. First let's look at the ABCs of Darwinism.

Darwin's Two-Part Theory

Many of the main ideas that Darwin developed in *The Origin of Species* are still regarded by scientists as correct, but others have been refined or expanded. Still others have been junked entirely. Although evolutionary theory has developed considerably since Darwin's time, I'll take his basic ideas as a point of departure. Darwin's theory contains two main elements. First, there is the idea that all present-day living things are genealogically related. The organisms we see didn't come into existence independently by separate creation. Rather, organisms are related to each other by a family tree. You and I are related. If we go back far enough in time, we'll find a human being who is an ancestor of both of us. The same is true of us and a chimp, though, of course, we must go back even further in time to reach a common ancestor. And so it is for any two present-day organisms. Life evolved from nonlife, and then descent with modification gave rise to the diversity we now observe.

Notice that this first hypothesis of Darwin's says nothing about *why* new characteristics arose in the course of evolution. If all life is related, why aren't all living things identical? The second part of Darwin's theory is the idea of natural selection. This hypothesis tries to explain why new characteristics appear and become common and why some old characteristics disappear. It is very important to keep these two elements in Darwin's theory separate. The idea that all present-day living things are genealogically related isn't at all controversial in modern science. The idea that natural selection is the principal cause of evolutionary change is *somewhat* controversial, although it is still by far the majority view among biologists. One reason it is important to keep these ideas separate is that some creationists have tried to score points by confusing them. Creationists sometimes suggest that the whole idea of evolution is something even biologists regard with great doubt and suspicion. However, the idea that all life is related isn't at all controversial. What is controversial, at least to some degree, are ideas about natural selection.

Natural Selection

Here's a simple example of how natural selection works. Imagine a population of zebras that all have the same top speed. They can't run faster than 38 mph. Now imagine that a novelty appears in the population. A mutation occurs—a change in the genes found in some zebra— that allows that newfangled zebra to run faster (at 42 mph), say. Suppose running faster is advantageous, because a fast zebra is less likely to be caught and eaten by a predator than a slow one is. Running fast enhances the organism's *fitness*—its ability to survive and reproduce. If running speed is passed on from parent to offspring, what will happen? What will occur (probably) is that the fast zebra will have more offspring than the average slow zebra. As a result, the percentage of fast zebras in the population increases. In the next generation, fast zebras enjoy the same advantage, and so the characteristic of being fast will again increase in frequency. After a number of generations, we expect all the zebras to have this new characteristic. Initially, all the zebras ran at 38 mph. After the selection process runs its course, all run at 42 mph. So the process comes in two stages. First, a novel mutation occurs, creating the variation upon which natural selection operates. Then, natural selection goes to work changing the composition of the population:

Start		*Then*		*Finish*
100% run at 38 mph	$\longrightarrow$	A novel mutant runs at 42 mph; the rest run at 38 mph	$\longrightarrow$	100% run at 42 mph

We may summarize how this process works by saying that natural selection occurs in a population of organisms when there is *inherited variation in fitness*. Let's analyze what this means. The organisms must *vary*; if all the organisms are the same, then there will be no variants to select among. What is more, the variations must be passed down from parents to offspring. This is the requirement of *inheritance*. Last, it must be true that the varying characteristics in a population affect an organism's *fitness*—its chance of surviving and reproducing. If these three conditions are met, the population will evolve. By this, I mean that the frequency of characteristics will change.

The idea of natural selection is really quite simple. What Darwin did was to show how this simple idea has many implications and applications. Merely stating this simple idea wouldn't have convinced anyone that natural selection is the right explanation of life's diversity. The power of the idea comes from the numerous detailed applications.

Notice that the introduction of novel characteristics into a population is a precondition for natural selection to occur. Darwin didn't have a very accurate picture of how novel traits arise. He theorized about this, but didn't come up with anything of lasting importance. Rather, it was later in the nineteenth century that Mendel started to fill in this detail. Genetic mutations, we now understand, are the source of the variation on which natural selection depends. One central idea that Darwin had about mutation, which twentieth-century genetics has vindicated, is that mutations do not occur because they would be useful to the organism; this is what biologists mean when they say that mutations occur "at random."

Creationists sometimes say that the process of evolution by natural selection is like a tornado blowing through a junkyard. The latter process cannot sweep together the scraps of metal lying around on the ground and assemble them into a functioning automobile. From this, creationists conclude that the former process is likewise incapable of creating novel adaptations. This analogy is fundamentally misleading. The tornado is a totally random process, like the spinning of a huge roulette wheel. However, evolution by natural selection has two parts; mutations appear randomly, but then it is not a random matter which mutations increase in frequency and which decline. Selection is nonrandom. A better analogy than the tornado in the junkyard is one that Darwin proposed in his 1873 book *The Variation of Animals and Plants Under Domestication*:

> Let an architect be compelled to build an edifice with uncut stones, fallen from a precipice. The shape of each fragment may be called accidental; yet the shape of each has been determined by the force of gravity, the nature of the rock, and the slope of the precipice—events and circumstances all of which depend on natural laws; but there is no relation between these laws and the purpose for which each fragment is used by the builder. In the same manner, the variations of each creature are determined by fixed and immutable laws; but these bear no relation to the living structure which is slowly built up through the power of natural selection.
>
> (Darwin 1876, p. 236)

Notice that the little story I've told about zebra running speed describes a rather modest change that occurs *within* an existing species. Yet Darwin's 1859 book was called *The Origin of Species*. How does change within a species help explain the coming into existence of new species?

Speciation

Darwin's hypothesis was that small changes in a population (like the one I just described) add up. Given enough little changes, the organisms will become very different. Modern evolutionists usually tell a story like the following one. Think of a single population of zebras. Imagine that a small number of zebras are separated from the rest of the population for some reason; maybe they wander off or a river changes course and splits the old population in two. If the resulting populations live in different environments, selection will lead them to become increasingly different. Characteristics that are advantageous in one population may not be advantageous in the other. After a long time, the populations will have diverged. They will have become so different from each other that individuals from the one can't breed with individuals from the other. Because of this, they will be two species, not two populations belonging to the same species.

Pretty much everybody in Darwin's day, including those who thought that God created each species separately, would have agreed that the little story about zebras evolving a greater speed could be true. The real resistance to Darwin's theory focused on his thesis that the mechanism responsible for small-scale changes *within* species also gives rise to large-scale changes, namely, to the origin of *new* species. This was a daring hypothesis, but it is now the mainstream view in evolutionary theory. Even so, biologists continue to debate the importance that natural selection has had in the evolutionary process. Modern evolutionary theory describes other possible causes of evolutionary change. Which traits were due to natural selection and which were due to other evolutionary processes? There are a number of still unanswered questions in evolutionary biology about natural selection. Even biologists who hold that natural selection is the major cause of evolution are sometimes puzzled about how it applies in particular cases. For example, it is still rather unclear why sexual reproduction evolved. Some creatures reproduce sexually, others asexually. Why is this? Although there are open questions pertaining to natural selection, I want to emphasize that it isn't at all controversial that human beings share common ancestors with chimps. Don't confuse the idea of common ancestry with the idea of natural selection; these are separate elements in Darwin's theory.

The Tree of Life

I now turn to this uncontroversial idea. Why do biologists think it is so clear that living things are related to each other—that there is a family tree of life on Earth just as there is a family tree of your family? Two kinds of evidence have seemed persuasive. I won't give the details here; rather, I want to describe the *kinds* of arguments biologists deploy. As a philosopher, I'm more interested that you grasp the logic of the arguments; for the biological details, you should consult a biology book.

To illustrate how one line of argument works, consider this simple problem. Suppose I assign a philosophy class the job of writing an essay on the meaning of life. As I read through the papers, I notice that two students have handed in papers that are word-for-word identical. How should I explain this striking similarity? One possibility, of course, is that the students worked independently and by coincidence arrived at exactly the same result. The independent origin of the two papers isn't impossible. But I would regard this hypothesis as extremely implausible. Far more convincing is the idea that one student copied from the other or that each of them copied from a common source—an article downloaded from the Internet, perhaps. This hypothesis is a more plausible explanation of the observed similarity of the two papers.

The Principle of the Common Cause

The plagiarism example illustrates an idea that the philosopher Hans Reichenbach (in *The Direction of Time*, University of California Press, 1956) called the *Principle of the Common Cause*. Let's analyze the example more carefully to understand the rationale of the principle.

Why, in the case just described, is it more plausible that the students copied from a common source than that they wrote their papers independently? Consider how probable the matching of the two papers is, according to each of the two hypotheses. If the two students copied from a common source, then it is rather probable that the papers should closely resemble each other. If, however, the students worked independently, then it is enormously improbable that the two papers should be so similar. Here we have an application of the Surprise Principle described in Chapter 3: if one hypothesis says that the observations are very probable whereas the other hypothesis says that the observations are very improbable, then the observations strongly favor the first hypothesis over the second. The Principle of the Common Cause makes sense because it is a consequence of the Surprise Principle.

The example just described involves hypotheses that describe mental activity—when students plagiarize they use their minds, and the same is true when they write papers independently. However, it is important to see that the Principle of the Common Cause also makes excellent sense when the hypotheses considered do not describe mental processes. Here's an example: I have a barometer at my house. I notice that when it says "low," there is usually a storm the next day, and when it says "high," there is usually no storm the next day. The barometer reading on one day and the weather on the next are *correlated*. It may be that this correlation is just a coincidence; perhaps the two events are entirely independent. However, a far more plausible hypothesis is that the reading on one day and the weather on the next trace back to a common cause—namely, the weather at the time the reading is taken:

The common cause hypothesis is more plausible because it leads you to expect the correlation of the two observed effects. The separate cause hypothesis is less plausible because it says that the observed correlation is a very improbable coincidence. Notice that the hypotheses in this example do not describe the mental activities of agents.

Arbitrary Similarities among Organisms

I'll now apply this principle to the evolutionary idea of common ancestry. One reason biologists think all life is related is that all organisms (with some minor exceptions) have the same genetic code. To understand what this means, think of the genes in your body as a set of instructions for constructing more complex biological items—amino acids and then proteins. The total sequence of genes in your body and the sequence in a frog's are different. The striking fact, however, is that the gene that codes for a given amino acid in a frog codes for that very same amino acid in people. As far as we know now, there is no reason why the genes that code for a given amino acid had to code for that acid rather than some other. The code is arbitrary; there is no functional reason why it has to be the way it is. (Don't be misled by my talk of codes here. This word may suggest intelligent design, but this isn't what biologists mean. Genes *cause* amino acids to form; for present purposes, this is a perfectly satisfactory way to understand what it means for genes to "code for" this or that amino acid.)

How are we to explain the detailed similarity among the genetic codes that different species use? If the species arose independently of each other, we would expect them to use different genetic codes. But if those species all trace back to a common ancestor, it is to be expected that they will share the same genetic code. The Principle of the Common Cause underlies the belief that evolutionary biologists have that all living things on Earth have common ancestors.

Useful Similarities among Organisms

The reason a shared genetic code is evidence of common ancestry is that the code is arbitrary. There are lots of possible codes that would work. If there were only a single functional code, the fact that different species use this one code would not be evidence of common ancestry. Consider, for example, the fact that sharks and dolphins both have a streamlined body shape. Both are shaped like torpedoes. Is this strong evidence that they have a common ancestor? I would say not. There is an obvious functional reason why large predators that spend their lives swimming through water should be shaped like this. If there is life in other galaxies that includes large aquatic predators, we would probably expect those organisms to have this torpedo shape. Even if life on Earth and life on other galaxies are not descended from common ancestors, there are *some* similarities we would still expect to find. I conclude that the streamlined shape of dolphins and sharks isn't strong evidence that they evolved from a common ancestor. The Surprise Principle explains why some similarities, but not others, are good evidence for the hypothesis that there is a tree of life uniting all organisms on Earth.

The genetic code is just one example of a similarity that can't be explained by its usefulness to the organism. There are lots of others. Consider the fact that human beings have tail bones and that human fetuses have gill slits. Neither of these features is useful. Biologists interpret these features as evidence that we share common ancestors with nonhuman organisms. This and lots of other evidence point to the conclusion that we share common ancestors with monkeys, with other mammals, with fish, and with all other living things. In drawing this conclusion, biologists are using the Surprise Principle and the Principle of the Common Cause.

Irreducible Complexity

Although creationists have usually rejected the Darwinian hypothesis of common ancestry, not all have done so. What creationists universally reject is the thesis that natural selection is the correct explanation of the complex adaptations we observe in nature. Modern-day creationists are usually willing to grant that selection can explain small modifications in existing species, as in my earlier example about zebra running speed. But how can the gradual accumulation of modifications explain a feature like the vertebrate eye? This is the key objection that Michael Behe develops in his 1996 book *Darwin's Black Box* when he introduces the concept of *irreducible complexity*. Behe defines an irreducibly complex system as one in which the whole system has a function, the system is made of many parts, and the system would not be able to perform its function if any of the parts were removed. Behe's idea is that the Darwinian process of natural selection involves adding one small part to another, with each modification improving the fitness of the organism. But what good is 1 percent of an eye? Creationists, Behe included, think that the answer is obvious—no good at all—and that this shows that evolutionary theory can't explain complex adaptations.

---

6 Humans from Nonhumans, Life from Nonlife

When people hear about the idea of evolution, there are two parts of the theory that sometimes strike them as puzzling. First, there is the idea that human beings are descended from apelike ancestors. Second, there is the idea that life evolved from nonliving materials.

Scientists believe the first of these statements because there are so many striking similarities between apes and human beings. This isn't to deny that there are differences. However, the similarities (for example, the fact that both have tail bones) would be expected if humans and apes have a common ancestor, but would be quite surprising if they came into existence independently.

There is a big difference between having evidence that humans are descended from apelike ancestors and *having an explanation of precisely why this happened*. The evidence for a common ancestor is pretty overwhelming, but the details of why evolution proceeded in just the way it did are less certain. Students of human evolution continue to investigate why our species evolved as it did. In contrast, the claim that we did evolve isn't a matter of contemporary scientific debate.

What about the second idea—that life arose from nonlife? Why not maintain that God created the first living thing and then let evolution by natural selection produce the diversity we now observe? Notice that this is a very different idea from what creationists maintain. They hold that each species (or "basic kind" of organism) is the result of separate creation by God. They deny that present-day species are united by common descent from earlier life forms.

One main sort of evidence for thinking that life evolved from nonlife on Earth about 4 billion years ago comes from laboratory experiments. Scientists have created laboratory conditions that resemble the ones they believe were present shortly after the earth came into existence about 4.5 billion years ago. They find that the nonliving ingredients present then can enter into chemical reactions, the products of which are simple organic materials. For example, it is possible to run electricity (lightning) through a "soup" of inorganic molecules and produce amino acids. Why is this significant? Amino acids are an essential stage in the process whereby genes construct an organism. Similar experiments have generated a variety of promising results. This subject in biology—*prebiotic evolution*—is very much open and incomplete. No one has yet been able to get inorganic materials to produce DNA, but the promising successes to date suggest that further work will shed more light on how life arose from nonlife.

Laboratory experiments don't aim to create a multicellular organism from inorganic materials. No one wants to make a chicken out of carbon, ammonia, and water. Evolution by natural selection proceeds by the accumulation of very small changes. So the transition from nonlife to life must involve the creation of a rather simple self-replicating molecule. Chickens came much later.

A self-replicating molecule is a molecule that makes copies of itself. A molecule of this sort is able to reproduce. With accurate replication, the offspring of a molecule will resemble its parent. Once a simple self-replicating molecule is in place, evolution by natural selection can begin. It may sound strange to describe a simple self-replicating molecule as being "alive." Such a molecule will do few of the things that a chicken does. But from the biological point of view, reproduction and heredity (that is, similarity between parents and offspring) are fundamental properties.

Biologists sometimes respond to this creationist claim by arguing that gradual modification *can* explain structures like the eye. A piece of light-sensitive skin allows the organism to tell the difference between light and dark, and this is advantageous. Then, if this skin is shaped into a cup, the organism can tell not only whether it is light or dark, but also from what direction the light is coming, and this provides a further advantage. Maybe it is plausible that the eye could have evolved one small step at a time. However, there is another, more fundamental, problem with Behe's argument. What we call "the parts" of a system may or may not correspond to the historical sequence of accumulating details. Consider the horse and its four legs. A horse with zero, one, or two legs cannot walk or run; suppose the same is true of a horse with three. In contrast, a horse with four legs can walk and run, and it thereby gains a fitness advantage. So far so good—the four-legged arrangement satisfies the definition of irreducible complexity. The mistake comes from thinking that horses (or their ancestors) had to evolve their four legs one leg at a time. In fact, it's a mistake to think that a separate set of genes controls the development of each leg; rather, there is a single set that controls the development of appendages. A division of a system into parts that entails that the system is irreducibly complex may or may not correspond to the historical sequence of events through which the lineage passed. This point is obvious with respect to the horse's four legs, but needs to be borne in mind when other, less familiar, organic features are considered. What we call the "parts" of the eye may not correspond to the sequence of events that occurred in the eye's evolution.

Is Creationism Testable?

So far I have outlined what Darwin's theory of evolution amounts to, the kind of evidence that biologists take seriously for the claim of common ancestry, and some objections that creationists make to this theory. The question I want to consider now concerns the theory that creationists themselves present. What is it? What predictions does it make? What evidence is there for the theory they present?

Here we need to consider some of the different versions that creationism might take. To get started, let's consider:

> H_1: A superintelligent designer fashioned all the complex adaptations we observe organisms to have so that organisms would be perfectly adapted to their environment.

This hypothesis is disconfirmed by what we observe. Organisms often have highly imperfect adaptations. The eye that human beings use has a blind spot, though the eye of the octopus does not. And many spiders have eyes with built-in sunglasses, though human beings do not. Our eye is imperfect and so are lots of features that we and other organisms possess. Can we repair this defect in H_1? One way to do so is to make the hypothesis of intelligent design more modest in what it says:

> H_2: An intelligent designer fashioned all the complex adaptations we observe organisms to have.

The problem with H_2 is not that it makes false predictions, but that it makes none at all. H_2 is consistent with what we observe, no matter what our observations turn out to be. Features that are useful are consistent with H_2, as are features that are neutral and features that are harmful. Scientists expect scientific theories to be testable, which means that theories should make predictions that can be checked against observations. H_2, it appears, is not testable. This defect can also be remedied. Consider, for example, a third version of creationism:

> H_3: Organisms did not evolve. Rather, God created each species separately and endowed them with the very characteristics they would have had if they had evolved by natural selection.

H_3 is a wild card; it makes the same predictions that evolutionary theory makes. If so, what reason can there be to choose between these two theories?

Predictive Equivalence

Evolutionary theory and H_3 are *predictively equivalent*. If evolutionary theory predicts that life will have a particular feature, so does H_3. Although imperfect adaptations disconfirm H_1, they are perfectly consistent with H_3. Does this mean that evolutionary theory is not well supported? I would say not. Consider the following pair of hypotheses:

> J_1: You are now looking at a printed page.
> J_2: You are now looking at a salami.

You have excellent evidence that J_1 is true and that J_2 is false. J_1 predicts that you are having particular sensory experiences; if J_1 is true, you should be having certain visual, tactile, and gustatory sensations (please take a bite of this page). J_2 makes different predictions about these matters. The sensory experiences you are now having strongly favor J_1 over J_2. Now, however, let's introduce a wild card. What evidence do you have that J_1 *as opposed to J_3* is true:

J_3:   There is no printed page in front of you, but someone is now systematically misleading you into thinking that there is a printed page in front of you.

J_1 and J_3 are predictively equivalent. The experiences you are having now tell you that J_1 is
more plausible than J_2, but they don't strongly favor J_1 over J_3. In the section of this book
that focuses on Descartes's *Meditations* (Chapter 13), the problem of choosing between J_1
and J_3 will be examined in detail. For now, what I want you to see is this: when you ask
whether some hypothesis is strongly supported by the evidence, you must ask yourself what
the alternatives are against which the hypothesis is to be compared. If you compare J_1 with
J_2, you'll conclude that J_1 is extremely well supported. However, the problem takes on a
different character if you compare J_1 with J_3. The point applies to the competition between
evolutionary theory and creationism. When you compare evolutionary theory with creationism, everything depends on which version of creationism you consider. Some versions
make false predictions, some make no predictions, and some "piggy-back" on evolutionary
theory, relying on that theory's ability to make predictions and then using those predictions.

Prediction versus Accommodation

A fourth version of creationism raises interesting questions. Suppose we examine the human
eye in detail and observe that it has a set of features that we'll call F. We can then construct
the following version of creationism:

H_4: An intelligent designer made the human eye and gave it the set of features F.

Does H_4 make predictions? Well, it entails that we should observe that the eye has features
F. In fact, no theory can do a better job than H_4 does of fitting what we observe, as H_4 hits
the nail precisely on the head. The problem is that H_4 merely accommodates the observations; it does not provide novel predictions. It is easy—too easy—to construct hypotheses
such as H_4. Whenever you observe that O is true, you just construct the hypothesis that "an
intelligent designer wanted O to be true and had the means to bring this about." If such
hypotheses were satisfactory, there would be no need to do real science; we could shut
down all of the costly research now underway and just invoke this tidy formula.

This suggests that we should supplement the two rules for abduction presented in
Chapter 3. In addition to the Surprise Principle and the Only Game in Town Fallacy, we
should require that a good theory makes predictions that were not used in the construction
of that theory. This is the requirement that theories shouldn't merely accommodate what
we observe after the fact; in addition, they should make some predictions that are novel.

Does Evolutionary Theory Make Novel Predictions?

What is sauce for the goose is sauce for the gander. If we demand that creationism make
novel predictions, we should demand that evolutionary theory do the same. By "prediction," I do not restrict myself to saying what will happen in the future. A prediction can
involve observations that have not yet been made that reflect events that took place in the
past. For example, the part of evolutionary theory that says that organisms possess common
ancestors predicts that we should find intermediate fossil forms. Biology says that whales and
cows have a common ancestor, so there should be fossils that have characteristics that are
"in between." And if birds and dinosaurs have a common ancestor, there should be fossils
that are intermediate here as well. Darwin worried about "the incompleteness of the fossil

record," but there have been numerous fossil finds that fulfill the predictions of the hypothesis of common ancestry.

What about the other part of Darwin's theory, the hypothesis of natural selection? What does it predict? Here it is important to realize that there are many detailed theories in evolutionary theory that predict which traits will be favored by natural selection in which circumstances. For example, in human beings, slightly more boys than girls are born. In other species, there is a more extreme male bias, or a female bias, in the sex ratio at birth. Evolutionary theory provides theories that predict when a species should evolve one sex ratio and when it should evolve another. Another example concerns the nature of infectious disease. Suppose you are infected with a disease that is spread through the air; if you get sick, you will take to your bed and you will spread the disease less frequently. Compare this with a disease like diarrhea that is spread through feces. Even if you take to your bed, your feces will be taken from your room and sent into the environment, just as if you were well. Now think about these two patterns from the point of view of the organism that causes the disease. In the case of an airborne disease, selection favors infections that are mild over ones that are severe; in the case of a waterborne disease, selection favors just the opposite pattern. The *vector* of the disease—the mechanism that spreads the disease from infected to uninfected individuals—allows biologists to predict what traits the disease should evolve. These evolutionary ideas have recently been important in biological thinking about AIDS-HIV; see Paul Ewald's *The Evolution of Infectious Disease* (Oxford University Press, 1993) for discussion.

When I say that evolutionary theory makes predictions, I do not mean that it is now in a position to predict the whole detailed future of the planet's biosphere, or that every detail of the past can be predicted. There are many open questions in evolutionary biology, as there are in any science. However, the theory has made impressive strides since 1859. The same is not true of creationism. Paley compared the random hypothesis with the hypothesis of intelligent design and argued that the latter was better supported; Behe compares evolutionary theory to the hypothesis of intelligent design and draws the same conclusion. Creationists, then and now, criticize the theories that they dislike. But they have not developed a positive theory of their own.

Concluding Remarks

Creationism comes in many forms. Some of them make very definite predictions about what we observe. The version that says that God made organisms so that they are perfectly adapted to their environments makes predictions that do not accord with what we observe. Young earth creationism, which says that the earth is ten thousand years old, also makes predictions that conflict with what scientists observe. A third version of creationism says that God made organisms to look exactly as they would if they had evolved by the mindless process of natural selection; this makes the same predictions that evolutionary theory makes, and so our observations do not allow us to discriminate between evolutionary theory and this "mimicking" or "piggy-backing" version of creationism. Finally, the bare, minimalistic version of creationism that says that God had some (unspecified) impact on the traits of living things is, I suggest, untestable. We have not found a version of creationism that makes definite predictions about what we observe *and* that is better supported by the observations than evolutionary theory is. What is wanted here is not just a version of creationism that can accommodate the observations after we have made them, but one that tells us what we will observe before we make those observations. Is there a version of creationism that can do this?

Review Questions

1 What are the two main elements of Darwin's theory?
2 Describe what the Principle of the Common Cause says. How is this principle related to the Surprise Principle? How is it used by biologists to decide whether different species have a common ancestor?
3 The geneticist François Jacob said (in "Evolution and Tinkering," *Science* Vol. 196, 1977, pp. 1161–66) that "natural selection does not work as an engineer works. It works like a tinkerer—a tinkerer who does not know exactly what he is going to produce but uses whatever he finds around him." What does Jacob mean here? How is this point relevant to evaluating whether the hypothesis of evolution or the hypothesis of intelligent design is a more plausible explanation of the characteristics of living things?
4 What does it mean to say that two theories are predictively equivalent? Can the design hypothesis be formulated so that the existence of imperfect adaptations isn't evidence against it?
5 How is the Principle of the Common Cause related to the Surprise Principle? (Hint: why do evolutionary biologists typically appeal to both of them, rather than just one?)
6 Why is it important for a hypothesis to generate novel predictions, rather than predictions that merely "accommodate" past observations?
7 Do all creationists reject the Darwinian hypothesis of common ancestry? If not, why not?
8 Does the Principle of the Common Cause entail that, for any case of correlation between two observed effects, a hypothesis that stipulates a common cause is always more plausible than a hypothesis that stipulates separate causes?

Problems for Further Thought

1 Louis Pasteur (1822–1895) developed scientific evidence against the hypothesis of "spontaneous generation." For example, he argued that maggots developing on rotten meat aren't the result of life springing spontaneously from nonliving materials; the maggots were hatched from eggs laid there by their parents. Does Pasteur's discovery mean life couldn't have evolved from nonliving materials?
2 Suppose you are a crew member on the starship *Enterprise*, bound for a new planet. You know there is intelligent life there; the question you want to answer is whether these life forms have ever had any contact with Earth. Which sorts of observations would be relevant and which irrelevant to this question? Defend your interpretation. How does the Principle of the Common Cause apply to this problem?
3 Compare what Paley says about the watch with what Behe says about irreducible complexity.

Recommended Readings, Video, and Audio

Visit the companion website at www.routledge.com/cw/sober for suggestions of readings, video, and audio, for this chapter.

Chapter 7

Can Science Explain Everything?

In the previous chapter, we failed to identify a version of the design hypothesis that not only makes predictions, but also makes *novel* predictions, about the features we should observe in living things. It is a further question whether there are versions of creationism that do better than the versions I described. If there are not, then creationism should be discarded as an explanation of the characteristics that organisms possess. But this result would not show that the design hypothesis has no role to play at all. Perhaps there are other features of the universe, distinct from the ones discussed in biology, that we should explain by postulating the existence of an intelligent designer.

Here is another way to pose this problem: A *naturalistic* explanation seeks to explain features of the world by describing the processes in nature that produced them. A *super-naturalistic* explanation, on the other hand, attempts to explain features of the world by describing the supernatural processes (the processes that occur outside of nature) that produced them. Is there reason to think that every feature of the natural world has a naturalistic explanation? If so, the hypothesis of a supernatural God isn't needed to explain anything.

The question I want to explore in this chapter is this: should we expect that science will sooner or later explain everything that's true about the world we inhabit? That is, will science sooner or later be able to explain everything and do this without needing to postulate the existence of a supernatural God?

Scientific Ignorance

It is easy to find facts about the world that science can't explain now. Every scientific discipline has its open questions. These are the things that keep present-day scientists busy. Scientists don't spend their time repeating to each other things everybody already knows; rather, they devote their energies to trying to puzzle out answers to heretofore unanswered questions.

Because there are plenty of facts about the world that science can't explain now, it is easy to construct a particular kind of abductive argument for the existence of God. I mentioned in Chapter 6 that evolutionary theory is currently unable to explain why *some* species reproduce sexually while others do not. Consider the following theological explanation for this puzzling fact: there is a God, and God decided to make organisms reproduce in precisely the way they do. Whereas evolutionists can't (now) explain patterns of reproduction, a theologian can do this just by saying "it was God's will." I doubt that any scientist would argue that patterns of reproduction will *never* be explained scientifically. To be sure, evolutionists cannot *now* explain certain facts about sex. But science isn't over yet; it is reasonable to suspect that this example of scientific ignorance is only temporary.

---

7 "But How Do You Explain God?"

Sometimes people object to the suggestion that the existence of God is the explanation of a fact by asking, "But how do you explain the existence of God?" The implication behind this question is that it isn't plausible to say that God explains something unless you are able to explain why God exists.

This criticism of abductive arguments for the existence of God isn't a good one. Mendel was right to think that the existence of genes explains something. However, Mendel had no idea how to explain the fact that genes exist. Here are two more examples that exhibit the same pattern. For hundreds of years before Newton's time, sailors had good evidence that the tides are correlated with the phases of the Moon, even though they had no very plausible explanation for why this should be so. As noted in Chapter 6, evolutionists have excellent evidence that human beings are descended from apelike ancestors, even though the explanation of this evolutionary event is still somewhat unclear. My conclusion is that if abductive arguments for the existence of God are defective, this isn't because no one knows how to explain why God exists.

The Only Game in Town Fallacy

What should we say *now*? Apparently, we now have two choices: We can accept the theological explanation sketched above, or we can admit that we have no explanation at all for why some species, but not others, reproduce sexually. I think it is clear that we aren't obliged to accept the theological explanation. To think we are required to accept the theological explanation just because it is the only one on the table is to commit the Only Game in Town Fallacy.

Recall the anecdote from Chapter 3. If you and I are sitting in a cabin and hear noises in the attic, it is easy to formulate an explanation of those noises. I suggest the noises are due to gremlins bowling. This hypothesis has the property that if it were true, it would explain why we heard the noises. But this fact about the gremlin hypothesis doesn't mean that the hypothesis is plausible.

Instead of accepting a theological explanation of why organisms reproduce as they do, we should consider the option of simply admitting that we at present don't understand why this is so. If my prediction about the future of evolutionary theory is correct, we will eventually have a satisfactory scientific explanation. We just have to be patient.

I now want to consider a very different kind of scientific ignorance. Suppose there are facts about the world that science *in principle* can't explain. It isn't a temporary gap, but a permanent one, that I now want to consider. If there are such facts, then the choice won't be between a theological explanation and a naturalistic explanation that science will eventually produce; the choice will be between a theological explanation and no explanation at all—not now and not in the future.

The Two Questions

There are two questions I want to consider: (1) Are there any facts about the world that science is inherently incapable of explaining? (2) If there are, can we plausibly argue that the best explanation of why those facts are true is that God exists? To answer the first of these questions, I'll sketch a picture of how scientific explanation works. I then will argue that this view of scientific explanation implies that there are certain facts about the world that science can't ever explain. It isn't just that scientists haven't worked out the explanation *yet*; the point is that the nature of scientific explanation precludes their ever doing so.

What Is a Scientific Explanation?

There are two kinds of things science aims to explain. It aims to explain particular *events*, and it aims to explain *generalizations*. An example of the first type of problem would be the astronomer's question, "Why did the solar system come into existence?" An example of the second type would be the chemist's question, "Why does it take two atoms of hydrogen and one of oxygen for hydrogen and oxygen to combine to form a molecule of water?" Don't confuse these two explanatory projects. Generalizations are true or false. Events aren't true or false; they happen or fail to happen. An event happens at a certain place and time. True generalizations, however, describe what is true of *all* places and times. I want to focus here on what scientists do when they explain *events*.

My thesis is that science explains an event by describing its causes. I'll assume further (although this isn't strictly necessary for what I want to conclude) that a cause must precede its effects. So the causal explanation of an event E_1 that happens now is provided by citing one or more events in the past and showing how those events produced E_1. Suppose we show that E_1 was caused by E_2. We then might be interested in explaining why E_2 occurred. This might lead us to describe a still earlier event, E_3, and so on. This project leads us to describe causal chains that trace back into the past. You'll recall that Aquinas (Chapter 4) believed that causal chains extending back into the past can have only a finite number of links. I make no assumption about this.

So far I've described two relationships that can obtain between events: (1) some events precede others in time and (2) some events cause others. There is a third relationship. Some events are *parts* of other events. Consider the relationship between the storming of the Bastille and the French Revolution. The storming of the Bastille marked the beginning of the French Revolution. Both of these are events; the first is *part* of the second.

I want to focus on what science does when it tries to explain a spatiotemporal event. By "spatiotemporal," I simply mean that the event in question happened at some place and at some time. Of course, lots of events are "spread out." They don't occur in an instant, but take some length of time to occur. And they take place in a volume of space, not at a single spatial point. For example, the French Revolution lasted about ten years, and it took place in France.

A Thesis about Explanation

My thesis is this: For science to be able to say why a spatiotemporal event E occurred, there must be events in space and time that aren't included in E. I assume that no event explains itself. So if science is to explain E, there must be some event outside of E (but still inside of space and time) that can be cited as the explanation.

It follows from this thesis that answerable questions about why this or that spatiotemporal event occurred must be about events that are *part* of what happens in the history of the spatiotemporal universe. Such questions can't be answered if they ask why the *whole history* of the spatiotemporal universe was as it was. Consider an exhaustive description of the past, present, and future of what happens in space and time:

$$\cdots \longrightarrow E_3 \longrightarrow E_2 \longrightarrow E_1 \longrightarrow \cdots$$

$$\text{Past} \qquad\qquad\qquad \text{Present} \qquad \text{Future}$$

E_1 is explicable because there is something besides E_1 in the world that can be cited to do the explaining. If E_1 is part of some bigger event (the way the storming of the Bastille is part of the French Revolution), then that more inclusive event will be explicable only if there is something outside of it that we can cite by way of explanation. Such answerable questions about spatiotemporal events I'll call *local why-questions*. They focus on part of what has happened in the world's history. In contrast to them are *global why-questions*—questions that ask for an explanation of the totality of what has happened in the whole universe's history. I claim science can't answer global why-questions.

Why Is There Something Rather than Nothing?

Here's an example of a global why-question: *Why is there something rather than nothing?* This question doesn't ask why there is something *now*. That, of course, is a local question, which can be answered by saying that the universe was nonempty in the past, and then perhaps citing a conservation law (as Aquinas did—see Chapter 4) that says that if the world is nonempty at one time, it will be nonempty forever after. What I have in mind here is the question of why the universe *ever* contained anything. That is, why wasn't the universe entirely devoid of material objects throughout its history?

The spatiotemporal universe is the totality of everything that was, is, or will be, anywhere. There is nothing impossible about a universe that contains no material objects. Obviously the actual world isn't this way. The actual world (the one we inhabit) corresponds to one total history. An empty universe corresponds to a different total history. Both of these totalities are possible, but only one is actual. The question of why there is something rather than nothing asks why the first of these possible worlds, rather than the second, is actual. My claim is that science can't answer this question.

Can Physics Explain the Origin of the Universe?

Don't be misled by the fact that physicists talk about explaining the "origin of the universe." This makes it sound as though they are explaining why the universe is nonempty. My view is that they are doing no such thing. Rather they are addressing a different question. The Big Bang Theory doesn't show why the universe, in my sense of the word, came into existence. The universe, according to the way I am using the term, includes *everything* that there ever was, is, or will be. If the Big Bang produced what came after it, then the universe includes two stages: First, there was a Big Bang and then there was what happened next. The Big Bang doesn't explain why the whole universe exists; the Big Bang is *part* of the universe. The scientific question addressed by physicists is local, not global.

So the question "Why this totality, rather than that one?" isn't scientifically answerable because it is global. Can a theological answer be provided? Let's imagine that God isn't a material object; he (or she or it) is outside the spatiotemporal totality I'm calling "the material universe." Can we explain why the material universe is nonempty by saying that God decided to make one totality actual rather than another?

Leibniz: God Chooses Which Possible World to Actualize

The seventeenth-century philosopher and scientist Gottfried Leibniz (1646–1716) thought this form of explanation is plausible. He said that God considered the set of all possible worlds and decided to make one of them actual. He did this by finding which world is best. This is why we live in the best of all possible worlds. If you think the world we inhabit is morally imperfect, you may doubt Leibniz's story. In Chapter 11, I'll consider this issue when I take up the problem of evil. However, the point of importance here is that Leibniz had another kind of perfection in mind in addition to moral perfection. Leibniz thought this is the best of all possible worlds in the sense that this world has the maximum diversity of phenomena and the maximum simplicity of laws. Scientific laws are simple, but the kinds of events that happen in our world are enormously rich. This joint property of our world is what makes it perfect in this nonmoral sense.

I won't discuss the details of Leibniz's theory. My point is that he proposed a theological explanation for why there is something rather than nothing in the world of space and time. This fact about the world, being global, can't be scientifically explained. The question I want to pose is this: If a fact can be explained by the hypothesis that there is a God, but can't be explained scientifically, is this a good enough reason to conclude there is a God?

Clarke: God Explains Why the Actual World Consists of One Total History Rather than Another

Another anticipation of the argument for the existence of God we are considering is due to the British philosopher Samuel Clarke (1675–1729). Clarke thought he saw a way to improve an argument that Aquinas proposed. As noted in Chapter 4, Aquinas's second argument for the existence of God depends on the universe's being finitely old. Clarke's argument, presented in his 1705 book *A Demonstration of the Being and Attributes of God*, does not depend on that assumption. He asks us to consider the entire totality of events that occur in the world of space and time. Why did this history occur rather than some other? Clarke says that there are two possibilities: The entire history occurred for no reason at all, or it was brought into existence by a being who exists outside of space and time, namely, God. Clarke rejected the first suggestion as patently absurd; there *must* be a reason why the world is comprised of one total history rather than another. That reason is God. Clarke's argument is an instance of the cosmological argument.

If science is incapable of explaining why the world of space and time includes one total history rather than another, should we accept the claim that God exists because this hypothesis, if true, would explain this global fact? In similar fashion, should we accept the claim that God exists because it is able to explain why there is something rather than nothing (a fact that science is unable to explain)?

The Only Game in Town Fallacy, Again

I think the answer to these questions is *no*. Once again, the Only Game in Town Fallacy needs to be considered. There is a second option besides accepting the only explanation available. This is to admit that there are things about the universe we don't understand *and never will*. Why there is something rather than nothing may be inherently inexplicable; the same may be true of the question of why the world contains one total set of events rather than another. I grant that *if* (1) there were an all-powerful God who exists outside of space and time and *if* (2) a God outside of the material world could nonetheless create a material world and *if* (3) God wanted to make the world nonempty, then this would explain why there is something rather than nothing in the spatiotemporal universe. These suppositions would explain the fact in question, but that doesn't show that this explanatory story is at all plausible.

Causality

To see what is problematic about this suggested explanation, consider the causal relationship it says exists between God and the totality of the material universe. God is outside of space and time, but nonetheless manages to bring the whole material world into existence. This causal relationship is extremely hard to understand.

Think of the causal relationships we discuss in science and in everyday life. For example, we say that throwing the rock at the window caused the window to break. Here a causal relationship is said to obtain between two events, each of which occurred at a particular place and at a particular time. This is a characteristic of well-understood claims about causality; in this case, *causation is a relationship that obtains between events that occur within space and time*. This is why it is so puzzling to say that a God outside of space and time causes the world of space and time to come into being.

I think it is misleading to use the statement "God did it" as a substitute for the statement "I really can't explain why this or that fact is true." The first statement advances an explanation, while the second admits to not having one. If the existence of God is to explain something, it must have more going for it than the fact that the observation under consideration is otherwise inexplicable.

I said before that evolutionary theory currently cannot explain why some species reproduce sexually while others don't. This doesn't mean evolutionists can't make vague pronouncements such as "the pattern is due to natural selection." This vague remark is available to anyone who wants to make it. No scientist, however, would regard this single sentence as a satisfying explanation. The question—the main question—would be *how* natural selection managed to produce the results it did. What made sexual reproduction advantageous in some species and asexual reproduction advantageous in others? It is this more detailed question that, to date, has not been answered satisfactorily. There is an analogy here with the theological case. The theologian can say, "God did it." The evolutionist can say, "natural selection did it." A scientist would regard the latter explanation as unsatisfying because it is too short on details. Why should the theological explanation be taken any more seriously? Part of what is missing in the theological story is any indication of *how* or *why* God did what he did. This may help explain why the theological explanation of patterns of reproduction should not be embraced. A theological explanation so short on details leaves too many questions unanswered to be convincing. In this circumstance, perhaps it is more plausible to admit we don't understand than to pretend that "God did it" gives us much by way of understanding.

A similar diagnosis can be offered of why the theological explanation of why there is something rather than nothing is so unsatisfying. To say "God did it" is to leave too much unexplained. How is it possible for something outside of space and time to cause the entire spatiotemporal universe to come into being? Why should God have preferred to actualize this possible world rather than any of the others? To the degree that we don't understand these matters, we should conclude that the theological explanation is really not much of an explanation at all.

My conclusion is that science may not be able to explain everything. There are facts now known to be true that science has not been able to account for. And even if science progresses, as I expect it to do, there will remain facts that are intrinsically resistant to scientific treatment. Not only has science not explained them yet, but it never will, because it can't. Of course, we should be open to the possibility that explanations from outside of science may have some plausibility. My point here is that bringing in the existence of God is often to trade one mystery for another, with no net gain in our understanding.

The Principle of Sufficient Reason

Clarke's argument makes use of an idea that has long been influential in philosophy. It is called *The Principle of Sufficient Reason*. This principle asserts that everything that happens in nature has an explanation; nothing happens for no reason at all. What can be said in favor of this principle? Scientists seem to assume it, or something like it, when they address a new problem. Consider some body of facts that science is currently not able to explain. For example, what is it about the organization of the human brain that allows us to have *conscious experience*? Neuroscientists assume that there is an answer to this question. This is why they set themselves the task of finding a scientific explanation of consciousness. But what assurance do they have that such an explanation exists?

Maybe it makes sense for scientists to assume that consciousness has an explanation even if they have no evidence at all that such an explanation exists. After all, if they look for an explanation, they may find one (if such an explanation exists). But if they don't even look for an explanation, they will certainly fail to find it, even if there is one to be had. This is a strategic argument for its being sensible to look for an explanation of consciousness. It is not an argument that offers evidence that such an explanation exists. The fact that scientists search for explanations without a guarantee that they will succeed is not evidence that the Principle of Sufficient Reason is true.

Review Questions

1   What is the difference between a global why-question and a local why-question?
2   Can science answer global why-questions? Why or why not?
3   Is it possible to have evidence that something exists without having an explanation for why the thing exists?
4   Consider the following argument: "If science can't explain some fact that a theological story can explain, then that fact is strong abductive evidence that the theological story is true." How is the Only Game in Town Fallacy relevant to assessing this argument?
5   What does it mean to say that causation is a relationship that obtains between events in space and time? If this were a correct claim about causation, what implications would it have for the idea that God explains the sorts of global facts discussed in this chapter?
6   What is the Principle of Sufficient Reason? Do you find it plausible? Why or why not?

7   How does the Principle of Sufficient Reason inform Leibniz's and/or Clarke's arguments for the existence of God?
8   Can you think of any plausible explanations that aren't either theological or scientific?
9   The identification of causes seems to be a central feature of scientific explanation. But are we always satisfied to explain an event by appealing to its cause(s) alone? For example, imagine that someone explained the Big Bang by arguing that God, who exists outside of space and time, caused the Big Bang to occur; and suppose, for the sake of argument, that all the premises of this argument are true (such that God does exist, and did in fact cause the Big Bang to occur). Why might we still not accept this as a meaningful explanation? What more might we want to know?

Problems for Further Thought

1   Philosophers sometimes use the term *brute fact* to describe a fact that is so simple and obvious that it can't be justified or explained by appeal to any other fact. Consider the relationship between *x* and *y* described in the statement "*x* = *y*." This is the relationship of *identity*. This is a relationship that everything bears to itself; "the Eiffel Tower = the Eiffel Tower" is true, but "the Eiffel Tower = the Statue of Liberty" is false. What explains the fact that everything is self-identical? Is this true because of the way we use the identity sign "="? Is it a brute fact?
2   In this chapter, I claimed that nothing explains itself. In everyday speech, however, we talk about something's being "self-explanatory." What does this mean? Is there a conflict between what I've said about explanation and the everyday idea? We also use the term "self-starter" to describe some people. Does this conflict with the idea that nothing causes itself?
3   Blaise Pascal, a seventeenth-century philosopher whom I'll discuss in Chapter 10, once said, "The truth of religion lies in its very obscurity." What does this mean, and is it true?
4   I argued in this chapter that science can't explain everything. In particular, it can't explain why there is something rather than nothing. The physicist Lawrence Krauss published a book called *A Universe from Nothing—Why There Is Something Rather than Nothing* (Free Press) in which he claims to do what I say is impossible. The philosopher David Albert reviewed the book in the *New York Times* (Sunday, March 25, 2012). Read Albert's review and think about how Krauss's argument (as described by Albert) relates to the argument presented in this chapter. A link to the review can be found on the companion website.

Recommended Readings, Video, and Audio

Visit the companion website at www.routledge.com/cw/sober for suggestions of readings, video, and audio, for this chapter.

Chapter 8

The Ontological Argument

The various arguments I've considered so far for the existence of God include premises we know to be true by experience. By using our senses (of sight, hearing, touch, etc.), we know that objects are in motion and that organisms are intricate and adapted to their environments. What is more, there is no other way to know these things; sensory experience is indispensable. Such propositions are called *a posteriori*. Notice the prefix *post*, meaning "after." An *a posteriori* truth is a truth that requires experience to be known (or justified). Accordingly, the arguments for the existence of God considered thus far are called *a posteriori* arguments.

A Posteriori and A Priori

Are all propositions *a posteriori*? Many philosophers have thought there are propositions that can be known to be true by reason alone. These propositions are termed *a priori*. Note the word "prior"; such propositions are knowable prior to, or independently of, experience. Standard examples are mathematical truths and definitions. We can know that $7 + 3 = 10$ and that bachelors are unmarried merely by thinking about the concepts involved. You don't have to do experiments or conduct surveys to find out whether such statements are true. Reason suffices.

Let's be clear on what it means to claim that a given proposition is *a priori*. To say that we know *a priori* that bachelors are unmarried doesn't mean we were born with the concepts of bachelorhood and marriage. For a proposition to be *a priori*, it isn't essential that the concepts contained in the proposition be *innate*. Maybe none of us is born with an understanding of the concept of a bachelor; maybe we need to have various experiences if we are to acquire that concept. Even if the concepts were acquired through experience, however, that wouldn't show the proposition fails to be *a priori*. To say that a proposition is *a priori* true means that *IF* you understand the concepts involved, then reason will suffice for you to decide that the proposition is true. Don't forget the *IF* in this idea. The idea that there is *a priori* knowledge doesn't require that there be innate concepts.

The Ontological Argument for the existence of God is an *a priori* argument. It aims to establish the truth of theism without reliance on any *a posteriori* premise. In particular, the idea is that we can prove that God must exist simply by examining the definition of the concept of God.

Definitions and Existence

This should strike you as a very surprising thing to try to do. Consider other definitions. For example, a bachelor is by definition an adult unmarried male. The thing to notice about this definition is that it doesn't imply there are any bachelors. The same point seems to be true of most definitions. You can define what it is to be a unicorn or a golden mountain, but the definitions won't settle whether there are such things. When we consider concepts such as *bachelor, unicorn,* or *golden mountain,* the definitions specify what it would take to be an individual of the kind in question; the definitions don't say whether there are zero, one, or many things of that kind. The Ontological Argument claims the concept of God is different: from the definition of the concept of God, the existence of God is supposed to follow.

So the proposition that bachelors are unmarried is *a priori*, whereas the proposition that bachelors exist is *a posteriori*. The definition doesn't imply the existence claim. Are there any nontheistic examples of existence claims that can be known *a priori*? Perhaps existence claims in mathematics furnish examples. If mathematics is *a priori*, then mathematical existence claims are *a priori*. So it is an *a priori* truth that there exists a prime number between 12 and 14. It is philosophically debatable whether there are any *a priori* truths at all. I won't discuss that issue here, however, but will go along with the idea that mathematical truths are *a priori*. This means that since mathematics contains existence claims, there are some existence statements that are *a priori* true. It follows that if there is a mistake in the Ontological Argument for the existence of God, it isn't to be found in the fact that the argument maintains that some existence claims are *a priori* true.

Anselm's Argument

The Ontological Argument was formulated by Anselm (1033–1109), who became archbishop of Canterbury. Aquinas, who lived in the thirteenth century, rejected this argument and recommended in its stead the five *a posteriori* arguments that we examined in Chapters 4 and 5. Philosophers down to the present (including Descartes, whose *Meditations on First Philosophy* we'll discuss in Part III) have discussed the Ontological Argument and have constructed different versions of it. Here I'll consider a simplified formulation of the argument:

(1) God is by definition the greatest being possible.
(2) A being who fails to exist in the actual world (while existing in other possible worlds) is less perfect than a being who exists in all possible worlds.

(O) ——————————

Hence, God exists, necessarily.

I label the argument "O" for future reference.

Premise (1): Conceivability and Possibility

Premise (1) is intended to capture what Anselm meant by saying that God is a being "than which none greater can be conceived." It isn't just that God is the most perfect being that happens to exist in the actual world. The actual world, after all, might contain only grossly imperfect beings, so that God's being the best of these wouldn't mean he is *all*-powerful, *all*-knowing, and *perfectly* good. The idea is that God is a being who is the best possible being. There is no more perfect being in any possible world. (If you're a bit vague on the idea of a "possible world," go back to Chapter 4 and review.)

Although I gloss Anselm's first premise by saying that God is the best possible being, I want to note an important difference between possibility and conceivability. What is possible is an objective question; it doesn't depend on what people know or believe. Whether we can conceive of something, however, is a fact about us as knowing subjects. Hence, conceivability is a subjective notion. (This should remind you of the point made in Chapter 4 that necessity and certainty are different.)

What can be conceived of may vary from individual to individual. We can conceive of things that dogs can't conceive of; perhaps there are superintelligent beings elsewhere in the universe who can conceive of things that are beyond our grasp. In contrast, there is a sense of the term *possible*, which I am using here, according to which what is possible doesn't vary from one thinker to another.

It is impossible, according to Einstein's special theory of relativity, for an object that has positive mass to go faster than the speed of light. This simply can't be done, no matter how powerful a rocket ship you build. Yet, I think this is something we can conceive of; we can describe what it would mean to go faster than the speed of light. Newton thought that travel faster than the speed of light was possible. He not only could conceive of what this would be, he thought it was possible. We now view Newton as mistaken. It isn't possible to do this, and it never has been. For something to be possible, it isn't enough that you can conceive of its happening or that you can't see any reason why it wouldn't happen.

If the human mind is limited in various ways, then maybe the most perfect being we can conceive of is still grossly imperfect in many ways. Maybe an ant can't conceive of a creature greater than an anteater, but that doesn't mean that anteaters are the most perfect possible beings. Anselm, though he used the word "conceivable," really meant possible, I think. God isn't just the best being we frail human beings can conceptualize; God is supposed to be the best possible being.

Premise (2): Necessary Existence Is a Perfection

If a being exists in all possible worlds, it is a necessary being, not a contingent one. Why does Anselm think God's perfection demands that God be a necessary being? A contingent thing depends for its existence on other things. You and I are contingent things; we exist only because certain other contingent beings acted as they did. But a truly perfect being, Anselm thinks, wouldn't depend for its existence on anything contingent. It would exist unconditionally. According to Anselm's second premise, a necessary being is more perfect than a contingent one. So if God has all the perfections, he must be a necessary being, not a contingent one.

The Ontological Argument *looks* like it is deductively valid: if God has all the perfections and if necessary existence is a perfection, then God exists necessarily. But from Anselm's time down to the present, there have been doubters. Many philosophers (both theists and atheists) have thought that the Ontological Argument must involve a mistake.

Gaunilo's Criticism

Anselm describes a criticism formulated by his contemporary, Gaunilo. Gaunilo says the argument must be defective, since if it were not, you could prove the existence of a perfect island by a similar *a priori* argument. What did Gaunilo have in mind?

Let's start with the concept of an island. The first point is that the concept of island-hood resembles the concept of bachelorhood. Its definition doesn't deductively imply that there are any objects of the kind defined. So any attempt to provide an *a priori* proof that islands exist must fail. Now let's define a new concept: Call it a *P*-island. A *P*-island is an island than which no greater island can be conceived. *P*-islands are just like ordinary islands, except that they are, by definition, the best possible islands. Gaunilo thought there can be no *a priori* demonstration that there are *P*-islands. Perhaps no such thing exists, and if there happen to be *P*-islands, this isn't something that could be discovered by reason alone.

---

8 *A Priori/A Posteriori* and Necessity/Contingency

In Chapter 4, the ideas of necessity and contingency were introduced. A possible world, roughly, is a way the world might be. A necessary truth is a proposition that is true in all possible worlds; a contingent truth is a proposition that is true in the actual world, but not in all possible worlds.

In this chapter, the ideas of *a priori* and *a posteriori* propositions were introduced. An *a priori* proposition can be known (or justified) independent of experience. How is the distinction between necessary and contingent propositions related to the distinction between *a priori* and *a posteriori* propositions?

This is a deep, controversial, and fundamental philosophical question. Some philosophers hold that the two distinctions divide up the propositions in exactly the same way. That is, they hold that all necessary propositions are *a priori* and that all contingent propositions are *a posteriori*. According to this theory, all the propositions that natural science discovers by observation are contingent.

Some of what I've said in previous chapters has assumed that this theory is false. I've suggested that empirical science (that is, science that relies on observation) is able to discover what is really possible. In Chapter 4, I mentioned some examples. I said that thermodynamics has discovered that perpetual motion machines are impossible (that is, it is a necessary truth that there are no perpetual motion machines); I also stated that Einstein's theories of relativity say that no particle (with positive rest mass) can go faster than the speed of light (that is, that objects with positive rest mass necessarily go slower than the speed of light). In other words, I've suggested that some *a posteriori* propositions are necessary, even though other *a posteriori* propositions are contingent.

What about *a priori* propositions? The examples discussed so far of *a priori* propositions (such as "bachelors are unmarried" and "2 + 3 = 5") are all cases of necessary truths. So the question remains: Are there any *a priori* propositions that are contingent? The examples I'll give provide a preview of material that will be discussed in Chapter 13. Consider the proposition each of us formulates when we say to ourselves "I exist." You know this proposition to be true without using sight, hearing, taste, touch, or smell. Thought alone allows you to see that it is true. So it is *a priori*. The same seems to be true for the proposition you formulate by saying to yourself "I am thinking." Yet, it isn't a necessary truth that you exist. You might have failed to do so. If this line of thinking is right, we may conclude that the proposition each of us considers when we say to ourselves "I exist" or "I am thinking" is *a priori* and contingent.

> Fill in the following table with examples of the four types of propositions indicated:
>
> | | Necessary | Contingent |
> |---|---|---|
> | A priori | | |
> | A posteriori | | |

Consider, however, the following argument, which mimics the structure of the Ontological Argument:

(1) A *P*-island is by definition the greatest possible island.
(2) An island that fails to exist in the actual world (while existing in other possible worlds) is less perfect than an island that exists in all possible worlds.

(I) ─────────────
    Hence, a *P*-island exists necessarily.

I label this argument "I" for future reference.

Gaunilo's conclusion wasn't that there are *P*-islands (as well as *P*-bagels, *P*-comedians, and so on). Rather, he thought this argument about islands must be defective. It seems crazy to think the existence of a perfect island could be established *a priori*. Gaunilo concluded that Anselm's argument must have a mistake in it as well. What sort of mistake did Gaunilo think these two arguments commit? He believed that the two premises of the Island Argument are true. But Gaunilo holds that these premises don't deductively imply the conclusion; the existence of a perfect island doesn't follow from these *a priori* premises. Gaunilo concludes that the Island Argument (I) is invalid. He takes this to show that the Ontological Argument (O) is also invalid.

How Are the Ontological Argument and the Island Argument Related?

Notice that Gaunilo's argument was obtained from Anselm's by substituting "*P*-island" for "God" and "island" for "being." We saw in Chapter 2 that the validity of an argument depends on its form, not on its subject matter. Gaunilo was suggesting that since his Island Argument is invalid, so too is Anselm's argument about God, since they have the same logical form. Gaunilo thought the Island Conclusion doesn't follow from the Island Premises. By parity of reasoning, he claims that Anselm's conclusion doesn't follow from Anselm's premises.

Gaunilo is making an argument about these two arguments. In particular, he attempts to show that Anselm's argument is invalid by *reductio* (see Chapter 4 for this piece of terminology). Gaunilo argues as follows:

> If the Ontological Argument is deductively valid, then the Island Argument is deductively valid.
> The Island Argument is not deductively valid.
>
> ─────────────
> The Ontological Argument is not deductively valid.

Anselm's Reply

Anselm scornfully replies to this criticism. He says that his argument applies to God—the greatest possible being. It doesn't apply to a *P*-island—the greatest possible island. His idea is that islands are not the kind of thing that could have all the perfections. For example, islands can't have the perfection of intelligence. I think this criticism of Gaunilo misses the mark. Islands can have some perfections (shady places, beautiful beaches, nice drinking water, tropical fruit), even if they can't have all of them. A *P*-island is an island that is the most perfect possible island; this does not require that it be intelligent. As long as existence is one of the perfections that an island can have, Gaunilo's point seems correct.

Even so, Gaunilo's objection is, to my mind, incomplete. His *reductio* argument, if it works, shows that there has to be a mistake somewhere in Anselm's reasoning, but it doesn't show exactly where the mistake occurs. As noted before, Anselm's argument *looks* valid; if it isn't, we would like to see exactly where it goes wrong.

When Anselm dismisses Gaunilo's Island Argument, maybe he means that the Ontological Argument is deductively valid, while the Island Argument is not. However, this suggestion seems implausible, since deductive validity doesn't depend on an argument's subject matter, only on its form, and the two arguments seem to have the same logical form. Or maybe Anselm is claiming the premises of the Island Argument are implausible, though the premises of the Ontological Argument are quite plausible. If this were correct, the two arguments would be disanalogous. But the first premise of the Ontological Argument and the first premise of the Island Argument seem to be on a par. Anselm holds that his own definition of God is correct; it is hard to see how Gaunilo's definition of a *P*-island could be mistaken.

What about the second premises of the two arguments? If necessary existence is a perfection for beings in general, why isn't it a perfection for islands in particular? I feel a little shaky about my ability to make such judgments about "perfection," but I don't see why the second premise of the Ontological Argument should be accepted and the second premise of the Island Argument rejected. I conclude that the two arguments are fully parallel, contrary to what Anselm says in reply to Gaunilo. Gaunilo, I think, is on to something.

Dispensing with Perfection

Anselm's argument (O) makes use of the idea that God is perfect. Gaunilo's parody of Anselm—Gaunilo's Island Argument (I)—also makes use of that concept. Gaunilo and Anselm shared a worldview according to which everything in the universe occupies a particular position on the Great Chain of Being. At the top is God, next come the angels, then human beings, then animals, and then plants. Anselm and Gaunilo believed it was an entirely objective question how perfect a given thing is.

I want to suggest that we can see a defect in the Ontological Argument more clearly once we set aside the concept of perfection. Let's not worry about inferring a being's existence from its being perfect. Let's not worry about how perfect a particular thing is or about whether perfection is objective. Let's simply build the property of existence into the definition of a being and see what happens.

Unicorns don't exist. The concept of unicornhood isn't exemplified in the actual world. Consider, however, a new concept, which I call *E*-unicornhood. An *E*-unicorn is by definition something that is an existing unicorn. Does it follow from the definition of an *E*-unicorn that there are *E*-unicorns? Not at all. The concept includes the property of existence, but that doesn't imply that the concept is actually exemplified. The definition simply describes what a thing must be like if it is to count as an *E*-unicorn. The definition tells us that if something is an *E*-unicorn, then that thing will have the property of existing. Now let's define the concept of an *E*-God. An *E*-God is a being who is all-powerful, all-knowing, all-good, and who actually exists. Does it follow from the definition of an *E*-God that there is an *E*-God? Not at all. The definition simply describes what a thing must be like if it is to count as an *E*-God. The definition tells us that if something is an *E*-God, then that thing will have the property of existing.

Conclusion

When we define God, we are saying what properties a being must have to be God. Parallel remarks apply to defining unicorns or golden mountains. Anselm argued that our concept of God has built into it the idea that God necessarily exists. Just as God is by definition omnipotent, it also is true that God, by definition, necessarily exists. My criticism of the Ontological Argument comes to this: let's grant that God is by definition the greatest possible being. And let us grant that necessary existence is a perfection. What follows from this is that necessary existence is part of the concept of God. Necessary existence is built into the concept of God, just as omnipotence is. But the fact that existence is built into a concept doesn't imply there are things to which the concept applies.

If we concede that God is defined as an omnipotent being, all this means is that if God exists, then that being must be omnipotent. Likewise, if we concede that God is defined as a necessarily existent being, we are merely saying that if there is a God, then that being necessarily exists. The definitions don't entail the existence of anything that is omnipotent nor do they entail the existence of anything that necessarily exists. It is for this reason that the Ontological Argument is invalid.

Review Questions

1 What is the logical difference between an argument about the definition of a concept and an argument for the existence of an object(s) to which such a concept applies?
2 Why do you think Anselm argues that God is "the greatest possible being," rather than "the greatest actually existing being"?
3 Suppose that Anselm's formulation of the ontological argument is both valid and sound. What kind of God does it guarantee exists? Do you think, for example, that God's perfection entails properties like "omniscience" or "omnibenevolence"? Why or why not?
4 Do you think that the attributes that Anselm takes to constitute "perfection," such as "necessary existence," are an objective or subjective matter? Are they universal or relative? Why? For example, do you think that the "perfection" we attribute to, say, a perfect watch is the same perfection—i.e., implies all the same properties as—the "perfection" we ascribe to a perfect book?
5 How do you think a skeptic might respond to the claim that, if we grant that the concept of God entails that God is perfect, we must also grant that God necessarily exists?
6 Do you think there is an important conceptual difference between an *E*-God concept and an *E*-unicorn or *P*-island concept? Why or why not?
7 What is the difference between an *a posteriori* proposition and an *a priori* proposition? What is the difference between saying that a proposition is *a priori* and saying that it is innate? Give an example of an *a posteriori* existence claim and an example of an *a priori* existence claim.

8 What is the difference between saying that a proposition is possible and saying that it is conceivable?

9 How does Gaunilo's point about islands bear on Anselm's argument about God? What is a *reductio* argument? Describe how Gaunilo uses this form of argumentation.

10 Suppose God is, by definition, a being that exists in all possible worlds. Does it follow that God exists?

Problems for Further Thought

1 Consult the original text of Anselm's argument and Gaunilo's reply. Give a formulation of the argument that is more true to the text than the one presented in this chapter.

2 I've argued that building the idea of existence into a concept doesn't ensure that anything actually exemplifies the concept. That is the point I made by considering *E*-unicorns. Now, however, consider the opposite problem. Is it possible to define a concept so that the definition ensures that *nothing* can exemplify it? Construct a definition that does this. How is it possible that definitions can have negative implications about existence, but not positive implications?

3 Do the following arguments have the same logical form? Explain your answer.

God has every perfection.
Existence is a perfection.
──────────────────
God exists.

Sam has every novel by Dickens.
David Copperfield is a novel by Dickens.
──────────────────
Sam has *David Copperfield*.

4 Suppose I define God as a necessarily existing being. Does it follow that God exists? If I assume that it is possible that God exists, would it then follow that God exists? If so, is this a convincing proof of God's existence?

5 In the selection from Hume's *Dialogues Concerning Natural Religion*, Philo, Demea, and Cleanthes discuss *a priori* and *a posteriori* arguments for the existence of God. What are their views on whether there can be an *a priori* proof that God exists?

Recommended Readings, Video, and Audio

Visit the companion website at www.routledge.com/cw/sober for suggestions of readings, video, and audio, for this chapter.

Is the Existence of God Testable?

Up to this point, I've taken the question of whether God exists to be perfectly meaningful. It may be difficult to answer, but I've assumed that there *is* an answer. Theists, atheists, and agnostics agree on this. I've assumed the sentence "God exists" says something; the question is whether what it says is true, and whether we can know this.

Logical Positivism

Some philosophers—advocates of the position called *logical positivism*—have an altogether different view of this problem. They hold that the sentence "God exists" is meaningless. It isn't true and it isn't false either. They hold that it is misguided to argue about whether God exists. It isn't that there is a true answer to the question "Does God exist?" but we'll never discover what that a true answer is. Rather, positivists hold that the question has no factual answer at all. Their idea is that we have been misled by a superficial grammatical similarity between the sentence "God exists" and the sentence "Genes exist." The latter expresses a scientific statement that can be justified or rejected by appeal to evidence. In contrast, the former sentence expresses no proposition at all. Positivism maintains that we shouldn't try to answer the question of whether God exists, but should reject it as meaningless. According to positivism, theists, atheists, and agnostics are all mistaken.

The Testability Theory of Meaning

Positivists advanced a theory that is supposed to justify this philosophical thesis. This is the *Testability Theory of Meaning*. It holds that for a sentence to be meaningful, it must be either *a priori* or *a posteriori*. The Testability Theory of Meaning also includes specific proposals for how these two categories should be understood.

As explained in Chapter 8, a truth is *a priori* if it can be justified without appeal to sense experience—it can be justified by reason alone. And a truth is *a posteriori* if sense experience is needed for it to be justifiably believed. This is what it means for a *truth* to be *a priori* or *a posteriori*. *Falsehoods* can fall into these categories as well. A mathematical truth like "2 + 3 = 5" can be justified by reason alone, but the mathematical falsehood "2 + 4 = 7" can be *disproved* by reason alone. Just as the statement "There is a book in front of you now" is an *a posteriori* truth, so the statement "There is no book in front of you now" is an *a posteriori* falsehood.

Some meaningful statements are true; others are false. In saying that each meaningful sentence is either *a priori* or *a posteriori*, positivists are saying that every meaningful sentence is *decidable in principle*. That is, they maintain that if S is a meaningful sentence, then it is possible to figure out whether S is true. If there is no way in principle to figure out whether S is true, positivists conclude that S is meaningless.

I now turn to the positivists' account of what makes a sentence *a priori* or *a posteriori*. Once each of these categories is clarified, they think the claim that God exists can be seen to fall into neither category. Positivists conclude the claim is meaningless.

Analyticity

Positivists (and some other philosophers besides) hold that all *a priori* statements are *analytic*. An analytic truth (as opposed to a *synthetic* one) is a definition or a deductive consequence of a definition. The truth of "All bachelors are unmarried" follows from the definitions of the terms that occur in it. "Either it is raining or it is not raining" similarly follows from the definitions of "or" and "not." Symmetrically, positivism maintains that all *a posteriori* statements are *synthetic*—if a sentence depends on sense experience for its justification, its truth doesn't follow from definitions alone.

Where does the sentence "God exists" fit into this classification? Positivists reject the whole strategy behind the Ontological Argument. They hold that "God exists" isn't decidable from definitions alone. So the sentence isn't *a priori*. This means that if "God exists" is meaningful, it must be *a posteriori*. We must now examine the account that positivists give of what makes a sentence *a posteriori*.

Falsifiability

Positivists say that the sentence "God exists" is *untestable*. There is no way to use observations to decide whether it is true. Defenders of the Testability Theory of Meaning have argued that sentences are tested by deducing predictions from them that can be checked by making observations. Mendel tested his genetic theory by deducing from it a prediction about the proportions of different characteristics that there should be in the pea plants he grew in his garden. He then was able to check these predictions observationally. Positivists argue that the sentence "God exists" makes no predictions whatsoever, so it is untestable.

Sometimes the idea of observational testability is developed with reference to the concept of *falsification*. If a theory makes a prediction that can be checked observationally, the theory runs the risk of being refuted by observations. This is what the influential philosopher of science Karl Popper (not a positivist himself) meant by saying that a scientific theory should be falsifiable. This doesn't mean a scientific theory should be false. *Falsifiable* doesn't mean *false*. What is crucial is that the theory rules out at least some possible observations. It must "stick its neck out."

In science, confirmation and disconfirmation are intimately connected. An experiment has different possible outcomes. If some outcomes would be evidence *in favor of* the hypothesis, then other outcomes would be evidence *against* it. If you propose an experiment for testing a hypothesis and you think that every possible result would indicate the hypothesis is true, there is no reason to run the experiment. The only way the experiment could offer you real evidence in favor of the hypothesis is if there were some possible results that would undermine the hypothesis. You then get evidence supporting the hypothesis if you run the experiment and find that those possible refuting outcomes don't come to pass. Getting evidence in favor of a hypothesis requires that the hypothesis rule out something. But what does the sentence "God exists" rule out? Is there anything we can imagine observing that would be evidence against theism? For example, if we observed that there are many moral evils in the world, would that count against the hypothesis that there is a God? In Chapter 11, I'll discuss this question in some detail. For now, I'll merely note that theists have usually not taken the existence of evil to count against theism. They say that if the world had been morally perfect, that would be consistent with the existence of God; if the world happens to contain moral evil, that too can be reconciled with theism. It seems that theists usually can reconcile their belief in God with just about anything they observe.

Consider the doomsday pronouncements that pop up from time to time in different religions. Every so often, some religious group gets the idea that God is about to bring the world to an end. Such predictions have yet to come true. What has been the result of these failed predictions? A few end-of-the-worlders have had their faith shaken. But, after some reflection, most theists have decided that the failed predictions of the end-of-the-worlders don't count against the hypothesis that there is a God. If the world had come to an end, theists would have taken this to support their belief that there is a God; but when the world fails to come to an end, these same people continue to believe that God exists.

I hope these remarks convey the flavor of what positivists are getting at when they claim that the hypothesis that God exists is untestable. I now want to be a little more precise about these ideas. I begin with two definitions:

A hypothesis *H* is *falsifiable* if and only if *H* deductively implies at least one observation statement *O*.

An *observation statement* is a statement whose truth or falsehood can be determined by direct observation. Notice that if a hypothesis is falsifiable, it can be refuted by a valid deductive argument if the observational prediction it makes turns out to be false:

If *H*, then *O*.
Not-*O*
_____

Not-*H*

Auxiliary Assumptions Needed

I agree that the hypothesis that God exists isn't falsifiable. The same is true, however, of most of the hypotheses that science investigates. *Hypotheses rarely deductively imply predictions all by themselves.* Rather, the usual pattern is that you must conjoin auxiliary assumptions *A* to a hypothesis *H* to get *H* to deductively imply an observational prediction *O*. It isn't *H* that implies *O*, but *H&A* that does the trick.

I'll illustrate this idea with an example from outside science. Consider Sherlock Holmes again. Holmes wishes to test the hypothesis that Moriarty is the murderer. Does this hypothesis, all by itself, tell Holmes what he will observe at the scene of the crime? Not at all. Auxiliary assumptions are needed. If Holmes knows that Moriarty wears a size 12 shoe, smokes El Supremo cigars, and fires a gun of type X, these auxiliary assumptions may lead him to expect to find certain clues. If he discovers a size 12 footprint, an El Supremo butt on the carpet next to the victim, and a bullet from a type X gun, his auxiliary assumptions may lead him to think that Moriarty is probably the murderer. On the other hand, if Holmes were to make *other* auxiliary assumptions, then the hypothesis that Moriarty is the murderer would lead Holmes to make quite different predictions. If Holmes thought that Moriarty didn't smoke, that he has a size 8 shoe, and that he prefers to use a knife, then the hypothesis that Moriarty is the murderer would *not* predict the clues Holmes found. The clues found at the scene of the crime don't say anything one way or the other about whether Moriarty is the murderer until auxiliary assumptions are added.

So most of the hypotheses we test don't, all by themselves, deductively imply observationally checkable statements. They do so only when supplemented with auxiliary assumptions. Where does this leave the thesis that the hypothesis that God exists isn't testable?

The sentence "God exists" is not falsifiable, but that is uninteresting, since most scientific hypotheses aren't falsifiable either. This brings us to the next question: Is the hypothesis that God exists testable when it is supplemented with auxiliary assumptions? The answer is *yes*. Consider the following candidates:

A_1: If there is a God, there will be living things in the world and they will be perfectly adapted to their environments.

A_2: If there is a God, there will be no living things.

A_3: If there is a God, there will be living things in the world, but they will not be perfectly adapted to their environments.

The hypothesis that there is a God, when conjoined with A_1, predicts something we can check by making observations. The same is true if we conjoin the theistic hypothesis with A_2 or with A_3. So there is a twofold parallel between the hypothesis that God exists and a scientific hypothesis (or a detective's hypothesis): The hypothesis isn't falsifiable, but it is testable when conjoined with auxiliary assumptions. Does this mean that the hypothesis that God exists is no less testable than the hypotheses of science?

There does seem to be a difference between these cases, although it isn't to be characterized in terms of the idea of falsifiability. In the case of Holmes testing whether Moriarty is the murderer, I noted that different sets of auxiliary assumptions entail different predictions about what Holmes will find at the scene of the crime. If A_4 is true, we get one set of predictions; if A_5 is true, we get a very different set.

A_4: Moriarty smokes El Supremo cigars, has a size 12 shoe, and uses a type X gun.

A_5: Moriarty does not smoke, has a size 8 shoe, and uses a knife as his preferred murder weapon.

If Holmes is to say whether the clues at the scene of the crime count for or against the hypothesis that Moriarty is the murderer, he must decide which of A_4 and A_5 is true.

9 Neptune and Vulcan

Most hypotheses in science don't entail predictions all by themselves; they need to be conjoined with auxiliary assumptions to do so. This means that if the prediction turns out to be false, scientists face a choice. They can reject the hypothesis, or they can reject the auxiliary assumptions.

Two episodes in nineteenth-century astronomy illustrate these two options. Working separately, John Adams and Urbain Leverrier used Newtonian physics plus assumptions about the planets then known to exist to predict where the orbit of Uranus should be. These assumptions included the idea that Uranus is the planet farthest from the sun. The prediction about Uranus' orbit obtained by conjoining Newton's theory with this assumption came out wrong. Adams and Leverrier therefore had to choose between rejecting Newtonian physics and rejecting one or more of the auxiliary assumptions. Because Newtonian theory was well supported by other observations, they were reluctant to reject it. They therefore suspected that the auxiliary assumptions were the culprit. They conjectured that Uranus isn't the last planet. Two years later, astronomers were able to confirm this conjecture; they observed the planet that we now call Neptune.

This same pattern of reasoning was subsequently applied to the planet Mercury. Newtonian physics plus auxiliary assumptions (including the assumption that there is no planet between Mercury and the Sun) predict where Mercury's orbit should be. This prediction turned out to be false. Scientists therefore faced a choice. Either Newton's theory is wrong or at least one auxiliary assumption is mistaken. Following the pattern of reasoning that worked so well for the case of Uranus, some scientists conjectured that there is a planet lying between Mercury and the Sun. It was given the name "Vulcan."

As it turned out, this conjecture was mistaken. There is no such planet. It wasn't the auxiliary assumption (that there is no planet between Mercury and the Sun) that was responsible for the false prediction about Mercury's orbit; it was Newtonian physics itself that led to the error. Only when Newton's theories were replaced by Einstein's theories of relativity could the departure of Mercury's orbit from Newtonian values be explained.

In the reasoning about Uranus and the reasoning about Mercury, three sorts of statement play a role. There are theories (T), auxiliary assumptions (A), and predictions (P). Describe the logical form of the arguments that the scientists formulated in the two cases.

Auxiliary Assumptions Must Be Independently Established

In the scientific case, as well as in the case of detective work, there is an important fact about auxiliary assumptions that goes beyond what I've said so far. Not only are auxiliary assumptions needed if the hypothesis is to make observational predictions, in addition, *those auxiliary assumptions must be checkable independent of the hypothesis under test*. For example, Holmes can interpret the clues found at the scene of the crime once he decides whether A_4 or A_5 is true. Furthermore, he can find out whether A_4 or A_5 is true without his having to already know if Moriarty is the murderer.

Can the same be done for auxiliary hypotheses about God's nature, such as A_1, A_2, or A_3? This isn't so clear. It is easy enough to *invent* auxiliary hypotheses that reconcile what we observe with the hypothesis that God is responsible for what we observe. If we find that an organism is perfectly adapted to its environment, we can construct an auxiliary assumption that effects this reconciliation. If we find that the organism is imperfectly adapted, a different auxiliary assumption can be invented that does the same thing. The problem is: How do we figure out which of these auxiliary assumptions is true without assuming at the outset that God is responsible for what we observe? This is the problem we ran into in Chapter 5 when we considered different versions of creationism.

In the detective case, Holmes wouldn't endlessly revise his opinions about auxiliary assumptions just to preserve his faith that Moriarty must be the murderer. To do so would be to fall prey to an obsession, not to do good detective work. Holmes would find out which of A_4 and A_5 is true, and then use these independently confirmed auxiliary assumptions to test the hypothesis that Moriarty is the murderer. The result may be that Holmes is forced to conclude Moriarty is probably innocent of the crime. It is difficult to test the hypothesis that God exists because it is hard to determine which auxiliary assumptions to accept if you don't already believe that God exists.

How is what I'm saying different from what the Testability Theory of Meaning maintains? To begin with, I'm not using the idea of falsifiability to criticize the hypothesis that God exists. Nor am I claiming that no one will ever figure out how the hypothesis that God exists can be tested. Perhaps someday auxiliary assumptions will be independently discovered that can tell us what the hypothesis that God exists predicts about the observable world. My claim is just that this hasn't happened *yet*. In summary, positivists used the Testability Theory of Meaning to try to derive a *timeless* verdict concerning the sentence "God exists." In contrast, I've used a different idea about testability (one that emphasizes the role of auxiliary assumptions) to argue for a verdict concerning how the issue of testability stands *now*.

"God Exists" Is Meaningful

I disagree with positivism on another count. I think the hypothesis that there is a God is meaningful. It is possible to discuss whether there is evidence for or against it. Also, the hypothesis obviously has various logical properties; I noted before that it, in conjunction with various auxiliary statements, deductively implies various predictions. This is enough to show that the sentence "God exists" isn't meaningless gibberish. A meaningful statement need not be decidable in principle.

Summary

I'll summarize my assessment of the Testability Theory of Meaning as follows. I think there are difficulties in testing the hypothesis that God exists. This, however, isn't because I endorse the criterion of falsifiability; I don't. The bare statement "God exists" does not entail observational predictions, but neither does the bare statement "electrons exist." The typical situation in science is that theoretical statements have observational consequences only when they are conjoined with auxiliary assumptions. It is easy to invent auxiliary assumptions that permit the hypothesis that God exists to make predictions. It is also easy to invent such assumptions so that the result is that the hypothesis makes true predictions. What is not so easy is to show that the auxiliary assumptions that permit the theistic hypothesis to make predictions are themselves well confirmed. Scientific testing requires that the auxiliary assumptions used be well supported by evidence; inventing them isn't enough.

Review Questions

1   What does it mean to say that a hypothesis is falsifiable? Does this mean it is false? Is the hypothesis that organisms contain genes falsifiable?
2   What is an auxiliary assumption? How does testing the hypothesis that God exists depend on a choice of auxiliary assumptions?
3   What does it mean to say that Holmes could independently confirm the auxiliary assumptions he needs concerning Moriarty? Independent of what?
4   How does the Surprise Principle explain why the existence of miracles would be strong evidence for the existence of God? In what way are auxiliary assumptions needed if one wants to interpret miracles as evidence favoring the hypothesis that God exists?
5   What are two weaknesses of the logical positivists' "testability theory of meaning," particularly as it relates to an analysis of the meaning of the statement "God exists"?
6   How, and why, are auxiliary assumptions independently established or confirmed?
7   Do you think the statement "God exists" should admit of a timeless verdict, rather than a temporally-indexed (or historically contingent) one? Why or why not?
8   How does falsifiability differ from testability? Can a hypothesis be testable without being falsifiable?

Problems for Further Thought

1   Consider the following passage from David Hume's "Essay on Miracles":

> That no testimony is sufficient to establish a miracle unless the testimony be of such a kind, that its falsehood would be more miraculous than the fact which it endeavors to establish.... When any one tells me that he saw a dead man restored to life, I immediately consider with myself whether it be more probable that this person should either deceive or be deceived, or that the fact which he related should really have happened. I weigh the one miracle against the other, and according to the superiority which I discover, I pronounce my decision, and always reject the greater miracle. If the falsehood of his testimony would be more miraculous than the event which he relates, then, and only then, can he pretend to commend my belief or opinion.

   What general point about eyewitness testimony is Hume making here? Does Hume's argument show that miracles never happen?
2   Can positivists say that a sentence is meaningful even though we will never actually find out whether it is true? Can they say that a sentence is meaningful if it is impossible for us to discover whether it is true? Does this mean that sentences about the prehistoric past are meaningless?
3   The concept of falsifiability was defined in this chapter. Define the parallel concept of verifiability. What problems are there with the claim that statements that are not *a priori* must be verifiable?
4   Is the Testability Theory of Meaning meaningful according to the standards it specifies? That is, is the theory either a consequence of definitions or testable via sense experience?

Recommended Readings, Video, and Audio

Visit the companion website at www.routledge.com/cw/sober for suggestions of readings, video, and audio, for this chapter.

Chapter 10

Pascal and Irrationality

Blaise Pascal (1623–1662), a French physicist, philosopher, mathematician, and mystic, was interested in the question of whether it could be rational to believe in God even if you think it is enormously improbable that God exists. Suppose all the evidence is *against* God's existence—you regard the existence of God as a possibility, although you think it is extremely implausible. Can it still make sense to be a theist? Pascal was one of the founders of the modern mathematical theory of probability. His argument has come to be called *Pascal's Wager*, because Pascal argues that believing that God exists is a sensible wager, even if there is no evidence that God exists.

Prudential and Evidential Reasons for Belief

Before analyzing Pascal's argument, I want to describe two kinds of reasons someone might have for believing some proposition or for performing some action. Suppose one day we meet for lunch. I'm carrying a machine gun and a briefcase. I open the briefcase and show you that it contains $1,000,000. I show you that the gun is loaded. Then, I make you an offer that I think you can't refuse. You probably do not believe the president of the United States is juggling candy bars at this very moment. You regard this proposition as very improbable, though you grant that it isn't entirely impossible. Here is my offer: If you can get yourself to believe that the president is juggling candy bars right now, I'll give you $1,000,000. If you don't believe this proposition, I'll shoot you with the machine gun. What is it reasonable for you to do, supposing that you think I'm entirely sincere in my threats and promises?

In one sense, it is rational to try to believe, even though you think the proposition in question is very improbable. It would be prudent (that is, in your self-interest) to try to believe, supposing that you don't want to die and would like to have the million dollars. I'll call this kind of reason a *prudential reason*.

In another sense, however, you don't have any reason to believe that the president of the United States is juggling candy bars right now. You have no evidence at all that the proposition is true. Let's describe this fact by saying that you don't have an *evidential reason* for believing the proposition in question.

Pascal's Wager is intended to provide you with a *prudential* reason for believing that God exists even if you think there is no *evidence* that there is a God. Even if you think all the evidence is against the existence of God, Pascal thinks he can give you a prudential reason for theism, so long as you grant that the existence of God is at least possible.

When Does It Make Sense to Gamble?

Before analyzing Pascal's argument, I need to mention one detail about gambling. Here is a fact about reasonable gambles: *It can make sense to bet on improbable outcomes if the payoff is big enough.* Suppose I offer you the following wager. If you pay me $1, you will be allowed to draw a single card from a standard deck of cards. If the card drawn is the ace of spades, I'll give you $1,000,000. If it is some other card, you receive nothing; you simply forfeit the dollar you paid to play. Question: Does it make sense to buy into this gamble, assuming you can trust me to pay you if you win and that your goal is to maximize the amount of money you possess? The answer is *yes*. Although the probability of winning is only 1/52, the payoff if you win is so huge and the cost to you if you lose is so small that this is a great gamble to make. Bear this fact in mind as you consider Pascal's argument.

---

10 The Expected Value of an Action

You have to decide between two actions: buying a lottery ticket and not buying one. If you buy the ticket, a card is drawn at random from a standard deck of cards. If the card is the ace of spades, you win $1,000,000. If not, you lose. The ticket costs $1. Should you buy the ticket, if your only goal is to maximize your cash resources?

The *expected value* (expected utility) of an action is the *average* payoff you would receive if you performed the action again and again. If you buy the ticket, there is a 51/52 chance that the ace of spades will not appear; in this case, your resources will have dropped by $1 (the cost of the ticket). On the other hand, if you buy the ticket, there is a 1/52 chance that you will win the million; in this case, your resources (taking account of the cost of the ticket) will have increased by $999,999. So the expected value of buying the ticket is

($1)(51/52) + ($999,999)(1/52) = $19,230

What is the expected value of the alternative action—of *not* buying the ticket? That depends on what you would do with the $1 in question. Suppose that you would simply put it in your pocket if you didn't buy into the lottery. In this case, you can be certain that your resources will neither increase nor decline. So the expected value of not buying a ticket is $0. Notice that buying the ticket has a higher expected value than not buying. So the rule in decision theory tells you to buy the ticket because this is how you maximize your expected utility (or value).

The expected value of buying the ticket is *not* the amount of money you can expect to get. If you enter the lottery, you'll either end up a dollar behind or

$999,999 ahead. The expected value is what you would average if you bought into the lottery again and again. Most of the time, you'll lose; occasionally, you'll win. The average payoff per ticket over the long run is about $19,230.

The mathematical idea of an expectation also applies to quantities other than value or utility. A probability theorist might say that the expected number of off-spring for parents in the United States today is about 2.2. This doesn't mean that a couple can expect to have precisely this number of children. Rather, 2.2 is the expected number because it is the average. The same is true when life insurance companies describe the life expectancy of a person who is now nineteen years old.

Pascal's Argument

Pascal's Wager can be represented as a solution to a problem in decision theory. This is a modern theory that describes how an agent should choose among different available actions on the basis of the *utilities* of different possible *outcomes*. Be sure to get clear on how each of these italicized terms figures in Pascal's argument.

You have to decide whether or not to believe there is a God. These are the two possible actions—believing in God or not believing. Separate from what you believe, there is the way the world is—either there is a God or there isn't. Hence, there are four possible outcomes—an outcome being composed of your performing an action when the world is a particular way. The four outcomes are represented in the following two-by-two table:

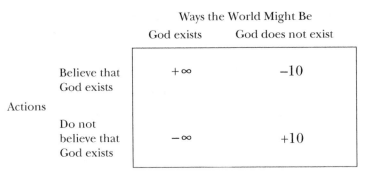

The upper-left entry represents the outcome in which you believe in God and there is a God. What is the result, if this should come to pass? Pascal says that the payoff to you is an infinite reward—you go to heaven. Suppose, on the other hand, that you occupy the lower-left cell. This is the outcome in which you don't believe there is a God, but God in fact exists. Here Pascal says you suffer an infinite punishment—you receive eternal damnation. What about the other two entries? If you believe in God, but there is no God, perhaps you will have wasted your time with religious rituals and observances you might have preferred to skip had you only known there is no God listening to your prayers. This isn't a horrible result, though it should be represented as a modest disutility—hence my entry of −10. On the other hand, if you don't believe in God and there is no God (the lower-right cell), you receive a modest benefit. Instead of engaging in religious practices that you may find boring at times, you can get involved in activities that are more rewarding. Pascal says that the entry in this cell represents a modest benefit; my chosen value for the utility here is +10.

To summarize the structure of the problem: you must decide which action to perform. The possible outcomes are the possible pairings of an available action with a different way the world might be. With each possible outcome, you associate a utility (a payoff) that represents how good or bad the outcome is for you.

How should the utilities of the different possible outcomes be assessed to reach a decision about which act is preferable? The *expected utility* of believing that there is a God needs to take account of two possibilities: There is the utility you receive if you believe and there is a God, and the quite different utility you receive if you believe and there is no God. Similarly, the expected utility of not believing must take account of both outcome possibilities (represented in the bottom row). Here is Pascal's solution. Even if you think the existence of God is very improbable (say, you assign it a probability of only 1/1,000,000), the expected utility of believing is higher than the expected utility of not believing. The reason is that, although the existence of God is very improbable, there is a huge benefit if you are a theist and God exists, but only a small cost if you are a theist and there is no God. It makes sense to bet on the existence of God, even if the existence of God is very improbable, for reasons that parallel the gamble I mentioned before. The gamble makes sense even though it is improbable that there is a God.

First Criticism of Pascal's Argument

Two criticisms have been made of this wager, but only one of them is decisive. First, some philosophers have objected to treating belief as an action. We can't decide to believe a proposition; belief isn't an action we control in this way. In my story about the president, you may recognize that it is in your interest to believe that the president is now juggling candy bars. Believing this would be good for you, but that doesn't mean you can automatically make yourself believe the proposition. The objection to Pascal's argument is that it is a mistake to treat belief as a problem in decision theory, since decision theory is about choosing actions that you can perform if you want to.

Pascal recognized this difficulty. After stating his wager, he comments that people who are convinced his reasoning is sound may not be able to suddenly start being theists. He suggests to them that they go live among religious people. By doing this, habits of faith will gradually take hold. Pascal realized you can't simply decide to believe something. But he did see that you can choose to live your life in such a way that belief will come naturally after a while.

Pascal's comment means that the wager can be reformulated so that the actions considered really are things under our control. Rather than treating belief and nonbelief as things we can choose to do directly, let's recognize that sincere belief can only occur in the right setting, where the right habits have been developed. It is also worth mentioning that Pascal's Wager concerns what it is best for you to believe. The question of whether you can do what is best for you is a separate question.

Second Criticism of Pascal's Argument

The second objection to Pascal's argument is more telling. In Chapter 9, I discussed the difficulty of establishing what God would be like if such a being existed. This is the problem of independently confirming auxiliary hypotheses, as I called them, about God's nature.

Pascal's Wager makes very specific assumptions about what God would be like if there were such a being. The assumption is that God would send believers to heaven and nonbelievers to hell. But there are other conceptions to consider. For example, maybe God would reward those who lead a good life and would punish those who are bad, independently of what those individuals' theological opinions happen to be. Or consider another possibility:

Perhaps God will send everyone to heaven except those who are convinced by Pascal's Wager.

The main problem with the wager is that it makes assumptions about God's nature that are part of one religious tradition but not part of many others. How can one tell which assumptions are true? In the absence of a convincing argument, I see no reason to think Pascal's description of the payoffs is correct.

The Role of Reason

Pascal argued that it can make sense to believe things that are totally unsupported by evidence. If you think evidence is the hallmark of rational belief, then you'll interpret Pascal as giving a justification of irrationality. Of course, he didn't abandon the standard of rationality altogether. He tried to provide a *rational argument* that we should believe in God even if there is no evidence that God exists. Pascal aimed to provide a prudential reason, not an evidential reason.

Pascal rejected the idea that evidential reasoning should determine whether or not we believe in God. Other religious thinkers have done the same thing, but for reasons that differ from Pascal's. For example, it has been suggested that God is so radically different from all the other beings that we know about that the methods of reasoning appropriate for discussing these other beings are no longer appropriate when the question is a theological one. God is said to be an infinite being, one who may stand outside of space and time and yet be able to influence what happens inside of space and time. God is also supposed to be all-powerful, all-knowing, and all-good. In all these respects, God is far different from the familiar objects about which we are accustomed to reasoning.

Let's grant that God is supposed to have these special features. Why do they show that reason isn't an appropriate tool to use in thinking about whether God exists? I noted in Chapter 2 and again in Chapter 9 that deductive validity depends on an argument's form, not on its subject matter. If this is right, then deductive reasoning should apply to the question of God's existence in the same way that it applies to other questions.

Sometimes, it is suggested that God is so shrouded in mystery that we can't hope to understand God by rational inquiry. Maybe this is right—maybe the issues are so mysterious that you'll never be able to see that God exists if you adhere to rational standards of argument. But why does this mean that those standards should be abandoned? Why not take this to mean that you shouldn't believe that God exists, precisely because no good argument can be produced for this conclusion?

I won't pursue these questions any further. Maybe it can be explained why usual standards of evidence and argument should be abandoned when the question is whether God exists. However, I know of no reason to think this.

Freud's Psychological Explanation of Theism

There is a curious fact here, one that really does require an explanation. If we were talking about virtually any topic from everyday or scientific life, no one would be very attracted by the advice that we should believe something on the basis of no evidence. Yet, when the question is whether God exists, people sometimes lower their critical standards. This isn't true of everyone, of course. It wasn't true of Anselm, Aquinas, Hume, or Paley, for example. Still, the idea of switching from reason to faith has been attractive to many.

There is a psychological question I want to pose here, even though I will not try to answer it. Why are people sometimes inclined to believe without evidence when the question is whether God exists, but are much less willing to take this attitude when the question is a different one?

In his essay, "The Future of an Illusion," Sigmund Freud (1856–1939), the founder of psychoanalysis, gave an answer that is worth pondering. Freud points out that the world is in many ways a frightening place. It is a relatively recent event in human history that people have come to exercise some mastery over nature, and even this recent mastery is enormously incomplete. Even if you aren't threatened every day by wild animals, lightning, drought, famine, and flood, you still have to face the inevitability of your own death. In this ultimate sense, we are as helpless as our ancient ancestors. With so much of nature out of our control, beyond our understanding, and threatening our survival, it isn't surprising that human beings should invent myths that provide a different and more appealing picture of our place in the cosmos. Instead of viewing the universe as indifferent to us, impersonal, incomprehensible, and dangerous, we construct a comprehensible picture of forces more powerful than ourselves who take an interest in our fate. Freud's hypothesis was that believing in God persists in human history because of the psychological benefits it provides to believers.

Pascal aimed to provide a prudential argument for believing that God exists. Freud was an atheist, but aimed to provide an explanation for why many people believe that God exists. Pascal sought to justify theism; Freud didn't seek to justify it, but to explain it.

A New Prudential Argument

In spite of these differences, we can use some of Freud's observations to formulate a prudential argument for theism that is stronger than the one that Pascal provided. The stumbling block for Pascal was the assumptions he made about what God would be like if he existed. We can avoid these difficult questions about God's nature, however, and focus on something that is more familiar and closer to home—our own minds.

Suppose you are the sort of person who derives comfort and fulfillment from believing in God. Your belief in God provides your life with meaning. It gives you the courage to face adversity. Moreover, let's suppose that without believing in God, you would plunge into despair. You would become depressed, unable to live a productive life.

There are many people in the world who aren't like this. First, there are cheerful agnostics and atheists—people who manage to make a meaningful life for themselves without needing a theological framework. Second, there are people who remain tormented by despair even after they become theists. In both these cases, I'm talking about people whose general outlook is rather independent of the theological opinions they happen to have. Nevertheless, let's suppose there are some people for whom belief in God makes all the difference. Perhaps you are a person of this sort. If so, you can use these psychological facts to formulate a prudential argument for theism:

> If you believe in God, you will lead a happy and productive life.
> If you don't believe in God, you will fall into depression and despair.
> ———————————————————————————————
> The way to maximize expected utility is for you to be a theist.

This argument resembles Pascal's in that it doesn't focus on whatever evidence there may be concerning whether God exists. But unlike Pascal's argument, this prudential argument doesn't make assumptions about what God would do to theists and atheists. This argument focuses on the psychological consequences of theism, not on speculations about heaven and hell. This argument is more difficult to refute than Pascal's. The major issue it raises is difficult and general. Should we allow prudential reasons to influence what we believe, or should we require that our beliefs be regulated by evidence alone?

Pragmatism

Pragmatism is a general philosophical position that has implications for this question. This philosophical idea was developed in the nineteenth and twentieth centuries principally by Charles Sanders Peirce, William James, and John Dewey. In ordinary speech, "being pragmatic" means *being practical*. The philosophical position, however, isn't fully captured by the everyday meaning of the word. Pragmatists say that we should believe propositions that are useful to us. In everyday life, this usually means that we should be attentive to evidence. Suppose you are about to cross the street and want to know whether a bus is coming. The most useful thing to do here is to use your senses (sight, hearing, etc.). It would be silly to engage in wishful thinking—to refuse to consult any evidence and simply believe the proposition you'd like to be true. In cases of this sort, the prudent thing to do is to attend to evidence. There are cases, however, in which prudential considerations can lead in one direction and evidential considerations in another. My story about the president juggling candy bars provides one example. A prudential argument for theism may provide another.

In *The Will to Believe* (1897), William James (1842–1910) says that a person is entitled to believe in God for purely prudential reasons (of the psychological sort described earlier) if the belief provides a "vital benefit" and if no decision about theism can be made on the basis of the evidence available. But why shouldn't a pragmatist be more liberal? Even if there were *substantial* evidence against there being a God, why shouldn't sufficiently large prudential benefits outweigh the evidential considerations? James's position doesn't provide a blanket justification of theism. As mentioned before, people who could lead happy productive lives without being theists can't claim they *need* to believe in God to avoid falling into despair. Yet, the spirit of pragmatism (if not the letter of James's formulation) seems to sanction believing in God if belief would be useful.

To do justice to the problems pragmatism raises, we would need to consider a variety of cases. If it is a matter of life and death, is it reasonable for someone to be a theist on purely prudential grounds? In less extreme cases, is the comfort provided by theism reason enough to believe in God? This raises complex questions about the attitudes we should take towards our lives. Someone might reject pragmatic arguments for theism by saying that they prefer to look the universe square in the face without the benefit of comforting illusions. This person might prefer a life of honest uncertainty and doubt over a life made comfortable by beliefs that have no evidential basis.

The pragmatist says that we should believe what it is useful to believe. An opponent of pragmatism might insist that prudential considerations are always irrelevant; we should believe only those propositions that are well supported by evidence. This is the position that W. K. Clifford defended in his essay "The Ethics of Belief" (1877). He rejected James's position and maintained that "it is wrong always, everywhere, and for anyone, to believe anything upon insufficient evidence." Here is one of the arguments that Clifford gives:

> If I let myself believe anything on insufficient evidence, there may be no great harm done by the mere belief; it may be true after all, or I may never have occasion to exhibit it in outward acts. But I cannot help doing this great wrong towards Man, that I make myself credulous. The danger to society is not merely that it should believe wrong things, though

that is great enough, but that it should become credulous and lose the habit of testing things and inquiring into them; for then it must sink back into savagery.

(p. 79)

Clifford's warning is exaggerated. It just isn't true that society will "sink back into savagery" if you believe a proposition without having any evidence for it. People in benign and progressive societies have been believing various propositions without having evidence for them for a long time. Clifford is here advancing a *consequentialist* argument; he is suggesting that the action in question is wrong because it has bad consequences. Another possible argument for Clifford's position would be that it is wrong *in itself* to believe upon insufficient evidence, regardless of whether this has good or bad consequences. This raises the question of why it is wrong in itself to so believe.

Review Questions

1 What is the difference between a prudential reason and an evidential reason for believing something?
2 Can it ever make sense to bet on something that probably won't happen?
3 Given the payoffs Pascal assigns to outcomes, what is the expected value of believing in God? Of not believing?
4 Do people believe what they do because they "decide to believe"? If not, does it follow that Pascal's argument is mistaken?
5 How does Pascal's argument depend on a set of auxiliary assumptions (in the sense of Chapter 9) about God's nature?
6 Describe a prudential argument for believing in God that avoids the problem that Pascal's argument confronts.
7 Why did Clifford reject James's pragmatic argument for theism? Evaluate the argument that Clifford presents for his position.
8 Pascal sought to show that it is rational to believe in God without sufficient evidence, whereas Freud and James both sought to show that it may be reasonable—that is, that it may make good psychological sense—to believe in God without sufficient evidence. Do you think there is an important difference between justifying and explaining beliefs? Why?
9 What implications does Pascal's argument have for our conceptions of the role of reason in belief-formation?
10 How broad is the scope of Pascal's argument? Can it be used to justify beliefs in (e.g.) vampires or zombies, or is its use restricted to beliefs about God? Explain your answer.

Problems for Further Thought

1 In Chapter 7, I explained what the Principle of Sufficient Reason is and sketched an argument for why it might be useful to believe the principle even if there is no evidence that it is true. Work out the details of this decision-theoretic argument by constructing a two-by-two table for this problem that resembles the one used for Pascal's Wager. Is the argument successful?
2 In Chapter 7, I argued that there is a kind of question (a global question about why the whole history of the universe is as it is) that science cannot answer. Can science answer the question of whether we should accept James's or Clifford's position on the ethics of belief? If so, which scientific theory provides an answer to this question?

3   Ethicists often distinguish duties from superogatory acts. An action is a duty if it is something you must perform; an action is superogatory if it would be a good thing to do, but is not a duty. How does this distinction apply to Clifford's argument against James?

Recommended Readings, Video, and Audio

Visit the companion website at www.routledge.com/cw/sober for suggestions of readings, video, and audio, for this chapter.

The Argument from Evil

Most of the arguments considered so far concerning the existence of God have had theistic conclusions. I now turn to an issue many regard as providing an argument for atheism. Sometimes it is thought that the fact that there is evil in the world (or that there is so much of it) proves there is no God. An argument to this effect is called an Argument from Evil. I'll consider three forms this argument might take. I think none of these successfully proves there is no God. Then I'll consider a fourth version of the argument from evil; here, instead of trying to prove that there is no God, the argument attempts to show something more modest—that the existence of evil is evidence against the hypothesis that God exists.

First Version of the Argument

The first form of the Argument from Evil is simple:

(1) If God were to exist, then that being would be all-powerful, all-knowing, and all-good (all-PKG, for short).
(2) If an all-PKG being existed, then there would be no evil.
(3) There is evil.

───────────

Hence, there is no God.

The argument is deductively valid; convince yourself of this by identifying the argument's logical form.

Sometimes it is said that the first premise is a definition of what we mean by the concept of God. I'll say in a minute why I don't think (1) is a definition. Premise (2) is usually defended as follows. If God is all-good, he wants to prevent evil. If he is all-knowing, he knows the difference between right and wrong and knows how to prevent evil from coming into existence. And if he is all-powerful, he can prevent evil, should he wish to do so. So God, if he is all-PKG, has both the inclination and the ability to prevent evil from occurring.

Two Kinds of Evil

What does *evil* mean in premise (3)? Discussion of the Argument from Evil usually divides existing evils into two categories. There are the evils that are brought into existence by human actions, and there are the evils that exist because of natural events that aren't under human control. The first category includes the suffering that human beings inflict on each other; the second includes the suffering that human beings (and other creatures) experience because of natural disasters, such as earthquakes and plagues.

Possible Reactions to the Argument

As mentioned before, the argument is valid. Hence, if you wish to reject the conclusion, you must reject one or more of the premises. What options are available?

One option is to deny the existence of evil (premise 3). For example, you could take the view that there really is no difference between right and wrong. This is the idea that the universe is morally neutral and that we human beings impose illusory moral categories upon it. This view about morality will be discussed in the fifth section of the book, especially in Chapters 29 and 30. For now I'll ignore this option. I'll assume that some of the murders, tortures, and other brutalities that have peppered human history really are morally bad. I will also assume that the world would have been a better place if some of the suffering caused by natural disasters hadn't occurred. This assumption—that premise (3) is correct—is shared by many, if not all, religious traditions.

Another option is to reject premise (1). You could interpret the existence of evil as showing merely that if there is a God, then God isn't all-PKG. This strategy grants premises (2) and (3), but then concludes that if God exists, he can't be exactly the way one religious tradition says he is.

The fact that this strategy is available shows, I think, that (1) isn't "true by definition." If the first premise really did define what the term "God" means, then the existence of evil couldn't be explained by rejecting this premise. But this does seem to be a real option. What we need to recognize is that premise (1) doesn't have the same status as the following sentence: "A bachelor is an unmarried man." Suppose we found that a man whom we thought is a bachelor in fact is married. Would this lead us to consider the possibility that maybe bachelors could be married? I think not. Premise (1) embodies one theory about what God's nature is. It is one theory among many possible theories, none of which deserves to be viewed as "true by definition." The ancient Greeks denied that the gods are all-PKG. Manichaeism and Zoroastrianism deny that God is all-powerful. So rejecting premise (1) is an option we need to consider as a way of explaining why evil exists.

Theodicy and Defense

One other option remains: reject premise (2). This is the strategy pursued by theists who think premises (1) and (3) are true. If you think God is all-PKG and that evil is a reality, you need to show how God's being all-PKG doesn't imply that there should be no evil in the world.

There are two types of criticism that might be offered of premise (2). You could try to explain why it is false. This is the project known as "theodicy" in traditional Christian theology. Here you try to explain why an all-PKG God would allow evil to exist. Alternatively, there is the more modest criticism in which you try to show that we don't have a good reason to think that the premise is true. Contemporary philosophers of religion use the term "defense" to describe this second type of reply to the Argument from Evil. The distinction that separates theodicy from defense can be seen in the discussion of other arguments for the existence of God. For example, in Chapter 4, we considered an objection to the design argument that maintains that if God built organisms, they would be perfectly adapted to their environments. One way to criticize this argument is to suggest that there is no reason to think that God would have wanted each organism to be perfectly adapted. A more ambitious criticism would be the attempt to demonstrate what God's motives would be.

In any event, I think there is some plausibility in rejecting premise (2). Notice that premise (2) makes a very ambitious claim. It says that if an all-PKG God existed, there would be zero evil in the world.

Soul-Building Evils

Traditional theodicy has claimed that some evils have the property of being "soul-building." Soul-building evils are the ones that make us better people. Living through adversity strengthens our character; it makes us better people than we would have been if we had never suffered hardship.

I want to be careful about what I'm conceding here. I grant that *some* evils are soul-building. But I think it is a gross exaggeration to say this of *all* the evils that human beings have experienced. Sometimes suffering doesn't make the victim stronger; sometimes suffering destroys people. And even when people survive brutal tortures, do we really think that they are always better people for it? Sometimes they survive as mere shells. Even when torture victims in some sense are made stronger by their ordeals, do we still want to say that the experience has been worth it? If you think it was worthwhile for *them*, would *you* choose to undergo the torture yourself, or choose it for someone you love? There are some "strengths" that aren't worth having because they cost too much to acquire.

Sometimes it is suggested that when people are destroyed by the sufferings they endure, the souls of other people are strengthened by watching this happen. I think this is sometimes true, but it is often false. Sometimes the only effect on witnesses is that they are sickened by having to watch events they know full well are horrible. Sometimes people who witness the suffering of others react with callousness and indifference, and some suffering occurs in private. In these cases, there is no audience whose souls are made stronger by watching the spectacle. Just as suffering often doesn't make the sufferer a better person, it also is true that one person's suffering often fails to improve the characters of witnesses. So in granting that *some* suffering is soul-building, I'm granting something about a rather small portion of the huge mountain of agony the human race has experienced.

Is the fact that some evils are soul-building enough to refute premise (2)? This isn't so clear. If it is desirable that we be strong of heart, why couldn't God have made us this way without us having to experience evil? The need for soul-building experiences is sometimes defended by an analogy concerning the way a benevolent parent treats a child. If you really care about your children, you won't shield them from all adversity. There are some experiences that involve pain and suffering that children need to have if they are to mature into morally sensitive and autonomous adults. If your child is being picked on by a bully at school, maybe you will decide that your daughter needs to tough it out for herself. Intervening would save her a few scrapes and bruises *now*, but you might decide as a parent that this wouldn't be in her long-term best interests.

You, as a parent, have the goal of seeing your children develop in a certain way. You choose not to prevent some bad things from happening to your child because you recognize that there is no other way for her to mature as you intend. Suppose, however, that you could have your child become a virtuous adult without her having to be kicked around by the bully. In this case, why would you allow the bully to continue to harass your child? A parent might allow soul-building evils to befall a child when there is no other way to have the child's soul grow strong, but the limitations that might justify a parent's choice aren't supposed to be present where God is concerned. If God is all-PKG, why couldn't he simply make us with strong souls? Defenders of the soul-building idea reply that God wants us to be able to be proud of our own achievements. If we suffer through adversity, we get credit for the strong souls that result. If, however, God simply gave us strong souls *gratis*, we would deserve no such credit. We couldn't be proud of ourselves; at best, we would simply be grateful to a benevolent deity. To evaluate this suggestion, we must ask why it is so important that we be able to take credit for having strong characters. Why is it better to experience an evil and then get credit for having endured it? Why is this better than having a strong character because God made us that way from the start? I raise this question, but won't attempt to answer it. I'll concede for now that an all-PKG God would allow at least some evils to exist. Some soul-building evils are of this sort. In other words, I'll concede that premise (2) is false.

Does this mean there is no problem of evil—that the existence of evil poses no difficulty for the conception of God as an all-PKG being? I think not. The soul-building evils an all-PKG God would allow us to experience are a tiny portion of the evils we need to explain. What needs to be explained isn't why there is some evil *rather than none at all*. The deeper problem is to explain why there is so much evil, *rather than one ounce less*.

Second Version of the Argument

The second Argument from Evil is more difficult to refute than the first. It takes the following form:

(1) If God were to exist, then that being would be all-PKG.
(4) If an all-PKG being existed, then the amount of evil would not exceed a soul-building minimum.
(5) The amount of evil does exceed a soul-building minimum.

———————————————————

Hence, there is no God.

By "soul-building minimum," I mean the minimum amount of evil that would suffice to make us have strength of character. This argument is valid. Hence, if the conclusion is false, at least one of the premises must be false. The project of theodicy is to show that premise (4) is mistaken.

Free Will

Is there a reason that an all-PKG being might have for permitting evils to exist that go beyond the soul-building minimum? It is sometimes suggested that this reason is to be found in the idea of *free will*. God made us free; this means that it is up to us whether we do good or do evil. A consequence of this freedom is that there is more evil than would be strictly necessary for soul-building.

There is a question here that we will examine in detail in the section of this book on philosophy of mind. Why couldn't God have made us free agents who always freely choose to do what is right? Why assume that free people must sometimes perform evil actions? If an evil doer can have free will, why can't someone who behaves better? After all, God is supposed to be a free being who never does evil things. This seems to show that being free and always doing what's right are not incompatible. Even if being free implies that you *could* do evil things, why does freedom imply that you *actually* choose to do so?

However, let's now set this point aside and assume, for the sake of argument, that human freedom requires that people sometimes produce evil and that this evil exceeds the soul-building minimum. This means that premise (4) in the second argument is mistaken. But again, I want to emphasize that this doesn't fully solve the problem of evil. The problem is to account for the quantity of evil that exists. Let's grant that some evil must exist for soul-building and some more evil will be a consequence of human freedom. Does this explain the quantity of evil that the world contains?

Examples and a Third Version of the Argument

Let's single out some horrendous evil that has befallen the human race. Think of all the suffering Hitler caused. How could an all-PKG God have allowed this to happen? Is the answer that God gave each of us free will? I think this appeal to the importance of human freedom doesn't begin to address the difficulty. Why didn't God intervene in human affairs on those rare occasions on which it would have made a dramatic difference? When the sperm and egg came together that produced Hitler, why didn't God prevent that fertilization event from happening? To do so would still have allowed human beings to be free; in addition, that brief intervention would allow there to be soul-building evils aplenty. Here I'm considering a minor foray into human affairs, not some major restructuring of human nature. Suppose that if Hitler had never existed, many of the terrible things he did would never have happened. The world would have been a much better place. Most theists would agree with this. So why didn't God influence the course of human history for the better? What you must see here is that appeals to soul-building and to freedom don't provide an answer. Causing Hitler to never be born would not have robbed his parents of free will.

Another way to make this point is to consider horrendous evils that come into existence for reasons having nothing to do with human action. Consider the bubonic plague. If God had prevented that disease from existing, much suffering and death would have been avoided. To intervene in the lives of the relevant microorganisms doesn't rob them of free will, since they don't have wills (minds) to begin with. Also, the amount of suffering that occurred because of the plague far exceeded what could be explained by the goal of soul-building. About one-third of the European population died agonizing deaths from bubonic plague. Would our souls have been less strong if some smaller percentage had perished?

These considerations lead to a third version of the Argument from Evil:

(1)   If God were to exist, then that being would be all-PKG.
(6)   If an all-PKG being existed, then there would be no more evil than the minimum required for soul-building and as a consequence of human freedom.
(7)   The quantity of evil found in human history exceeds the minimum required for soul-building and as a consequence of human freedom.

Hence, there is no God.

A Criticism of the Argument

How might this third argument be criticized? If there is a God, and if premises (1) and (7) are true, what grounds can there be for rejecting premise (6)? The project of *theodicy* needs to produce a reason for thinking that (6) is false. The more modest project of *defense* merely needs to show that we don't have a good reason to think that (6) is true. Although soul-building and free will were just presented in the context of a theodicy, I'll now shift gears and formulate a reply to this last argument that has the character of a defense.

Premise (6), like premises (2) and (4) in the preceding arguments, attempts to specify an upper bound on the amount of evil that an all-PKG God would allow to exist. But why think that we mere humans have the ability to figure this out? After all, God, if he exists, is vastly more intelligent than we are. Therefore, it is entirely possible that his plan for the world contains elements that we cannot understand or even imagine. Perhaps God allowed evils into the world beyond those required for soul-building and as a consequence of human freedom because these additional evils are required to obtain some greater good of which we are unaware. We need to be careful in how we formulate this criticism of the Argument from Evil. I am not asserting that premise (6) is false. I am giving a reason for thinking that we don't know that (6) is true. All of the versions of the Argument from Evil that I have surveyed attempt to pinpoint exactly how much evil there should be if an all-PKG being existed. To do this requires that we know a lot about what an all-PKG being would do. To the degree that we lack knowledge of what God's plan would be if he existed, we also lack the sort of knowledge that is needed for these arguments for atheism to succeed.

Testability, Again

In Chapters 6 and 9, I discussed whether the existence of God is testable. The reply I just formulated to the Argument from Evil raises the same issue. How much evil should we expect there to be if there were a God? Atheists who advance the Argument from Evil just described think they can answer this question. However, if we can't answer this question, we can't test the proposition that God exists by examining how much evil there is in the world.

Another Kind of Argument—The Evidential Argument from Evil

The arguments from evil formulated so far are deductively valid; the goal is to prove that an all-PKG God cannot exist, given this or that fact about the evils that there are.

There is reason to think that no such deductive argument can be made to work. Such an argument would have the following form:

If an all–PKG God exists, then evils of kind X will not exist.
Evils of kind X do exist.

No all–PKG God exists.

This argument is deductively valid (what is its logical form?). The problem with this kind of argument is that it is hard to show that the first premise is true. Atheists might object to this argument by asserting that human beings are in no position to understand why an all–PKG God would allow evils of kind X to exist. The theist's point is not to assert that the first premise is false but to say that we can't tell whether it is true.

I now turn to a more modest formulation of the argument from evil. It is called the evidential argument from evil (see W. Rowe's article, "The Problem of Evil and Some Varieties of Atheism," *American Philosophical Quarterly* [1979] 16: 335–41). The goal here is merely to show that this or that kind of evil is evidence against the hypothesis that an all–PKG being exists; the argument does not claim that these evils prove that no such being exists. We can use the Surprise Principle to formulate the argument. Let E be a proposition that describes in some detail the kinds and quantities of evil that exist:

If an all–PKG God existed, you would expect E not to be true.
If an all–PKG God did not exist, you would expect E to be true.
The Surprise Principle.

E is strong evidence against there being an all–PKG being.

The Surprise Principle describes what "strong" evidence means. It can be reformulated to define what evidence (strong or weak) means, and this allows us to construct an even more modest version of the evidential argument from evil:

The truth of proposition E is more surprising if an all–PKG God exists than it would be if there were no such being.
The Modest Surprise Principle.

E is evidence against there being an all–PKG being.

As an exercise, write down what the Modest Surprise Principle says. This modest evidential argument from evil says that E favors the hypothesis that no all–PKG God exists. Is it true that the kinds and quantities of evil that exist are evidence against the existence of an all–PKG God? If not, what could count as evidence against this hypothesis?

Review Questions

1   Consider the proposition that God is all-powerful, all-knowing, and all-good. Should we regard this proposition as a definition of what the word "God" means? If it isn't a definition, does this mean that the proposition is false?
2   It sometimes is suggested that imperfections must exist if human beings are to be able to form the idea of God (a perfect being). Is this a solution to the problem of evil?
3   Does the fact that some evils are soul-building while others are consequences of human freedom solve the problem of evil?

4   What is the difference between theodicy and defense as criticisms of the Argument from Evil? Illustrate this distinction by constructing an argument of each kind that has nothing to do with the existence of God.

5   A criticism was presented of the third Argument from Evil. The argument is valid. And the criticism did not claim that any of the premises are false. What, then, is the criticism?

6   What is the evidential argument from evil? Is it more successful than the arguments that attempt to prove that there is no God?

7   Can someone reasonably believe both that the statement "God exists" is testable but that the statement "If God exists, then evil should not exist" is not testable? Why or why not?

8   Why might even a committed atheist worry that arguments about the incompatibility of an all-PKG god and the existence of evil rest on shaky ground? (Hint: What would we have to know in order to prove that they are genuinely incompatible?)

Problems for Further Thought

1   The appeal to free will, which is part of the project of theodicy, includes the claim that (a) God is omnipotent (all-powerful) and the claim that (b) God cannot give us free will without there also being evil in the world. Are (a) and (b) compatible? How should the concept of "omnipotence" be understood?

2   Are there reasons beyond the goal of soul-building and the goal of giving us free will that an all-PKG God would have for allowing evil to exist? If so, would those additional reasons solve the problem of evil?

3   Some people interpret the Bible as providing an adequate theodicy. According to their interpretation, Adam and Eve freely chose to sin in the Garden of Eden. When they did so, this effectively unleashed all of the rest of the evils that we find in the world. This theodicy apparently can explain *all* of the evil that there is, not just the evils that can be attributed to soul-building and to free will. Is this theodicy an adequate reply to the Argument from Evil?

4   Here's a question about the free will solution to the problem of evil. If God knows in advance what we'll do (which he must, if he is all-knowing), how can it be true that we have free will? This is a question we'll address in Part IV.

Recommended Readings, Video, and Audio

Visit the companion website at www.routledge.com/cw/sober for suggestions of readings, video, and audio, for this chapter.

Part III

Theory of Knowledge

What Is Knowledge?

Epistemology

In everyday life, in science, and in philosophy as well, we talk of "knowing" things. We also say that some beliefs are "strongly supported by evidence"; we say that they are "justified" or "well confirmed." We apply these phrases not only to ourselves, but also to others.

Epistemology is the part of philosophy that tries to understand such concepts. Epistemologists try to evaluate the common-sense idea that we (often, if not always) have knowledge and that we are (often, if not always) rationally justified in the beliefs we have. Some philosophers have tried to defend these common-sense ideas with philosophical argumentation. Others have developed a philosophical position that involves denying these common-sense ideas. A philosopher who claims that we don't have knowledge, or that our beliefs aren't rationally justified, is defending some version of *philosophical skepticism*.

In this chapter, I'll begin with some remarks about the problem of knowledge. In the next chapter, I'll examine the views of the seventeenth-century French philosopher René Descartes. Descartes tried to show that we really do possess knowledge of the world; he tried to refute the skeptic. After evaluating Descartes' views about knowledge, I'll turn to an alternative way of thinking about knowledge, the Reliability Theory of Knowledge (Chapter 14).

After this discussion of the problem of knowledge, I'll examine the idea of rational justification. The eighteenth-century Scottish philosopher David Hume, whose views on the Argument from Design we considered in Chapter 5, argued that the beliefs we have that are based on induction aren't rationally justified. Hume was a skeptic about induction.

We'll consider his argument for this philosophical position and also the attempts some philosophers have made to show that Hume's startling thesis is mistaken. The last chapter in this part of the book discusses a central problem in epistemology—how do we know that things outside our own minds exist?

So let's get started with the problem of knowledge. Before we can ask whether we know anything, we have to get clear on what knowledge is. To focus ideas, I want to distinguish three different ways we talk about knowledge. Only one of these will be our concern in what follows.

Three Kinds of Knowledge

Consider the differences that separate the following three statements, each concerning an individual, whom I'll call S (the subject):

(1) S knows how to ride a bicycle.
(2) S knows the President of the United States.
(3) S knows that the Rocky Mountains are in North America.

Right now I'm not interested in saying which of these statements is true. The point is that they involve different kinds of knowledge.

The kind of knowledge described in (3) I'll call *propositional knowledge*. Notice that the object of the verb in (3) is a proposition—something that is either true or false. There is a proposition—the Rockies are in North America—and (3) asserts that S knows that that proposition is true. Statements (1) and (2) don't have this structure. For example, the object of the verb in (2) is a person, not a proposition. A similar kind of knowledge would be involved if I said that S knows Chicago. Statement (2) says that S is related to an object—a person, place, or thing—so I'll say that (2) describes an instance of *object knowledge*. Is there a connection between object knowledge and propositional knowledge? Maybe to know the president of the United States, you must know some propositions that are about him. But which propositions? To know the president, do you have to know what state he comes from? This doesn't seem essential. The same holds true for each other fact about the man; there doesn't seem to be any particular proposition you've got to know for you to know him.

There is another aspect of the idea of object knowledge, one that is rather curious. Suppose I've read lots of books about the president. I know as many propositions about him as you might wish. Still, it won't be true that I know him, because I've never met him. Knowing people seems to require some sort of direct acquaintance. But it is hard to say exactly what is needed here. If I once was introduced to the president at some large party, that wouldn't be enough for me to say that I "know" him. It isn't just direct acquaintance, but something more, that is required. I won't try to describe this further. I'll merely conclude that propositional knowledge, no matter how voluminous, isn't sufficient for object knowledge. Object knowledge requires some sort of direct acquaintance with the object. In contrast propositional knowledge does not require that you have direct acquaintance with the objects that the proposition is about; S can know that the Rockies are in North America though she has never seen them.

I turn next to the kind of knowledge described in statement (1). I'll call this *know-how* knowledge. What does it mean to know how to do something? I think this idea has little connection with propositional knowledge. My son Aaron knew how to ride a bike when he was five years old. This means that he had certain abilities—he knew how to keep his balance, how to pedal, and so on. If you asked a physicist to describe what Aaron was doing that allowed him to ride the bike, the physicist could write out a set of propositions. There would be facts about gravity, forward momentum, and balancing of forces. But Aaron wasn't a physicist at age five. He didn't know the propositions that the physicist specifies. Aaron *obeyed* the physical principles that the physicist describes—his behavior conformed to what they say—but he didn't do this by learning the propositions in question. Aaron had know-how knowledge, but little in the way of propositional knowledge.

---

11 Necessary and Sufficient Conditions

Consider the following suggested definition of what a bachelor is:

For any S, S is a bachelor if and only if

(1) S is an adult.
(2) S is male.
(3) S is unmarried.

I'm not claiming that this definition precisely captures what "bachelor" means in ordinary English. Rather, I want to use it as an example of a proposed definition.

The definition is a generalization. It concerns any individual you care to consider. The definition makes two claims. The first is that IF the individual has characteristics (1), (2), and (3), then the individual is a bachelor. In other words, (1), (2), and (3) are together *sufficient* for being a bachelor. The second claim is that IF the individual is a bachelor, then the individual has all three characteristics. In other words, (1), (2), and (3) are each *necessary* for being a bachelor.

We can define what a necessary condition is and what a sufficient condition is as follows:

"X is a necessary condition for Y" means that if Y is true, then X is true.
"X is a sufficient condition for Y" means that if X is true, then Y is true.

What does the expression "if and only if" mean in the proposed definition of bachelorhood? It means that the conditions listed are both necessary and sufficient. A good definition will specify necessary and sufficient conditions for the concept one wishes to define.

This means that there can be two sorts of defect in a proposed definition. A definition can fail to provide conditions that are sufficient. It can also provide conditions that aren't necessary. And, of course, it can fall down on both counts. Which sorts of defects are present in the following suggested definitions?

- S is a bachelor if and only if S is male.
- S is a bachelor if and only if S is an unmarried human adult male who is tall and lives in Ohio.

The first definition is said to be "too broad"; it admits too much. The second is "too narrow"; it admits too little.

Conversely, it is possible for a physicist to have detailed knowledge of the physical principles that describe successful bike riding and yet not know how to ride a bike. The physicist may lack the ability to perform the behaviors, but not because there is some proposition he or she fails to grasp. I conclude that propositional knowledge is neither necessary nor sufficient for knowing how to perform some task. The two concepts of knowledge are quite separate.

The subject of this and the following two chapters is *propositional knowledge*, not *object knowledge* or *know-how knowledge*. The goal is to understand what propositional knowledge is. We want to answer the following question: What are the necessary and sufficient conditions for it to be true that S knows that p, where p is some proposition—for example, the proposition that the Rockies are in North America?

Two Requirements for Knowledge: Belief and Truth

Two ideas that form part of the concept of knowledge should be noted at the outset. First, if S knows that p, then S must believe that p. Second, if S knows that p, then p must be true. Knowledge requires both *belief* and *truth*.

I won't try to argue for the first of these requirements, but will just assume it is correct. The second does require some explanation, however. People sometimes say they know things that, in fact, turn out to be false. However, this isn't a case of knowing things that are untrue, but of people *thinking* they know things that happen to be untrue.

Knowledge has an objective and a subjective side. You should remember this pair of concepts from Chapter 1. A fact is objective if its truth doesn't depend on the way anyone's mind is. It is an objective fact that the Rocky Mountains are more than ten thousand feet above sea level. A fact is subjective, on the other hand, if it isn't objective. The most obvious example of a subjective fact is a description of what's going on in someone's mind. Whether someone believes that the Rockies are more than ten thousand feet above sea level is a subjective matter, but whether the mountains really are that high is an objective matter. Knowledge requires both an objective and a subjective element. For S to know that p, p must be true and the subject, S, must believe that p is true.

I've just cited two necessary conditions for knowledge: Knowledge requires belief, and knowledge requires truth. Is that it? That is, are these two conditions not just separately necessary but also jointly sufficient? Is true belief enough for knowledge?

Plato: True Belief Isn't Sufficient for Knowledge

In the dialogue called *The Theaetetus*, the Greek philosopher Plato (ca. 430–345 B.C.), who was Aristotle's teacher, argues that the answer is *no*. Orators and lawyers sometimes trick people into believing things; sometimes those things happen to be true. According to Plato, people who have been duped in this way have true beliefs, but they don't have knowledge.

Of course, the fact that orators and lawyers intend to deceive isn't crucial for Plato's point. Think of an individual, Clyde, who believes the story about Groundhog Day. Clyde thinks that if the groundhog sees its shadow, then spring will come late. Clyde puts this silly principle to work this year. He receives the news about the behavior of the Official Designated Groundhog, and so he believes that spring will come late. Suppose Clyde turns out to be right about the late spring. If there is no real connection between the groundhog seeing its shadow and the coming of a late spring, then Clyde will have a true belief (that spring will come late), but he won't have knowledge.

So what else is needed, besides true belief, for someone to have knowledge? A natural suggestion is that knowledge requires justification. The problem with Clyde is that he didn't satisfy this further requirement (though perhaps he thought he did). Justification, notice, can't just mean that the subject *thinks* he has a reason; otherwise we'd have to conclude that Clyde knows how long winter will last just because he believes that he has a reason for thinking this.

Justification

What does it mean to say that an individual is "justified" in believing a proposition? Sometimes we start believing that a proposition is true because we consider an argument that describes the evidence available. Mendel believed that genes exist because of the data he collected from his pea plants. Sherlock Holmes believed that Moriarty was the murderer because of the evidence he found at the crime scene. Should we conclude that people are justified in believing a proposition only when their belief in the proposition was caused by their considering an argument? This isn't always plausible. When I believe that I have a headache, I don't construct an argument in which the evidence is laid out in a set of propositions that constitute the argument's premises. Still, it would seem that I am justified in believing that I have a headache. This suggests that there is such a thing as *noninferential justification*. Some of the propositions we believe are apprehended more or less "directly"; they are not inferred from other propositions that we believe.

What, then, does "justification" mean when it is used in accounts of what knowledge is? When we talk about someone's action being *morally* justified, we mean that the action does not violate any *moral* duties that the person has. Perhaps "justified belief" should be understood in a similar way. We should think of individuals as having certain duties concerning how their beliefs should be formed. A belief is justified if the process by which it was formed does not violate any duties that the person has. To make sense of this suggestion, we'd have to say what duties we have that govern how we are supposed to form our beliefs. Are we obliged to base our beliefs on the evidence that is available, and only on the evidence? This, I take it, is what I do when I believe that I have a headache. However, this suggestion requires further exploration; some of the issues were touched on in Chapter 10, on Pascal's Wager.

Even though the concept of "justification" requires further attention, it is plausible to think that this is one of the necessary ingredients that defines what knowledge is. Knowing that a proposition is true requires more than just having a true belief. The third requirement is that your belief be "justified."

The JTB Theory

Suppose knowledge requires these three conditions. Is that it? That is, are these conditions not just separately necessary, but jointly sufficient? I'll call the theory of knowledge that asserts this the *JTB Theory*. It says that knowledge is one and the same thing as justified true belief: (JTB) For any individual S and any proposition p, S knows that p if and only if

(1) S believes that p.
(2) p is true.
(3) S is justified in believing that p.

The JTB Theory states a generalization. It says what knowledge is for *any* person S and *any* proposition p. For example, let S be you and let p = "the moon is made of green cheese." The JTB Theory says this: If you know that the moon is made of green cheese, then statements (1)–(3) must be true as well. And if you don't know the moon is made of green cheese, then at least one of statements (1)–(3) must be false. As in the definition of bachelorhood discussed in the preceding box, the expression "if and only if" says that we are being given necessary and sufficient conditions for the defined concept.

Three Counterexamples to the JTB Theory

In 1963, the U.S. philosopher Edmund Gettier published a pair of counterexamples to the JTB Theory ("Is Justified True Belief Knowledge?" *Analysis*, 1963, Vol. 23, pp. 121–23). What is a *counterexample*? It is an example that goes counter to what some general theory says. A counterexample to a generalization shows that the generalization is false. The JTB Theory says that *all* cases of justified true belief are cases of knowledge. Gettier thought his two examples show that an individual can have justified true belief without having knowledge. If Gettier is right, then the three conditions given by the JTB Theory aren't sufficient, even if they are necessary.

Here is one of Gettier's examples: Smith works in an office. He knows that someone will soon be promoted. The boss, who is very reliable, tells Smith that Jones is going to get the promotion. Smith has just counted the coins in Jones' pocket, finding there to be ten coins there. Smith therefore has excellent evidence for the following proposition:

(a) Jones will get the promotion and Jones has ten coins in his pocket.

Smith then deduces from this statement the following:

(b) The man who will get the promotion has ten coins in his pocket.

Now suppose that, unknown to Smith, Jones will *not* get the promotion. Rather, it is Smith himself who will be promoted. And suppose Smith also happens to have ten coins in his pocket. Smith believes (b), and (b) is true. Gettier also claims that Smith is justified in believing (b), since Smith deduced (b) from (a). Although (a) is false, Smith had excellent reason to think that it is true. Gettier concludes that Smith has a justified true belief in (b), but Smith does not know that (b) is true.

Gettier's other example exhibits the same pattern. The subject validly deduces a true proposition from a proposition that is very well supported by evidence even though it is, unbeknownst to the subject, false. I now want to describe a kind of counterexample to the JTB Theory in which the subject reasons *non*deductively.

The British philosopher, logician, and social critic Bertrand Russell (1872–1970) described a very reliable clock that stands in a town square. This morning you walk by it and glance up to find out what the time is. As a result, you come to believe that the time is 9:55. You are justified in believing this, based on your correct assumption that the clock has been very reliable in the past. But suppose that, unbeknownst to you, the clock stopped exactly twenty-four hours ago. You now have a justified true belief that it is 9:55, but you don't know that this is the correct time.

Let me add a third example to Gettier's Smith/Jones story and to Russell's clock. You buy a ticket in a fair lottery. "Fair" means that one ticket will win and every ticket has the same chance of winning. There are one thousand tickets and you get ticket number 452. You look at this ticket, think for a moment, and then believe the following proposition: Ticket number 452 will not win. Suppose that when the drawing occurs a week later, you are right. Your belief was true. In addition, it was extremely well justified; after all, its probability was extremely close to unity—there was only one chance in a thousand that you would be mistaken. Yet, I think we want to say in this case that you didn't *know* that the ticket would fail to win. Here is a third case of justified true belief that isn't knowledge. Note that the reasoning here is nondeductive.

What the Counterexamples Have in Common

In all three of these cases, the subject has *highly reliable*, but not *infallible*, evidence for the proposition believed. The boss *usually* is right about who will be promoted; the clock *usually* is right as to what the time is; and it *usually* is true that a ticket drawn at random in a fair lottery doesn't win. But *usually* doesn't mean *always*. The sources of information that the subjects exploit in these three examples are *highly* reliable, but not *perfectly* reliable. All the sources of information are prone to error to at least some degree.

Do these examples really refute the JTB Theory? That depends on how we understand the idea of justification. If highly reliable evidence is enough to justify a belief, then the counterexamples do refute the JTB Theory. But if justification requires perfectly infallible evidence, then these examples don't undermine the JTB Theory.

My view is that evidence can justify belief without the evidence being infallible. I think we can have rational and well-supported beliefs even when we aren't entitled to be absolutely certain that what we believe is true. This is the point of strong inductive and abductive arguments (Chapter 3). From this, I conclude that justified true belief is not sufficient for knowledge. The counterexamples have refuted the JTB Theory.

An Argument for Skepticism

What more is required? The lottery example suggests the following idea. In this case, you *probably* won't be mistaken when you believe that ticket number 452 will lose, but high probability isn't enough. To know that the ticket will lose, it must be *impossible* for you to be mistaken. You don't have knowledge in this example, because there is a chance (small though it may be) that you will be wrong.

There is some plausibility to this suggestion about what knowledge requires. The problem is that this idea seems to lead immediately to skepticism—to the conclusion that we don't know anything. For it seems that virtually all the beliefs we have are based on evidence that isn't infallible. Consider, just briefly, the beliefs we have that depend on the testimony of our senses. We use vision, hearing, touch, and so forth, to gather evidence about the way the world is. Do the resulting beliefs count as knowledge? The problem is that the senses are sometimes misleading.

Right now, you believe you are looking at a printed page. You believe this because of the visual experiences you are having now. Do you *know* that there is a printed page in front of you? According to the present suggestion, for this to be true, it must be the case that you couldn't possibly be mistaken in believing what you do. But the fact of the matter seems to be that you *could* be mistaken. You might be hallucinating, or dreaming, or your senses might be malfunctioning in some other way.

So here's where we are. The JTB Theory is mistaken. JTB doesn't suffice for knowledge. As an alternative to the JTB Theory, we have this suggestion: knowledge requires the impossibility of error. This suggestion, plausible though it may be as a diagnosis of why you don't have knowledge in the lottery example, allows us to formulate the following argument for skepticism:

If *S* knows that *p*, then it isn't possible that *S* is mistaken in believing that *p*.
It is possible that *S* is mistaken in believing that *p*.

S doesn't know that *p*.

This form of argument can be used to argue that *a posteriori* knowledge does not exist. Recall from Chapter 8 that a proposition is *a posteriori* if it can be known only through the testimony of sense experience. The skeptic claims that beliefs based on sense experience aren't totally immune from the possibility of error. People make perceptual mistakes—for example, in cases of illusion, hallucination, and dreaming. Since we can't absolutely rule out the possibility of error, the skeptic concludes that our senses do not provide us with knowledge.

---

12 Is Skepticism Self-Refuting?

Skeptics claim that people don't know anything. Can skeptics claim to know that what they say is true? If not, does that show that their philosophical thesis is false?

It is a contradiction to say that you know that no one (including yourself) knows anything. But a skeptic can *assert* that people lack knowledge without claiming to *know* that this is so. In addition, a skeptic can claim to provide a *good argument* for skepticism. This isn't contradictory.

The thesis that no one knows anything, if true, can't be known to be true. But that doesn't show that the position is false. If you think that all truths are knowable, you will say that this skeptical thesis can't be true. But why think that all truths are knowable? Why not think, instead, that the universe may contain truths that we are incapable of knowing?

Another way for skeptics to avoid contradicting themselves is to be modest. Instead of claiming that no one knows *anything*, they could limit themselves to the claim that no one ever knows anything *through the testimony of the senses*. If this more limited kind of skepticism could be supported by an *a priori* argument, the position would not be self-refuting.

This argument for skepticism is deductively valid. (Identify its logical form.) The first premise seems to describe a plausible requirement for knowing the proposition in question. The second premise also seems plausible; it just says that the beliefs we have aren't absolutely immune from the possibility of error. If you want to reject skepticism, you must refute one or both of these premises.

Although the above argument has fairly plausible premises, its conclusion is pretty outrageous. I think I know lots of things and I believe this is true of you as well. It is hard to accept the idea that I don't know that I have a hand. If you think that you now know there is a printed page in front of you, you too should balk at this argument for skepticism. The skeptical argument contradicts a fundamental part of our common-sense picture of the way we are related to the world around us. Common sense says that people sometimes have knowledge of the world they inhabit; the skeptical argument says that common sense is mistaken in this respect. If there is a mistake in the argument, where is it?

Review Questions

1   Explain how object knowledge, know-how knowledge, and propositional knowledge differ.

2   What do the following pieces of terminology mean? (i) *X* is a necessary condition for *Y*; (ii) *X* is a sufficient condition for *Y*; (iii) *X* is true if and only if *Y* is true; (iv) *O* is a counterexample to the statement "All emeralds are green."

3   Why think that true belief isn't sufficient for knowledge? What is the JTB Theory? What is the difference between highly reliable evidence and absolutely infallible evidence?

4 Describe the three counterexamples to the JTB Theory (Gettier's, Russell's, and the lottery example). Do these counterexamples show that JTB isn't necessary or that it isn't sufficient for knowledge?

5 What is skepticism? What is the argument for skepticism given at the end of this chapter? Is the argument deductively valid?

Problems for Further Thought

1 People sometimes say, concerning a proposition that is difficult to take to heart, "I know it is true, but I don't believe it." Does this refute the claim that if *S* knows that *p*, then *S* believes that *p*?

2 I suggested that we lack knowledge in the lottery example because knowledge requires the impossibility of error. Can you think of a different explanation for why we lack knowledge in this or in the other two examples that were used against the JTB Theory?

Recommended Readings, Video, and Audio

Visit the companion website at www.routledge.com/cw/sober for suggestions of readings, video, and audio, for this chapter.

Descartes' Foundationalism

René Descartes (1596–1650) is sometimes described as the father of modern philosophy. The kind of epistemology he tried to develop is called *foundationalism*. Before launching into the details of Descartes' philosophy, I want to describe the kind of approach to the problem of knowledge that foundationalism provides.

Foundationalism

The word *foundationalism* should make you think of a building. What keeps a building from falling over? The answer has two parts. First, there is a solid foundation. Second, the rest of the building, which I'll call the superstructure, is attached securely to that solid foundation. Descartes wanted to show that (many if not all of) the beliefs we have about the world are cases of genuine knowledge. To show this, he wanted to divide our beliefs into two categories. There are the foundational beliefs, which are perfectly solid. Then, there are the superstructural beliefs, which count as knowledge because they rest securely on that solid foundation.

Besides this metaphor from architecture, there is another that should help you understand what Descartes' project is. You probably had a geometry course in high school where you studied Euclid's development of the subject. Recall that Euclid, who lived about 2,200 years ago, divided the propositions of geometry into two categories. First, there are the axioms of geometry. These are supposed to be simple and totally obvious truths. Second, there are the theorems, which at first glance are somewhat less obvious. Euclid shows that the theorems are true by showing how they can be deduced from the axioms.

A foundationalist theory of knowledge could also be called a Euclidean theory of knowledge. To show that a given body of beliefs counts as knowledge, we use the following strategy: First, we identify the beliefs that will provide the foundations of knowledge (the axioms). These must be shown to have some special property, such as being totally beyond doubt. In a moment, I'll clarify what Descartes had in mind by this "special property." Second, we show that the rest of our beliefs count as knowledge because they bear some special relationship to the foundational items. In Euclid's geometry, the special relationship was deductive implication.

Euclid, of course, was interested only in the beliefs we have about geometry. Descartes had a wider ambition. He was interested in the totality of what we believe. But whether the problem is to describe the foundations of geometry or the foundations of knowledge as a whole, there are two ideas that must be clarified. We need to identify what the foundational items are and we need to describe the relationship that must obtain between foundational and superstructural items that qualifies the latter as knowledge. In doing so, we need to remember that the building metaphor is only a metaphor. What makes the foundation of a house solid is that the walls are thick and hard and are set deeply into solid ground. But foundational beliefs aren't foundational because they are thick and hard and planted deeply in dirt. What, then, does it mean, for a belief to be "foundational"?

Euclid's Parallel Postulate

If your high school geometry course was like mine, you spent most of your time seeing what theorems could be proved from the axioms. You spent little or no time seeing why the axioms should be regarded as true. You were told that they are "obvious," or that they should just be accepted on faith. Maybe your teacher said that geometry is just a game and the axioms are the rules. In fact, the question about the axioms is a serious one. One of Euclid's starting assumptions—his so-called fifth postulate—bothered geometers for about two thousand years. This postulate says that if you have a straight line (call it S) and a point not on that line, then there is exactly one straight line that goes through that point and is parallel to S. In other words, the parallel postulate says that if you extend all the lines passing through this point to infinity, exactly one of them will fail to intersect the initial line.

A number of subsequent geometers felt that this assumption of Euclid's was less obvious than the other assumptions he used. As a result, they tried to show that it could be proved from the other axioms. Geometers repeatedly failed to do this, and eventually it was established that the parallel postulate cannot be proved from Euclid's other assumptions. That is, they showed that the parallel postulate is *independent* of the other assumptions. This means that the denial of the parallel postulate is logically consistent with Euclid's other assumptions. It then transpired that non-Euclidean geometries could be developed, ones that retain Euclid's other assumptions but reject his parallel postulate.

The details of this story don't matter here. The history of geometry does show, however, that it sometimes isn't so clear whether a given statement is "obviously true." Perhaps Euclid thought that the parallel postulate was obvious. If so, that would have been his justification for treating it as something that doesn't need to be proved; it would stand on its own as an axiom/postulate. This doesn't mean, however, that subsequent geometers had to regard Euclid's judgment as beyond question. What strikes one person as obvious may not be so obvious to someone else.

Descartes' Method of Doubt

Now let's consider Descartes' approach to the problem of knowledge. Descartes' goal is to refute skepticism. He wants to show that we really do have knowledge of the world we inhabit. His strategy for achieving this goal is foundationalist in character. This means the first item on his agenda is to identify the beliefs that are foundational.

At the beginning of his *Meditations on First Philosophy* (1641), Descartes proposes a method for determining which of his beliefs are foundational. He called this the *method of doubt*. For each proposition you believe, you see whether it is possible to doubt that proposition. If it is possible to do this, you set the belief aside—it isn't foundational. If it isn't possible to do so (that is, if the belief is *indubitable*), then the belief is foundational. Notice that failing the method of doubt test doesn't show that the belief is *false*. It just means the belief isn't *absolutely certain*.

Descartes doesn't try to apply this method to beliefs one at a time. Think of all the beliefs you have—there are millions (at least). You believe that 1 is a number. You believe that 2 is a number. And so on. It would be time consuming and also boring to try to consider each belief separately. Rather, Descartes considers *kinds* of beliefs; he considers whether all the beliefs in this or that category pass or fail the method of doubt test.

---

13 Indubitability

Very few propositions are made true just by your believing them. You can believe that there are unicorns, but that doesn't make such creatures pop into existence.

Consider the proposition "I am thinking." If you believe that this is true, then it must be true. Believing is a kind of thinking. Descartes thinks that the same is true for propositions of the form "I seem to see that *p*." He also thinks that this is true for propositions that say that you believe that *p* or want it to be true that *q* (where *p* and *q* are propositions). If you believe them, they must be true.

If a proposition is made true by your believing it, then you can't describe a situation in which you believe the proposition but the proposition is false. Descartes determines whether a proposition is dubitable by seeing whether he can describe a situation of this kind. This means that a proposition is indubitable if the proposition is made true by the act of believing it (or doubting it).

Are there indubitable propositions that aren't made true by your believing them? Some philosophers have held that simple logical truths, such as "It is raining or it is not raining," are beyond doubt. Is it plausible to maintain that these are made true by your believing them?

The Method Applied to *a Posteriori* Beliefs

The first category Descartes considers is the set of beliefs that depend for their justification on sense experience. Many of our beliefs are based on sight, hearing, touch, taste, and smell. These propositions are *a posteriori*; recall this piece of vocabulary from Chapter 8. Is it possible to doubt these beliefs? Descartes says that the answer is *yes*. Your present belief that there is a printed page in front of you is based on vision. Vision, however, can be misleading. Psychologists tell us about hallucinations and illusions. Maybe you've had such experiences yourself. If not, remember Macbeth, who was certain that a dagger was hovering in front of him. Besides hallucinations, there is the fact of dreaming. In a dream you may find yourself believing that there is a printed page in front of you. You may find yourself having visual experiences just like the ones you are having now. But in the dream, your belief is mistaken. Descartes takes this to show that the belief you have right now might be mistaken.

So beliefs that rest on the testimony of the senses fail the method of doubt test. Let's be clear on why Descartes thinks they do so. Descartes shows such beliefs are dubitable by constructing a story of a particular kind. You now believe that there is a printed page in front of you on the basis of a set of visual experiences. Let's call the proposition you believe *B* and the experiences you now are having *E*. Your belief that *B* is true rests on your having experiences *E*. Descartes holds that *B* can be doubted because he can describe a situation in which you have *E* and believe *B* and yet *B* is false. Dreams and hallucinations show how this can happen. Descartes shows that a class of beliefs is dubitable by constructing a story of this sort.

Dubitability Is a Logical, Not a Psychological, Property

In saying that a belief is dubitable, Descartes isn't saying that we are able to take seriously the idea that it might be false. The proposition that there is a page in front of you is dubitable in Descartes' sense; this doesn't mean that you are now about to take seriously the possibility that no page is present. A proposition is dubitable when a certain sort of story can be constructed; dubitability is thus a logical property that a proposition has. It has nothing to do with whether we can get ourselves to believe that the proposition might be false.

The Method Applied to Beliefs Based on Rational Calculation

Descartes next turns his attention to propositions of mathematics. I believe that 2 + 3 = 5. I believe that squares have four sides. Descartes remarks that these are true "whether I'm awake or asleep." These propositions are *a priori* (recall this piece of vocabulary from Chapter 8). They don't depend for their justification on sensory experience. Do propositions justified by reason, independent of sense experience, pass the method of doubt test? Descartes thinks they fail. To demonstrate that such beliefs are dubitable, Descartes asks us to imagine that our minds are deceived by an "evil demon." Imagine that an evil demon causes our faculty of reasoning to find propositions totally obvious that in fact are false. If this were so, we might believe that 2 + 3 = 5 even though the proposition isn't true.

These conclusions—all reached in the first of the *Meditations*—are entirely negative. *A posteriori* beliefs about the character of the world outside the mind are dubitable. We see this by considering dreams and hallucinations. *A priori* propositions also are dubitable. We see this by considering the evil demon. If no belief in these two categories passes the method of doubt test, which beliefs could be the foundations of knowledge? What category of belief could possibly satisfy this very stringent requirement?

I Am Thinking, Therefore I Exist

In an earlier work, the *Discourse on the Method* (1637), Descartes identifies a pair of propositions that pass the test:

> I noticed that while I was trying to think everything false, it must be that I, who was thinking this, was something. And observing that this truth, *I am thinking, therefore I exist* [*Je pense, donc je suis* in French; *Cogito ergo sum* in Latin], was so solid and secure that the

most extravagant suppositions of the skeptics could not overthrow it, I judged that I need not scruple to accept it as the first principle of the philosophy I was seeking.

In the *Second Meditation*, Descartes focuses on the belief "I am, I exist" as the first proposition that he thinks is beyond doubt.

To understand what Descartes is driving at, you must think about yourself, formulating your thoughts in the first person. When Descartes considers the proposition "I am thinking," you aren't supposed to consider the proposition "Descartes is thinking." Rather, you should say to yourself precisely what Descartes says to himself.

Consider my belief that I am thinking. I can't doubt this. It is impossible for me to construct a story in which I believe this proposition, though it is false. For if I *believe* the proposition, then I am thinking, and so the proposition is true. So the attempt to doubt the proposition fails; the attempt to doubt the proposition proves that the proposition must be true. The proposition "I am thinking" passes the method of doubt test.

There are two important characteristics of the proposition "I am thinking" that you should note. First, it is important that the proposition is in the first person. When Descartes considers "I am thinking," he concludes that this proposition passes the method of doubt test. However, if he had considered "Descartes is thinking," the result would have been different. It *is* possible for Descartes to doubt that there is someone named "Descartes." He can invent a story in which there is no such person as Descartes; the fact that such a story can be constructed shows that the proposition is dubitable. The second feature of the proposition "I am thinking" is that it involves a psychological property. I can't doubt that I am thinking, but I can doubt that I am now in North America. Both beliefs are first-person, but only the former is psychological.

As noted, Descartes maintains that the proposition "I exist" also passes the method of doubt test. Take a few minutes to formulate an argument, similar to the one just described for "I am thinking," that shows that this is so.

So far, we have two propositions that Descartes thinks can serve as foundations for the rest of what we know. I can't doubt that I am thinking and I can't doubt that I exist. This is a meager foundation. Just as it would be hard to erect a big building on a foundation made of two bricks, so it would be difficult to ground the whole of what we know about the world on this paltry foundation of two beliefs.

There is more, however. Consider propositions solely about the contents of your own present sensory experiences. Such propositions describe the way things *seem* to be, not the way they in fact *are*. You now seem to see a page in front of you. Descartes thinks that all such first-person descriptions of the way things seem are indubitable. To understand Descartes' point, it is essential to recognize the difference between the following two propositions:

- There is a page in front of me.
- I seem to see a page in front of me.

It is pretty clear, as noted earlier, that the first of these can be doubted. That's the point about dreams and illusions. Descartes maintains that the second proposition is different. He holds that it has the property that if you believe that the proposition is true, then you can't be mistaken. If you *believe* that you seem to see a page in front of you, then you *do* seem to see a page in front of you. You can't be mistaken in your beliefs about the way things seem.

So the foundation of knowledge has just been augmented. "I am thinking" and "I exist" are indubitable, and so are the many first-person beliefs about the way things seem.

Thesis of the Incorrigibility of the Mental

Descartes went even further. He thought that people have infallible access to what they believe and desire. Introspection ("looking inward") is a method that the mind can use to accurately grasp its own contents. This is sometimes expressed by saying that Descartes believed in *the thesis of the incorrigibility of the mental*. Although "There is a page in front of me" isn't indubitable, Descartes thought "I believe that there is a page in front of me" is indubitable. If you believe that you have that belief, then it must be true that you do have that belief. Ditto for desires. If you believe that you want some ice cream, then it must be true that you want some ice cream.

A great deal of work in psychology in the last hundred years shows that this incorrigibility thesis isn't plausible. Sigmund Freud, whose views on religion came up in Chapter 10, argued that we often misunderstand what we really believe and what we really want. At times, our beliefs and desires would be very upsetting to us if we were conscious of them. So, as a defense mechanism, our minds repress them. The result is that we often have mistaken beliefs about what we really think and want. An example of this is Freud's theory of the Oedipus complex. Freud held that little boys want to kill their fathers and marry their mothers. If you asked a little boy whether he wanted to do this, however, he probably would sincerely answer *no*. You might well ask: What evidence can there be for this theory? If little boys deny having these desires, why think they have them? Freud's answer is that his theory is a plausible explanation of what little boys *do*. It is their behavior that we must consider, not just what they say they believe and desire. Verbal reports about what we think and want are evidence as to what our beliefs and desires really are. Sincere reports, however, don't settle the matter, since behavior may provide *other* evidence that is relevant.

Although this idea—that we often have a false picture of our own beliefs and desires—is very important in Freud's theories, it isn't unique to them. A great deal of other work in psychology also denies Descartes' thesis of incorrigibility. See, for example, the 1977 article by R. Nisbett and T. Wilson called "Telling More Than We Can Know" (*Psychological Review* 84: 231–59). Descartes wants to include *all* first-person reports of his own beliefs and desires as foundations. Each, he thought, passes the method of doubt test. Freud and many other psychologists would disagree. I'm on their side.

Where does this leave Descartes' project of identifying the foundations of knowledge? The foundations include *I am thinking* and *I exist* and all first-person reports about the way the world seems to be. Another example of an indubitable belief might be "I am in pain." Descartes' view was that if you believe that you are in pain, then you are in pain.

In Chapter 2, I pointed out that for a very large class of our beliefs, there is a huge difference between believing a proposition and that proposition's actually being true. To believe that the Rockies are over ten thousand feet is one thing; for the mountains to actually be that high is another. It is misguided wishful thinking to hold that believing the proposition guarantees that it is true. This sensible separation of belief and truth, which seems right for a wide class of propositions, is called into question by the special examples that Descartes thought pass the method of doubt test. According to Descartes, "I am in pain" must be true if I think it is. The same holds for "I am thinking" and "I seem to see a page in front of me." These are cases in which wishful thinking seems to work.

Do First-Person Psychological Beliefs Provide a Sufficient Foundation?

These propositions, Descartes thought, are foundational. We can't be mistaken in believing them. Some philosophers have disagreed with Descartes' claim. They have maintained that it is possible to be mistaken in holding some of these beliefs. I'm not going to address that matter here. Instead, I want to consider another problem. Recall the architectural metaphor discussed at the beginning of this chapter. An adequate foundation for a building must have two properties. It must be (1) secure and (2) sufficient to support the superstructure. The foundations of knowledge are subject to the same requirements. According to Descartes, they must be indubitable. In addition, it must be possible to rest everything else we know on them. Don't forget that the method of doubt is intended to identify the foundations; the entire superstructure is supposed to rest on that basis.

Descartes, as I mentioned before, wasn't a skeptic. He thought that we know lots of things about the world outside our own minds. For example, you know that there is a page in front of you now. This belief about the external world isn't indubitable; it didn't pass the method of doubt test. Nevertheless, it is (Descartes would agree) something you know. How can Descartes show that this is true? Recall the Euclidean analogy. We've just identified some axioms of the system of knowledge. Do these suffice to prove some theorems? We must show how you know there is a page in front of you by showing how this proposition is connected with foundational ones. In Euclidean geometry, we justify theorems by deducing them from axioms. How can a superstructural belief be shown to be knowledge? We must show that it is connected with foundational pieces of knowledge in the right way. But what is this special connection supposed to be?

Can deduction do the trick? Euclid deduced theorems from axioms. Can Descartes deduce propositions about the world outside the mind from beliefs that are first-person psychological reports? To show that you know that there is a page in front of you, maybe we should try to deduce that proposition in the following way:

I seem to see a page in front of me.

There is a page in front of me.

The premise of this argument is foundational. The problem is that it does not deductively imply the conclusion. The existence of a page in front of me does not deductively follow from the way things seem to me now. That's the point noted before about dreams and hallucinations. The above argument is not deductively valid.

The premise given isn't enough. Even if I augmented it with other reports about my present psychological state (for example, "I seem to feel a page," "I seem to taste a page," etc.), that still would not be enough. Such premises might be ones about which I'm perfectly certain, but they don't provide a sufficient foundation for the beliefs I have about the world outside my mind. Such arguments are not deductively valid.

An Additional Foundational Belief: God Exists and Is No Deceiver

Descartes saw quite clearly that the argument just described needs an additional premise, one that will bridge the gap between first-person psychological premises and a conclusion that describes the world outside the mind. Descartes thought the proposition that *God exists and is no deceiver* provides the additional premise that he needs.

How would this additional premise solve Descartes' problem? Descartes had the following picture in mind: God created your mind and situated you in the world. What sort of mind did God give you? Obviously, he didn't give you a mind that reaches true conclusions about the world on each and every occasion. Your mind isn't infallible. On the other hand,

God would not have furnished you with a mind that leads you to false beliefs about the world no matter how carefully you reason and no matter how much evidence you consult. If God had done this, he would have been a deceiver. Descartes thinks that God created us with minds that have the capacity to attain true beliefs about the world. We are neither infallible nor hopelessly trapped by falsehood. Rather, we are somewhere in between: We can reach true beliefs if we are careful about how we use the minds that God bestowed upon us. This is the kind of mind that an all-PKG god would have given us. But why think that such a being exists?

How to Prove that God Exists

I've just explained what role the proposition that God exists and is no deceiver is supposed to play in Descartes' theory of knowledge. However, if this proposition is to be a part of the foundations, it must be indubitable. It must pass the method of doubt test. Descartes has to show that the proposition that God exists and is no deceiver is not just true, but that it is indubitable. Here Descartes seems to be trying to do the impossible. Isn't it obvious that it is possible to doubt that God exists and is no deceiver? After all, atheists or agnostics don't believe that God exists. Isn't this enough to show that it is *possible* to doubt that God exists and is no deceiver?

Descartes thinks that atheists and agnostics have not considered the matter carefully enough. They *think* they can doubt the proposition, but they have not really grasped what this would really involve. (Recall Anselm's comment about the "fool" who "said in his heart what cannot be conceived.") Descartes believes that he has a proof of the existence of God whose premises are *indubitable*. In addition, the proof is so simple that once you attend carefully to it, you can't doubt that there is a god. This is the proof that Descartes lays out in the *Third Meditation*. Here it is, in outline:

(1) My idea of God is an idea of a perfect being.
(2) There must be at least as much perfection in the cause as there is in the effect.
_____

Hence, the cause of my idea is a perfect being—namely, God himself.

Once you inspect this proof, the proposition that God exists is like the proposition *I am thinking*—it is impossible to doubt that it is true.

Descartes thinks he knows premise (1) of this argument by introspection. By looking inward at the contents of his own mind, he can discern this fact about himself. Premise (1), Descartes believes, is indubitable. As to premise (2), Descartes thinks that it is an indubitable principle about causality. It can be broken into two components. First, there is the idea that every event has a cause. Second, there is the idea that the cause must be at least as perfect as the effect. It isn't clear why we should accept these principles about causality. For example, why couldn't some events occur for no reason at all? This is a question we explored in Chapters 4 and 7. Descartes needs to show not only that it is *true* that every event has a cause, but that this proposition is *indubitably* true. This is something that he does not succeed in doing.

Premise (2) needs to be clarified. Descartes distinguishes two kinds of perfection (or "reality") that an idea or representation might possess. To find out how *objectively* perfect a representation is, you must find out how perfect the thing is that the representation represents. Two photographs of a saint must have the same degree of objective perfection; two photographs of a trash can will have the same degree of objective perfection as well. If saints are more perfect than trash cans, the first pair will have more objective perfection than the second.

This characterization of objective perfection requires a little fine-tuning. A picture of a unicorn has a certain degree of objective perfection, even though there are no unicorns. So, to determine how objectively perfect the picture is, you must ask yourself this question: If the picture represented something that actually existed, how perfect would that thing be?

I hope you can see from the definition of objective perfection why Descartes thinks that his concept of God has the maximum amount of objective perfection. This is something that Descartes can say just by examining his concept of God. Indeed, it is something that an atheist might agree to as well. If there were a God, then that being would have all the perfections; this means that the atheist's concept of God is objectively perfect.

The concept of objective perfection allows some representations to be ranked higher than others. My idea of God is at the top. Somewhere below that is my idea of a saint. And still further down the list is my idea of a trash can. The second kind of perfection that Descartes discusses is different. This is what Descartes calls an idea's *formal perfection*. All mental contents have the same degree of formal perfection because they are all made of the same stuff. To see what Descartes has in mind here, consider paintings. These may differ in their degree of objective perfection, but all are made of canvas and paint. In this sense, they have the same degree of formal perfection. Descartes thinks the same holds for all the ideas I may have.

In the argument for the existence of God that I just sketched, Descartes is talking about the *objective* perfection of his idea of God. Let's reformulate the argument to make this explicit:

(1) My idea of God is objectively perfect.
(2) If an idea is objectively perfect, then the cause of that idea must be a perfect being.

———————————

Hence, God exists.

Premise (2) strikes me as implausible. Here is a way to see that it is false. I claim that people could form their concept of God (a perfect being) in the following way. They could look at *imperfect* things in the world and thereby form the idea of *limited* intelligence, *limited* goodness, and *limited* power. Then, by applying the concept of negation (the concept we express by the word "not") to these ideas, they would obtain the idea of a being who has *unlimited* intelligence, goodness, and power. This seems to be an entirely possible causal explanation for why we have the idea of a perfect being. If it is possible, then (2) is false.

In the *Third Meditation*, Descartes explicitly considers this suggestion. He rejects the idea that we might have acquired the concept of perfection by seeing imperfect things and then applying the concept of negation. You should consider Descartes' argument and decide whether you think it works. Descartes thinks that the only possible explanation for the fact that we have an idea of a perfect being is that a perfect being actually exists and caused us to have this idea. Leaving this exercise to you, I'll conclude that Descartes' causal argument for the existence of God is defective. Descartes wanted to show that "God exists" isn't just true, but indubitably true. This proposition was to be a foundational element in the structure of our knowledge. The argument he gave falls short of this ambitious goal.

The Clarity and Distinctness Criterion

If God is no deceiver, how can we tell whether the beliefs we have are true? Descartes thought that if we inspect them carefully, and make sure that they are clear and distinct, we can be certain that they are correct. Descartes maintained that *clear and distinct* beliefs must be true. If you reason carefully and use your mental faculties in the way that God intended them to be used, you will obtain knowledge of the world you inhabit. Descartes thinks you have an indubitable grasp of the contents of your own mind; he also thinks that you can know indubitably that God exists and is no deceiver. This foundation, he believes, provides a sufficient and secure basis for you to gain knowledge of the world you inhabit.

The Cartesian Circle

Philosophers argue over whether Descartes' argument for the existence of God has a defect that goes beyond the fact that some of his premises are dubious. They have suggested that the argument is circular, given its place in Descartes' larger philosophical program. Recall that Descartes wants to prove that God exists and is no deceiver in order to be able to conclude that clear and distinct ideas must be true.

Descartes' argument for the existence of God, like all arguments, involves the use of reason. For us to recognize that the argument establishes the existence of God, we must use the faculty of reasoning we possess. Descartes' argument begins by examining his concept of God and determining that this is the idea of a perfect being. Descartes therefore seems to be using the clarity and distinctness criterion in arguing that God exists. Descartes vehemently denied that he was guilty of circular reasoning. This problem has come to be known as the Problem of the Cartesian Circle.

Here's how I see this issue: Descartes is using the method of doubt test to assemble foundations for knowledge. His goal is to assemble enough premises by this procedure so that he can show that we have knowledge of the world outside our minds. The existence of a God who is no deceiver is supposed to be one of these indubitable premises. Descartes thought his causal argument for the existence of God is beyond doubt; he thought that if you reason your way through the argument, you must find it irresistible.

Why should we agree that the proposition that every event has a cause is beyond doubt? Descartes' view seems to be that when we consider the proposition carefully, using the full resources of clarification and logic that we possess, we will be driven to conclude that the proposition must be true. This seems to mean that we are applying the clarity and distinctness criterion. If so, Descartes is reasoning in a circle.

Conclusion

Where does this leave the project of refuting skepticism? Descartes thought that first-person psychological beliefs are indubitable. He recognized that this, by itself, isn't enough to show that we have genuine knowledge of the world outside the mind. Additional premises are needed. The following example argument shows how Descartes wanted to bridge the gap between the indubitable knowledge we have of our own minds and the beliefs we have about the world outside our minds:

(1) I now believe that the object in front of me is a page.
(2) My present belief is clear and distinct.
(3) Clear and distinct ideas are true.
_____

There is a page in front of me.

The argument is valid. If the premises are true, the conclusion also must be true. Descartes' foundationalism can be understood as a pair of claims about this argument. First, he claims that the premises of this argument are *indubitable*. Second, he thinks that the conclusion of the argument is a proposition we *know* because it follows from these indubitable premises. I've already discussed premise (1). What of the next two premises? There is a tension between these two claims.

Suppose we grant Descartes that premise (3) is right—that a clear and distinct idea can't fail to be true. If we grant this, then it isn't so obvious that my present belief about what is in front of me really is clear and distinct. I may *think* that it is, but this appearance may be deceiving. So if (3) is right, (2) can't be beyond doubt. Alternatively, suppose we are able to tell, by introspection, whether a belief is clear and distinct. That will be enough to underwrite the truth of (2). In that case, there is no longer any absolute assurance that (3) is right. The problem here concerns whether we should see "clarity and distinctness" as a purely subjective characteristic of a belief. If I can tell just by examining the contents of my own beliefs whether they are "clear and distinct," I see no reason to say that a clear and distinct belief must be true. On the other hand, if we treat "clarity and distinctness" as a characteristic that is necessarily connected with truth, I don't see how I can tell whether a belief is "clear and distinct" just by introspection.

Descartes tried to refute the following skeptical argument, which I described at the end of the previous chapter:

> Knowledge requires the impossibility of error.
> It is now possible that I am mistaken in believing that there is a page in front of me.
> _____
> Hence, I don't know that there is a page in front of me.

Descartes accepted the first premise but denied the second. Descartes concedes that we often make mistakes. The senses sometimes play tricks on us, and so does our faculty of reasoning. But the fact that this *sometimes* happens doesn't show that it is happening *now*. If I am reasoning now in a careful and logically rigorous way, then I can't now be mistaken in what I believe, or so Descartes maintained. So Descartes' reply to the skeptic's argument can be put like this:

If God exists and is no deceiver and I now have a clear and distinct belief that there is a page in front of me, then I can't be mistaken in thinking that there is a page in front of me.

> God exists and is no deceiver and I now have a clear and distinct belief that there is a page in front of me.
> _____
> I can't be mistaken in thinking that there is a page in front of me.

The problem is that Descartes' argument for the second premise of this last argument wasn't successful. He wasn't able to prove that we are embedded in the world in the special way described by the hypothesis that God exists and is no deceiver. Consequently, he wasn't able to refute the skeptic's argument.

Review Questions

1   What is foundationalism in epistemology? What does it have to do with Euclidean geometry? With building a house?
2   What is the method of doubt test? What does Descartes use this method to do? What fails the test? What passes?

3   What does it mean to say that there is a "gap" between our first-person psychological beliefs and the beliefs we have about the world outside the mind?

4   Descartes thought that proving that God exists would help show why we are able to have knowledge of the world around us. Why did he think this? Is the proposition that "God exists and is no deceiver" foundational, according to Descartes?

5   Analyze Descartes' causal argument for the existence of God. Suppose that one of Aquinas's arguments for the existence of God is valid and has true premises. Could Descartes have used it, instead of his causal argument, to prove that God exists?

6   What is the Problem of the Cartesian Circle?

7   In the previous chapter, an argument for skepticism was presented. How would Descartes evaluate this argument?

8   What is the "clarity and distinctness criterion"? Why do you think Descartes found it plausible? Do you find it plausible?

9   Can Descartes' foundationalist project succeed without appeal to the additional premise that "God exists and is no deceiver"? Why or why not?

Problems for Further Thought

1   Which of the following propositions pass the method of doubt test? How are they different from each other?

- •   I saw Joe run.
- •   I seem to remember seeing Joe run.
- •   I remember seeming to see Joe run.

2   Can someone mistakenly believe that he or she seems to see a coffee cup? Can someone mistakenly believe that he or she is in pain?

3   I suggested that our idea of a perfect being might be obtained by observing imperfect things and then using the concept of negation. Descartes considers this suggestion in the *Third Meditation* and rejects it (consult the paragraph that begins "Nor should I imagine that I do not perceive … "). What reason does Descartes give for rejecting this explanation? Are his reasons plausible?

4   In his book *The Principles of Philosophy* (1644), Descartes defines clarity and distinctness as follows:

> I term that "clear" which is present and apparent to an attentive mind, in the same way that we see objects clearly when, being present to the regarding eye, they operate upon it with sufficient strength. But the "distinct" is that which is so precise and different from all other objects that it contains within itself nothing but what is not clear…. Perceptions may be clear without being distinct, but cannot be distinct without also being clear.

Given this definition, can a clear and distinct idea be false?

Recommended Readings, Video, and Audio

Visit the companion website at www.routledge.com/cw/sober for suggestions of readings, video, and audio, for this chapter.

Chapter 14

The Reliability Theory of Knowledge

Descartes: Knowledge Is Internally Certifiable

According to Descartes, *knowledge is internally certifiable*. What does this mean? It means that if I know some proposition *p*, then there exists an argument that shows that *p* must be true, *whose premises are either* a priori *true or knowable by introspection*. Recall how Descartes would explain why I now know that there is a page in front of me:

> I believe that there is a page in front of me.
> My belief that there is a page in front of me is clear and distinct.
> Clear and distinct ideas are true.
> _____
> There is a page in front of me.

The first two premises I know by *introspection*—by gazing within my own mind and examining its contents. How do I know that the third premise is true? I know by introspection that I have an idea of a perfect God; I (supposedly) know a priori that an idea of a perfect being must be caused by a perfect being. Putting these two thoughts together, I deduce that God—a perfect being—must exist. The third premise is supposed to follow from this.

Notice that the word "knowledge" does not appear in the displayed argument. So what does this argument have to do with the issue of whether I *know* that there is a page in front of me? For Descartes, I know that the concluding proposition is true because I know the premises are true. And how do I know the premises? I know these by introspection and *a priori* reasoning.

I want to name the elements in this argument. There is a *subjective premise*, an *objective conclusion*, and a *linking premise*. The subjective premise describes what is going on in the subject's mind ("I believe that there is a page in front of me"). The objective conclusion makes a claim about the world outside the subject's mind ("There is a page in front of me"). The linking premise (or premises) shows how the subjective premise necessitates the objective conclusion ("If I have a particular belief and it is clear and distinct, then it is true").

This vocabulary can be used to say what is characteristic of Descartes' approach to the problem of knowledge. His idea—that knowledge is internally certifiable—comes to this: *If the subject knows that the objective conclusion is true, then the subject must know that the linking premise is true and must know this independently of sense experience.* By introspection and *a priori* reasoning, I can establish the required connection between what is inside the mind and what is outside it.

The theory of knowledge I'll discuss in this chapter is very different from Descartes'. It agrees with Descartes that knowledge requires the existence of a connection between what is going on inside the mind and what is going on outside it. Knowledge requires that a particular linking premise be true. But according to the *Reliability Theory of Knowledge*, the linking premise doesn't have to be knowable by introspection and *a priori* reasoning. In fact, this theory maintains that the subject doesn't have to know that the linking premise is true at all. It just has to *be* true. This approach to the problem of knowledge was first proposed by Alvin Goldman (in "A Causal theory of Knowing," *Journal of Philosophy*, Vol. 64, 1967), Fred Dretske (in "Conclusive Reasons," *Australasian Journal of Philosophy*, Vol. 49, 1971), and David Armstrong (in *Belief, Truth, and Knowledge*, Cambridge University Press, 1973).

What Makes a Thermometer Reliable?

The Reliability Theory of Knowledge claims that there is an important analogy between knowledge and a reliable measuring device. If you know that there is a page in front of you now, then your belief is related to the world outside your mind in the same way that the reading of a reliable thermometer is related to the temperature.

Thermometers are devices that form representations of temperature. The height of the mercury column is the representation; the ambient temperature is the thing represented. Thermometer readings represent temperature, just as your beliefs represent the world outside your mind. Thermometer readings can be accurate or inaccurate, just as beliefs can be true or false. What makes a thermometer reliable? Does this just mean that its readings are accurate? To see why this isn't enough, consider a thermometer that is used just once. Suppose, on that one occasion, the thermometer said "98°F" and the temperature happened to be 98°F. The reading was accurate, but that doesn't mean that the thermometer was reliable. For all I've said, the thermometer may be broken—perhaps it would say "98°F" no matter what the true temperature is. If so, it isn't reliable, even though its one and only reading was accurate. A reliable thermometer is one for which there is a connection between readings and temperatures. If the thermometer reads n degrees Fahrenheit, then the temperature must be n degrees Fahrenheit. If a thermometer is reliable, then its reading must be correct; it can't be mistaken in what it says. A stuck thermometer isn't reliable, even when its readings happen to be correct. It is unreliable because its readings are correct only *by accident*.

Do reliable thermometers exist? I think so. The mercury thermometers we use to check whether we have fevers are examples. In saying this, I'm not denying two obvious facts.

First, a thermometer can be reliable in one set of circumstances but not in another. A mercury thermometer wouldn't be very useful for measuring temperature if it were wrapped in insulation before being placed in your mouth. The second point is that in saying that a thermometer is reliable, I'm not denying that it would be unreliable if it were broken. Hitting a reliable thermometer with a hammer will usually be enough to make it unreliable. So there are two things that help make a thermometer reliable. First, it has to be used in the right environment (for example, don't wrap it in insulation if you want to take somebody's temperature). Second, the internal makeup of the device has to be right (for example, the glass tube that holds the mercury can't be broken).

Notice that reliability is an objective feature of the relationship between the thermometer and its environment. The question is whether the thermometer and its environment make the following claim true: *If the thermometer says that the temperature is n degrees Fahrenheit, then the temperature must be n degrees Fahrenheit*. It is an entirely separate question whether anybody realizes that this thermometer/environment relationship obtains. Whether we notice this fact is a subjective question, but whether the relationship obtains is an objective matter.

Let's imagine that you take a thermometer out of a child's mouth, see that it reads 99°F, and then announce: "The thermometer is reliable, and so the baby's temperature is 99°F." Suppose a contentious philosopher (like me) comes along and tries to refute your claim. I say:

> Your thermometer isn't reliable. It is unreliable because I can conceive of a circumstance in which its reading would be false. For example, I can conceive of a situation in which the thermometer is wrapped in insulation. In that case, the thermometer reading wouldn't be correct. I also can conceive of the thermometer's being broken. In that case as well, the thermometer reading wouldn't be correct. It follows from the fact that I can conceive of these things that your thermometer isn't reliable.

Should you be convinced by my argument? I think not. Whether the thermometer is reliable *here and now* has nothing to do with what I can imagine. Granted, if the situations I described actually obtained, then the thermometer wouldn't be reliable. But from this it doesn't follow that the thermometer is unreliable in the actual circumstances in which it is used.

Relevance to the Problem of Knowledge

How does this discussion of reliable thermometers bear on the problem of knowledge? The Reliability Theory of Knowledge says that an individual knows a proposition if the individual is related to the proposition the way a reliable thermometer is related to the temperature it measures. A reliable thermometer wouldn't say *n* degrees Fahrenheit unless the temperature were *n* degrees Fahrenheit. An individual knows that there is a page in front of her precisely when she wouldn't have believed that there is a page in front of her unless there were one there. Another way to express this idea is by using the concept of *causality*. A thermometer is reliable in a given circumstance if the only thing that could cause the thermometer to read *n* degrees Fahrenheit is that the temperature really is *n* degrees Fahrenheit. Similarly, *S* knows that there is a page in front of her in a given circumstance if the only thing that could cause *S* to believe this is that there really is a page in front of her.

I hope that the connection between thermometers and knowledge is starting to become clear. Suppose *S* believes that there is a page in front of her. We want to know whether this belief is an instance of knowledge. The answer should depend on the *actual* relationship that obtains between S and her environment. Suppose S's sensory system is functioning normally; she isn't hallucinating, for example. In addition, suppose that there are no evil demons around who might choose to provide S with misleading evidence. If so, it may be true that S's sensory system is a reliable indicator of the presence of a page. If you want to answer the question of whether S knows that there is a page present, it will be entirely irrelevant to point out that if S had taken a hallucinatory drug or if S were plagued by an evil demon, then S's belief would be (or might be) false. These *hypothetical* considerations do nothing to undermine the claim that S's sensory state is a reliable indicator of what is going on in her environment.

Here's how the Reliability Theory of Knowledge characterizes what knowledge is:

S knows that p if and only if

(1) S believes that p.
(2) p is true.
(3) in the circumstances that S occupies, if S believes that p, then p must be true.

The third condition can also be formulated in either of the following two ways:

• In the circumstances that S occupies, S wouldn't believe that p unless p were true.
• In the circumstances that S occupies, it is impossible that S believes p and p is false.

Notice that the Reliability Theory of Knowledge makes use of the concepts of *necessity* and *impossibility*. To understand this theory of knowledge, we need to look more carefully at what these concepts mean.

Three Concepts of Impossibility

I want to discuss three kinds of impossibility. Consider the following three statements:

(1) Joe can't be a married bachelor.
(2) Joe can't go faster than the speed of light.
(3) Joe can't tie his shoes now.

The word "can't" in each of these indicates that something is *impossible*, but different kinds of impossibility are involved.

The first statement is logically necessary. It has to be true, just by virtue of logic and the definitions of the terms involved. If definitions and their deductive consequences are *a priori* true (Chapter 8), then (1) expresses a necessary truth that is *a priori*.

In contrast, statement (2) isn't *a priori*. We know that it is true because Einstein's theory of relativity—an *a posteriori* theory—says that it is so. Statement (2) is said to be *nomologically necessary* (from *nomos*, meaning "law"). It is necessary because of a law of nature, in this case, an *a posteriori* law of physics.

Statement (3) differs from the first two examples. Its truth doesn't follow from logic or definitions. Nor does its truth follow from any law of nature—physical or biological or whatever. Rather, to see that (3) is true, you have to take into account particular facts about Joe. For example, suppose that Joe can't tie his shoes now because he is carrying several bags of groceries. I'll call this third sort of necessity *circumstantial necessity*. By this I mean that the statement is necessarily true because of facts about the circumstances in which Joe finds himself. There is an additional fact about type (3) necessity that I should note. Whether we judge (3) true or false depends on how we interpret it. That is, (3) is ambiguous. If we interpret it to mean that Joe can't tie his shoes because he is otherwise occupied, (3) may be true. Suppose, however, we take (3) to mean that even if Joe put down the bags of groceries, he still couldn't tie his shoes. If that is how we interpret (3), we may judge it to be false. This is an important feature of statements that are circumstantially necessary—they are *ambiguous*.

When I say that a thermometer is reliable, I mean that it and its environment are related in a special way. I'm saying that its circumstances are such that its readings *must* be correct. In saying this, I'm using the concept of *circumstantial necessity*. Similarly, when I say that *S* knows that there is a page in front of her, I'm saying that she is related to her environment in a special way. I'm saying that she can't be mistaken in believing what she does. Here again, I'm using the concept of circumstantial necessity.

Suppose that a real printed page is the only thing that could get *S* to believe that a printed page is in front of her. Her senses are functioning normally. There are no evil demons lurking about who provide misleading evidence. If this is so, and if *S* subsequently believes the proposition in question, then *S* will *know* that there is a printed page in front of her. This is what the reliability theory says. In this circumstance, her belief will be related to the world the way the reading of a reliable thermometer is related to the temperature.

To Have Knowledge, You Don't Have to Be Able to Construct a Philosophical Argument Refuting the Skeptic

It is important to notice that the claim that *S* knows some proposition *p* isn't refuted by the fact that *S* may not be able to defend her knowledge claim against clever philosophical interrogation. If I asked *S* how she knows that her impressions aren't caused by an evil demon, she may draw a blank. If I ask her how she knows that she isn't dreaming, she may admit that she can't construct an argument proving that she isn't dreaming. Such philosophical puzzles may even lead *S* to say, "I guess I don't know that there is a printed page in front of me." But her comment doesn't show that she lacks knowledge. Rather, it shows only that *S* doesn't believe that she knows there is a printed page in front of her.

If *S* is like a reliable thermometer, she has knowledge. Being like a reliable thermometer, however, doesn't require that *S* has the ability to construct fancy philosophical arguments that show she is like a thermometer. Thermometers can't construct philosophical arguments, yet they are sometimes reliable. *S* may be similar. She may be unable to refute the skeptic, but that doesn't show she lacks knowledge. *S* may even be a skeptic herself. She may believe that she lacks knowledge, but that doesn't entail that she really lacks it. Just as it is possible to mistakenly believe that a thermometer is unreliable, so it is possible to mistakenly believe that an individual lacks knowledge. In fact, it is possible to have false beliefs about one's own situation; *S* can believe that she lacks knowledge and yet be mistaken.

14 The KK-Principle

According to the Reliability Theory of Knowledge, knowing a proposition doesn't imply that you know that you know it. That is, the reliability theory rejects what is called the *KK-principle*. The following several paragraphs about this principle will be somewhat tough to grasp—so take a deep breath, read them slowly, and then read them again.

The *KK-principle* says that if S knows that p, then S knows that she knows that p. But I've just argued that the following is possible: S knows that p, but S doesn't believe that she knows that p. It follows that S might know that p even though she doesn't know that she knows that p. So if I'm right, the KK-principle is false.

If the KK-principle were true, S could prove that she lacked knowledge just by becoming a philosophical skeptic. This would be very *convenient*—wouldn't it be nice to be able to prove some thesis just by believing it?

Suppose S believed, maybe for no reason at all, that she didn't know that p is true. The KK-principle would conclude from this that, indeed, S failed to know that p is true. To see why, consider the following argument:

(1) If you don't believe that you know that p, then you don't know that you know that p.
(2) If you don't know that you know that p, then you don't know that p.

_____

If you do not believe that you know that p, then you don't know that p.

The argument can be symbolized as follows:

(1) If −B[K(p)], then −K[K(p)].
(2) If −K[K(p)], then −K(p).

_____

If −B[K(p)], then −K(p).

The argument is deductively valid (what is its logical form?). Notice that premise (1) is correct; it follows from the fact that knowing a proposition requires that you believe the proposition. Premise (2) would be true if the KK-principle were correct. So if the KK-principle were correct, believing that skepticism is true would be enough to ensure that skepticism is true. However, if knowing is like being a reliable thermometer, this has got to be wrong.

The Reliability Theory of Knowledge holds that whether an agent knows something is settled by the objective relationship that obtains between the agent's belief and the environment. Whether the agent believes that this relationship obtains is irrelevant. The reliability theory rejects the KK-principle.

In summary, the Reliability Theory of Knowledge explains why S knows that there is a page in front of her by describing the following argument:

S believes that there is a page in front of her.
In the circumstances S occupies, she wouldn't believe that there is a page in front of her unless there were a page in front of her.

_____

There is a page in front of S.

This argument doesn't use the word "know." So what does it have to do with knowledge? According to the reliability theory, S knows that the concluding proposition is true because the premises are true. But S doesn't have to *know* that the premises are true, nor does S have to produce an argument independent of sense experience for the premises. This shows why the reliability theory rejects Descartes' claim that knowledge is internally certifiable.

One virtue of the reliability theory is that it explains what is wrong with a standard skeptical argument. The skeptic claims that S doesn't know that there is a printed page in front of her on the grounds that it is possible to imagine that S is deluded in some way. You can imagine a situation in which S believes what she does but she is mistaken. The reliability theory shows why this act of imagination is irrelevant to the question of whether S has knowledge *in the real world situation that she occupies.*

A Consequence of the Reliability Theory

To conclude this discussion, I want to consider an implication that the reliability theory has. It involves a fact about circumstantial necessity that I mentioned before. This is the fact that claims of circumstantial necessity are often ambiguous. I'll restate the point and then show how it is relevant to the reliability theory.

Consider the statement "Joe can't tie his shoes now." Suppose I make this comment to you while we are looking at Joe, who is carrying two heavy bags of groceries. Is the quoted remark true? Here are two ways of interpreting it:

1   If Joe tries to tie his shoes while holding the bags of groceries, he will fail.
2   If Joe tries to tie his shoes after first putting down the groceries, he will fail.

If we interpreted "Joe can't tie his shoes now" to mean (1), it will be true; if we interpreted it to mean (2), it will be false. Which reading you choose affects whether you will say that the quoted claim is true.

To see how this idea applies to the Reliability Theory of Knowledge, let's switch examples—from knowing that there is a printed page in front of you to knowing that there is a barn in the field next to the road on which you are driving. Suppose one day you go for a drive in Dane County, which is where Madison, Wisconsin is located. On your drive, you look at a field and say, "There is a barn in that field." Suppose that the proposition you've asserted is true. You believe the proposition. Do you know that it is true? The reliability theory says that we must ask whether, in the circumstances you occupy, there is anything besides a real barn that could have caused you to believe a barn is present. The problem I want to focus on is that it isn't clear how to decide what is included and what is excluded by the expression "in the circumstances you occupy."

First, I need to define the idea of a *fool's barn.* Fool's gold looks like gold, but isn't gold at all. A fool's barn is something that looks like a barn but isn't one. Suppose there are no fool's barns in Dane County. The only things that look like barns are real barns. This means that if I describe the circumstances you occupy by saying that you are in Dane County, then it will be true that the only thing that could have made you think a barn is present is a real barn. Hence, you know that there is a barn in the field.

Now let's broaden our vision. In Hollywood, there are fool's barns. These are the facades used in movie sets. When viewed from one angle, they look just like barns, but they aren't buildings at all. If you were driving around Hollywood and came to believe that a barn is present, your belief would not count as knowledge (even if your belief happened to be true). The reason is that, around Hollywood, there are things besides real barns that can make you believe that a barn is present.

So if your circumstances are restricted to Dane County, you might know that a barn is present; if your circumstances are restricted to Hollywood, you wouldn't. But now consider a puzzle. I initially suggested that the circumstances you occupy are limited to the objects in Dane County. Given this array of objects, I argued that a real barn is the only thing (in the circumstances you occupy) that could cause you to think that a barn is present. But why describe your circumstances so narrowly? Why not describe your circumstances as including all the objects in the United States? If I describe your situation in this way, it will be false that the only thing that could cause you to believe a barn is present is a real barn.

Here is the point: When we assert or deny that the only thing *in the circumstances* that could cause you to believe that a barn is present is a real barn, we are making reference to the environment you occupy. The environment may be thought of as composed of a set of objects. If we describe that set narrowly, it may be true that the only thing in the set that could cause you to believe that a barn is present is a real barn. If we describe the set more broadly, this may no longer be true. So whether you know, on your drive through Dane County, that there is a barn on the hill next to the road depends on how we choose to describe the "circumstances you occupy." There are many true descriptions we might select. Narrow ones will entail that you have knowledge; broader ones will entail that you do not.

Thesis of the Relativity of Knowledge

The claim I just made about knowledge may be put this way: *Knowledge is relative*. Whether S knows that p depends on (is relative to) a choice. "S is in Dane County" and "S is in the United States" are equally correct descriptions of the circumstances that S occupies. Which one we consider depends on our interests.

Let's be clear what this relativity thesis asserts. When you say that something is relative, you should always be prepared to say *what* it is relative to. The thesis that knowledge is relative is the thesis that whether an agent knows a proposition depends on (is relative to) a specification of his or her circumstances. These circumstances can be specified in different equally correct ways, and so there is no unique answer to the question of whether the agent has knowledge.

Let's consider a down-to-earth example of relativity that does not concern knowledge. Mary and Alice are walking down the street, side by side. Is Mary walking to the left of Alice? Well, that depends on the point of view. If you look at them from the front, you get one answer. If you look at them from the back, you get the other. The key thing to notice is that x's being to the left of y isn't a relation between x and y alone. It involves some third item, z.

Does S know that p? The suggestion now being considered is that the question is incomplete, that is, whether S knows that p depends on a third item besides the agent S and the proposition p. It depends on a specification of S's environment. There are different true ways to describe S's environment. S is in Dane County. But it is also true that S is in the United States. Relative to one specification of the environment—call it E_1—S knows that p. But relative to another equally true specification of the environment—call it E_2—S doesn't know that p.

What Does the Relativity Thesis Say about Skepticism?

The thesis that knowledge is relative has an interesting implication about skepticism. Skepticism, recall, is the position that people don't have knowledge. Its opposite is the more common-sense idea that people often (if not always) know the propositions they believe. If the relativity thesis is true, then each of these theses is true in one sense but false in another. If the agent's environment is given a very broad specification, then skepticism is true. If the environment is given a narrower specification, then the common-sense position will be correct. Notice, however, that there is no conflict between the following two claims:

(1) S knows that p, relative to E_1.
(2) S doesn't know that p, relative to E_2.

These statements don't conflict with each other, any more than the next pair conflicts with each other.

(3) Mary is walking to the left of Sue, when they are viewed from the front.
(4) Mary is not walking to the left of Sue, when they are viewed from the back.

So the dispute between skepticism and common sense seems to end in a stalemate, not in a victory for either side, if the relativity thesis is correct. Each position is correct in one sense but incorrect in another. This consequence follows from the Reliability Theory of Knowledge once we acknowledge that claims about circumstantial necessity are ambiguous.

---

15 What's Relative about Einstein's Theory of Relativity?

Sometimes people say that Einstein proved that "Everything is relative." This isn't true. Neither is the more modest claim that Einstein proved that everything in physics is relative.

To say that a statement is relative isn't to say that it is subjective or arbitrary. Rather, it is to say that the statement is incomplete in a particular way. Whether Sue is walking to the left of Mary is a relative matter. That means that there exists some third item, beyond the two people mentioned, that must be referred to if the statement is to be true or false. To say just that Sue is to the left of Mary is to fail to express a complete thought.

It takes no enormous insight or creativity to see that whether one person is walking to the left of another is a relative, not an absolute, matter. In contrast, Einstein's idea that simultaneity is relative is anything but obvious. It was a brilliant theoretical conjecture, something that isn't at all suggested by our common-sense talk about space and time. Consider two events that occur at different places. Common sense suggests that either the events are simultaneous with each other or they aren't. Einstein's theory says that this isn't true. Whether two events are simultaneous depends on the choice of some third item—something called a *rest frame*. Relative to one rest frame, the events are simultaneous, but relative to another equally correct rest frame, they aren't. Simultaneity is relative, not absolute.

Einstein didn't say that everything in physics is relative. For example, in the special theory of relativity he defines a quantity called *the space-time interval*. This quantity measures the amount of separation that there is between events; it takes account of both spatial and temporal distances. The space-time interval between two events isn't relative to the choice of a rest frame. The space-time interval is absolute, not relative.

Review Questions

1 At the beginning of this chapter, I said that Descartes held that knowledge is "internally certifiable." What does this mean? Does the Reliability Theory of Knowledge agree?

2 What is the difference between logical necessity, nomological necessity, and circumstantial necessity?

3 What does it mean to say that claims about circumstantial necessity are "ambiguous"?

4 What does it mean to say that a thermometer is "reliable"? What analogy does the Reliability Theory of Knowledge see between reliable thermometers and knowledge?

5   How does the Reliability Theory of Knowledge assess the following skeptical argument: "I can imagine that my senses are now malfunctioning. Hence, I don't know now that there is a printed page in front of me."

6   What does it mean to say that knowledge is "relative"? Relative to what?

7   Does the relativity thesis entail that skepticism is correct?

8   What is the difference between "accuracy" and "reliability"? Can an instrument be accurate but not reliable? Can it be reliable but not accurate?

9   What are the two minimal conditions that have to be met in order for a mechanism or instrument (e.g., a thermometer) to function reliably? (Hint: Under which conditions would we expect an otherwise reliable mechanism to fail to be reliable?)

10 Why do reliabilists about knowledge argue that hypothetical considerations are not (or at least not necessarily) relevant to determining whether a subject has knowledge?

Problems for Further Thought

1   For any proposition p, we can construct the sentence "S knows that p." Since "S knows that lemons are yellow" is a sentence, we can construct the sentence "S knows that S knows that lemons are yellow." We can repeat this operation as many times as we please. The KK-principle says that if S knows that p, then S knows that S knows that p. Formulate similar principles for truth (the TT-principle), belief (the BB-principle), and surprise (the SS-principle). Are any of these principles plausible? Defend your answers.

2   Whether a ring is made of gold depends on the materials that the jeweler chooses when the ring is made. Does this mean that whether a ring is made of gold is a relative matter? How is this example different from the two claims about relativity discussed in this chapter?

3   Do you think that nonhuman organisms have knowledge? For example, do dogs? What is required for dogs to have knowledge, according to the reliability theory? How do these requirements differ from what would be demanded by the view that knowledge is internally certifiable? If dogs have knowledge, does this count for or against the Reliability Theory of Knowledge?

Recommended Readings, Video, and Audio

Visit the companion website at www.routledge.com/cw/sober for suggestions of readings, video, and audio, for this chapter.

Chapter 15

Justified Belief and Hume's Problem of Induction

In this chapter, I will present a new problem in epistemology. So far, I've discussed the concept of *knowledge*, examining Descartes' foundationalism (Chapter 13) and the Reliability Theory of Knowledge (Chapter 14). The problem to be considered here concerns the idea of justified belief.

Knowledge versus Justified Belief

Before starting, let's be clear on how this problem differs from the previous one. What is the difference between knowledge and justified belief? Two differences should be clear. First, if S knows that p, then p must be true; whereas S's having a justified belief that p doesn't require that p be true. Knowledge requires truth, but justified belief does not. The second difference is that knowledge requires the impossibility of error; justified belief does not. Recall the lottery example discussed in Chapter 12. Suppose you believe, before the drawing, that ticket number 346 will not win in a fair lottery containing one thousand tickets. Suppose your belief turns out (after the drawing) to be true. You didn't *know* before the drawing that that ticket wouldn't win, but you nonetheless had strong evidence for thinking the ticket would lose. Your belief was reasonable, or justified. (I'll use these two terms interchangeably.)

These comparisons of knowledge and justified belief are summarized in the following table:

	Is truth required?	Is the impossibility of error required?
Knowledge	Yes	Yes
Justified belief	No	No

As the lottery example illustrates, the evidence you have for many of your beliefs falls short of providing absolute certainty. We sometimes use the concept of *probability* to describe such cases. We say that ticket number 346 *probably* won't win, to indicate that we aren't absolutely sure that it will not. Similarly, you might also say that your present experiences make the beliefs you have about the world outside your mind highly probable. Your present experiences don't make it absolutely certain that there is a printed page in front of you, but it does seem plausible to say that your experiences make it very probable that there is a printed page before you.

Skepticism about Justified Belief

Until now I've talked about skepticism as if it were a single thesis. Now I want to distinguish skepticism about knowledge from a second kind of skepticism, which concerns the idea of justified belief.

Although skepticism about knowledge sounds like a shocking thesis at first hearing, once one grasps what it says, it doesn't fundamentally undermine our picture of ourselves and the world we inhabit. If knowledge requires the *impossibility* of error, perhaps we should concede that we don't know many things. True, we often talk about the knowledge we have, but perhaps this is just sloppy talk. This concession to skepticism isn't terribly threatening because it allows us to hold onto the idea that our beliefs about the world aren't groundless and arbitrary. We can still say that they are "reasonable" and "well justified," even if they aren't entitled to be labeled "knowledge." Skepticism about knowledge doesn't entail skepticism about rational belief. This is why it is possible to abandon the claim that we have knowledge without thereby giving up the idea that our beliefs are rational.

There is a second form of skepticism that is far more disturbing. This form of skepticism rejects our claim to rationality. According to this more radical form of skepticism, we aren't rationally justified in believing what we do. It is this type of skepticism that is involved in Hume's views on induction. Hume claimed that the beliefs we have about the future and the beliefs we have concerning generalizations can't be rationally justified. For example, it isn't just that we can't be *certain* that the sun will rise tomorrow. And it's not just that we don't *know* that the sun will rise tomorrow. According to Hume, we have no rational justification at all for this or for any other expectation we have about the future.

Hume's Skeptical Thesis about Induction

We constantly form expectations about what the future will be like or about which generalizations (statements of the form "All *A*s are *B*") are true based on evidence that isn't deductively conclusive. Our beliefs about the future are based on perception and memory, but you can't deduce what the future will be like from premises that describe just the present and the past. Let's focus on an example in order to get clear on this simple point. Suppose I have observed many emeralds and have found each of them to be green. I then formulate the prediction "The next emerald I observe will be green", or maybe I formulate the generalization "All emeralds are green." (Just so this can be an example of the kind I want, suppose that it isn't a definitional truth that all emeralds are green.)

Common sense says that we are rational in believing the predictions and generalizations we do if those beliefs are based on lots of evidence. Looking at lots of emeralds and finding that each is green seems to justify my expectation that the next emerald I examine will be green. Now it is obvious that we can't *deduce* generalizations or predictions from our past observations. Yet, the following appear to be perfectly sensible *nondeductive* arguments:

(GEN)

> I've observed numerous emeralds, and each has been green.
> ===============================
> Hence, all emeralds are green.

(PRED)

> I've observed numerous emeralds, and each has been green.
> ===============================
> Hence, the next emerald I observe will be green.

I've drawn a double line between premises and conclusions to indicate that these arguments aren't deductively valid. In both the generalization (GEN) argument and the prediction (PRED) argument, we think that the conclusion reached is rationally justified by the premises. We think that it isn't a mere prejudice to hold, in each case, that the premise provides good evidence for the truth of the conclusion. Hume's thesis is that this conviction can't be rationally defended.

It is important to see that Hume's thesis goes far beyond the undisturbing claim that the GEN and PRED arguments just given aren't deductively valid. That much is obvious. Rather, Hume is saying that the premises in those arguments don't rationally justify their conclusions. Hume's view is that there is absolutely no rational justification for the beliefs we have that are predictions or generalizations. He thinks it is merely a habit we have that we regard such premises as providing good reason to believe such conclusions. This is a habit we can't abandon; it is part of human nature to expect the future to resemble the past. But it is a habit we can't rationally defend. When challenged by the skeptic to rationally justify this pattern in our thinking, we can say only that this is the way human beings in fact operate. We can't produce a good argument to rationally justify this habit of mind.

Hume's Argument that Induction Can't Be Rationally Justified

Why did Hume reach this startling conclusion about induction? (Here I'll reconstruct the argument that Hume gives in Part II of the section from *An Enquiry Concerning Human Understanding* called "Skeptical Doubts Concerning the Operations of the Understanding.") Hume thought that the arguments GEN and PRED require an additional premise. As they stand, the premise doesn't support the conclusion. If the observation is to support the generalization or the prediction, then we must assume that the future will resemble the past. This assumption Hume calls the *Principle of the Uniformity of Nature* (PUN).

Hume thought that this principle plays an indispensable role in each and every inductive argument we make. The example described above concerns the color of emeralds. Consider, however, the belief that the sun will rise tomorrow. This predictive belief is based on the premise that the sun has risen on each of the days that we have bothered to make an observation. Why should these *past* observations support the prediction you make about *tomorrow*? Hume thought that you must be assuming that nature is uniform—that the future will resemble the past. Hume says that without this assumption, the past would be no guide to the future.

So each and every inductive argument presupposes PUN; we must assume PUN if the observational premise is to support the prediction or the generalization stated in the argument's conclusion. This means that if the conclusion we reach is rationally defensible, then a good argument must be available for thinking that PUN is true. If PUN can't be defended, then anything you believe that depends on assuming that PUN is true must likewise be indefensible.

We now can state Hume's skeptical argument:

(1) Every inductive argument requires PUN as a premise.

(2) If the conclusion of an inductive argument is rationally justified by the premises, then those premises must themselves be rationally justifiable.

(3) So, if the conclusion of an inductive argument is justified, there must be a rational justification for PUN.

(4) If PUN is rationally justifiable, then there must be a good inductive argument or a good deductive argument for PUN.

(5) There is no good inductive argument for PUN, since any inductive argument for PUN will be circular.

(6) There cannot be a good deductive argument for PUN, since PUN is not *a priori* true, nor does PUN deductively follow from the observations we have made to date.

(7) So, PUN is not rationally justifiable.

———————————

Hence, there is no rational justification for the beliefs we have that take the form of predictions or generalizations.

In a nutshell, Hume's claim is that the beliefs we have about emerald color and tomorrow's sunrise (and lots of other beliefs as well) aren't rationally justifiable. This is because they rest on an assumption that can't be rationally justified.

Why Can't PUN Be Justified?

Let's look more carefully at steps (4)–(6) in the argument. Consider what PUN asserts; it says that the future will resemble the past—that past uniformities will continue to obtain in the future. Is this something that we could know to be true on the basis of induction? If it were, the inductive argument would look like this:

Nature has been uniform in my past observations.
[insert double line]
Nature in general is uniform.

Recall that Hume claims that *all* inductive arguments require that PUN be assumed as a premise, but the above argument is inductive. Notice that if we insert PUN as a premise, as Hume requires, the argument becomes circular—it assumes as a premise the very proposition it tries to establish as a conclusion.

What about the other sort of justification? Can we give a deductive justification of PUN? Here again, Hume holds that the answer is *no*. The argument isn't deductively valid; the general uniformity principle can't be deduced from the observations I've made in the past.

Hume considers, and rejects, a second possible sort of deductive argument. Could PUN be a definitional truth, deducible from the definitions of the terms it uses? If PUN were a definitional truth, it would have the same sort of *a priori* justification that "All bachelors are unmarried" possesses. Hume rejects this idea by saying that there is "no contradiction" in supposing that the universe should suddenly cease to be uniform. It isn't a definitional truth that past regularities will continue into the future, Hume says.

Summary of Hume's Argument

It should now be clear how Hume's skeptical argument proceeds. First, there is a claim: Every inductive argument requires the premise that nature is uniform. Second, Hume argues that no rational justification can be given for that premise. He defends this assertion by considering three options: (1) an inductive argument in favor of PUN, (2) a deduction of PUN from past observations, and (3) a deduction of PUN from definitions. He asserts that none of these ways of defending PUN is going to work. This means that PUN can't be justified. Hume concludes that the inductive inferences we make aren't rationally justifiable.

Review Questions

1   What is the difference between knowledge and justified belief? Does skepticism about knowledge entail skepticism about rational justification? What do each of these skeptical theses assert?

2   It is obvious that we can't deduce what the future will be like from our present observations and memories. Does Hume's skeptical thesis say anything more than this?

3   What is the Principle of the Uniformity of Nature?

4   What is Hume's skeptical argument about induction?

5   Why, according to Hume, can't the Principle of the Uniformity of Nature be justified by a deductive argument? Why can't it be justified by an inductive argument? Do you find his arguments for each of these conclusions equally convincing?

6   Why does Hume claim that the Principle of the Uniformity of Nature can't be deduced from the definition of (e.g.) "nature"? Do you agree? Why or why not?

7   According to Hume, which kinds of arguments always require us to show that the Principle of the Uniformity of Nature is rationally justified? Why?

8   Hume argues that we have no justification for believing that the future will resemble the past. But it seems as though our beliefs about the past do, at least sometimes, enable us to accurately predict the future. For example, I believed that the sun would rise yesterday morning because the sun had risen every day before that; and it did rise yesterday morning. How do you think Hume would respond to an argument of this kind?

Problems for Further Thought

1   Is the claim that nature is uniform falsifiable (Chapter 9)? That is, can you describe a possible observation that would count against this claim?

2   Is it possible that *all* of our beliefs could be rationally justified? Would this be possible if we had a finite number of beliefs? In answering, explain what you think it means to say that a belief is rationally justified?

Recommended Readings, Video, and Audio

Visit the companion website at www.routledge.com/cw/sober for suggestions of readings, video, and audio, for this chapter.

Chapter 16

Can Hume's Skepticism Be Refuted?

In the previous chapter, I described Hume's skeptical argument about induction as focusing on the Principle of the Uniformity of Nature (PUN). This principle, recall, says that the future will resemble the past. In this chapter, I'll criticize this version of Hume's argument. Then I'll formulate Hume's argument in another way. After that, I'll examine two criticisms that have been made of Hume's startling argument. Again, you want to be clear on what Hume's conclusion is. He didn't merely say that our predictions are uncertain; he said that they have *no rational justification whatever*. These predictions are rationally indefensible, but we can't help making and believing them—they are consequences of a habit that is deeply entrenched in human nature.

What, Exactly, Does the Principle of the Uniformity of Nature Say?

PUN says that the future will resemble the past. Recall that Hume held that every time we make an induction—inferring that the sun will rise tomorrow or that the next emerald we observe will be green—we are assuming that nature is uniform. So PUN is supposed to be an assumption that is required by each and every inductive argument. But what, exactly, does PUN mean? Does it mean that nature is uniform *in each and every respect*? If so, it is pretty clear that we don't think that PUN is true. Summer leaves are green, but we don't expect autumn to resemble summer in this respect. So if we understand PUN in this way, the principle is not, contrary to Hume, something we are always assuming.

Let's try a second interpretation. Maybe PUN means merely that the future will resemble the past *in some respect*. This does seem to be something we believe. This is such a modest principle, however, that it is hard to see how it will help very much in the task of inferring what the future will be like. If I want to know whether future emeralds will be green or blue based on my observation that so far they all have been green, this modest version of PUN is pretty useless. It doesn't tell me whether it makes sense to expect emeralds to remain green or to expect a change.

These two attempts to clarify what PUN says illustrate a general problem. No one yet has been able to clarify the principle so that it has both of the following properties:

(1) PUN is something we believe.
(2) PUN gives definite advice about what we should infer from the observations we have made.

There is a third characteristic that Hume's argument about induction attributes to PUN. This is the idea that PUN plays an indispensable role in the way we think about the world:

(3) If we want to make inductive inferences about the world, PUN is something we must believe, no matter what else we believe.

This last condition expresses Hume's idea that PUN is an assumption—a presupposition—that underlies the whole project of inductive inference.

If it is hard to formulate PUN so that it satisfies (1) and (2), it will be even harder to clarify the principle so that it satisfies (1)–(3). I haven't proved that it is impossible to do this. But no one has done so yet. For this reason, I suggest we drop the formulation of Hume's argument that involves PUN. Instead, I'll now describe a different version of Hume's argument that induction can't be rationally justified.

A New Concept: Degrees of Reliability

This new version of Hume's argument involves the idea that a method of inference possesses *some degree of reliability*. Induction is a method of inference. It uses observations to make predictions and to say what generalizations are true. We can evaluate a method of inference by determining how often the predictions or generalizations it endorses have been true. A method that usually leads to truth is highly reliable; one that rarely does so is very unreliable.

This use of the concept of reliability departs somewhat from the one employed by the Reliability Theory of Knowledge (Chapter 14). There I discussed reliability as an on/off concept; a thermometer is either reliable or it isn't. Moreover, a reliable thermometer, in the sense employed there, *must* make true claims about the temperature. Notice that the concept of degrees of reliability isn't an on/off concept. In addition, a highly reliable method of inference can sometimes lead to falsehood. The point is that it does so *rarely*. A method of inference is highly reliable if the predictions it makes are *usually* true.

Induction is a rule of inference that scientists use to evaluate hypotheses in the light of evidence. A scientist makes a number of observations—call them O. The goal is to say which hypothesis among a set of competing hypotheses is most plausible in the light of those observations. For example, suppose you've examined numerous emeralds and all have been green. The problem is to say which of the following hypotheses is better supported in the light of those observations:

(H_1) All emeralds are green.
(H_2) All emeralds are green until the year 2050; thereafter, they are blue.

Common sense suggests that H_1 is more plausible than H_2 in the light of the observations O. The philosophical question is to explain why this is so. Hume denied that this evaluation of the competing hypotheses can be rationally defended.

What Is a Rule of Inference?

Rules of inference provide *licenses*. A fishing license permits you to fish. A rule of inference permits you to draw conclusions. In the previous example, induction permits you to conclude that H_1 is probably true, given O. That is, induction is a rule of inference that connects premise to conclusion in the following argument:

> I've examined lots of emeralds and all have been green.
>
> I[══════════════════
>
> All emeralds are green.

I've drawn a double line to indicate that the argument is not supposed to be deductively valid. I've written an "I" beside the double line to indicate that the rule of inference being used is induction. The problem of induction is to explain why we are entitled to use this inference rule.

Does the Past Reliability of Induction Provide an Answer?

Common sense may suggest that we are now entitled to use induction because induction has been reliable in the past. Induction has often been used to make predictions, and the predictions endorsed by inductive arguments usually turned out to be correct. This is why we rightly take seriously what induction tells us. Hume rejected this attempt to justify induction. Let's examine the attempted justification more carefully. Here is the argument we need to consider:

> Induction has been highly reliable in the past.
>
> ══════════════════
>
> Induction will be highly reliable now and in the future.

The premise of this argument is something we know by having observed the past track record of the inductive method. The conclusion makes a claim about what will be true now and in the future.

Every argument must use a rule of inference to license the transition from its premises to its conclusion. What rule of inference is used here? Can the conclusion be validly deduced from the premise? *No.* That is why I've drawn a double line. This is an *inductive* argument; induction (I) is the rule of inference that is being used, so an "I" should be inscribed next to the double line.

Hume's point about this argument is that it is *circular* or *question-begging*. The philosophical question is whether induction can be rationally justified. This argument simply assumes that induction is legitimate. You can't justify using induction now by appeal to the fact that induction has been successful in the past.

Hume's Argument Reformulated

So Hume's skeptical argument about induction can be formulated as follows:

(1) To rationally justify induction, you must show that induction will be reliable.
(2) To show that induction will be reliable, you must construct an inductive argument or a deductively valid argument.
(3) You can't show that induction will be reliable by giving an inductive argument; that would be question-begging.
(4) You can't validly deduce that induction will be reliable from premises describing the past reliability of induction (or from definitions).

Hence, induction cannot be rationally justified.

This argument doesn't say anything about the PUN. Can it be refuted?

Strawson: It Is Analytic that Induction Is Rational

Hume claimed that a rational justification for using induction must show that the method will probably be reliable. The British philosopher Peter Strawson (in *Introduction to Logical Theory*, Methuen, 1952) challenged this. Strawson rejects premise (1) of Hume's argument. Strawson's idea is simple. He thinks that the statement "Induction is rational" is like the statement "Bachelors are unmarried." Both are *a priori* truths. Both are deductive consequences of the definitions of the terms that occur in them. According to Strawson, induction is, by definition, a rational activity.

Strawson doesn't claim that "Induction will be reliable" is an *a priori* truth. He agrees with Hume that this isn't true by definition. But he thinks that you don't need to establish that an inference rule will be reliable if you want to show that using the rule is rational. Hume thought that rationality requires reliability. Strawson denies this. According to Strawson, it is entirely rational to use inductive methods to formulate our beliefs about the future, even though we can offer no good reason for expecting that the method will probably lead to true beliefs. If it turns out later that we were entirely mistaken about what we thought the world would be like, no one can accuse us of having been irrational. Even if we turn out to be mistaken in our beliefs, we still behaved perfectly reasonably when we formed them.

I find Strawson's argument unconvincing. Methods of inference are methods for doing things. Consider an analogy—*recipes*. Suppose I told you that I have a great recipe for making a cake. To determine whether this is true, you would want to see if the method is reliable. The point of the recipe is to produce nice cakes. You evaluate the recipe by seeing if it is a reliable instrument. It would puzzle you if I said that a particular recipe is excellent even though I granted that there is no reason whatever to think that using the recipe will probably result in a nice cake. This, however, is just what Strawson is saying about induction. The point of induction is to reach true beliefs about the world. That is the goal we have when we make inferences. Whether it is reasonable to use induction or some other method depends on whether the method is a reliable instrument for attaining the specified goal. If it can't be shown that the instrument will attain the goal, or even that it probably will, how can using the instrument be rationally justified? Strawson's mistake, I think, is to hold that the rationality of a method has nothing to do with its reliability.

Black: Induction Can Be Inductively Justified

I turn now to an attempt at providing an inductive justification of induction. The American philosopher Max Black (in "Inductive Support of Inductive Rules," *Problems of Analysis*, Cornell University Press, 1954) argued that once you look carefully at what *circularity* means, you'll see that the inductive justification of induction isn't circular at all. That is, Black holds that the following argument provides a perfectly good reason for accepting the conclusion:

> Induction has been highly reliable until now.
> I[=================================
> Probably, induction will be highly reliable if we use it now and in the future.

Once again, I use the letter "I" to indicate that the rule of inference that licenses passing from the premise to the conclusion is the principle of induction.

What does Black think it means for an argument to be circular? His suggestion is roughly as follows: if an argument is circular, then the conclusion occurs as one of the premises. This isn't Black's exact formulation, but it captures the spirit of what he says. For Black, circularity involves a relationship between the conclusion and the premises. It has nothing to do with what rule of inference is used to get from premise to conclusion. I hope it is clear, if you accept Black's definition of circularity, that the above inductive justification of induction isn't circular. The point I want to make, however, is that Black's definition is too narrow. I think there is a broader definition of circularity that shows that the above argument is defective. It is this: An argument is circular if it couldn't possibly convince people that the conclusion is true if they didn't believe the conclusion already. A circular argument can't change anybody's mind. If you have doubts about induction, the above argument is not going to lay those doubts to rest.

Besides this, there is another problem confronting Black's suggestion. Consider a bizarre rule of inference that is the mirror image of induction. It is called *counterinduction*. Induction tells you to expect past regularities to continue into the future. Counterinduction tells you to expect past regularities *not* to continue. For example, counterinduction licenses the following inference:

> I've examined lots of emeralds and all have been green.
> I[=================================
> Future emeralds will not all be green.

Of course, induction would lead to a quite different conclusion. The problem of induction is, in part, to explain why we should use induction rather than counterinduction to formulate our predictions about the future.

What has this to do with Black's proposal? Black claims that the inductive justification of induction isn't circular. If he is right, then neither is the following argument:

> Counterinduction has been highly unreliable until now.
> CI[=================================
> Probably, counterinduction will be highly reliable now and in the future.

Here we have a counterinductive justification of counterinduction.

Counterinduction has had a poor track record in the past. How should we expect it to do in the future? That depends on what rule of inference we use. If we use induction, we will expect counterinduction's dismal past track record to continue into the future. If, however, we use counterinduction, we expect the pattern to reverse. Since the method has been unreliable in the past, counterinduction tells us to expect that counterinduction will be *reliable* in the future. So we have two arguments to compare: the inductive justification of induction and the counterinductive justification of counterinduction. Which method of inference—induction or counterinduction—should we use now? The problem with Black's inductive justification of induction is that it gives us no reason to reject the counterinductive justification of counterinduction. This means that Black's favored inductive justification of induction, even if it is noncircular in Black's sense of the term, doesn't show why we should use induction rather than counterinduction. Hume's problem has not been solved.

Is it possible to refute Hume's argument? We have examined two attempts to do so. I think both fail. This does not mean that there is no way to prove Hume wrong. In the next chapter, I'll consider this problem from a different angle.

Review Questions

1   When we try to clarify exactly what the Principle of   the Uniformity of Nature says, we run into a problem. What is the problem?
2   How can Hume's skeptical argument about induction be formulated without mentioning PUN?
3   What is Strawson's justification of induction? What objection to it was presented in this chapter?
4   What is Black's inductive justification of induction? What two objections to it were presented in this chapter?
5   What does it mean to say that a rule of inference is a "license"? What is the difference between the license provided by induction and the license provided by counterinduction?
6   Why does Hume think that we can't justify inductive inference by appeal to the successes of past inductions? Do you find his line of reasoning convincing?
7   What three conditions must any reconstruction of the Principle of the Uniformity of Nature satisfy in order to support Hume's skeptical argument? Why?
8   Under what conditions will an argument be "circular," according to Black? Do you think Hume would be satisfied with Black's account of circularity? Why or why not?
9   How does Black's view compare to the alternative conception of circularity I've suggested above?

Problems for Further Thought

1   The problem of induction involves explaining why the observation of many emeralds, all of them green, supports H_1 better than H_2:

H_1: All emeralds are green.
H_2: All emeralds are green until 2050; thereafter, they are blue.

Can the Surprise Principle (Chapter 3) be used to show that the observations strongly favor H_1 over H_2? Explain your answer.
2   Hume considers, and rejects, two kinds of arguments that might justify induction—deductive arguments and inductive arguments. Would considering abductive arguments change the sort of conclusion that Hume reaches about induction?
3   Consider the rules of inference that are used in arguments we think are deductively valid. How can these rules be justified? Formulate a skeptical problem about deduction that is similar to Hume's problem about induction. Can this problem be solved?

4   Maybe Hume's Principle of the Uniformity of Nature should be formulated as the claim that the laws of nature are the same at all times and places. Is this claim true? Does it give definite advice about what we should infer from a given body of observations? Is it an assumption of all inductive reasoning?

Recommended Readings, Video, and Audio

Visit the companion website at www.routledge.com/cw/sober for suggestions of readings, video, and audio, for this chapter.

Chapter 17

Beyond Foundationalism

In the previous chapter, I briefly considered two attempts to refute Hume's skeptical argument about induction. I argued that neither is successful. However, the failures of these two criticisms don't show that Hume was right, so the question remains: Can Hume's skepticism be refuted?

Hume's Problem and Descartes' Problem

In this chapter, I'm going to argue that if we understand the idea of rational justification in the way Hume did, then he was right that induction can't be rationally justified. Notice that the thesis I'll be arguing for has an *IF* in it. I won't claim that Hume's skepticism is correct. My conclusion will be more modest: skepticism is correct, *IF* the task of rational justification is understood in the way Hume understood it.

To defend this thesis, I want to describe a similarity between a problem that Descartes tried to solve and the problem that Hume addressed. Descartes asked, "How does my present mental state justify the beliefs I have about the world outside my mind?" Hume asked, "How do the observations I have made of my physical environment justify the beliefs I have about the future?" The parallelism between these two problems is illustrated in the following diagram:

	Level	Kind of Belief	Examples
Hume's problem	3	Predictions and generalizations	"The sun will rise tomorrow."
	2	Present and past observations	"The sun is now rising." "The sun has risen each day that I have made an observation."
Descartes' problem	1	Indubitable beliefs	"I now seem to see a sunrise." "I now seem to remember that the sun has risen each day that I have made an observation." "God exists and is no deceiver."

In this diagram, I've divided beliefs into three categories. Hume was asking how beliefs at level 3 can be justified. Descartes was asking how beliefs in level 2 can be justified.

Both Descartes and Hume were foundationalists in the way they approached questions about knowledge and justification. By this, I mean that each held that IF a belief is rationally justified or known, then it is justified or known solely on the basis of its relationship to beliefs at lower levels. Foundationalism holds that justification flows from bottom to top, not in the other direction. Beliefs are justified because of their relationship to other beliefs that are more certain.

Hume thought that IF beliefs in category 3 were justified, they would have to be justified solely on the basis of items in category 2. Descartes thought that IF beliefs in category 2 were justified, they would have to be justified solely on the basis of items in category 1. Notice that both of these points are IF statements. They don't assert that the beliefs in question actually are justified; the point is that Descartes and Hume agreed about what would need to be true IF the items in question were justified. This is something on which a skeptic and a nonskeptic might agree.

In spite of this similarity between the way Descartes and Hume formulated their respective problems about justification, they ended up defending very different solutions. Remember that Hume was a skeptic, whereas Descartes was not. Hume claimed that level 3 beliefs cannot be justified, whereas Descartes argued that level 2 beliefs can be justified.

I now want to advance a thesis about Descartes' problem and then extend that thesis so that it applies to Hume's problem as well. Let's grant Descartes that each of us is absolutely certain about his or her own present psychological state. My point is that these level 1 beliefs aren't enough to justify the beliefs I have about the physical environment I inhabit (level 2). I need an additional assumption concerning the relationship between levels 1 and 2. This connecting principle might take the form of claiming that God exists and is no deceiver, or it might take some other form. Hume thought that it is indubitable that God exists and is no deceiver. I argued before that he was mistaken in claiming this. But Descartes was right that the contents of my own experience are simply not enough, taken all by themselves, to justify the beliefs I have at level 2.

The parallel thesis about Hume's problem is as follows: if my beliefs about my present and past environment (items at level 2) are to justify the predictions and generalizations I believe (items at level 3), then I need to assume something about the relationship between levels 2 and 3. The principle of the uniformity of nature ("the future will resemble the past") is an example of this type of bridge principle. Or some other bridge principle might be proposed. The point is that my present perceptions and memories are simply not enough, taken all by themselves, to justify the beliefs I have at level 3.

Let's be clear on what I'm suggesting. First, note an obvious point: Level 1 statements don't deductively imply level 2 statements, and level 2 statements don't deductively imply level 3 statements. My point isn't this obvious fact about deductive relationships. I want to make a more ambitious claim. Not only do lower-level statements fail to deductively imply higher-level statements; I additionally claim that lower-level statements, all by themselves, are not enough to provide a justification for higher-level statements. Lower-level statements, taken by themselves, don't even provide good evidence for higher-level statements.

Whether *X* Is Evidence for *Y* Depends on Background Assumptions *Z*

This is a pretty radical thesis, I admit. Do your present experiences provide evidence about the physical environment you occupy? For example, does statement (a) below provide a rational justification for believing statement (b)?

> (a)   You seem to see a printed page in front of you now.
> (b)   There is a printed page in front of you now.

I claim that the answer depends on what you assume about the *relationship* between your present experiences and the world outside your mind. Given one set of assumptions, statement (a) might be excellent evidence that statement (b) is true. But given a different set of assumptions, statement (a) would be good evidence that statement (b) is false. The point is that these assumptions go beyond what is contained in level 1. Assumptions about the relationship of levels 1 and 2 aren't, properly speaking, contained in level 1. I hope my discussion of Descartes makes plausible what I'm saying about the relationship of (a) and (b). If you assume that the environment is "normal" and that your senses are functioning properly, then (a) is evidence favoring (b). If you assume that your senses are misleading you, however, then (a) would be evidence against (b).

What would the parallel claim be about the relationship of statements at levels 2 and 3? For example, does statement (c) provide strong evidence for statement (d)?

> (c)   I've examined lots of emeralds and all have been green.
> (d)   All emeralds are green.

We naturally take (c) to be evidence favoring (d). How could this be otherwise? Well, suppose you believed the following statement (the example is due to I. J. Good, "The White Shoe Is a Red Herring," *British Journal for the Philosophy of Science*, Vol. 17, 1967, p. 322):

> Either there are lots of emeralds, of which 99 percent are green, or there are very few emeralds, and all of them are green.

If you believed this, then (c) would be evidence *against* (d). On the other hand, if you believed the following statement, then (c) would provide evidence in favor of (d):

> If you examine lots of emeralds and all have been found to be green, then probably all emeralds are green.

Notice that the two possible assumptions just listed aren't strictly at level 2.

Whether (c) is evidence for or against (d) depends on what assumptions you make. If you make no assumptions about the relationship of levels 2 and 3, then the evidence described in (c) can't be interpreted as either favorable or unfavorable to (d). In a way, the present idea is something that has already come up in this book. I've already pointed out that hypotheses are testable only when background assumptions are added to them (Chapter 9). Here's an elaboration of that idea: When you test a hypothesis H and obtain some observations O, it will usually be true that O is evidence for or against H only because of the background assumptions (A) you made.

Another Relativity Thesis

We have here another example of a relativity thesis in philosophy. The idea of relativity, recall, came up in Chapter 14 in connection with the problem of knowledge. There it was argued that the Reliability Theory of Knowledge leads to the conclusion that whether S knows some proposition p depends on how one chooses to describe the environment that S inhabits. Different equally true descriptions of S's circumstances lead to opposite conclusions about whether S has knowledge. The present point concerns the concept of evidence, not the concept of knowledge. Is statement (c) evidence for statement (d)? No answer can be given until a third term is specified. Relative to one set of assumptions, the answer is *no*, but relative to another the answer is *yes*. We shouldn't ask whether one statement is evidence for another; rather, we should ask whether one statement is evidence for another relative to a stated set of background assumptions.

Foundationalism Leads to Skepticism

I'm claiming that the evidence relationship involves three things, not just two. Whether O is evidence for H depends on background assumptions (A). What impact does this point have on the problems that Hume and Descartes pursued about the concept of rational justification? My suggestion is that the problems they posed lead right to skepticism. If the challenge is to see if level 3 beliefs can be justified *solely by level 2 beliefs*, we must conclude that this can't be done. Similarly, if the problem is to see if level 2 beliefs can be justified *solely by level 1 beliefs*, we are forced to reach a negative conclusion in this case as well. Descartes wasn't a skeptic about the rational justifiability of level 2 beliefs. Hume was a skeptic about the rational justifiability of level 3 beliefs. My claim is that if we adopt a foundationalist understanding of what rational justification involves, then Descartes was wrong and Hume was right. In both Descartes' problem and Hume's problem, foundationalism leads to skepticism.

A Nonfoundationalist Approach to Justification

However, I don't think this shows that our beliefs are totally lacking in rational justification. Rather, I believe that the foundationalist misunderstands what it takes to rationally justify a belief. We *can* justify a level 3 belief. We do this by appealing to the other beliefs we have, some of which will themselves be at level 3. The same holds for the beliefs we have at level 2.

Think of how the task of justification works in everyday life and in science. If a scientist makes a prediction, or if we do this in our everyday lives, how are these predictions to be defended? If we say that the sun will rise tomorrow, we can support this prediction by appealing to other beliefs we have about the way the solar system has worked *and will continue to work*. In everyday life and science, we allow people to justify their beliefs at level 3 by appealing to other beliefs that are also at level 3. Often, predictions are justified by citing generalizations. In doing this, we aren't following the rules that foundationalism lays down. We aren't justifying a belief at one level strictly in terms of beliefs that are at lower levels.

What does this imply about whether our beliefs about the world are rationally justified? My point is to focus on what it means to ask for a rational justification. If we understand that idea in a foundationalist way, we will be led straight to skepticism—to the conclusion that the beliefs we have aren't rationally justifiable. On the other hand, if we recognize that the idea of rational justification needn't be understood in the way that foundationalism demands, skepticism doesn't threaten. In everyday life and in science, we frequently say that our beliefs are justified. When we do this, we aren't using a foundationalist understanding of the idea of rational justification. I'm suggesting that we are often perfectly correct when we say that this or that belief is well justified. Such claims are correct, in part, because rational justification is usually not understood in the way the foundationalist demands.

Standards of Justification Often Depend on the Audience

Our standards of rational justification often depend on the audience we have in mind. Suppose you believe some proposition that some other person does not. Your goal is to rationally persuade the other individual that you are right. In doing this, you will feel free to use as a premise in your argument any belief that the two of you share. If you agree about lots of things, there will be many propositions that you can use as premises. If, however, your disagreement with the other person is more pervasive, you will be much more limited in the premises you can use. And if the two of you somehow disagree about *everything*, it will be impossible for you to construct a rational argument that shows this person that the proposition in question is correct.

In everyday life, it is a familiar occurrence that one person rationally justifies some proposition to another. The same is true in science and in courts of law. This can happen because the two parties agree about enough; what they share is sufficient to allow an argument to be constructed that shows whether the proposition under dispute is correct. Matters change, however, when we ask someone to justify a proposition *to a skeptic*. A skeptic won't agree with you about many of the things you take for granted. If skeptics differ with you on sufficiently many beliefs, perhaps it will be impossible for you to rationally convince them that the proposition is true.

Foundationalists say that when you try to provide a rational justification of some proposition *p*, you must construct an argument that would be compelling *to a skeptic who doubts all the propositions that are at the same level as p*. This is one sort of activity, but there are others. A more familiar problem of rational justification is to construct an argument that would convince someone who doesn't already believe *p*, but who has lots of other beliefs at the same level as *p*. Even if the foundationalist's problem is insoluble, this doesn't mean that more familiar problems of rational justification are too.

Two Metaphors—Building a Building and Repairing a Raft

In Chapter 13, we examined the foundationalist idea that justifying our beliefs resembles building a building on solid foundations. The foundations must be perfectly solid; otherwise, the entire superstructure will be insecure. This is a good metaphor for foundationalism. Antifoundationalists think that it is fundamentally misleading. When we take up philosophical problems about rational justification, we already have many beliefs. Our job is not to strip them down to an indubitable core and then build them back up. Rather, what we need to do is to ask if we should change any of the beliefs we already have.

Otto Neurath (1882–1945) expressed this view of philosophy in the following analogy: "We are like sailors who must rebuild their ship on the open sea, without being able to dismantle the ship in dry dock or being able to reconstruct it from the best components." Solid foundations are impossible, but that doesn't mean that our beliefs are completely unjustified.

Review Questions

1   What is meant by saying that we have beliefs at levels 1–3? How does a foundationalist understand what it means for a belief at a level to be rationally justified? Are there any beliefs that are located at none of these three levels?

2   A relativity thesis is advanced in this chapter concerning the idea of evidence. What is that thesis? How does it go beyond the "obvious" fact that level 2 beliefs don't deductively imply beliefs at level 3?

3   How could the observation of lots of green emeralds be evidence against the claim that all emeralds are green?

4   Foundationalists understand the problem of rational justification in one way, but people in ordinary life usually think of the problem in another. What is the difference?

5   In what respect(s) do standards of justification depend on the audience to which the justification of a given belief is addressed? How might justificatory standards vary across audiences?

6   Does the observation that people typically don't attempt to justify their beliefs in a foundationalist manner in either daily life or scientific practice give us good reason to reject the foundationalist's central commitments? Why or why not?

7   Identify two problems that confront the foundationalist project in epistemology. Do you think these problems are sufficient reason to abandon any such project?

A Problem for Further Thought

In Chapter 7, I argued that scientific explanation is possible only for local why-questions. In the present chapter, I argued that you can rationally justify a proposition to someone only if you agree with that person about something. What similarities are there between these two theses?

Recommended Readings, Video, and Audio

Visit the companion website at www.routledge.com/cw/sober for suggestions of readings, video, and audio, for this chapter.

Locke on the Existence of External Objects

The last problem I want to discuss in this section of the book on epistemology concerns the beliefs we have about the physical objects in our environment. Consider your present belief that there is a book in front of you. There are several epistemological questions we could ask about this belief. Does this belief count as knowledge? Are you justified in believing the proposition that there is a book before you? What evidence do you have that this proposition is true? In Chapters 13 and 17, I discussed the first of these questions—the one about knowledge—in connection with Descartes' foundationalism. We discussed Descartes' theistic answer, that God is no deceiver, which means that if I am careful in my reasoning, I will not err in trusting the testimony of my senses. In the present lecture, I want to take up the third of these questions—the one about evidence. I'll do so by examining some ideas that the English philosopher John Locke (1632–1704) presents in his *Essay Concerning Human Understanding*.

Philosophers call the book in front of you an "external" object, meaning that it is not in your mind. Your mind can be thought of as "an internal world." It is populated by beliefs, desires, and feelings. Books and tables are physical objects in the external world. The experiences you are now having—for example, your present visual and tactile sensations—seem to provide you with evidence that there is a book in front of you. But how can what transpires in the internal world of your mind provide evidence concerning what is going on in the external world of physical objects? Locke read and learned from Descartes, but he does not argue for the existence of a God who is no deceiver to answer the question he wanted to address. In Book 4, Chapter 11, of the *Essay Concerning Human Understanding*, Locke tries to show that there are features that we can discern in our experience that show that those experiences provide evidence for the existence of external objects.

Before we get started on the details of Locke's argument, it is worth considering the kind of argument that Locke is attempting to construct. Suppose you are walking through an art gallery and are looking at several paintings that were all painted by a single artist. You wonder whether these paintings are pictures of real-world scenes or are fantasies produced by the artist's imagination. It seems that you can't answer this question just by looking at the paintings themselves. If the paintings are similar to each other, that doesn't seem to help, since an artist can produce similar paintings by looking at a single part of the external world, or by merely imagining a series of similar scenes. But suppose the paintings all contain unicorns and mermaids. Isn't this evidence that the paintings are fantasies, not paintings of a real-world scene? Maybe so, but here you are relying on information you have—that there are no unicorns and mermaids. This information isn't something you learned just by looking at the paintings. If this is the right thing to say about the paintings in the gallery, how can Locke successfully defend his thesis that the content of our experience provides evidence that there are external, physical objects?

Locke points out that "nobody can, in earnest, be so skeptical as to be uncertain of the existence of those things which he sees and feels." This is a correct psychological point. None of us is capable of seriously doubting that there are physical objects in our environment. One might say that it is part of *human nature* to think that an external world exists. However, this *psychological* point does not address the question of *epistemology*. Why *should* you think that the content of your experience provides evidence for the existence of external things? Locke gives the following answer: "This is certain: the confidence that our faculties do not herein deceive us is the greatest assurance we are capable of concerning the existence of material beings." This isn't much of an argument. Locke is talking about the following two propositions:

- Your sense organs do not deceive you.
- There are external objects.

He is saying that you are entitled to be confident that the first is true, and that this assures you that the second proposition is true as well. The problem is that the two propositions aren't separable in the way Locke suggests. Given the experiences you are having now, the first entails the second. Someone who questions the second proposition will also want to question the first; the brief argument of Locke's that I just quoted *begs the question* (Chapter 2). Locke then provides four more "concurrent reasons" for thinking that our experience provides evidence for the existence of external objects. Let's see if he does a better job of solving this problem.

Locke's First Argument—"Those That Want the Organs of Any Sense"

Locke's first reason has to do with people who are blind or lack some other (functioning) sense organ:

Those that want the organs of any sense, never can have the ideas belonging to that sense produced in their minds. This is too evident to be doubted: and therefore we cannot but be assured that they come in by the organs of that sense, and no other way. The organs themselves, it is plain, do not produce them: for then the eyes of a man in the dark would produce colours, and his nose smell roses in the winter: but we see nobody gets the relish of a pineapple, till he goes to the Indies, where it is, and tastes it.

Locke is arguing as follows:

> People who are blind do not have visual sensations.
> The visual experiences of sighted people are not caused by their having eyes.
> _____
> The visual experiences of sighted people are caused by external things.

Is the argument valid? If not, maybe a double line should be drawn between premises and conclusion to indicate that the premises are supposed to show that the conclusion is plausible or probable, not that it must be true. Also, are the premises true?

Locke's Second Argument—"Ideas Which Force Themselves upon Me"

Locke notes that sensation and memory are experienced differently:

> When my eyes are shut, or windows fast, I can at pleasure recall to my mind the ideas of light, or the sun, which former sensations had lodged in my memory; so I can at pleasure lay by that idea, and take into my view that of the smell of a rose, or taste of sugar. But, if I turn my eyes at noon towards the sun, I cannot avoid the ideas which the light or sun then produces in me. So that there is a manifest difference between the ideas laid up in my memory (over which, if they were there only, I should have constantly the same power to dispose of them, and lay them by at pleasure), and those which force themselves upon me, and I cannot avoid having. And therefore it must needs be some exterior cause, and the brisk acting of some objects without me, whose efficacy I cannot resist, that produces those ideas in my mind, whether I will or no.

Locke's argument might be put like this:

> I cannot mentally control whether I have the visual experiences I have.
> Those visual experiences have causes.
> _____
> The causes of those visual experiences are external to my mind.

Again, assess this argument: Do the premises provide a good reason to believe the conclusion? Are the premises true?

Locke's Third Argument—"Pleasure or Pain"

Locke's next argument also focuses on a difference between sensation and memory—in this case, the memory of a sensation:

> Pleasure or pain, which accompanies actual sensation, accompanies not the returning of those ideas without the external objects. Add to this, that many of those ideas are produced in us with pain, which afterwards we remember without the least offence. Thus, the pain of heat or cold, when the idea of it is revived in our minds, gives us no disturbance; which, when felt, was very troublesome; and is again, when actually repeated: which is occasioned by the disorder the external object causes in our bodies when applied to them: and we remember the pains of hunger, thirst, or the headache, without any pain

at all; which would either never disturb us, or else constantly do it, as often as we thought of it, were there nothing more but ideas floating in our minds, and appearances entertaining our fancies, without the real existence of things affecting us from abroad.

Locke then adds that "the same may be said of pleasure." Here is how I see Locke's argument:

> When I have a headache, I feel pain.
> When I remember the headache, I don't feel pain.
> This difference must have a cause.
> _____
>
> The difference is that an external object causes the headache, but not the memory of the headache.

Yes, same old drill—evaluate Locke's argument.

Locke's Fourth Argument—"Our Senses Assist One Another's Testimony"

This is my favorite:

> Our senses assist one another's testimony of the existence of outward things, and enable us to predict. Our senses in many cases bear witness to the truth of each other's report, concerning the existence of sensible things without us. He that sees a fire, may, if he doubt whether it be anything more than a bare fancy, feel it too; and be convinced, by putting his hand in it.

In Chapter 6, on evolution and creationism, I discussed the Principle of the Common Cause. Locke is using this principle here. When two students submit word-for-word identical essays, it is possible that they wrote their essays independently. However, it is far more plausible to think that they copied their essays from a common source—say, from a website on the Internet. Another example discussed in that chapter is the striking resemblance between the words in French, Spanish, and Italian for the numbers. This similarity might be a coincidence, but it is far more plausible to think that the similarities exist because these different languages are descendants of a common ancestor—Latin.

In Locke's example, the visual experience of fire tends to be accompanied by a tactile sensation of warmth. Why are these correlated? True, it might be a coincidence. However, it is far more plausible to think that the correlation is due to a common cause—an external object that causes both the visual impression _and_ the feeling of warmth. The same kind of argument can be developed concerning the different memories you have that are in agreement. Your visual impression right now resembles the experience you had a second ago, and also resembles the experience you had the second before that. You know that this resemblance exists by accessing your memories. The resemblance is plausibly explained by postulating the existence of an external object that persists through time—the book before you—which is the common cause of various experiences and of subsequent memory traces.

These considerations don't _prove_ that there are external objects, but the argument that makes use of the Principle of the Common Cause does seem to establish something more modest—that the content of your experience is _evidence_ for the existence of things that are outside of your experience—an external world.

Review Questions

1   How is Locke's approach to the question of how we have knowledge of (or evidence for) the existence of physical objects external to the mind different from that of Descartes?
2   Describe Locke's four arguments and evaluate them. Are they deductive, inductive, or abductive?
3   In Chapter 6, the Principle of the Common Cause was presented and it was said to be a consequence of the Surprise Principle, introduced in Chapter 3. How does the Surprise Principle apply to the fourth of Locke's arguments?
4   Which of Locke's four arguments discussed here do you find most convincing? Why?
5   Would a radical skeptic be convinced by Locke's arguments? If not, do you think this presents a problem for Locke? Why or why not?

A Problem for Further Thought

In discussing Locke's fourth argument, I describe two possible hypotheses. What are they? Are there other possibilities? If so, does considering them affect the conclusion of the argument?

Recommended Readings, Video, and Audio

Visit the companion website at www.routledge.com/cw/sober for suggestions of readings, video, and audio, for this chapter.

Part IV

Philosophy of Mind

Chapter 19

Dualism and the Mind/Body Problem

In this fourth part of the book, on philosophy of mind, I'll discuss three problems—the mind/body problem (Chapters 19–23), the problem of free will (Chapters 24–26), and the problem of psychological egoism (Chapter 27). The mind/body problem and the problem of free will both address the broad issue of how the mind is related to the physical world of cause and effect. Are minds physical things (for example, are they identical with brains?), or are they nonmaterial? If your beliefs and desires are caused by physical events outside of yourself, how can it be true that you act the way you do of your own free will? The last problem—the problem of psychological egoism—concerns the motives that drive us to act. Are people genuinely moved by the welfare of others, or is all behavior, in reality, selfish?

These three problems concern different stages in the causal chain that leads from genes and environment, to the mind, and then to action:

Mind

Genes	$\rightarrow$	Beliefs		
			$\rightarrow$	Actions
Environment	$\rightarrow$	Desires		
(1)		(2)		(3)

The mind/body problem concerns the nature of the objects and events that exist at stage 2 in this diagram. What is a mind? What are beliefs and desires? The problem of free will concerns the relation of stage 1 and stage 2. If our beliefs and desires are caused by the genes we possess and the environments we have inhabited, how can we possess free will? The problem of psychological egoism concerns the relationship of stages 2 and 3. If the actions we perform are caused by the desires we have, won't it be true that all action is fundamentally selfish—aimed at satisfying the actor's own desires, not at satisfying the needs of others? These are preliminary statements of the three philosophical problems. Each needs to be refined.

What Is the Mind/Body Problem?

The question posed by the mind/body problem is simple: What is the relationship between the mental and the physical? You have a mind, which contains various beliefs, desires, sensations, and emotions. You also have a brain; this physical thing is a structured piece of tissue containing an intricate web of neurons. Are your mind and your brain one and the same thing? Are your beliefs, desires, emotions, and sensations identical with physical things found in your brain? Or are your mind and your brain different objects? Perhaps the mind isn't a physical thing at all.

Descartes' Dualism

In the previous section, the discussion of Descartes focused on his epistemology. Descartes also advanced a solution to the mind/body problem. It is this view, now called Cartesian Dualism, that I'll now discuss. Dualism is the idea that there are two kinds of things in the world. There are physical objects on the one hand, and, on the other, there are mental objects (like minds, pains, and beliefs). According to dualism, brains and the bodies in which they are found are physical things; the mind, which is a nonphysical object, is distinct from both the whole body and is also distinct from all of the body's physical parts. Descartes didn't deny that there are causal interactions between the mental and the physical; taking aspirin can cure headaches, and the sound of trumpets can lift your spirits. In the other direction, it seems undeniable that beliefs and desires can cause the parts of your body to move in various ways (speaking, walking, etc.). But granting this two-way interaction did not lead Descartes to abandon dualism.

The Mind/Brain Identity Theory

One alternative to dualism is provided by the Mind/Brain Identity Theory. This theory makes a claim about objects and also about the properties those objects possess. First, it says that your mind and your brain are one and the same object. Second, it claims that the mental properties you have (for example, believing that fire is hot, or wanting some ice cream, or being in pain) are physical properties; to be in pain is to have a certain type of physical event occur in your central nervous system.

The identity theory asserts that mental terminology and physical terminology describe the same items in the world. The following analogy may be instructive. For a long time, people used the term "water" to denote various items in the world. This term was used in everyday life. At a certain point in the history of science, it was discovered that water is made of H_2O molecules. The discovery was that water and H_2O are one and the same thing. There certainly is a difference between the two pieces of terminology "water" and

"H$_2$O." The first word has been used by ordinary people for a very long time. The second term was introduced much more recently, as part of a scientific theory. Yet it does not follow from these facts about the two terms that the terms denote different things. Water is identical with H$_2$O, as chemists have discovered.

Philosophers who defend the Mind/Brain Identity Theory say that the same point applies to the relationship of mental terms and neurophysiological terms. Common sense has for a very long time deployed such terms as "belief," "desire," "pain," and "mind." The identity theory suggests that what happened to water will happen to the mind. Eventually neurophysiology will discover the nature of the mind, just as chemistry discovered the nature of water. Once various scientific theories have been developed, we will understand what it is to believe that snow is white, what it is to want some coffee, what it is to feel pain, what it is to have a mind. In each case, the answer will be given in the vocabulary provided by brain science. We now have only a very partial picture of what these neurophysiological theories will be like. However, the identity theory predicts that science is headed in the direction of a purely materialistic account of the mind. The mind is a physical thing, even though we now have only an incomplete picture of what its physical nature is.

In addition to dualism and the Mind/Brain Identity Theory, there are other solutions to the mind/body problem that I'll discuss. These are logical behaviorism (Chapter 20) and functionalism (Chapter 23). Rather than describing them right now, I'll turn to the task of analyzing Cartesian Dualism.

Immortality of the Soul

Before I present Descartes' arguments for dualism, I should note a connection between the mind/body problem and an issue in the philosophy of religion. If you believe the doctrine of the immortality of the soul but also hold that the body disintegrates at death, you may be attracted by dualism. The issue of whether the soul is immortal, of course, isn't the same as the question of whether there is a God. After all, there are many religions that deny the immortality of the soul. Conversely, someone might hold that the soul survives the death of the body and yet deny that there is a God. But historically it is worth remembering that what we might call "traditional" Christianity (this includes the Christianity of Descartes' time) espouses the doctrine of immortality. Dualism makes room for this possibility.

If the soul is part of the mind (even if it isn't the entirety of the mind) and if the soul lives forever and the body does not, we have an argument for dualism. However, this isn't Descartes' argument for dualism. Why not? Perhaps the reason is that anyone who doubts dualism will also probably doubt that any part of the mind survives the death of the body. So you aren't going to convince anyone that dualism is true by beginning with the premise that the soul is immortal.

Leibniz's Law

Note a structural feature of the argument for dualism that I just described. The argument defends dualism by trying to find a property that the mind has but the brain lacks; the property in question is immortality. Quite apart from whether this argument is successful, we should note a perfectly sensible principle that it uses. The idea is that if m and b are identical, then they must have all the same properties. This principle is called Leibniz's Law, after the seventeenth-century philosopher/mathematician (who, incidentally, co-invented the calculus with Newton. In Chapter 7, I briefly discussed Leibniz's belief that we live in the best of all possible worlds). Leibniz's Law is sometimes called the principle of the *indiscernibility of identicals*. It states that if you can find even one property that *m* has and *b* lacks, then you will have shown that *m* and *b* are distinct entities. You'll see this principle at work in both of the arguments that Descartes presents for dualism. The following form of argument is deductively valid:

> *m* has property *P*.
> *b* does not have property *P*.
> If *m* has a property that *b* lacks, then *m* ≠ *b*.
> _____
>
> *m* ≠ *b*.

Be sure you see how the argument concerning immortality has this logical form. The argument is valid. This means that if you reject the conclusion, you must reject at least one of the premises. I suggest that the third premise (Leibniz's Law) is true. Therefore, if you reject the conclusion, you must reject one of the first two premises.

Descartes' First Argument for Dualism—The Indubitable Existence Argument

Now let's look at Descartes' first argument for dualism. In Chapter 13, I discussed how Descartes uses the method of doubt in his epistemology. He also uses the idea of doubt in his discussion of the mind/body problem.

In the *Second Meditation*, Descartes claims you can't doubt that you have a mind. If you try to doubt that you have a mind, you will find yourself entertaining a thought, and so you must grant that you have a mind after all. Descartes thought that the existence of the body has a quite different status. He thought that it *is* possible for you to doubt that you have a body. After all, you *can* entertain the thought that you are a disembodied spirit. Descartes concludes that your mind has a property that your body lacks. You can doubt the existence of the one, but not the existence of the other. Dualism follows, by Leibniz's Law.

Perhaps you are suspicious of what Descartes says about your body. Is it really possible for you to doubt that you have a body? Can you conceive of yourself being a disembodied spirit? You should also consider Descartes' other premise. Is Descartes right that you can't doubt that you have a mind?

I'm not going to pursue these questions here. I'll grant Descartes that he *can't* doubt that he has a mind and that he *can* doubt that he has a body. I want to consider whether dualism validly follows from these premises. To see whether this follows, we must be very explicit about what the property is that the mind is said to have and the body is said to lack. Descartes claims that his mind has the property of *indubitable existence*, and that his body lacks that property. Let's look more closely at this property. For an object *X* to have this property means that the "owner" of *X* can't doubt that *X* exists. I say "owner" since *my* mind does not have indubitable existence *for you*. I take it that *you* have no trouble entertaining the thought that *I* don't have a mind. It is the first-person case that matters here—a person can't doubt the existence of his or her own mind.

An Analogy

There is a subtle mistake in Descartes' argument. I'm going to argue that indubitable existence is not a genuine property at all.

I'll illustrate this idea by an example. Lois Lane wants to marry Superman. She doesn't realize that Superman and Clark Kent are one and the same person. Clark Kent, you'll recall, is the most incompetent reporter at the *Daily Planet*. If you ask Lois whether she wants to marry Clark Kent, she will say "No!" Does it follow from this (via Leibniz's Law) that Superman and Clark Kent are two different people? Of course not. The following argument is not valid:

> Lois Lane wants to marry Superman.
> Lois Lane does not want to marry Clark Kent.
> ───────────────
> Superman is not identical with Clark Kent.

On the surface, it looks as if this argument is valid, given Leibniz's Law. It describes a property that Superman has and Clark Kent lacks and concludes that they are nonidentical. What you must see is that the argument does not describe any such property. Leibniz's Law, properly understood, does not license the conclusion of nonidentity. The two premises are true, but the conclusion does not follow from them; it is false.

Superman and Clark Kent have exactly the same properties. This isn't contradicted by the fact that Lois Lane wants one of the following *propositions* to be true and the other to be false:

> Lois Lane marries Superman.
> Lois Lane marries Clark Kent.

The fact that Lois desires one of these propositions to be true and the other to be false does not show that Superman and Clark Kent have different properties. The propositions are different; the people are identical.

Likewise, Descartes says that I am able to doubt one, but not the other, of the following two *propositions*:

> I have a brain.
> I have a mind.

But from this, it does not follow that my brain has a different property from my mind. The *propositions* are different, but that doesn't show that your brain and your mind are different objects.

Propositional Attitudes and Aboutness

The crucial distinction we have to note here is this: doubting and desiring are attitudes we have towards *propositions*; doubting, desiring, and believing are examples of *propositional attitudes*. Perhaps there are some propositions whose truth cannot be doubted, whereas there are other propositions that we are able to doubt. Surely we desire that some propositions, but not others, should be true. But separate from this issue concerning propositions is the issue of what *objects* those propositions are about. Here is the lesson I draw from the example about Lois Lane: *Even if one proposition is desired whereas another is not, it does not follow that what the first proposition is about differs from what the second proposition is about.* The same point holds when we consider other propositional attitudes, like doubting. What follows from these two statements?

Lois Lane wants it to be true that Lois Lane marries Superman.
Lois Lane does not want it to be true that Lois Lane marries Clark Kent.

What follows is that the proposition *Lois Lane marries Superman* is a different proposition from the proposition *Lois Lane marries Clark Kent*. What does *not* follow is that the person the first proposition is about (Superman) differs from the person the second proposition is about (Clark Kent). (Note to the reader: if you think that Superman and Clark Kent are different individuals, please invent an example in which a single person has two names and show how this example illustrates the relevant point about propositional attitudes and aboutness.)

What follows from these two statements?

I can't doubt that I have a mind.
I can doubt that I have a body.

What follows is that the proposition *I have a mind* is a different proposition from the proposition *I have a body*. What does *not* follow is that the object the first proposition is about (my mind) differs from the object the second proposition is about (my body).

With this diagnosis in hand, let's go back to Descartes' argument for dualism. He says that his mind has the property of indubitable existence, whereas his body does not have that property. It *sounds* as if Descartes is describing a property that the one thing has but the other thing lacks. But this, I claim, is deceptive. Indubitable existence is not a property of an object; rather, doubting is something we do or fail to do to propositions. To say that my mind indubitably exists is just to say that I cannot doubt a particular proposition. To say that my body does not indubitably exist is just to say that I can doubt a particular proposition. From this difference between propositions, however, nothing follows concerning whether those propositions are about the same or different things. Descartes' first argument for dualism is invalid.

16 Sense and Reference

The philosopher/logician Gottlob Frege (1848–1925) wanted to explain a difference that separates the following two statements:

The Evening Star is the Evening Star.
The Evening Star is the Morning Star.

The first of these is obviously true; it is a logical truth of the form "$a = a$." It is *a priori*; anyone who understands the meanings of the terms in this sentence will be able to see that it is true, there being no need for astronomical observation. The second statement is different. It describes a discovery that astronomers made; it is *a posteriori*. The phrase "*the Evening Star*" is used to refer to the first star to appear in the evening. "*The Morning Star*" is an expression that is used to refer to the last star to disappear in the morning. It was discovered that these are one and the same object—namely, the planet Venus.

Notice that the terms occurring in the two statements refer to exactly the same thing. How, then, can the statements express different thoughts? Frege said that the explanation of this fact is that terms have sense (meaning) as well as reference. Although "*the Morning Star*" and "*the Evening Star*" are terms that refer to the same thing (the planet Venus), the two expressions aren't synonymous; they have different meanings. Frege thought that synonymous terms must refer to the same thing, but that terms that refer to the same thing need not be synonymous.

The meaning of a term determines its reference, but not conversely. He also believed that the "truth value" of a statement (that is, whether the statement is true or false) is settled just by the reference of the terms it contains.

Consider the statement "The inventor of bifocals is dead." This statement is true. If Frege were right to say that the truth value of a statement is determined by the reference of the terms it contains, then we should be able to remove a term from this statement, replace it with a coreferring term, and have the resulting statement still be true. We can do this: "the inventor of bifocals" and "the first U.S. ambassador to France" are coreferential. Substituting one for the other, we obtain the following sentence: "The first U.S. ambassador to France is dead." This statement is true. In this case, a true statement remains true if one of its terms is replaced by another that is coreferring.

Statements describing propositional attitudes posed a problem for Frege. Even though "*Superman*" and "*Clark Kent*" refer to the same person, the first, but not the second, of the following statements is true:

Lois Lane wanted to marry Superman.
Lois Lane wanted to marry Clark Kent.

To account for this fact, Frege suggested that terms in such sentences don't refer to the objects that they normally refer to. Normally, "Superman" and "Clark Kent" refer to a person. But in the above pair of sentences, Frege claimed that a shift occurs; the first refers to the meaning of the term "Superman," whereas the second refers to the meaning of the term "Clark Kent." Since these terms have different meanings, it won't be true that the terms in the first sentence refer to precisely the same things that the terms in the second sentence refer to. This makes it possible for the first sentence to be true and the second false. In this way, Frege was able to retain his principle that the truth value of a sentence is determined by the reference of its constituent terms.

When you say, "Lois Lane shook hands with Superman," you are referring to Superman. When you say "Lois Lane wanted to marry Superman," you aren't referring to Superman, according to this proposal of Frege's. If you believe that you are referring to Superman in both statements, then you will reject Frege's account of how statements about propositional attitudes should be understood.

Descartes' Second Argument for Dualism—The Divisibility Argument

I now turn to Descartes' second argument for dualism. It is far simpler than the one just analyzed. In the *Sixth Meditation*, Descartes claims that physical things have spatial parts. For example, a surgeon could divide my brain into pieces. My mind, however, does not have spatial parts. If so, dualism follows, by Leibniz's Law. Descartes also says that the body, but not the mind, has *extension*. By this he means that the body, but not the mind, takes up physical space; it has spatial location. This also leads to dualism, by Leibniz's Law.

I'll treat these two arguments together: if the body has the properties of divisibility and extension, but the mind does not, dualism follows. I think that Descartes' argument here is valid. The question is whether his premises are true. I'll grant Descartes that it sounds odd to say that my mind has spatial parts and that it is located between my ears. It also sounds strange to say that my mind weighs about five pounds and has blood vessels running through it. How are we to explain the fact that such claims sound funny to us? One explanation is that they can't be true. If this were right, dualism would follow, since we then would have cited properties that my brain has but my mind does not. However, there is another possible explanation for why it sounds odd to say that my mind has spatial parts, or weighs five pounds, or has blood vessels running through it. The explanation is that these ideas are unfamiliar. The assertions sound jarring because they radically depart from what we happen to believe.

Consider the claim that water is H_2O. Before the advent of the atomic theory, the claim that a liquid is made of numerous tiny particles that are too small to see may have sounded pretty strange to some people. But this, of course, does not mean that water could not be made of molecules of H_2O. For this reason, I claim that Descartes' second argument for dualism is inconclusive. If the mind and the brain are really identical, then many surprising facts may follow.

I conclude that Descartes' arguments for dualism do not work. The first argument (involving the idea of indubitable existence) is invalid. The second argument (involving the ideas of divisibility and extension) is valid, but it begs the question. There seems to be no reason to accept the premises (that the mind is indivisible and lacks extension) unless you already believe that the conclusion (dualism) is true. These negative verdicts don't show that dualism is false. All I've claimed so far is that these two arguments for dualism are unsuccessful. I now turn to a criticism that has been made of dualism.

Causality between the Physical and the Nonphysical

One of the main stumbling blocks for dualism has been the idea, endorsed by Cartesian Dualism, that there can be causal interactions between physical and nonphysical things. Descartes thought that physical events in your body can cause sensations in your mind. These sensations, like all mental events, allegedly lack spatial location. But how can events that are located in space bring about events that lack spatial location? And how are causal relations in the opposite direction possible? In *The Passions of the Soul*, Descartes claimed that the pineal gland in the brain is the jumping-off point for this interaction. Nerve impulses reach the pineal gland and then manage to affect the mind, even though the mind is not located anywhere at all. Conversely, your mind (which is no place at all) influences your body by making an impact on the pineal gland. This is pretty mysterious, and dualists since Descartes have not managed to make this process any more comprehensible.

Causality is something we understand best when we consider two physical events that are linked by a physical signal. When we say that throwing the switch on the wall caused the ceiling light to go on, we are talking about two physical events that occur at different times and at different places. These two events are connected by the flow of electricity. We not only know *that* throwing the switch caused the light to go on; we also know *how* throwing the switch managed to bring this about. If we were unable to detect a physical signal passing from the switch to the light, we would be puzzled about how the first event was able to cause the second. Similarly, if I said that throwing the switch caused an event that isn't located anywhere at all, you would be puzzled how electricity or any other physical signal could reach an event that has no spatial location.

In light of the difficulty of understanding how causality can "cross over" from the mental to the physical and back again, wouldn't it be simpler to account for the causal interaction of the mind and the body by adopting the identity theory? If the mind and the brain are identical, it isn't terribly puzzling how your beliefs and desires can cause you to behave in various ways. This doesn't prove that the Mind/Brain Identity Theory is correct; the point is just that what is a hard question for dualism to answer isn't especially hard for the identity theory.

Review Questions

1 What does dualism assert? What is the Mind/Brain Identity Theory?
2 What is Leibniz's Law? How is it used in arguments supporting dualism?
3 "I can't doubt that I have a mind, but I can doubt that I have a body. Hence, my mind isn't identical with my body." Is this argument valid?
4 "My brain is divisible into spatial parts, is located between my ears, weighs about five pounds, and has blood vessels running through it. My mind has none of these properties. Hence, my brain and my mind are nonidentical." Is this argument valid? If it is valid, must dualism be true?
5 Dualism has been thought to make mysterious how the mind and the body can causally interact. What problem is involved here?
6 According to the Mind/Brain Identity Theory, do mentalistic terms like "belief" or "pain" compete with physical terms like "neuronal impulse" or "synaptic cleft"? Should we aim to preserve the use of both mental terms and physical terms? Why or why not?
7 Reconstruct Descartes' first argument for dualism. Is it valid? If not, why not? (Are the premises true? Is the conclusion true? Explain your answers.)
8 Descartes' first and second arguments for dualism both appeal to the same principle: namely, Leibniz's Law. Will the same objection suffice to undermine both? If not, why not?
9 What is a propositional attitude? Give three examples that aren't discussed above.
10 Consider the following set of propositions: (1) "Linda remembers receiving an autograph from Muhammad Ali." (2) "Linda does not remember receiving an autograph from Cassius Clay."

   • Do these propositions contain any reference to propositional attitudes? If so, which?
   • Do these propositions attribute any properties to objects? If so, which objects?
   • What conclusion, if any, can you derive from these two propositions? (Does it follow that Muhammad Ali and Cassius Clay are different people?)

Problems for Further Thought

1 Descartes says that he can conceive of himself being a disembodied spirit (that is, having a mind but not a body). What does conceiving of something mean? Does Descartes' claim entail that it is possible for him to be a disembodied spirit? (See discussion of conceivability and possibility in Chapter 8.)
2 Is a statue identical with the stone it is made of? Is an organism identical with the collection of cells in its body? Can Leibniz's Law be used to show that either of these claims of identity is false?
3 In the *Sixth Meditation*, Descartes argues that he is *essentially* a thinking thing. An essential property of a thing is a property that the thing must have if it is to exist. Could Descartes be deprived of thought and still be Descartes? Could Descartes have been born without the capacity of thought and still be Descartes? If Descartes can't doubt that he thinks, is that enough to show that Descartes is essentially a thinking thing?
4 It was suggested in this chapter that we understand causality best when there is a physical signal that passes from cause to effect (the electricity example). However, the fact that "absences" are sometimes causes suggests that causality need *not* involve a physical

signal. For example, suppose a patient dies because his doctor fails to give him medicine. There is no "physical signal" between doctor and patient in this case, but there is causation. Does this point solve the objection to dualism that concerns the nature of causality?

Recommended Readings, Video, and Audio

Visit the companion website at www.routledge.com/cw/sober for suggestions of readings, video, and audio, for this chapter.

Chapter 20

Logical Behaviorism

In 1949, Gilbert Ryle, a philosopher at Oxford University, published an influential book called *The Concept of Mind*. In it he presented a solution to the mind/body problem that has come to be called logical behaviorism. His views have something in common with those expressed by Ludwig Wittgenstein in his posthumously published *Philosophical Investigations* (1953). Later, an American philosopher deeply influenced by Wittgenstein, Norman Malcolm, elaborated this philosophical position in his book *Dreaming* (1959).

Logical behaviorism is a thesis about the meaning of the mentalistic terms we use in ordinary speech. Logical behaviorism tries to describe what we mean when we talk of an individual's thoughts, beliefs, intentions, dreams, and sensations. This thesis about meaning is quite different from a doctrine called methodological behaviorism, which I'll discuss in the next chapter. Methodological behaviorism is a thesis about science. It doesn't offer a linguistic analysis of ordinary speech; rather, it gives advice about how a productive science of psychology should be developed. Logical behaviorism advances both negative and positive claims. The negative part criticizes other views of the mind; the positive part offers an account of what mentalistic terminology means.

The Attack on "the Ghost in the Machine"

Ryle thought that the common-sense view of the mind is deeply confused. According to Ryle, common sense is committed to the idea that mental states are inner causes of behavior. To see what he means, suppose we ask why Joe lifted the cup to his lips. A common-sense answer might be that he did this because he *wanted* a drink of water and *believed* that there was water in the cup. This common sense explanation says that mental states are inner states that Joe occupies, ones which cause his outward behavior. According to common-sense, we see the behavior (the drinking), but we don't see the beliefs and desires that cause it. The beliefs and desires are "inside"; they can't be directly observed by third parties, though their effects—behavior—can be. I'll use the term "mentalism" to name this common-sense idea that mental states are inner causes of behavior. Ryle thought that this natural picture is deeply confused—mentalism is one-half of what he called the myth of "the Ghost in the Machine."

Ryle also held that common sense embraces *dualism*. This is the other half of what Ryle calls the myth of the Ghost in the Machine. Although Ryle lumped mentalism and dualism together, we need to keep them separate. Mentalism and dualism are different. Someone who thinks that the mind and the brain are identical—that mental states are states of the central nervous system—would reject dualism but would agree that mental states are inner causes of behavior. So mentalism does not imply dualism.

Why did Ryle reject mentalism—that minds exist and are quite different from the behaviors they cause? I'll discuss one of his main reasons. Ryle thought that the view of minds as inner causes leads to what I'll call *third-person skepticism*.

Logical Behaviorism Says Mentalism Is False Because It Leads to Skepticism

Ryle's argument goes as follows. If mental states were inner, then the mental states of others would be hidden from us. Each of us would be able to observe the behaviors of others, but not the beliefs and desires that others have. Because of this, we wouldn't be able to know what others think or want. At best, the only facts we would know about the mind would come to us via *first-person introspection*. I can tell by examining my own mind what I think, want, and feel. However, if mental states were inner, I would have no way of knowing anything about what mental states you occupy. Ryle thought we clearly *do* have knowledge of the mental characteristics of others. He concluded that mental states can't be inner causes of behavior.

The deductively valid argument that Ryle advances goes like this:

(1) If mental states were inner causes of behavior, we would not have knowledge of the mental states of others.
(2) We do have knowledge of the mental states of others.

———————————

Hence, mental states are not inner causes of behavior.

Since the argument is valid, if you want to reject the conclusion, you must reject one or both of the premises. My view is that premise (2) is true. I also think that the conclusion is false. This means that I must reject premise (1). To do this, I must explain how we can have knowledge of the inner mental states of others.

Do We Know about the Mental States of Others by Analogy with Our Own Case?

A traditional explanation of how we are able to have knowledge of the mental states of others is via an *argument by analogy*. In 1948, Bertrand Russell advanced this argument in his book *Human Knowledge: Its Scope and Limits*, but the argument has been put forward by many philosophers. It is offered as a solution to the so-called "problem of other minds." I know by introspection that I have a mind. I also see by observing my own body that I behave in certain ways. I note that some of my behaviors tend to be associated with some of my mental states. For example, when I hurt my finger by stabbing it with a pin, I tend to say "Ouch!" I then look at others and notice that they produce certain behaviors. They say "Ouch!" on some occasions. I reason, by analogy, that others probably have minds and occupy the mental states that I do when I produce the same behaviors.

So the analogy argument goes like this:

> In my own case, I notice that when I produce behavior *B*, I usually am in mental state *M*.
> I observe that another individual (*O*) is now producing behavior *B*.
> [════════════════]
> So, *O* is now in mental state *M*.

The double line indicates that the argument isn't supposed to be deductively valid. Rather, the analogy argument says that the conclusion is probable if the premises are true. The analogy argument aims to show how we can have knowledge of the inner mental states of others. If the argument works, it refutes Ryle's claim that mentalism leads to third-person skepticism. But is the analogy argument persuasive?

The usual criticism of this argument is that it is very weak because the evidence is limited to my own case. It is like arguing that since *I* own a green chair, probably *everyone* has one. I agree with this criticism: An induction from one's own case to a conclusion about *all* human beings bases too ambitious a conclusion on too slender an evidential basis. The sample size is too small. Although the analogy argument does not refute premise (1) in Ryle's argument, I still think this premise of Ryle's is mistaken. We can see why by thinking about abduction, not induction.

Abduction

Let's view the beliefs and desires we attribute to others as theoretical postulates. We don't directly observe what other individuals think and want; we observe their behavior. We then invent a "theory" whose adequacy is judged by its ability to explain and predict behavior. My suggestion is that there are many cases in which the ascription of mental states to others is well confirmed by the behaviors we observe. (Of course, there also are cases in which our claims about what people think and want are undermined by what we subsequently observe them do, but that isn't in dispute.)

What's the difference between this solution to the problem of other minds and the analogy argument? In the analogy argument, I begin with an observation of myself and then seek to extend that description to other individuals. In the abductive argument, I make no mention of introspection. Mendel never observed a gene, but that is no objection to his theory. The fact that genes are inner causes of how tall a pea plant grows, or of whether its peas will be wrinkled or smooth, does not mean that we can't know about genes (see Chapter 3). Likewise, the view that mental states are inner causes of behavior does not lead to third-person skepticism. Ryle's criticism of mentalism is mistaken.

There is a simple but important distinction that needs to be drawn here. The following two questions are different; they need not have the same answers:

(1)   Is proposition *P* about observable things and only observable things?
(2)   Is proposition *P* testable by observation?

The Mendelian case and the case of claims about the mental states of others provide examples in which the answers are (1) *no* and (2) *yes*.

This discussion of the problem of other minds should remind you of material discussed in Chapter 5 concerning the role of analogy and induction in the Argument from Design for the existence of God. Hume criticized the Argument from Design for being a weak analogy argument and for being a weak induction. How is my reply to Hume similar to the reply I just made to Ryle?

Logical Behaviorism's Positive Thesis—Its Analysis of Mentalistic Vocabulary

In addition to criticizing mentalism, Ryle also advances a positive thesis about how statements about beliefs and desires should be understood. Logical behaviorists maintain not just that belief is *not* an inner state; they also make a positive claim about what it *is* for an agent to believe something.

Logical behaviorism says that the meanings of mentalistic terms can be specified purely in terms of behavior. For example, what does it mean to say that someone wants a drink of water? The following proposal, though false, at least is consistent with the requirements that logical behaviorism imposes on the problem:

S wants to drink water $=_{df}$ S drinks.

The subscript "df" means that the two statements are said to be equivalent by definition. This proposal is false; people who want a drink of water don't always get to drink. Notice, however, that the proposal obeys the rules that logical behaviorism lays down. The proposal analyzes the meaning of a mentalistic term ("wants to drink water") in purely behavioral language ("drinks"). Behaviorists usually admit that proposals like this one are too crude. They suggest, instead, that the meaning of mentalistic terminology cannot be given in terms of *actual* behavior, but can be given in terms of *dispositions* to behave. A more satisfactory suggestion, logical behaviorists maintain, is the following:

S wants to drink some water $=_{df}$ S is disposed to drink water.

I have two criticisms of this proposal. First, it is incomplete. When the proposal is fleshed out, it turns out not to be consistent with the requirements of logical behaviorism. Second, I'll claim that even if the proposal were true, it would not establish what logical behaviorists hold—namely, that mentalistic terminology does not describe inner causes of outward behavior.

The Dispositional Analysis of Desire Is Incomplete

I begin with the charge of incompleteness. Wanting to drink water is supposed to be a disposition to drink water. Suppose Joe wants to drink some water and we place a cup of water before him, but he does not drink. Why not? The answer might be that he does not *believe* the cup contains water. However, this means that the behaviorist's proposed definition must be corrected so that it reads as follows:

S wants to drink water = $_{df}$ S is disposed to drink those things that S believes are water

Notice that the proposal now is not consistent with behaviorist requirements. The present proposal analyzes a desire in terms of a disposition to behave *and* a belief. So we have not analyzed the mentalistic concept in *purely* behavioral terms.

I doubt that behaviorists can overcome this problem. Our common-sense mentalistic concepts seem to have the following property: attributing a *single* mentalistic property to an agent does not, by itself, have implications concerning how the agent will behave. What has such implications are *batches* of mentalistic properties. If an agent wants, above all else, to drink water *and* believes that the cup before him contains water, perhaps this implies that he will reach for the cup and drink its contents (but what if he is paralyzed?). However, the desire *by itself* has no such implication and neither does the belief.

A Dispositional Analysis Does Not Refute Mentalism

My second objection to logical behaviorism's proposal for how mentalistic terms are to be analyzed is this: even if mentalistic concepts could be analyzed purely in terms of behavioral dispositions, that would not disprove the mentalistic thesis that mental states are inner causes of outward behavior. To see why, I want to describe an analogy that David Armstrong (whose views on the Reliability Theory of Knowledge were discussed in Chapter 14) noticed between the supposed dispositional property of wanting a drink and other nonmental properties that clearly are dispositional in character. Dispositional properties are often named in English with "ible" or "able" suffixes. For example, to say that a lump of sugar is *soluble* is to say that it is disposed to dissolve. Solubility is a dispositional property. It is not hard to give a "behavioral analysis" of solubility. To say that something is water-soluble is to say that it is disposed to behave in a certain way when placed in a certain situation:

X is soluble (in water) = $_{df}$ If X were immersed (in water), then X would dissolve.

Dissolving is a behavior; to immerse something is to place it in a particular sort of environment. This definition of solubility conforms to behavioristic requirements, since it makes no mention of the inner state that soluble substances might occupy. I have no objection to this behaviorist definition of solubility. My point is that the adequacy of this definition does not mean that there is no inner state of lumps of sugar that makes them dissolve when immersed. In fact, chemistry provides a scientific description of the inner features of sugar that make sugar dissolve when immersed in water. Solubility is a dispositional property, but this is consistent with the fact that soluble substances have internal, structural properties that make them behave as they do.

How is this relevant to the logical behaviorist's attempt to analyze mental states? Even if wanting to drink water were a behavioral disposition—one that could be described without mentioning any inner state of the organism—this would not show that wants aren't inner states. On the contrary, there is every reason to think that when something has a dispositional property, there is a *physical basis* of that disposition. When an organism is disposed to drink water, it is entirely appropriate to ask what it is about the organism's internal makeup that disposes it to act in this way.

This completes my criticism of logical behaviorism's positive thesis. I claim that the meanings of mentalistic terms (like "wants," "believes") cannot be analyzed in purely behavioral language. In addition, I have argued that even if such an analysis could be provided (by describing mental states as "dispositions to behave"), it would not follow that mental states aren't inner causes of behavior.

---

17 Pain without Pain Behavior?

Curare, the poison that some South American Indians traditionally used on their darts, paralyzes its subject. In the 1930s and 1940s, scientists purified curare and studied its effects on the central nervous system. At first, some doctors thought that curare was a painkiller; they noticed that if you give curare to your patient before surgery, the patient will not move under the knife. After surgery, the patients complained that they experienced great pain, but for a time, the physicians didn't believe them (many of the patients were children). Eventually a physician volunteered to undergo surgery with curare; he reported that the pain was vivid and excruciating. After that, doctors realized that curare isn't a painkiller; it simply immobilizes the patient.

Daniel Dennett (in "Why You Can't Make a Computer That Feels Pain," *Brainstorms*, MIT Press, 1978) suggests the following puzzle. An amnesiac is a drug that makes you forget. Suppose that you gave someone curare and an amnesiac before surgery. Would the individual feel pain? The patient would not say "ouch" or writhe during surgery. And after surgery, the patient would not say "that was horribly painful." Let's use the term "pain behavior" to name any behavior that usually accompanies pain. In Dennett's puzzle, there is no pain behavior, either during the surgery or after. The question is, can there be pain without pain behavior? Dennett's example suggests that the answer is yes. Would you be prepared to undergo surgery with curare and an amnesiac as the only drugs you get? If not, the reason is probably that you think that you would still feel pain.

What does this example show about the claim that mentalistic terms do not describe the inner causes of behavior, but describe only the behavior itself?

Review Questions

1   What is the "problem of other minds"? Does the analogy argument from one's own case solve this problem? Ryle thought that the mental states of others would be unknowable if mental states were inner causes of behavior. Why did Ryle think this?

2   What is logical behaviorism? Can a logical behaviorist analysis be given of the statement "Jones believes that there is rat poison in the gravy"?

3   Suppose that a mentalistic concept (like wanting to drink water) could be analyzed as a disposition to behave. Would that show that wants aren't inner causes of behavior?

4   What is "the problem of other minds"? How do advocates of the analogy argument attempt to resolve this problem? How convincing do you find their strategy?

5   Why does Ryle claim that we cannot have knowledge of other persons' mental states if such states are inner causes of behavior? Is his argument valid? Is it sound?

6   What, according to Ryle, is the core commitment that underpins both "mentalism" and the use of mentalistic terminology? Why does Ryle insist that we reject this commitment?

7   Are all propositions that can be tested by observation necessarily about observable things, and only observable things? Can you think of a proposition, in addition to the ones discussed above, that is both (1) testable via observation and (2) not about observables?

8   What is the positive thesis advanced by Logical Behaviorism? How, if at all, does it relate to its negative counterpart? Can one reasonably accept the negative thesis while rejecting the positive thesis, or vice versa?

9   Identify and explain two problems with the dispositional analysis of mentalistic terms. Which, if any, do you think is most problematic for the logical behaviorist?

Problems for Further Thought

1   I've suggested that an abductive argument can solve the problem of other minds. Construct such an argument, making clear how the Surprise Principle (Chapter 3) applies.

2   What does it mean to say that X is "nothing but" Y? It can't mean just that X wouldn't exist if Y didn't. We wouldn't exist without oxygen. It doesn't follow that we are "nothing but" oxygen.

Recommended Readings, Video, and Audio

Visit the companion website at www.routledge.com/cw/sober for suggestions of readings, video, and audio, for this chapter.

Chapter 21

Methodological Behaviorism

Logical behaviorism was the subject of the last chapter; methodological behaviorism is the subject of the present one. Although the names sound similar, the doctrines themselves are very different. Logical behaviorism says that the meanings of common-sense mentalistic concepts can be analyzed in purely behavioral terms. Methodological behaviorism is not a thesis about what such common-sense terms mean; rather, it is a recommendation for how the science of psychology ought to be pursued.

In a curious way, methodological and logical behaviorisms take opposite views on the nature of common-sense mentalistic language. As noted earlier, logical behaviorism *rejects* the idea that beliefs and desires are inner states that cause behavior. Methodological behaviorism, by contrast, *accepts* the idea that our common-sense mentalistic vocabulary refers to inner states. Methodological behaviorism then argues that a scientific psychology should avoid talking about beliefs and desires precisely because they are inner states.

In this chapter, I'll divide methodological behaviorism into a negative and a positive thesis. (This is similar to my division of logical behaviorism into a negative and a positive thesis in the previous chapter.) First, I'll analyze the negative thesis; this is the claim that psychology should *not* attempt to explain behavior in terms of people's beliefs and desires. Then, I'll consider methodological behaviorism's positive thesis; this is the idea that people's behavior *can* be explained solely in terms of their history of conditioning.

The Negative Thesis: Psychology Should Avoid Belief/Desire Explanations

Why should psychology avoid explaining the behavior of agents by attributing beliefs and desires to them? B. F. Skinner, who was a leading proponent of behaviorism, provided several answers to this question in his books *Science and Human Behavior* (New York, Free Press, 1953), *Beyond Freedom and Dignity* (New York, Knopf, 1971), and *About Behaviorism* (New York, Random House, 1974). Skinner's first objection to mentalistic explanation is that beliefs and desires aren't observable. They are hidden. All we can directly observe is the behaviors of others, not what goes on in their minds. By now, my view of this kind of argument should be clear. Science legitimately talks about things that aren't or can't be observed. The fact that beliefs and desires can't be observed directly doesn't mean that claims about an individual's beliefs and desires can't be tested by observing behavior. For example, suppose I claim that Jane wants a drink of water and believes that there is water in the cup before her. Suppose I further claim that she has no other desires that would override her desire for the water. These claims about the agent's mind predict that she will reach for the water and drink it. If that prediction fails, I've gained evidence against the description just formulated about Jane's mind. As in the Mendelian case, claims about what is not observed can be tested by examining what they imply about what can be observed.

Another reason that Skinner gives for rejecting mentalistic theories is that they are "too easy." In the example, I attributed to Jane a combination of beliefs and desires that predict something about her behavior. Suppose she doesn't reach for the water. What will I do? I'll modify my claim about what she thinks and wants. I won't abandon my assumption that Jane has beliefs and desires and that these cause her behavior. So, apparently, the assumption of mentalism—that behavior is caused by beliefs and desires of some sort—isn't tested by observing behavior. Indeed, it appears that no matter what Jane does, I can always formulate a belief/desire story that is consistent with what I observe.

I want to clarify this point of Skinner's by distinguishing *specific belief/desire hypotheses* from what I'll call *the mentalistic thesis*, which is the claim that an individual's behaviors are caused by the beliefs and desires he or she possesses. The specific attributions are testable against the data of behavior; however, the mentalistic thesis does not seem to be. Skinner believes that the claims of science must be testable by observation; hence, he concludes, the mentalistic thesis does not deserve to be part of a scientific psychology. Notice that even if the mentalistic thesis is untestable, this would not imply that *specific belief/desire attributions* are untestable. The requirement that scientists should only put forward theories that are testable has the curious consequence that they are allowed to advance specific belief/desire explanations but are not allowed to say that mentalism is true. But mentalism is *logically entailed* by each specific belief/desire explanation. Can't we assert what our confirmed theories entail?

In Chapter 9, I discussed the idea that scientific claims should be testable. I argued that the thesis of falsifiability is implausible. I now want to make a related point: *There are many perfectly respectable scientific statements that cannot be refuted by the result of a single experiment*. In the present case, we have an example of this kind of statement. Statements that describe the basic tenets of a *research program* are not falsifiable. Mentalism is such a thesis; it says that theories explaining behavior can be developed by extending and refining the ordinary concepts of belief and desire. Time will tell whether this is a good idea for psychology or a dead end. The fact that a single theory within this framework fails does not show that the whole framework is bankrupt. One rotten apple need not show that the entire barrel is spoiled.

Curiously enough, precisely the same point applies to Skinner's own research program. Skinner rejects mentalism and espouses behaviorism. This is the thesis that behaviors can be explained by describing the stimuli people have received from their environments. Skinner says we don't need to describe the inner states—mental or physical—of individuals in order to explain their behavior. This behaviorist thesis states the framework of the Skinnerian research program. Suppose I follow its dictates and construct a detailed behaviorist explanation of why you are now reading this page. Suppose further that this explanation turns out to be mistaken. Does that refute behaviorism as a general research program? I would say not (and Skinner would probably agree).

It is appropriate to demand that *specific explanations* be testable against the data of observations. It is not appropriate to demand that *theses about the framework of a research program* should be falsifiable. Mentalism can't be faulted on the ground that it isn't testable. Specific mentalistic hypotheses can be tested. Time will tell whether the general thesis of mentalism will turn out to be correct. In this sense, the framework of mentalism, like the framework of behaviorism, *is* testable—it is testable "in the long run."

Methodological Behaviorism's Positive Thesis

I'll now consider methodological behaviorism's positive claim—that behavior can be explained without describing the inner states of the organism. I believe that there is a simple fact about people that shows that behaviorism can't be successful—that the explanations it demands do not exist. Recall that methodological behaviorism does not deny that we have inner mental states. It claims, rather, that psychology does not need to discuss them in its attempt to explain behavior. So behaviorism grants that the causal chain linking environmental stimuli to behavior has the following structure:

Environment $\longrightarrow$ Inner state of organism $\longrightarrow$ Behavior

Methodological behaviorism maintains that my present behavior can be explained in terms of (1) the past environments I've occupied and the behaviors I produced in them and (2) my present environment.

Skinner's theory of stimulus conditioning shows how such explanations can be constructed. In his research, Skinner manipulated the behavior of chickens and other organisms by placing them into a totally controlled environment—a *Skinner box*. For example, a chicken can be conditioned to peck at a key in its cage when the light is on. This is how the conditioning is done. When the chicken is first placed in the box, it will peck occasionally. The box is so arranged that if the chicken pecks when the light is on, it receives a pellet of food. If it pecks when the light is off, it obtains no reward. After some time, the chicken's pecking starts to happen pretty much only when the light goes on. In this stimulus/response experiment, the chicken is conditioned to peck when and only when the light is on. The conditioning works by rewarding the chicken in some circumstances but not in others.

Suppose that this conditioning process has taken place. You then look into the cage and see that the chicken is pecking. How might you explain this behavior? A mentalistic explanation might say that the chicken is now pecking because it wants food and believes, based on its past experience, that pecking produces pellets of food. This is a mentalistic explanation—it is stated in terms of beliefs and desires. Skinner believes that this mentalistic story is entirely unnecessary. You can give a behaviorist explanation of the present behavior as follows: (1) in the past, the chicken was conditioned to peck when the light was on and

(2) right now, the light is on. Notice that Skinner's explanation makes no mention of beliefs and desires. We can formulate the behaviorist explanation as a deductive argument:

> If the light is on, then the chicken pecks.
> The light is on now.
>
> _____
>
> Hence, the chicken now pecks.

You explain the present behavior by deducing it from the two facts listed as premises.

Skinner thinks that what is true of the chicken's pecking in the experiment is true of all the chicken's behaviors, both those produced in the experiment and those that occur in less controlled environments (like the barnyard). In addition, Skinner believes that human beings are like the chicken in relevant respects. Each of our behaviors can be explained by describing our history of stimulus conditioning. This is the thesis on which the behaviorist research program rests. We don't need to talk about what human beings think and want if we are to explain what human beings do.

First Objection to Behaviorism's Positive Thesis: Novel Behaviors

Are we like the chicken in a Skinner box? Critics of behaviorism, like the linguist Noam Chomsky, have claimed that *novel behaviors* cannot be explained in the way the behaviorist demands. Let's look with some care at an example of Skinner's to see what this criticism means.

Suppose you are walking down the street one day and a robber jumps out of the shadows, sticks a gun in your face, and says "your money or your life." You fumble nervously and then hand over your wallet. How should your behavior be explained? What makes the behavior novel is that you have never been robbed before. The only time anyone ever waved a gun in your face was when you were a child and the gun was a water gun. In that case, you didn't hand over your wallet; rather, you giggled and ran away. So why didn't you do the same thing this time?

The behaviorist needs to show that the present stimulus situation is similar to past ones in which you behaved similarly. Skinner explains the chicken's present pecking by saying that the *present* situation is like *past* situations in which the chicken pecked. The similarity is that the light is on in the Skinner box. The problem is that the present robbery is similar to many past situations you have been in. It is similar to your childhood playing with water guns. It is also similar to the time your mother threatened to spank you if you didn't clean up your room. After all, the robbery involved a gun *and* a threat. Which of these past experiences is the right one to appeal to in explaining your present behavior?

Remember that you have never been robbed before. The only time anyone waved a gun in your face it was a water gun and you giggled and ran away. And when your mom threatened to spank you, you apologized and cleaned up your room; you did not hand her your wallet. What past episodes can a behaviorist say are similar to, and also explain, your current behavior? An obvious answer is that you learned in the past that you should accommodate those who threaten you. Perhaps you were rewarded in the past for doing this and so the behavioral pattern became fixed. Although this sounds like the right sort of explanation to develop, it isn't true to the demands of behaviorism.

In the chicken case, there was a *physical property* of the earlier stimulus situations that recurs in the present. In the past, *the light was on.* In the present case, *the light is on.* It is perfectly permissible for a behaviorist to describe the history of conditioning in terms of such physical properties. What the behaviorist can't say, however, is that you are the sort of individual who behaves in ways you *believe* are accommodating when you *believe* that you are being threatened. This description of your stimulus history refers to inner mental states. These are just the items that the behaviorist says should *not* be included in the explanation.

I doubt that there is a physical similarity between past threats and the present one. In the past, your mom may have said, "If you don't clean up your room, I'll give you a spanking." Your behavioral response was not to hand your wallet over, but to apologize and tidy things up. The only way to describe how this past event is similar to the present robbery is to describe your beliefs and desires.

If our behaviors always obeyed patterns that were describable in terms of *physical similarities* between past and present stimulus conditions, behaviorism might work. But this often seems to be radically untrue. In lots of cases, what makes the past similar to the present is that we conceptualize past and present in similar ways. Take this mentalistic similarity away and behaviorism delivers radically mistaken predictions. In terms of purely physical similarities, I suppose that your participation in a water gun battle as a child may be more similar to the present robbery than your being scolded by your mother. If you were to behave now in ways that are similar to the ways you behaved in previous *physically similar* past events, the prediction would be that you would giggle and run away.

It is an important fact about human beings that small physical differences in a stimulus often make enormous differences in the response, and huge physical differences in the stimulus often make no difference in the response. If a robber walks into a bank and hands the teller a note that says "You give me the cash," the teller produces one response. If the note had said "Me give you the cash," the response might be very different. The notes aren't *that* different physically, so why was the response so different? Likewise, receiving a paper with a few marks on it can produce the same result as hearing a verbal command. But the marks on paper ("You give me the cash") and a verbal message ("Empty the cash drawers into this sack") are physically very different.

---

18 Minimal Explanation versus Deep Explanation

The behavior of a conditioned chicken in a Skinner box can be explained without describing the chicken's internal state. Why is the chicken now pecking the key? Skinner's answer is that the chicken pecks whenever the light is on, and the light is now on.

Since we have explained the behavior without mentioning the chicken's internal state, Skinner concludes that describing the internal state would be of no explanatory relevance. You don't need to describe what is going on inside, so why bother?

I grant that the purely behavioral account is an adequate explanation. However, I think that there can be a deeper explanation of the chicken's behavior.

Consider an analogy. Why did this white cube just dissolve? A behaviorist might answer by noting that (1) the cube was made of sugar, (2) it was just immersed in water, and (3) all sugar dissolves when immersed in water. Granted, this is an explanation. But it is possible to do better.

What is it about sugar that makes it dissolve when immersed? Here we request information about the internal structure of the sugar lump. Since sugar is water-soluble but wood is not, we expect that the one has an internal state that the other lacks. Once described, this internal state of the lump of sugar is relevant to explaining why it just dissolved.

The chicken pecks when the light is on. Surely we can ask what it is about this chicken that makes it peck when the light is on. A conditioned chicken has a disposition to behave that an unconditioned chicken does not have. It is legitimate to expect that the one has an internal state that the other lacks. Once described, this internal state of the conditioned chicken is relevant to explaining why it is now pecking.

Perhaps it is possible to explain the chicken's behavior in the way the methodological behaviorist demands. However, this does not mean that other explanations that violate behaviorist principles are irrelevant to understanding why the chicken pecks.

Behaviorism sounds plausible for two reasons. First, it is true that claims about the mental states of individuals should be tested against behavioral data. Second, an individual's behavior is importantly influenced by the environments he or she has experienced. Neither of these truisms, however, shows what methodological behaviorism maintains—that it is possible to explain (and predict) behavior without mentioning mental states.

Second Objection to Behaviorism's Positive Thesis: It Assumes that Environmental Determinism Is True

One final shortcoming of methodological behaviorism should be noted. Behaviorism is a radically environmentalist doctrine. That is, when it comes to the nature/nurture problem—the problem of saying how much a behavior is explained by genes and how much by environment—the behaviorist is entirely on the side of the environment. By saying that *inner states* need not be described in explaining behavior, the behaviorist is excluding genes as well as environmentally acquired mental states. My point is that environmentalism may be true in some cases, but not in others.

Returning to the example of the chicken, it is interesting to note that there are some behaviors that you can't condition a chicken to perform. Speaking English is something that human beings learn to do when they are in the right kind of environment. A chicken in the same environment will not acquire this skill. Why not? Since the environments are the same, the answer can't be environmental. Presumably, there is a genetic difference between chickens and human beings that explains this behavioral difference.

What is true between species may also be true, in some cases, within a species. There may be genetic differences between human beings that are relevant to explaining differences in their behaviors. This is now a controversial area of investigation. My point is that methodological behaviorism assumes in advance of any detailed scientific analysis that environmental variables suffice to explain behavior. This should not be assumed as a matter of doctrine, but should be empirically investigated on a case-by-case basis.

Scientists are now considering the possibility that there may be a significant genetic component in conditions such as depression and schizophrenia. That is, in addition to the environmental causes of these conditions, there may also be genetic causes. In contrast, no one now believes that there is a genetic component in explaining why some people speak one language while others speak another. In this case, variation in the behavior has an entirely environmental explanation.

Environmental determinism is the view that genetic differences do not help explain any behavioral differences. Genetic determinism is the view that environmental differences do not help explain any behavioral differences. Both of these views are too sweeping and extreme to be plausible. First, we must consider different behaviors separately. The kind of explanation we offer for schizophrenia may differ from the kind we want to give for speaking English. Second, we must recognize that there are "mixed" proposals that deserve a hearing; we want to consider the idea that some behaviors have both environmental and genetic causes.

The Two Objections Summarized

In conclusion, there are two kinds of questions that methodological behaviorism can't address. The first is the kind of question typified by the robbery example. When I ask how your present behavior of handing over the money is explained by your previous experiences, it seems essential to describe your beliefs and desires. There is no purely physical similarity between the present holdup and your previous environments that provides an explanation. Rather, the similarity exists only because you conceptualize the present situation in a way that resembles the way you conceptualized previous (physically different) situations. Second, there is the idea of genetic (nonenvironmental) causes of behavior. If these exist, then methodological behaviorism will be unable to explain in some cases why some organisms behave differently from others. Methodological behaviorism began by rejecting mentalism; it claimed that mental states are irrelevant to explaining behavior. But, in fact, its thesis excludes brain science and genetics as well. The real thrust of behaviorism is to claim that the explanation of behavior need not describe the *inner state* of the organism. Mentalism describes what goes on inside, but so do brain science and genetics.

By focusing on what happens in tightly controlled environments, behaviorism may seem to have established a general pattern for explaining all behavior. It is true that the pecking of the chicken in the Skinner box can be handled in the way Skinner demands. However, it is a mistake to think that successful explanation in this case can be generalized to all other behaviors. Take the chicken out of the Skinner box and perhaps it will produce novel behaviors, just as you did when the robber said "your money or your life." And apart from the issue of novel behaviors, there is the nature/nurture issue, which methodological behaviorism settles in advance of looking at the relevant data.

Review Questions

1   What is the difference between methodological behaviorism and logical behaviorism?
2   What is mentalism? Is mentalism testable? How does the distinction between specific explanations and framework assumptions about a research program bear on this question?
3   Why do so-called novel behaviors pose a problem for methodological behaviorism? What does *novel* mean? Isn't every behavior novel in some respect or other?
4   What does methodological behaviorism say about the relevance of genetics and brain science to the explanation of behavior? Why would innate differences in behavior be a problem for behaviorism?
5   What two objections have been raised against methodological behaviorism? Do you think a methodological behaviorist might be able to respond to one or both of them? If so, how?
6   What is environmental determinism? How does it differ from other forms of determinism?
7   Why do you think psychologists and philosophers might feel attracted to methodological behaviorism? What characteristic advantages does it offer?
8   Why does the stimulus-response model of human behavior seem an inadequate account of actual human behavior?
9   Are methodological behaviorists committed to the view that inner mental states don't exist?

Problems for Further Thought

1   Some psychotherapists call themselves "behaviorists." They treat patients with phobias (extreme fears) by helping them modify fear behavior (like increased heart rate, perspiration, anxiety) rather than by helping them understand why they have the array of beliefs and desires that produce the reaction. Consider people who are enormously afraid of being in closed areas (claustrophobia). Instead of trying to get a claustrophobic individual to understand why he or she has this fear, a behavioral therapist might concentrate on "desensitizing" the individual. The goal would be to modify the individual's behavior. Treatment might begin with very brief exposures to closed areas; gradually, as the patient gains confidence, longer exposures would be attempted. Here's the question: Do the criticisms I've made of methodological behaviorism imply that behavioral therapy will not be effective? Defend your answer.

2   *Saying that lemons are yellow* is a kind of event. Can it be defined by its physical characteristics? Is *saying the English sentence "lemons are yellow"* definable by its physical characteristics? What is the difference between these two kinds of events?

3   If I strike your knee with a hammer, it will jerk. Is this due to the beliefs and desires you have? If not, why is your going to a movie tonight any different?

Recommended Readings, Video, and Audio

Visit the companion website at www.routledge.com/cw/sober for suggestions of readings, video, and audio, for this chapter.

Chapter 22

The Mind/Brain Identity Theory

So far I've examined three approaches to the mind/body problem. These were Cartesian dualism (Chapter 19), logical behaviorism (Chapter 20), and methodological behaviorism (Chapter 21). Although dualism and methodological behaviorism agree that mental states are inner causes of outward behavior (a thesis that I have called "mentalism"), each says more than this. Dualism asserts that your mind is a nonphysical object; methodological behaviorism recommends that scientific explanations of behavior ignore the mind (in part because you allegedly can't have knowledge of another person's mind). Logical behaviorism is the one theory of these three that denies mentalism.

The Identity Theory Is an *A Posteriori* Claim

Cartesian dualism and logical behaviorism are very different positions. Yet the arguments that each presents have something in common: neither appeals to any scientific finding as evidence for what it maintains. Cartesian dualism says that we can recognize by introspection and philosophical reasoning that the mind has a property that the body lacks. Logical behaviorism says that we can see that mental states are not inner causes of behavior just by analyzing the meanings of common-sense mentalistic terms. Both theories are defended by arguments that are intended to be *a priori*.

The Mind/Brain Identity Theory isn't just a different theory from those surveyed so far; it is also a different *kind* of theory. The identity theory argues for its solution to the mind/body problem by describing the progress that science has made so far and by predicting the progress that science will make in the future. The relationship of the mind and the body, says the identity theory, is something that science discovers by observation and experiment. It isn't something that armchair philosophy—*a priori* reflection and linguistic analysis—can hope to resolve. The identity theory is offered as an *a posteriori* proposition about the relationship of mind and body.

Materialism

The identity theory asserts that the history of science has been marked by success after success for a doctrine called *materialism* or *physicalism*. This is the view that every object is a material (physical) object. But what does that mean? Does it just mean that every object has at least one physical property? There must be more to materialism than this. After all, Descartes and other dualists agree that your thoughts have temporal location. For example, yesterday, you wanted an ice cream cone; this is a physical property that your episode of desiring had. What distinguishes materialism from dualism is this: materialists hold that if two objects are different in any way at all, they must exhibit physical differences. If you love jazz and I do not, then there must be a physical difference between us. If we were physically exactly the same, either we'd both love jazz or neither of us would. The materialist's slogan is *no difference without a physical difference*. Dualists disagree with this principle. They think it is possible that two physically identical lumps of matter might be such that one of them has a mind while the other does not. A jazz lover and a jazz hater might be molecule-for-molecule identical; they would be physically identical but psychologically distinct. Dualists think this is possible because they think that the mind is a not a material object at all.

Progress in Science

Looking back on the history of human knowledge, we find phenomena that weren't well understood scientifically. For example, lightning was once profoundly perplexing. The ancient Greeks thought that lightning was Zeus's thunderbolt. But in the eighteenth and nineteenth centuries, scientists studying electricity established that lightning is an electrical discharge. Science was able to take a phenomenon that earlier had seemed to defy physical description and show that it can be understood within the framework of the laws of physics. Consider a statement that describes this scientific discovery:

Lightning is one and the same thing as a kind of electrical discharge.

This statement wasn't established by analyzing the meaning of the word *lightning*. The statement isn't an *a priori* truth, knowable by linguistic analysis; rather, it is an *a posteriori* truth, discovered by scientists using observational evidence. It could be established only by observation and experiment.

In the past century, there was a similar perplexity about the nature of life. What is the difference between living things and things that are not alive? A doctrine called *vitalism* held that living things contain a nonphysical substance that animates them with life—an *élan vital* (a vital fluid). In this century, vitalism has been undermined by the discoveries of molecular biology. We now know that life is a physico–chemical phenomenon. Organisms are made of the same basic elements (carbon, oxygen, etc.) as nonliving things. Life differs from nonlife because of how these basic physical constituents are arranged. There is no extra nonphysical ingredient that magically makes organisms "alive."

Biology in the last one hundred years has discredited vitalism. The discovery of the molecular basis of life has been a triumph for materialism. By this I don't mean that each and every detail of the physical basis of life is well understood; if this were true, there would no longer be a need for research in molecular biology and biochemistry. Rather, what I mean is that the details are sufficiently well understood that there is no longer any real doubt that metabolism, reproduction, digestion, respiration, and so on are all physical processes.

Dualism Resembles Vitalism

Cartesian dualism and vitalism are similar. Dualism says that an individual's mind is a non-material substance. Thinking beings therefore are said to contain a nonphysical ingredient not found in beings that don't have minds. Vitalism says that living things contain a non-physical substance—an *élan vital*—that is unique to them. Just as dualism opposes a materialistic solution to the mind/body problem, so vitalism opposes a materialistic answer to the question of how biological and physical processes are related to each other.

The Mind/Brain Identity Theory says that what has happened to the problem of life is in the process of happening to the problem of mind. We now have some knowledge of the physical basis—the neurophysiological basis—of the mind. If science progresses the way it has in other areas, this materialistic understanding will broaden and deepen. The identity theory predicts that science will fully vindicate the thesis that an individual's mind and brain are one and the same entity. Each mental characteristic (for example, believing that snow is white, wanting a drink of water, and feeling pain) is identical with some physical characteristic. The identity theory is a version of materialism: Mental objects are physical objects and mental characteristics are physical characteristics.

During the 1950s and 1960s, identity theorists—for example, U. T. Place, in "Is Consciousness a Brain Process?" and J. J. C. Smart, in "Sensations and Brain Processes" (both reprinted in V. Chappell [ed.], *The Philosophy of Mind*, Prentice-Hall, 1962)—gave the following as an example of what they meant. Brain scientists at that time suggested that feeling pain is one and the same event as having the c-fibers in one's brain fire. This neurophysiological hypothesis about the physical basis of pain later turned out to be untrue. This didn't deter identity theorists, however, who are quite happy to leave it to science to work out the details of the general hypotheses they formulate. The identity theorist claims that feeling pain is identical with being in *some physical state or other*; it is for science to tell us precisely what this physical state is.

A Correlation Experiment

Consider this example in more detail. How might a scientist investigate the connection of pain and c-fiber firing? The scientist would want to find out whether people experience pain whenever their c-fibers fire and whether people have their c-fibers fire whenever they experience pain. Here's a simple experiment that would help determine if these mental and physical events co-occur. A probe inserted into the subject's brain would indicate when the subject's c-fibers fire. Perhaps the subject's own testimony, based on introspection, would indicate when he or she experiences pain. The experimenter occasionally hits the subject's thumb with a hammer. Ignoring complications, suppose that different human subjects, when placed in this (morally questionable) experiment, generate the same data. Suppose that the data show a perfect correlation between experiences of pain and c-fiber firings—the one kind of event occurs if and only if the other does.

Does this, by itself, show that the identity theory is true? No. Dualism is consistent with there being a perfect correlation of mental events and physical events. Dualism claims that feeling pain and having your c-fibers fire are *two* distinct kinds of event. The identity theory, on the other hand, says that feeling a pain and having one's c-fibers fire are perfectly correlated because they are one and the same kind of event.

How are we to choose between dualism and the identity theory? One consideration, mentioned in Chapter 19, is that dualism makes it difficult to understand how mind and body can causally interact. The identity theory, on the other hand, has no difficulty accommodating this fact. However, the fourth Problem for Further Thought at the end of Chapter 19 suggests that this objection to dualism rests on a questionable assumption about what causality involves. Is there some other basis on which to choose between dualism and the identity theory?

The Principle of Parsimony

Identity theorists offer a second reason for rejecting dualism. They claim that the identity theory is more parsimonious (simpler) than dualism. Their idea is that the scientific method says that we should prefer simpler theories over more complex ones when both are consistent with the observations. It isn't just that more parsimonious ideas are easier to think about or are aesthetically more pleasing. Rather, their idea is that more parsimonious theories are more likely to be *true*.

The identity theory is more parsimonious because it claims (if the experiment just described were to yield a perfect correlation) that feeling pain and having one's c-fibers fire are one and the same event. A dualist, on the other hand, says that these are two different events. The Principle of Parsimony, sometimes called "Ockham's Razor" after the medieval philosopher William of Ockham, is an abductive principle. It says that we should prefer explanations that minimize the number of entities, processes, and events they postulate. The usual slogan is "don't multiply entities beyond necessity," though this isn't in Ockham's writings. Since one is a smaller number than two, the Mind/Brain Identity Theory is more parsimonious than dualism. Identity theorists count this as a reason for thinking that the identity theory is true and dualism is false, given that both are consistent with the observed correlation of mental and physical states.

In the vitalism controversy, no biologist took seriously the idea that an *élan vital* exists once the physical bases of life processes became reasonably clear. Rather, the conclusion was that an organism's being alive is nothing above and beyond its having certain physical processes going on in its body. To say otherwise would be to admit a further entity—an *élan vital*—without necessity. This would contradict the Principle of Parsimony. Biologists took this principle to heart once they obtained physical explanations of life processes. They realized that there was no reason to postulate the existence of an *élan vital*. For this reason, vitalism was rejected and materialism accepted. If a perfect correlation could be found between mental characteristics and physical ones, what reason could there be to postulate the existence of an immaterial mind—one that just happens to exhibit psychological characteristics that are correlated with the physical characteristics of the brain? This seems entirely gratuitous—a violation of the Principle of Parsimony. The identity theory asserts that dualism should be rejected and materialism accepted if science discovers perfect correlations between mental and physical characteristics.

Let's be clear on what the Principle of Parsimony recommends. In the problem of life, the principle leads one to *deny* the existence of an immaterial vital substance. It doesn't say that one should *suspend judgment* as to whether such a substance exists. Likewise, mind/brain identity theorists argue that parsimony offers a reason to think that immaterial minds do not exist. Their recommendation is not to suspend judgment about dualism, but to conclude that dualism is false. In both cases, Ockham's Razor leads one to conclude that X does not exist, not to conclude that one should suspend judgment as to whether X exists.

There is an interesting and difficult philosophical problem here, which I won't attempt to solve: Why should the greater simplicity or parsimony of a theory be a reason to think that the theory is true? Does using the Principle of Parsimony in this way require that we assume that nature is simple? This seems to be the rationale that Isaac Newton offers for using the principle in scientific reasoning (see the accompanying box). If using the principle requires that we assume that nature is simple, what evidence do we have that nature really is simple? This question should remind you of the question we explored in connection with Hume's views on induction in Chapters 15–17 concerning the principle of the uniformity of nature.

---

19 Newton on Parsimony

The Principle of Parsimony has been used in many scientific debates. In his *Principles of Natural Philosophy* (1690), Newton presents four "Rules of Reasoning in Philosophy." The first two concern abduction, the second two induction:

1   *We are to admit no more causes of natural things than such as are both true and sufficient to explain their appearances.* To this purpose, the philosophers say that Nature does nothing in vain, and more is in vain when less will serve; for Nature is pleased with simplicity and affects not the pomp of superfluous causes.

2   *Therefore to the same natural effects we must, as far as possible, assign the same causes.* As to respiration in a man and in a beast, the descent of stones in Europe and in America, the light of our culinary fire and of the sun, the reflection of light in the earth and in the planets.

3   *The qualities of bodies, which admit neither intensification nor remission of degrees, and which are found to belong to all bodies within the reach of our experiments, are to be esteemed the universal qualities of all bodies whatsoever.* For since the qualities of bodies are only known to us by experiments, we are to hold for universal all such as universally agree with experiments, and such as are not liable to diminution can never be quite taken away. We are certainly not to relinquish evidence of experiments for the sake of dreams and vain fictions of our own devising; nor are we to recede from the analogy of Nature, which is wont to be simple and always consonant to itself....

4   *In experimental philosophy we are to look upon propositions inferred by general induction from phenomena as accurately or very nearly true, notwithstanding any contrary hypotheses that may be imagined, till such time as other phenomena occur by which they may either be made more accurate or liable to exceptions.* This rule we must follow, that the argument of induction not be evaded by hypotheses.

Rule 1 is relevant to the debate between the identity theory and dualism. Rule 2 is similar to the Principle of the Common Cause discussed in connection with the Argument from Design (Chapter 6). Rule 3 bears on the relevance of Descartes' method of doubt (Chapter 13) to the progress of science.

There is an alternative argument for using the Principle of Parsimony that does not rest on the assumption that nature is simple. The history of science shows that using the Principle of Parsimony has repeatedly led to important scientific advances. In Aristotle's physics (which we considered briefly in Chapter 4), the motions of celestial bodies and the motions of objects here on Earth are said to follow different rules. One of the great achievements of Newton's physics is that it provided a single set of laws that covered both. Newton's theory is in this respect simpler than Aristotle's; it unifies diverse observations. The rejection of vitalism in the nineteenth and twentieth centuries provides another such example. These achievements are important scientific milestones. However, we must be careful not to attend only to episodes in which more parsimonious theories turned out to be better than their less parsimonious rivals. There also have been episodes in which the opposite turned out to be true.

Review Questions

1 What is materialism? Is it the view that money is the most important thing?
2 What is vitalism? Is vitalism shown to be true by the fact that living things contain DNA while nonliving things do not?
3 In what way is vitalism (as a solution to the problem of life) similar to dualism (as a solution to the problem of mind)? What is meant by "the problem of life" and "the problem of mind"?
4 What is the Principle of Parsimony? Why is dualism said to be less parsimonious than the identity theory?
5 Does the Principle of Parsimony agree with the following claim: "Since dualism and the identity theory both predict that mental events will be correlated with physical events, there is no way to choose between the two theories"?
6 Would the discovery of perfect correlations between certain mental events and physical events (say, between experiences of pain and c-fiber firings) be evidence against dualism? Why or why not?
7 What are the two central arguments that advocates of the Mind/Brain Identity thesis typically appeal to when defending their position?
8 Why might someone doubt that the Principle of Uniformity is a surefire guide to which theories we should pursue? Do you think this skepticism is well-founded, or is it just another example of philosophers' penchant for "radical doubt"?

Problems for Further Thought

1 Suppose we observe a perfect correlation between some mental property (like feeling pain) and some physical property (like having one's c-fibers fire). Apply the Surprise Principle (Chapter 3) to see whether this observation strongly favors the identity theory over dualism.
2 In the passage from *Principles of Natural Philosophy* quoted in this chapter, Newton defends the Principle of Parsimony by saying that "Nature does nothing in vain." Is this idea consistent with what we now know about natural selection (Chapter 6)?
3 The Principle of Parsimony is often thought to be relevant to the question of whether God exists. Formulate and evaluate an argument for atheism that makes use of this principle.
4 On the companion website, the psychologist U. T. Place defends the identity theory, but does not mention the Principle of Parsimony. He does so by describing a situation in which the correlation between two events justifies the conclusion that the two are identical. Evaluate Place's argument.

Recommended Readings, Video, and Audio

Visit the companion website at www.routledge.com/cw/sober for suggestions of readings, video, and audio, for this chapter.

Chapter 23

Functionalism

The Mind/Brain Identity Theory, our topic in the previous chapter, applies to the mind/body problem the general thesis that *everything is material*. Minds aren't made of an immaterial substance; rather, people have minds and mental characteristics by virtue of the fact that they have brains that possess various sorts of physical structure.

In the 1960s and 1970s, several philosophers—preeminently, Hilary Putnam (in "The Nature of Mental States" in H. Putnam, *Mind, Language, and Reality*, Cambridge University Press, 1975) and Jerry Fodor (in *Psychological Explanation*, Random House, 1968)—developed a criticism of the identity theory. They espoused a point of view that came to be called "functionalism." Although functionalism does not reject materialism, it does reject one important part of the identity theory. Functionalism has two parts—one negative, the other positive. The negative part describes what psychological states are *not*. This is the functionalist critique of the identity theory. The positive part advances a proposal about what psychological states *are*. I'll take these two ideas in order.

Functionalism's Negative Thesis: What's Wrong with the Identity Theory?

To begin with, I need to draw a common-sense distinction. Suppose someone says to you, looking at your clothing, "We own the same shirt." What might this mean? There are two choices. One is that you and this person own the same *kind* of shirt. The other is that the very shirt on your back is jointly owned by the two of you.

Let's introduce some terminology to mark this distinction. Unique physical objects are called *tokens*. Kinds (or properties) are called *types*. The unique physical object that you are now wearing is a token of many types. It is a token of the type *shirt*; it is also a token of the type *blue*, and a token of the type *clothing*. To say that a single token is a token of many types is merely to say that a single object has many properties.

Conversely, a given type may have zero, one, or many tokens that fall under it. *Unicorn* is a type of animal that has no instances; there are no tokens of that type. *Golden mountain* is a type of geological object, one that happens to have no exemplars. You can see just from this pair of examples that two types (properties) may apply to exactly the same tokens and still be distinct types. Being a unicorn isn't the same property as being a golden mountain, even though the set of unicorns has precisely the same members as the set of golden mountains.

How does the type/token distinction apply to the mind/body problem? The identity theory has two parts. It makes a claim about psychological tokens and also a claim about psychological types. The former category—of psychological tokens—includes the following: Descartes' mind, the pain I felt in my foot last Thursday, Jones's thinking to herself today that lemons are yellow. Each of these is a token, and the identity theory says that each is identical with some physical token.

In addition, there are psychological types (properties); the identity theory makes a claim about these as well. For example, there is the property of having a mind, the property of feeling pain, the property of believing that lemons are yellow, and so on. Note that these types each have numerous tokens falling under them. Each type, therefore, describes something that various tokens have in common. The identity theory says that each of these psychological types (properties) is identical with some physical property or other.

Multiple Realizability

Functionalism rejects what the identity theory says about psychological types. Functionalists hold that psychological properties are not identical with physical properties. Instead, functionalists argue that psychological types are *multiply realizable*. I'll explain this idea with an example.

Consider a type that isn't psychological—the property of *being a mousetrap*. Each token mousetrap is a physical object. But think of all the different ways there are to build a mousetrap. Some are made of wood and wire and are loaded with cheese. Others are made of plastic and catch mice by injecting them with curare. Still others are made of a team of philosophers, who stalk around armed with inverted wastepaper baskets. There are many, perhaps endlessly many, ways to build a mousetrap.

Is there a single physical characteristic that all mousetraps have in common, and which non-mousetraps lack? This seems highly dubious. Each token mousetrap is a physical thing, but the property of being a mousetrap (the type) doesn't seem to be a physical property at all.

How does this analogy bear on the plausibility of the Mind/Brain Identity Theory? There is more than one (physical) way to build a mousetrap. The analogy is that there may be many physical ways to build a creature that has a mind, and more than one way for a being with a mind to have this or that psychological property.

20 The Birthday Fallacy, Again

The Birthday Fallacy, introduced in Chapter 4, is the mistake you make if you confuse the following two statements:

Everyone has a birthday.
There is a single day on which everyone was born.

The first is true; the second false. It's a fallacy to think that the first entails the second. You'd be making the same mistake if you confused the following two statements:

Each mousetrap has physical properties that allow it to catch mice.
There is a single set of physical properties that all mousetraps have in common that allows them to catch mice.

The first is true; the second false. How can the Birthday Fallacy be used to describe functionalism's criticism of the identity theory?

Could a Computer Have Psychological Characteristics?

Consider computers. It isn't very plausible to regard very simple computers as having beliefs and desires. My desk calculator no more "knows" facts about simple arithmetic than my stove "knows" recipes for making soup. Rather, human beings use these devices to do arithmetic or to make soup. A desk calculator, in this respect, is like paper and pencil. It facilitates *our* calculations, but doesn't itself engage in mental activity.

Don't be misled by the fact that we sometimes use mentalistic terms to describe simple computers. For example, we talk about computer "memory." However, I don't think my home computer literally remembers anything. This is just a metaphor. If I write some thoughts on a piece of paper and those scribbles are not erased, it is true that the piece of paper has "retained" the inscriptions I placed there. But the piece of paper does not remember anything. In this respect, I think a simple computer is just like a piece of paper.

Very simple machines do not have minds or mental states. But let's now use our imaginations and think about what the future may bring. Could there be computers that have mental states? Could computers be built that perceive—see and hear, for example? Could computers be built that remember? Could a computer reason? Could a computer be built that has wants and needs and preferences? Functionalists regard these as very real possibilities. Perhaps current computers can't do these things, and perhaps computer scientists at times exaggerate how close they are to making computers with these abilities. But take seriously for a moment the possibility that computers eventually will be built that have one or more of these mental abilities.

This possibility has serious implications for the identity theory. These computers, let's suppose, won't be made of protein. Perhaps they will be made of silicon chips. There seems to be no reason to expect that these thinking machines must be physically very much like the brains we have. Just as there are many physical ways to build a mousetrap, so there seem to be many physical ways to have a mind and to have particular mental states.

Multiple Realizability within the Class of Living Things

We don't need to consider the future of computer science to see the point of the idea of multiple realizability. Organisms other than human beings have psychological states. Some can perceive and remember and feel pain, even if they aren't capable of all the complex thoughts and feelings that human beings can experience. Is it reasonable to suppose that these psychological states in other species must be based on precisely the same physical structures that are present in human beings?

Even within the human species, there may be variation in the physical structures used to encode this or that mental state. Indeed, even within a single human being, there may be many ways that the brain can encode a single piece of information. When you believe that lemons are yellow at two different times, maybe the brain structure that encodes your belief at the one time differs from the brain structure that encodes it at the other time.

This is functionalism's criticism of the identity theory. A given mental type—believing that lemons are yellow, wanting a drink of water, feeling pain—is not identical with any single physical type. The reason the identity theory is false is that psychological types have multiple physical realizations. This point might be formulated slightly sarcastically by saying that functionalism accuses the identity theory of being a "chauvinistic doctrine." (This quip is due to Ned Block, "Troubles with Functionalism," in W. Savage [ed.], *Perception and Cognition*, University of Minnesota Press, 1978.) Identity theorists say that a computer or another species must be like us physically if it is to have a mind and mental characteristics. Functionalism regards this as implausibly restrictive. This, then, is the negative thesis that functionalism advances. Mental properties are *not* identical with physical properties. Notice that this rejection of type-identity is consistent with accepting token-identity. Perhaps being a mousetrap isn't a physical property, but each mousetrap is a physical thing. Perhaps believing that lemons are yellow isn't a physical property, but my present state of believing that lemons are yellow might still be identical with a physical state that my brain occupies. Functionalism rejects the identity theory's thesis of *type*-identity, not its thesis of *token*-identity.

The identity theory is a version of materialism. So is functionalism. The identity theory denies that minds are made of an immaterial substance; it denies that disembodied spirits exist. Functionalism agrees. The following table shows how these two theories are related to each other, and also to dualism:

Types and Tokens: How Dualism, the Identity Theory, and Functionalism are Related			
	Dualism	*Functionalism*	*Identity theory*
Are all mental types identical with physical types?	No	No	Yes
Are all mental tokens identical with physical tokens?	No	Yes	Yes

Functionalism is an intermediate position; it is conceptually "in between" dualism and the identity theory.

Functionalism's Positive Thesis

So much for the negative thesis. What positive account does functionalism provide concerning what the mind and its properties are like? The name *functionalism* suggests what this positive account is. Let's return to the property of being a mousetrap. This property, I've argued, is not identical with any single physical property. What, then, makes something a mousetrap? What do the mousetraps have in common that makes them different from the non-mousetraps? A mousetrap is any device that functions to turn a free mouse into a caught one. Mousetraps are things that play a particular causal role. Any device that produces certain effects in certain circumstances counts as a mousetrap, regardless of what physical materials it is made of or how it is physically constructed. The property of being a mousetrap is a functional property.

What does it mean, then, to claim that psychological properties are "functional" properties? Let's consider a psychological state X that has the following characteristics:

When someone believes that there is water in a cup in front of her and the individual is in state X, she drinks from the cup.

When someone believes that a well contains water and she is in state X, then the individual will draw water from the well and drink it.

Each of these two statements is a *conditional*; it describes what an agent will do *if* the agent has a particular belief and is in state X. Can you guess from these two conditionals what state X is? A reasonable conjecture is that X is the state of wanting to drink water. Of course, there is more to this desire than what these two conditionals describe. Functionalism maintains that these conditionals, and others like them, describe what it is to have a particular desire. Any state that plays the right causal role will be the desire to drink water. The physical composition of the state does not matter. Psychological states are to be understood in terms of their causal relations to behavior and to other mental states. This example concerning state X suggests the following functionalist proposal for understanding what it is for an agent to have a desire:

S wants proposition P to be true if and only if, if S's beliefs are true, then S will cause P to become true.

Notice that this proposal describes desire as a state that plays a particular causal role: When added to beliefs, desires produce actions of certain sorts. As plausible as this suggestion might be at first glance, there are problems. First, people don't always get what they want when their beliefs are true. A pitcher may want to strike out a batter and may have true beliefs about how to achieve this, but still the pitcher may fail. The second objection is that people sometimes cause propositions to come true that they don't want to come true. When I drink from the cup, I cause my moustache to get damp, but this isn't something I want. So there is a defect in the functionalist proposal just stated for understanding what desire is. Perhaps it can be repaired. Maybe there is something right about the idea that mental states are to be understood in terms of their causal connections with behavior and with other mental states.

Sensations

The kind of difficulty we have been considering is especially prominent when we shift our attention from beliefs and desires to sensations. Consider what a functionalist says about the nature of pain, for example. When people are in pain, they are inclined to say "Ouch!" They are inclined to withdraw their bodies from the stimulus they think is causing the pain. And being in pain diminishes a person's attention span and has other psychological effects as well. Suppose I exhaustively described the causes and the effects of being in pain. These would involve the relationship of being in pain to external stimuli, to behavior, and to other psychological states. (Some of these I just mentioned.) It is sometimes suggested that this functionalist account of pain leaves out the most important fact about pain—the fact that pain *hurts*. A state may play the functional role of pain and still not be a pain state, or so this objection asserts. If this is right, then functionalism will fail as an account of the nature of pain.

I won't try to answer this question of whether functionalism is adequate. Perhaps there are some psychological phenomena that functionalism cannot adequately characterize. Maybe sensations (like pain) are counterexamples to functionalism. Even if this is true, however, there may be other psychological states for which functionalism is adequate; perhaps belief and desire can be understood along functionalist lines. This is now a controversial issue in philosophy.

Summary

I have argued that dualism, logical behaviorism, and the Mind/Brain Identity Theory are each inadequate. I think there is nothing wrong with mentalism—the view that beliefs and desires are inner causes of outward behavior. Behavior *provides evidence* about what an agent's mental states are, but behavior does not *define* what it is to be in a given mental state. To make sense of mentalism, we need not think that an agent's mind is made of some strange immaterial substance (as dualism maintains). Individuals have minds in virtue of the physical organization of their bodies. This, however, does not require that all the individuals who possess some psychological characteristic (like feeling pain or believing that lemons are yellow) have some single physical characteristic in common. My conclusion is that functionalism's negative thesis is correct; it is plausible to hold that psychological states are multiply realizable. As for the positive thesis that functionalism advances, it remains to be seen whether an adequate functionalist account of different mental states can be developed.

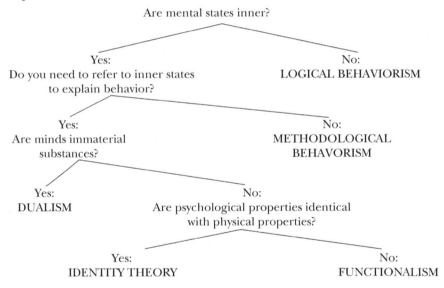

In the rest of this part of the book, I'll explore two other philosophical problems about the mind. If human beings act as they do because of what they think and want, and if what they think and want is caused by things outside of themselves, how can human beings have free will? This problem is addressed in Chapters 24–26. After that, I'll consider the problem of psychological egoism. If human beings act on the basis of what they think and want, doesn't it follow that people always act selfishly—that they try to satisfy their own wants and never care, ultimately, about the welfare of others?

Review Questions

1   I return home from a furniture store and report to my family, "They're selling our sofa." I look at the plate of food in front of my son and say, "That is what I ate for lunch." How does the type/token distinction help identify an ambiguity that is present in each of these two remarks?

2   What does it mean to say that a psychological property (a type) is multiply realizable?

3   Functionalists criticize the Mind/Brain Identity Theory for being "chauvinistic." What does this mean?

4   How is it possible to reject the identity theory without thinking that there are immaterial minds (disembodied spirits)?

5   Functionalists try to characterize what it is to have a psychological property (like feeling pain or believing that Washington is the capital of the United States) by describing that property's "causal role." What does that mean?

6   What is the negative thesis advanced by functionalists about mental states? What is their positive thesis? Do you find these theses plausible? Why or why not?

7   What are two reasons for thinking that the functionalist account of desire is not fully adequate? (In what sorts of cases do the characteristic "causal roles" associated with desire seem less relevant to understanding, explaining, or predicting human behaviour?)

8   How does functionalism differ from the Mind/Brain Identity Theory? Can someone be both an identity theorist and a functionalist about mental states? Why or why not?

9   How, if at all, can functionalists account for sensations like pleasure or pain? Why?

Problems for Further Thought

1   The fact that two types apply to exactly the same tokens isn't enough to ensure that they are identical. For example, *being a unicorn* and *being a golden mountain* are different types (properties), even though they apply to exactly the same objects (namely, to no objects at all). Can the same point be made with respect to types that are exemplified? Can two types be different, even though they apply to the same (nonempty) set of objects? Describe an example of this sort.

2   In Chapter 6, I discussed the concept of fitness that is used in evolutionary theory. What would it mean to say that fitness is *multiply realizable*? Is it plausible to claim that fitness has this characteristic?

3   Here is *the inverted spectrum problem*: You have a particular characteristic sensation when you look at red things and a quite different sensation when you look at green things. Is it possible that someone has precisely the reverse arrangement? This individual would have a red sensation when he looks at green things and a green sensation when he looks at red things. His behavior, including his use of language, would be precisely the same as yours. For example, he would apply the term "red" to fire engines and the term "green" to grasshoppers. If spectrum inversion is possible, what consequences does this have for functionalism's positive thesis about the nature of mental states?

Recommended Readings, Video, and Audio

Visit the companion website at www.routledge.com/cw/sober for suggestions of readings, video, and audio, for this chapter.

Chapter 24

Freedom, Determinism, and Causality

Although dualists, identity theorists, and functionalists disagree about a lot, they all grant that the mind and the physical world causally interact. Your beliefs and desires cause your body to move in various ways. In addition, mental states themselves have causal antecedents in the physical world. What you now believe and the preferences you now have—indeed, your personality as a whole—can be traced back to experiences you have had. These experiences were themselves caused by items in your physical environment. In addition, modern science recognizes that some features of your mind may be influenced by the genetic endowment you received from your parents.

So just as the human mind has effects on the physical environment, so too does the physical world affect our mental states. The following diagram represents these causal relationships:

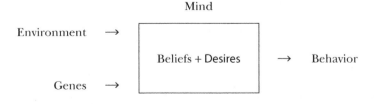

The Problem of Freedom

The puzzle about the existence of human freedom can now be given a preliminary formulation. Your beliefs and desires, and hence your behavior, are caused by things outside your control. You didn't freely choose the genes you have or the sequence of environments in which you grew up. If you didn't freely choose them, how can it be said that any of your behaviors is the result of free choices on your part? How can you be responsible for actions that were caused by events (long ago) over which you exercised no control? It looks like you are no more free than a computer; a computer behaves as it does because it was programmed to do so, and so, apparently, do you.

Another way to see the problem is to attend to a different feature of the above causal picture. Suppose your behavior is the result of your beliefs and desires just as a computer's behavior is the result of its programming. There is a feature of the computer's situation that seems also to characterize your own. Given the computer's program, it can't act differently from the way it does. Suppose a computer is programmed to compute the sum of two numbers. This means that if you input 7 and 5, then the computer can't fail to output 12. The computer can't act other than the way it does.

Are we like computers in this respect? Given the beliefs and desires we presently have, isn't it inevitable that we do precisely what we do? Our beliefs and desires leave open what we will do no more than a computer's program leaves open what it will do. This fact about the computer, and about ourselves if we are like the computer, seems to entail that we are not free agents. The reason is that if an action is performed freely, then it must have been possible for the agent to have done otherwise. If I freely lift a cup of coffee to my lips, then it must have been possible for me to refrain from lifting the cup to my lips. But given the beliefs and desires I had, I couldn't have done anything other than lift the cup to my lips. Our actions are the inevitable consequences of the minds we have, just as a computer's output is the inevitable consequence of its program.

I've just pointed out two features of the causal relationships depicted in the diagram on the preceding page. Each suggests its own argument for the thesis that no human action is free. I'll call the first argument the *Distant Causation Argument;* it focuses on the idea that our behaviors are caused by factors (our genes and our early childhood environment) that were beyond our control. I'll call the second argument the *Could-Not-Have-Done-Otherwise Argument;* it focuses on the claim that it is impossible for us to act other than the way our beliefs and desires cause us to act. Both these arguments will be discussed later. Before reading further, write out each of these arguments, with premises and conclusions stated carefully, and make sure that what you come up with is an argument that is deductively valid. Once you do this, it should be clear that if we sometimes act freely, at least one premise in each argument must be false. Notice also that both these arguments reach a conclusion of total generality; each concludes that *not one* of our actions is performed freely. This goes beyond the more modest idea that *some* of our actions aren't performed freely.

---

21 Transitivity

Some objects stand in relation to others. Alice *is taller than* Ben. David *loves* Edward. The italicized terms denote relationships. The names flanking the italicized term refer to objects that are said to be related to each other.

Some relations are transitive; others are not. If Alice is taller than Ben and Ben is taller than Cathy, then Alice is taller than Cathy. A relation R is said to be transitive precisely when it has this property:

For any three objects *a, b*, and *c*, if *a* bears R to *b*, and *b* bears R to *c*, then *a* must bear R to *c*.

Being taller than is a transitive relation. *Loving* is not a transitive relationship. The fact that David loves Edward and Edward loves Flo does not guarantee that David loves Flo.

Causality is a relation that obtains between events. Holmes's pulling the trigger caused Moriarty to die. Moriarty's death caused alarm to spread in the London underworld. Does it follow that Holmes's pulling the trigger caused alarm to spread in the London underworld? That is, is causality a transitive relation?

Does the Distant Causation Argument, discussed in this chapter, assume that causality is transitive?

Examples of Unfree Acts

It is controversial whether the Distant Causation Argument and the Could-Not-Have-Done-Otherwise Argument are right in their claim that human beings never act freely. However, it is not especially controversial that some human actions are not performed freely. Here I want to give two examples. The first is a behavior produced by *brainwashing*. Consider the case of Patty Hearst. Heiress to the newspaper fortune, Hearst was kidnaped and abused mentally and physically by her captors for several months in 1974. She then participated with them in a bank robbery. Later, she was caught and brought to trial. There was never any doubt that Hearst helped rob the bank. The question was whether she did so of her own free will. The defense attorneys tried to establish that Hearst didn't have free will at that time; they argued that her captors had so distorted her mental faculties that she was a mere pawn in their hands. Her actions were an expression of *their* wants, not of *hers*, or so they argued. The prosecution tried to show that Hearst was a free agent; they argued that even though she had been abused, she was still a willing participant in the bank robbery. The prosecution won the case, and Patty Hearst went to jail. Quite apart from whether this was the right outcome, I want to draw your attention to an idea on which both the defense and the prosecution agreed: People who do what they do because of brainwashing aren't acting of their own free will. Here, then, is one kind of behavior that I think we can safely regard as unfree.

The second category of unfree behavior was described by Freud. Freud describes a man who obsessively washes his hands. He is caught in the grip of a compulsion. Even after normal people would recognize that their hands are clean, the compulsive handwasher keeps scrubbing away. Sometimes the compulsion is so extreme that the person's flesh is eaten away, exposing the bone. "They can't help themselves," we may want to say. Another example of this sort is kleptomania. A kleptomaniac is someone driven by the compulsion to steal. Even when they recognize that stealing is ruining their lives, kleptomaniacs find themselves powerless to change their behavior. Perhaps some people steal of their own free will; this does not seem to be true of kleptomaniacs.

Even philosophers who think that we sometimes act freely usually concede that brainwashing and compulsions rob us of our freedom. The question is whether there are *other* categories of behavior that are genuinely free. The Distant Causation Argument and the Could-Not-Have-Done-Otherwise Argument answer this question in the negative.

Are All Behaviors Like Those Produced by Brainwashing and Compulsions?

To decide whether we ever act freely, you need to decide whether some of our behaviors differ significantly from the unfree behaviors just described. If brainwashing robs us of freedom, what should we say about the way a normal upbringing shapes us into the kinds of people we are? If indoctrination robs people of their freedom, what effect does education have on the possibility of free action? If a victim of brainwashing isn't responsible for what he or she does, how can we say that "normal" individuals are responsible for what they do?

Shifting now to the examples of compulsive behavior, we can ask—if compulsive behavior is unfree, what should we say about normal cases of rational deliberation in which people act on the basis of the wants they have? Perhaps the only difference between someone said to have a compulsion and a "normal" person is that they have different wants. It is unusual to want to wash your hands two hundred times a day, but not so unusual to want to wash them once after they get covered with dirt. If this is the only thing that distinguishes compulsive behavior from normal behavior, why say that the one is any less free than the other? To understand what freedom is, we need to answer questions such as these.

A Clash of Plausible Conceptions

The problem of freedom involves an apparent clash between two very fundamental ways we have of conceiving of ourselves. First, there is the idea that we are part of the causal network. Our actions don't spring from nothing; rather, they trace back to the beliefs, desires, and other mental features we possess. These mental characteristics also have their causal antecedents, in our genes and environment. Second, there is the idea that (at least sometimes) we perform actions of our own free will. Is there an unresolvable conflict between these two ideas, or can they be reconciled?

The arguments considered above concerned two different stages of the causal process represented in the figure. The Distant Causation Argument concerns the relationship of your actions to your genes and environment. The Could-Not-Have-Done-Otherwise Argument concerns the relationship of your actions to your beliefs and desires. In spite of this difference, the two arguments have something in common. Both assert that your actions are caused, and both assert that some fact about how your actions are caused shows that all of those actions are unfree. As noted before, if you think that some actions are performed freely, you must reject one or the other of these two premises.

What Is Causality?

For the rest of this chapter, I want to focus on the second of these key concepts. What does it mean to say that some events "cause" others? Understanding causality has been a very deep philosophical problem at least since David Hume's work in the eighteenth century. I won't attempt to get to the bottom of this cluster of problems. I will, however, try to clarify what causality is—enough so that we can better understand how causality and freedom are related.

What does it mean to say that striking a match caused the match to ignite? This doesn't mean that the striking was, all by itself, enough to get the match to light. After all, besides being struck, the match had to be dry and there had to be oxygen in the air. So the first fact about causality is this: *A cause need not be a sufficient condition for its effect.* The second fact about causality is that there are usually many ways to get a particular effect to occur. Striking the match caused it to light, but that doesn't mean that striking the match was the only way to get the match to catch fire. Using a magnifying glass to focus sunlight on the match head would have done the trick. And putting the match into a heated frying pan also would have worked. So the second fact is this: *Causes often are not necessary for their effects to occur.* (See Chapter 12 to review the definitions of necessary and sufficient conditions.)

I now want to note a difference between *a* cause of an event and what we may term *the whole cause* of that event. Striking the match is *a* cause of its lighting. It is, however, only part of the whole set of causally relevant facts. Suppose I somehow were able to list all the causally relevant facts about the match at a given time. At that time, the match is struck in a certain way, there is oxygen present, the match is dry, and so on. Given all this information, what can we conclude about what will happen next?

Determinism

Can we say that the match *may* light? Yes. Can we say something more—namely, that the match *must* light, given this complete specification of all the earlier causal facts? The idea that a complete description of the causal facts guarantees what will happen next is the thesis of *determinism*. This thesis says that if you list all the causally relevant facts pertaining to the match and its environment at a given time, these facts uniquely determine what will happen next. The match's future is not left open by its present state. Given a complete description of the match's present state, there is only one option as to what will happen next.

Sometimes, we describe the causally relevant facts about an object so that the description does leave open what will happen next. For example, suppose we say that a pair of dice is fair. If this is all we know, we should conclude that the probability that the dice will land double-six on the next roll is 1/36. The fact that the dice are fair and that you're now rolling them does not allow you to say what *must* happen. All you can say is that the dice *may* land double-six, but it is also true that they *may* fail to do so. This does not mean that the pair of dice violates the thesis of determinism. That thesis says only that a *complete* description of the system determines what will happen next. Perhaps causal determinism is true and my description of the dice is incomplete. This has some plausibility. For example, I didn't describe exactly how the dice are rolled, what the surface is like on which they land, or what the wind conditions are that affect them as they leave your hand. Causal determinism says only that if *all* the causally relevant facts are set out, these will leave open only one possible future for the pair of dice.

Indeterminism

Is determinism true? Before I answer this question, let's be clear on what it would be for determinism to be false. If determinism is false, then the world is indeterministic. This means that a complete description of the causal facts at one time leaves open what will happen next. In such a universe, all you can say is that the complete present state of a system makes some futures more probable than others; even a complete description of the present will leave open more than one possible future.

Until the twentieth century, determinism was a plausible and widely accepted thesis about the world. Newton's laws of motion, for example, are deterministic in character. You may recall from high school physics that those laws do not make use of the concept of probability. For example, Newton's law "$F = ma$" says that if a billiard ball of mass m is acted on by a force of magnitude F, the ball will have an acceleration equal to F/m. The law does not say that this will "probably" happen, as if there are other possibilities that could happen instead. Rather, the law says what must happen if the object is acted on in a certain way. This Newtonian picture about how physical objects move provides a suggestive model for how *all* events in nature ultimately will be described. Living things are more complicated than billiard balls; creatures with minds are more complicated than many living things. The idea I want to consider, however, says that all things that are made of matter are ultimately governed by the laws of physics. So, since Newtonian theory is deterministic, the idea is that the behaviors of living things and of things with minds must also be deterministic in character. The thought behind this generalized Newtonian thesis is that "determinism percolates up." If elementary particles are deterministic, so is everything that is made of elementary particles. If a person's mind is a material object, then his or her beliefs, desires, and subsequent behaviors are governed by deterministic laws. I'm not saying that Newton was right about elementary particles, and I'm not saying that the mind is a physical thing made of elementary particles (recall that dualism denies this). Rather, I want you to consider a certain idea: *If* all matter is deterministic and *if* a person's mind is a material thing, then human behavior is physically determined.

One of the if's in what I've just described—the idea that matter is deterministic—wasn't much questioned until the twentieth century. It was then that Niels Bohr, Werner Heisenberg, and Erwin Schrödinger developed the Quantum Theory. This theory is now interpreted in different ways by physicists, but the standard interpretation (which is called "the Copenhagen interpretation," for Bohr's hometown) is that the Quantum Theory says that the behavior of particles is not deterministic. According to this interpretation of the theory, even a complete description of a physical system leaves open what its future will be like. Some futures will be more probable than others, but the number of possibilities is always greater than one. In short, the present does not determine the future—chance is part of the way the world is.

It is by no means settled that the Copenhagen interpretation is the best interpretation of the Quantum Theory. Nor is it inconceivable that this very well-confirmed scientific theory will one day be replaced by another, which will say that the universe is deterministic. But what seems clear now is that one can't simply *assume* that determinism must be right. Perhaps the universe is deterministic, and then again, perhaps it is not. This is a scientific question to be settled by scientific investigation. One can't decide *a priori* whether determinism is true.

Suppose we are made of matter. Suppose that our psychological characteristics aren't due to the presence of some immaterial substance (as Cartesian Dualism asserts), but are consequences of how the matter we are made of is structured. If this is right, then I suggest that our behavior must be like the behaviors of physical particles. If chance influences the behavior of particles, then chance also influences the behavior of people. That is, I'm advancing the thesis that *in*determinism percolates up. If physical things don't obey deterministic laws, then our beliefs and desires don't determine what our actions will be. Rather, those beliefs and desires make some actions vastly more probable than others. Similarly our genes plus the environments we inhabit do not determine what our thoughts and wants will be. Again, the relationship is probabilistic, not deterministic.

Most philosophers who have written about the issue of human freedom have not worried about the implications of the Quantum Theory. Usually they have assumed that matter is deterministic and then have considered what this implies about the question of whether we are free. This is entirely understandable for people such as David Hume, who wrote about the issue of freedom long before the Quantum Theory came on the scene; Hume was writing in the heyday of the Newtonian world picture.

22 Two Uses of Probability

We often use the concept of probability to describe our *lack of knowledge*. When we say that a coin has an equal chance of landing heads or tails on the next toss, we often mean that the coin is evenly balanced (fair) and that we don't know exactly how it will be tossed or what the wind conditions will be.

If determinism is true, then the only reason we need to talk about probabilities is that we lack a complete description of the coin's initial state. Recall that determinism says that a complete description of a system at one time uniquely determines what will happen next; the present can't leave open different future possibilities each of which has some chance of coming true. If determinism is true, then we need the concept probability only to describe something subjective—namely, the fact that we sometimes (or always) lack complete information.

On the other hand, if determinism is false, then probability describes an objective fact about the world. Chance is a feature of the way things happen. In this case, probability talk isn't simply a way to represent our ignorance. In short, whether determinism is true affects how we should use the concept of probability.

Does Indeterminism Make Us Free?

If the world is indeterministic, how does that fact affect the issue of whether we are free? My suspicion is that the shift from determinism to indeterminism does not make much of a difference. The reason I say this is that if you suspect that determinism rules out freedom, you'll probably be inclined to think that we wouldn't be free if indeterminism were true instead.

Suppose you think we can't have free will on the grounds that our thoughts and wants are causally determined by factors outside our control. We don't freely choose the genes we have or the environments we inhabit in early childhood. These are thrust upon us. They shape the kinds of people we are as well as the specific beliefs and desires we have. Given all this, how can our actions be regarded as free? This is the thought expressed in the Distant Causation Argument. Maybe you find the Distant Causation Argument somewhat plausible. The question I want to ask is whether you would change your mind about freedom if chance were introduced into the above story. That is, suppose that your beliefs and desires were due to genes, environments, *and chance*. I suggest that if determinism robs you of freedom, chance seems to rob you of freedom as well.

The same point applies to the Could-Not-Have-Done-Otherwise Argument. Suppose you agree with this argument's thesis—that our actions can't be free, since they are inevitable, given the beliefs and desires we have. Would introducing chance into this story make more room for freedom? I think not. If the fact that your beliefs and desires determine your action makes you unfree, I think you'd still be unfree if your actions were caused by your beliefs, desires, *and chance*. To make this point graphic, consider a kind of brain surgery. Suppose you are now a deterministic system: Your beliefs and desires determine what you will do. I now offer you a brain implant, whereby a tiny roulette wheel is introduced into your deliberation processes. If you lack free will when you are a deterministic system, would the operation make you free? This seems implausible. Before the operation, you were a slave to your beliefs and desires. After the surgery, you are a slave to your beliefs, desires, and to the implanted roulette wheel. The shift from being a deterministic system to being an indeterministic system has not made a difference as far as the question of freedom is concerned.

Causality Is the Issue, Not Determinism

My suggestion is that determinism *and* indeterminism *both* pose a problem for human freedom. The reason is that causality can exist in an indeterministic universe just as much as it can in a deterministic one. If your mental states are caused by factors outside your control, how can you be a free agent? Whether these causal factors *determine* your behavior is not essential.

It isn't hard to visualize how some events can cause others in a deterministic universe. If striking the match causes the match to light, determinism tells us that the striking completed a set of causal conditions that determines that the match must light. But how can some events cause others if determinism is false? The following example (due to Fred Dretske and Aaron Snyder, "Causal Irregularity," *Philosophy of Science*, Vol. 39, 1972, pp. 69–71) shows, I think, that this is possible. Suppose a roulette wheel is connected to a gun, which is pointed at a cat. If I spin the roulette wheel and the ball lands on 00, this will cause the gun to fire, which then will kill the cat. Suppose that the roulette wheel is an indeterministic system—spinning the wheel does not determine where the ball will drop. Now suppose I spin the wheel and the ball happens to fall on 00, thereby killing the cat. It seems to me that my spinning the wheel caused the cat to die, even though the process is not deterministic. The death of the cat *traces back* to my spinning the wheel. For this to be true, it is not required that my spinning the wheel *made it inevitable* that the cat would die. This is why it is possible to have causation without determinism.

Thus, my suggestion is that the real problem is not to see whether determinism and freedom can be reconciled, but to see whether causality and freedom can be reconciled. However, since the traditional positions about freedom all focus on deterministic causation, I'll do the same.

What Does Determinism Say about the Causation of Behavior?

To fix ideas, let's be clear on how the thesis of determinism would apply to the diagram given earlier. This diagram represents the idea that your genes and environment cause your present mental state, and that this, in turn, causes your behavior. What do these causal relations mean if causality is understood deterministically? Let's suppose for a moment that this diagram is *complete*. That is, suppose it represents *all* the factors that influence your mental state and your subsequent behavior. What does the thesis of determinism say about this chain? It asserts the following: Given your genes and environment, you couldn't have had a set of beliefs and desires different from the set that you in fact possess, and given your beliefs and desires, you couldn't have performed an action different from the action that you in fact produced. Determinism, recall, is the thesis that the facts at one time uniquely determine what comes next.

Determinism Differs from Fatalism

Determinism is an entirely different doctrine from the idea termed *fatalism*. You can understand what fatalism says by seeing how it figures in the Greek myth about Oedipus. Oedipus was a victim of fate. The Fates decreed that he would kill his father and marry his mother. In the story, Oedipus does these things in spite of himself. The Fates somehow ensured that Oedipus would find himself in this sorry state of affairs no matter what choices he made and no matter what he did.

Determinism says that the present determines the future; it does *not* say that the future is cast in stone, unaffected by what is true of the present. Determinism is entirely consistent with the idea that what happens at a later time *depends* on what happened earlier. Determinism does not rule out the idea that if the past had been different, the present would be different. Determinism does not rule out the idea that I can affect what the future will be like by now acting one way rather than another. Fatalism denies this; it says that the future is *independent* of what you do in the present.

Newton said that billiard balls are deterministic systems. If you hit the ball in a certain way (call it W_1), then the ball will move to a certain position (call it P_1) on the table. But Newtonian physics also says that if you hit the ball in some *other* way (W_2), the ball will move to a *different* position (P_2). Notice that in this theory, the present *makes a difference* to the future. The future is controlled by the present.

What would it be for Oedipus to be a deterministic system? This does not require us to think that there are such things as the Fates. Oedipus would be a deterministic system if his actions were deterministically controlled by his beliefs and desires. If Oedipus has one set of beliefs and desires (call it S_1), then he produces one action (call it A_1). But if he had had a different set of beliefs and desires (S_2), his action would have been entirely different (A_2).

Here is a picture of Oedipus according to which he is a deterministic system, but fatalism is false: Oedipus's beliefs and desires, plus the environment he was in, ensured that he would kill his father and marry his mother. But if he had had a different set of beliefs and desires, he would not have done this.

It is easy to confuse determinism and fatalism, even though they are very different ideas. In fact, they are almost opposite in what they say. Fatalism says that our present beliefs and desires make no difference as far as what actions we will perform and as far as what will happen to us. In a sense, fatalism says that our beliefs and desires are impotent; they don't have the power to make a difference. But determinism, if we model it on the Newtonian idea, says that our beliefs and desires are *not* impotent; they causally control what we do and thereby powerfully influence what happens to us.

According to fatalism, there is no point in *trying* to do something. If it is fated that you will get an *A* in a course, you will get an *A* whether you try to get one or not; and if it is fated that you will get a *D*, you will, whether you try to avoid this fate or not. On the other hand, to think that your efforts influence what happens to you—to think that trying makes a difference to the grade you will receive—is to reject fatalism.

Greek mythology talked about the Fates. I'll assume that there are no such beings. I'll assume that fatalism is false. This leaves open the separate question of whether determinism is true. As I've noted, most previous writers on the free will problem have assumed that causality requires determinism. I hope you see why I reject this assumption; I think that causality is a fact about the world we inhabit, whether or not determinism turns out to be true.

Review Questions

1   What is the Distant Causation Argument? What is the Could-Not-Have-Done-Otherwise Argument? What do these arguments have in common? How do they differ?
2   Two examples of unfree actions were given. What were they?
3   What does the thesis of determinism assert? What is indeterminism? How do these theses employ the concept of a "sufficient condition" and the concept of a "complete description"?

4   An unusual sort of brain surgery was described in this chapter. What was it and what relevance does it have to the problem of free will?

5   What is fatalism? Is it accurately described by the saying, "que sera, sera" ("whatever will be, will be")? How does fatalism differ from determinism?

6   What is the difference between a cause of an action and the cause of an action? Does the fact that actions are always caused imply that actions are never free?

7   What does it mean to say that determinism or indeterminism "percolate upwards"?

8   Many philosophers have argued that, if the world is fundamentally deterministic, we cannot be genuinely free. Suppose we substituted "indeterministic" for "deterministic" in the conditional clause (such that "if the world is fundamentally indeterministic, then …"). Do you think the conclusion would change? Why or why not?

9   Why have I argued that causality, and not disputes over determinism vs. indeterminism, is the central issue in the free will debate? (Hint: Consider the structure of the Distant Causation and Could-Not-Have-Done-Otherwise arguments. What do both arguments suggest is a threat to free will?)

A Problem for Further Thought

Suppose the Fates decided to get Oedipus to kill his father and marry his mother by controlling what Oedipus thinks and wants. If this were so, would what happens to Oedipus be an example of determinism, fatalism, both or neither?

Recommended Readings, Video, and Audio

Visit the companion website at www.routledge.com/cw/sober for suggestions of readings, video, and audio, for this chapter.

A Menu of Positions on Free Will

In this chapter, I'll outline the standard philosophical positions on the relationship of freedom and determinism. I will then make some critical remarks about some of those positions. This will set the stage for the positive proposal I'll make in the next chapter about how the idea of freedom of the will should be understood.

"Compatibility" Defined

Before proceeding, I need to define a piece of terminology from logic. To say that two propositions are *compatible* is to say that the truth of one wouldn't rule out the truth of the other. Incompatibility means conflict; if one proposition were true, the other would have to be false. Two propositions can be compatible even though neither is, in fact, true. And two propositions can be incompatible even though both are false. Consider the following three statements:

(1) My shirt is green all over.
(2) My shirt is red all over.
(3) My shirt is torn.

Propositions (1) and (2) are incompatible; (1) and (3) are compatible. Do these facts about incompatibility and compatibility tell you what color my shirt is? Do they tell you whether the shirt is torn? The answer to both questions is *no*.

Incompatibilism and Compatibilism

Incompatibilism is a thesis about the problem of free will. It doesn't claim that determinism is true. It also doesn't claim that we are unfree. It merely asserts an if/then statement: *If determinism is true, then we aren't free.*

If two propositions (*D* and *F*) are incompatible, there are three possibilities: *D* is true and *F* is false; *D* is false and *F* is true; or *D* and *F* are both false. What is excluded by the claim of incompatibility is that both propositions are true. Of the three possible positions an incompatibilist can take, two have been prominent in philosophical discussion. The first holds that determinism is true and that we aren't free. This position has come to be called *hard determinism.* The second says that we are free and that our actions are not causally determined. This position is called *libertarianism.* These two positions agree that freedom and determinism can't both be true, but they disagree about which proposition is true and which is false.

Opposed to incompatibilism is the idea that determinism does not rule out the possibility that we are free. This view, not surprisingly, is called *compatibilism.* In principle, there are four possible subvarieties of compatibilism. If propositions *D* and *F* are compatible, then the options are (1) *D* and *F* are both true; (2) *D* and *F* are both false; (3) *D* is true and *F* is false; or (4) *D* is false and *F* is true. Of these four possible positions, only one has been discussed much in the philosophical literature. This view is called *soft determinism;* it holds that our actions are both free and causally determined. The basic idea here is that freedom does not require the absence of determinism, but rather requires that our actions be caused in a particular way.

So the basic menu of standard positions is as follows:

I   Incompatibilism (if determinism is true, then we lack freedom).

    A   Hard Determinism: Incompatibilism and determinism are true, so we lack freedom.

    B   Libertarianism: Incompatibilism is true and we are free, so determinism is false.

II Compatibilism (if determinism were true, that wouldn't rule out the possibility that we are free).

    A   Soft Determinism: Compatibilism and determinism are true, and we are free.

    B, C, D.

Note that this outline leaves some possible positions unlabeled. Be sure you understand what the unlabeled options are. My own view falls under II.B; I'm a compatibilist. As explained in the previous chapter, I don't think one can assume that determinism is true. I do, however, think that some of our actions are performed freely. The kind of compatibilist position I endorse will be described in the next chapter.

The three labeled positions display three patterns of similarity and difference. Soft determinism and libertarianism agree that we are free; hard and soft determinism agree that determinism is true; and hard determinism and libertarianism agree that incompatibilism is correct. To understand how these three positions are related, we can schematize each as endorsing an argument. Let *F* be the proposition that some of our actions are free, and let *D* be the proposition that determinism is true. Here is each position's characteristic argument:

Hard determinism:	*If D, then not-F* *D*
	————————————
	Not F
Libertarianism:	*If D, then not-F* *F*
	————————————
	Not D
Soft determinism:	*F* *D*
	————————————
	F and D are compatible

Note that each of these arguments is deductively valid. Our task is to figure out which of the premises are plausible.

Libertarianism

I'll begin by considering libertarianism. The philosopher C. A. Campbell (1897–1974) is the libertarian on whom I'll focus. Before I describe how Campbell defends libertarianism, let me note that "libertarianism" in the problem of free will is an entirely different doctrine from the idea that goes by that name in political philosophy. Libertarians in political philosophy argue that the state should not interfere in buying and selling or in other spheres of life. This is a *normative* view—a claim about the way things ought to be. On the other hand, libertarianism in the problem of free will is a *descriptive* claim, not a normative one. It asserts that we are free agents and that determinism is false. Libertarianism as a view about free will does not say whether it is good news or bad that we have free will.

---

23 The Normative Problem of Freedom

Libertarianism, soft determinism, and hard determinism take different stances on the question of whether we, in fact, are free. They don't advance claims as to whether it is a good thing or a bad thing to be free. In other words, these theories concern *descriptive*, not *normative*, issues.

There is a separate issue about freedom that arises in political philosophy. It involves the question of which freedoms people have a right to. Do people have rights to particular liberties, which may not be violated by other individuals or by the state? This is a normative question about what people should and shouldn't do. It isn't the same as the question of whether people have free will.

Freedoms, in this normative sense, can come into conflict. Some defenders of capitalism hold that people should be free to engage in buying and selling without regulation by the state. However, this can result in "boom and bust" cycles that produce widespread suffering. If freedom from want is an entitlement that people have, then certain economic freedoms may have to be regulated or curtailed. This and other normative questions about the freedoms that people are entitled to will be discussed in the section of this book on ethics.

Libertarians usually think they can tell by introspection that at least some of their actions aren't determined by the beliefs, desires, and other psychological characteristics they have; when we freely decide to do something, this decision is not causally determined by earlier events. For example, Campbell, in his book *Selfhood and Godhood* (Allen and Unwin, 1957), focuses on the fact that we sometimes perform actions that are "out of character." When we do this, he says, it isn't true that our actions are determined by the characters we have.

I have two objections to this line of thinking. First, as noted in Chapter 13, there is no reason to place such complete trust in introspection. The beliefs we form about ourselves by "gazing within" can be both incomplete and inaccurate. They can be incomplete because there may be facts about ourselves of which we aren't conscious—facts that introspection fails to detect. In addition, introspection can be inaccurate, since there are psychological mechanisms that systematically distort the way we appear to ourselves. Freud stressed both of these ideas. With respect to the latter category, he argued that some of our beliefs and desires would cause us great pain if we realized that we had them. As a "defense mechanism," introspection provides us with a false picture of what we really think and want. Although this view about introspection is characteristically Freudian, it is important to realize that many other approaches in psychology also endorse it. There is broad consensus that we shouldn't take the testimony of introspection at face value.

There is an additional difficulty with Campbell's view. He says that when we act out of character, our actions aren't determined by what our minds are like. I disagree. Consider a person who is usually cowardly but manages to act courageously on a given occasion. Is it plausible to think that the courageous act can't be explained by what the person's mind was like? I find this highly dubious. I suspect that there are aspects of the person's mind that came into play. Perhaps a combination of unusual circumstances led the person to muster his or her courage in a way that earlier had not been possible. So I really don't see that the actions we call "acting out of character" pose a problem for determinism. Campbell assumes that the phrase "acting out of character" means that the action isn't caused by the agent's character. But this is to misunderstand what the phrase really means. When people who usually are cowardly manage to act courageously, we might say "evidently, they had it in them." This testifies to the fact that "acting out of character" isn't something we think is uncaused.

Campbell accepts incompatibilism, he thinks that introspection shows that we sometimes produce free acts, and so he concludes that determinism must be false. I've suggested that this introspective argument against determinism is very weak. If you think that free will and determinism are incompatible, I don't see how the introspective impression we have that we are free can be decisive. The behaviorist psychologist B. F. Skinner, whose views I discussed in Chapter 21, wrote a book called *Beyond Freedom and Dignity* (Knopf, 1971). Like Campbell, Skinner is an incompatibilist; but, unlike Campbell, Skinner is a hard determinist. His view is that the introspective picture we have of ourselves as free agents is an illusion. It is a comforting idea—a fairy tale we tell ourselves. Although I don't agree with Skinner's hard determinism, I think that Skinner is right not to take introspection at face value. Baron d'Holbach, another hard determinist, took the same view of introspection in the eighteenth century; an excerpt from his book, *The System of Nature*, is available on-line.

If I thought that incompatibilism were true, I'd try to find out if human actions are determined. I would do this by seeing what science has to say about determinism and what psychology has to say about the causation of behavior. Campbell accepts incompatibilism, but argues in the opposite direction. He decides via introspection that some of our actions are free, and he concludes that our actions can't be causally determined. This, I think, is the wrong order in which to address the questions. Notice that Campbell's position, as I've presented it here, doesn't *argue* that incompatibilism is true. Rather, Campbell *assumes* that incompatibilism is true. He uses this as one of his premises to argue for the conclusion that our actions aren't causally determined.

Two Soft Determinist Theories

I turn now to the standard form that compatibilist theorizing takes—soft determinism. Soft determinist theories try to construct a plausible theory of what freedom is, one that shows why freedom is not ruled out by the alleged fact that our actions are determined. I think the two compatibilist theories I'll now consider are defective. However, they provide lessons concerning how a more successful compatibilist theory might be constructed.

The goal of a compatibilist theory is to show that an act is performed freely if it is caused in a particular sort of way; freedom doesn't require the absence of causality, but the right sort of causality. The goal of this theory is to make room for freedom in a world of causes.

Hume

I'll begin with the compatibilist account of freedom advanced by David Hume. His idea was that an action is performed freely when the agent could have done otherwise, had the agent wanted to. Suppose you accept an employer's offer of a summer job. Hume says you act freely if you could have declined the offer had you wanted to. By the same token, when you hand the robber your wallet after the robber says "your money or your life," you do so of your own free will, if the following were true: Had you wanted to die rather than stay alive, you could have refused to hand over your wallet. So Hume's theory is that free actions are ones that are under the causal control of the agent's beliefs and desires. When an action is under the agent's control in this way, it will be true that if the agent had had a different set of wants, the agent would have selected and performed a different action. Hume's is a compatibilist theory because it says that an action is free if it is causally related to the agent's beliefs and desires in a particular way.

What would an *unfree* action be like according to Hume's theory? Suppose you want to leave the room but you can't because you are handcuffed to the floor. In this case, you don't remain in the room freely. You stay in the room *whether you want to or not*. What you do is not under the control of your beliefs and desires.

Here is another example of unfreedom. Suppose I perform a brain operation on you. I disconnect your beliefs and desires from the nerves that send impulses to the rest of your body. I then implant a radio transmitter so that your body receives instructions from me. Now it is *my* beliefs and desires that dictate what *you* say and do. Your actions are no longer under the causal control of your own beliefs and desires. In this bizarre arrangement, your body would become a robot—a slave to my will. It would do what *I* want because I want it. After this operation, you do various things—you drink water, deposit money into my bank account, and so on. But you wouldn't be doing these things of your own free will. Hume's theory explains why your actions are unfree after the operation though many or all of them were free before.

First Objection to Hume's Theory: Compulsive Behavior

I think the main objection to Hume's theory is to be found in cases of *compulsive behavior*. Think of the kleptomaniac discussed in the previous chapter. A kleptomaniac is a thief whose desire to steal is overpoweringly strong. Kleptomaniacs want to steal even though they may be completely convinced that they will be caught and punished. Even with full knowledge that stealing will hurt them rather than help, they continue to steal. Kleptomaniacs are caught in the grip of an obsession. They are slaves to a desire that isn't diminished by the realization that acting on the desire does them more harm than good. There are thieves who aren't kleptomaniacs, of course. When they decide whether to steal, their decision is affected by information about the chance of being caught and punished. None of this information makes any difference to a kleptomaniac. The kleptomaniac is *stuck;* his desire isn't sensitive, in the familiar way, to considerations about self-interest.

I claim that when kleptomaniacs steal, they are not doing so freely. Kleptomaniacs lack freedom of will with respect to whether they steal. Yet, kleptomaniacs satisfy Hume's requirements for what it takes to be free. Kleptomaniacs want, above all, to steal things. When a kleptomaniac steals, he does so because of the desires he has. If he hadn't wanted to steal, he wouldn't have done so. The kleptomaniac's actions are under the control of his beliefs and desires. The problem is that there is something about the desires themselves and the way they work that make the kleptomaniac unfree.

The causal diagram from the previous chapter can be used to illustrate why Hume's account of freedom looks for freedom in the wrong place:

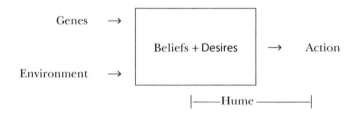

Hume's theory defines freedom in terms of a relation that obtains between beliefs and desires on the one hand and action on the other. For Hume, free actions are ones that are controlled by the agent's desires. The case of compulsive behavior provides an objection to Hume's account. It is the nature of the kleptomaniac's desires that makes him unfree. This suggests that a compatibilist theory shouldn't ignore the earlier links in the above causal chain.

Second Objection to Hume's Theory: Locke's Locked Room

There is a second, more subtle, problem with Hume's account. In his *Essay Concerning Human Understanding* (1690), John Locke (1632–1704) describes a man who decides to remain in a room in order to talk with a friend. Unbeknown to the man, the door of the room has been locked. The man remains in the room voluntarily, although it is false that he could have done otherwise had he chosen to do so. Locke's point is that an action can be voluntary even though the agent was not free to do otherwise. I think the man in the room stays there *of his own free will.* He freely chooses to stay in the room even though he is not free to exit it. If this is correct, Hume's theory is mistaken. For you to have performed some action of your own free will, it is not essential that you could have performed some other action if you had wanted to do so.

Here's another example that illustrates the same point. Take any action that an agent performed of his or her own free will. For example, suppose that Joe attended a concert last night of his own free will. Now imagine that if he hadn't decided to go to the concert, he would have been kidnapped and taken there against his will. Joe didn't know about this plot when he was deciding whether he would attend. The point is that Joe attended the concert of his own free will, even though he couldn't have done otherwise.

There is an important difference between the man locked in the room (though he doesn't know he is) and the kleptomaniac. The kleptomaniac's thought processes have malfunctioned; it is because of this malfunction that his stealing is not done freely. But the thought processes of the man in Locke's room have not malfunctioned. His will is free, although he isn't free to act in certain ways.

Does Coercion Rob Us of Free Will?

This contrast is important to bear in mind when you think about another important issue for the free will problem—coercion. Consider a robber who coerces you into handing over your cash by saying "your money or your life." The robber has robbed you of your money. But has he also robbed you of your free will?

The robber presents you with an option—you can keep your money and die, or hand over your wallet and live. One option he has taken away from you is for you to keep your money *and also* stay alive. You aren't free to do that. But has the robber robbed you of your free will?

This is a hard problem, but let me tentatively venture this answer: In many cases (if not in all), coerced actions don't rob their victims of free will. Of course, they can rob their victims of many things that are precious. And, of course, it is often wrong to place people in situations in which they have the choices (and only the choices) that the robber offers them. My point, however, is that the robbery victim's decision to surrendering his wallet is very different from the kleptomaniac's "decision" to steal. The robbery victim's mind is functioning well; it is the circumstances in which the victim finds himself that are objectionable. In contrast, something has gone wrong with the kleptomaniac's mind, and it is this mental incapacity that makes him lack free will.

A Second Compatibilist Proposal: The Relevance of Second-Order Desires

I now want to consider a second compatibilist theory, one that is intended to meet the problem posed by compulsive behavior. The theory I'll sketch is based somewhat loosely on ideas developed by Gerald Dworkin (in "Acting Freely," *Nous*, Vol. 4, 1970, pp. 367–83) and Harry Frankfurt (in "Freedom of the Will and the Concept of a Person," *Journal of Philosophy*, Vol. 68, 1971, pp. 5–20). The idea is that people in the grip of a compulsion are unfree because they act on the basis of desires they would rather not have, but are powerless to expunge. Suppose you ask a kleptomaniac whether he would like to get rid of his overpowering desire to steal and he replies that he would be glad to have this monkey off his back. This kleptomaniac has two desires: (1) he wants to steal and (2) he wants to stop having the desire to steal. The theory we are considering says that the kleptomaniac lacks free will because the second desire is unable to expunge the first.

The proposal we are considering requires us to distinguish first-order from second-order desires. A second-order desire is a desire about what one's desires should be. A first-order desire is a desire about what should be true in the world outside of one's mind. "I want some ice cream" is first-order; "I wish my desire for ice cream were less intense" is second-order.

The compatibilist theory we are considering says that people have free will when their second-order desires are related in a specific way to their first-order desires. According to this theory, it isn't enough that one's first- and second-order desires are in harmony. Suppose an alcoholic is so obsessed with alcohol that his addiction warps his ideas about what sort of person he wants to be. His craving for alcohol makes him want to have this craving; he can't even see the harm his alcoholism is doing. The lack of conflict between his first- and second-order desires does not entail that he has free will. The question is whether he would have the power to reshape his first-order desires if they were to conflict with his second-order desires. If he wanted to crave alcohol less, would this diminish the degree to which he wants to drink? If he has free will, the answer must be *yes*, or so this compatibilist theory maintains.

Although this proposal rightly says that many people who are in the grip of compulsions lack free will, it is still defective. Just as the kleptomaniac and the alcoholic have first-order desires that are compulsions, it is possible to have second-order desires that are compulsions. Consider a person who is brainwashed into thinking that sexual desire is always evil. This creates a second-order desire—they want to expunge all of their sexual desires. Suppose their second-order desire is so powerful that it transforms their first-order desires; after a while, they cease to have any sexual desires at all. This does not show that they have free-will. Just as a person can lack free will when their first-order desires are "stuck," a person can also lack free will when their second-order desires are "stuck."

In this chapter, I have outlined and criticized two compatibilist theories of freedom. In the next chapter, I outline a third compatibilist account.

Review Questions

1 What does it mean to say that X and Y are compatible? What does incompatibility mean? What do X and Y stand for?

2 Define compatibilism, incompatibilism, hard determinism, libertarianism, and soft determinism.

3 What argument have libertarians given for thinking that some actions are free? Assess this argument.

4 Explain Hume's theory of freedom. What makes it a compatibilist theory? Why does compulsive behavior provide a counterexample to this theory? Why does Locke's example of the man locked in the room provide a counterexample to Hume's theory? Hume suggests necessary and sufficient conditions for freedom. Which of these objections shows that the conditions aren't necessary? Which shows that they are not sufficient?

5 Are the following propositions equivalent in meaning? (I) S did A of her own free will; (II) S was free to not do A. How does Locke's example of the locked room bear on this question?

6 Describe and evaluate the Dworkin/Frankfurt theory of free will.

7 What makes Hume's theory of freedom compatibilist? Why do (1) compulsive behaviors and (2) Locke's thought experiment about the man unwittingly locked in a room serve as counterexamples to it?

8 Hume suggests both necessary and sufficient conditions for freedom. Which of the above objections suggests that his proposed conditions aren't necessary? Which shows that they are not sufficient?

9 Would a compulsive gambler who both wants to gamble and wishes he didn't want to gamble qualify as free according to Hume? According to Frankfurt? According to Campbell?

10   What does it mean to say that libertarianism (or soft determinism, or hard determinism) is a descriptive claim?

11   (A) Are all incompatibilists libertarians? Are all libertarians incompatibilists? (B) Are all compatibilists determinists? Are all determinists compatibilists?

Problems for Further Thought

1   In the selection from Campbell's *Selfhood and Godhood* reprinted at the end of this section of the book, Campbell argues that some actions occur neither by chance nor by necessity. These are examples of *creative activity*, "in which [...] nothing determines the act save the agent's doing it." According to Campbell, these are the acts that are free. Define what "chance" and "necessity" mean, taking into account the definitions of determinism and indeterminism provided in the previous chapter. Do your definitions allow that some actions may fall into neither category?

2   How does the idea of circumstantial necessity introduced in Chapter 14 apply to the present chapter?

3   In this lecture, I argued that the Dworkin/Frankfurt theory fails to provide a sufficient condition for having free will. This leaves it open whether the theory provides a necessary condition. See if you can construct an example that shows that the condition described in the theory is not necessary for having free will.

Recommended Readings, Video, and Audio

Visit the companion website at www.routledge.com/cw/sober for suggestions of readings, video, and audio, for this chapter.

Compatibilism

In the previous chapter, I presented and criticized two compatibilist theories of freedom. Each seeks to show that freedom doesn't require the absence of causality; both say that an action is free when it arises by a certain sort of causal process. In this chapter, I present a third compatibilist theory, one inspired by an idea suggested by my colleagues Dennis Stampe and Martha Gibson (in their "Of One's Own Free Will," *Philosophy and Phenomenological Research*, Vol. 52, 1992, pp. 529–56). After presenting a simplified version of this theory, I'll describe an objection to it. I won't propose a way of meeting this objection, but will leave the problem of free will unsolved. However, I do hope to convince you that compatibilism is a plausible view, even though I don't claim that a completely plausible compatibilist theory has yet been articulated.

The Weather Vane Analogy

I'll begin with an analogy. Consider a weather vane. This is a device that farmers put on top of their barns to tell them which direction the wind is blowing. We talk about weather vanes being "stuck." We also talk about weather vanes being "free." What does this mean?

A free weather vane is one that responds to certain causal influences. If the wind is blowing north, a free weather vane will point north. The behavior of a free weather vane isn't uncaused. A stuck weather vane, on the other hand, doesn't respond to the wind's direction. When a weather vane is stuck pointing due north, there is a causal explanation for why it is pointing in that direction. The explanation, however, has nothing to do with the direction of the wind. So the difference between a free weather vane and a stuck one isn't that the position of the former is uncaused, whereas the position of the latter has a causal explanation. Both are caused to point in a certain direction by something or other. The difference isn't in *whether* the behavior is caused, but in *what* causes it.

I've just described the ordinary meaning of "free" when it is applied to weather vanes. Notice that our common-sense understanding of this idea involves a compatibilist theory of what it is for a weather vane to be free. The idea is to use this as an analogy for constructing a compatibilist theory of what it is for the will to be free. Of course, we must remember that weather vanes don't have minds, whereas the issue of freedom of the will has to do with a feature of the mind. Let's press on, however, and see if the analogy can be developed.

Function and Malfunction

Why do we say that the vane is free when it is causally responsive to the wind's direction? Why don't we describe a weather vane whose swivel is rusted solid as free, since in that case the direction it points to isn't influenced by the wind? A stuck weather vane, after all, is free from the wind's influences. I suggest that the answer is to be found in the fact that the weather vane has a *function*. When the vane performs its function, its behavior is caused by the wind's direction. When it is stuck, it can't perform its function.

How can this idea about function be applied to the human mind? If we think of different parts of the mind as having functions, then freedom of the will exists when the mind is functioning properly. A malfunction, on the other hand, may result in a "stuck" will—one that is unfree.

Consider the following diagram, which shows how beliefs and desires are formed and then lead, via deliberation, to intentions and thence to action:

$$\left.\begin{array}{ll} \text{Evidence} \rightarrow & \text{BGD} \rightarrow \text{Beliefs} \\ \quad ? \quad \rightarrow & \text{DGD} \rightarrow \text{Desires} \end{array}\right\} \rightarrow \boxed{\text{Deliberation}} \rightarrow \text{Intention} \rightarrow \text{Action}$$

The box labeled "BGD" is the belief-generating device. It is the part of the mind that produces beliefs. Beliefs are its output. The BGD takes account of evidence (other beliefs and sensory experiences); these are its inputs. The BGD malfunctions when it isn't sensitive to evidence—when it outputs beliefs in a way that ignores the evidence at hand. Perhaps paranoia—the irrational and unshakable conviction that the whole world is conspiring against you—can be described as a malfunction of the BGD. In this situation, the person's beliefs are "stuck." The BGD has malfunctioned because it isn't responsive to evidence.

The DGD is the desire-generating device. It produces desires. Its inputs are the things that cause us to have the desires we do. I've put a question mark where the inputs to the DGD go; the inputs to this device are the things the device is sensitive to when it is functioning properly. Later, I'll discuss what function the DGD might have.

The BGD and the DGD output beliefs and desires, which are fed into a device that carries out deliberations. This device takes into account the agent's beliefs and desires and decides on the basis of them what the agent should do. This device completes its work when the agent forms the intention to perform some action.

By analogy with the weather vane, a person has free will when the various components involved in the process described in the diagram are functioning properly. Proper functioning is to be understood to mean that the BGD and the DGD are sensitive to certain sorts of causal influences.

What Does It Mean to Ascribe a Function to Something?

Before we can develop this idea much further, we need to have some understanding of what the word "function" means. In the case of the weather vane, we know what the function of that object is, because it was created by human beings for a certain purpose. If farmers put such objects on their barns for purely ornamental reasons, we might not regard them as malfunctioning when their swivels rust solid. But farmers want weather vanes to respond to the wind's direction; this is their intended function.

If the human mind were created by an Intelligent Designer (God), and if we could find out why that Designer gave people the kinds of minds they have, we could say what functions the mind and its components subserve. However, if we want a naturalistic, rather than a theological, account of what it is for parts of the mind to have functions, we must set this idea about an Intelligent Designer to one side.

Consider an analogous problem. We say that the function of the heart is to pump blood. What makes this true? After all, the heart does lots of things. It takes up space in your chest cavity. It also makes noise. But we don't say that the function of the heart is to take up space or to make noise. The problem is that the heart has many effects, but only some of these effects are what the heart is *for*—what it has as its function. If the heart were created by an Intelligent Designer, that would solve our problem. The Designer's intentions would settle what the function of the heart is. But I'll assume that we want a naturalistic, not a theological, account of heart function. We want to make sense of the idea of function without having to rely on the existence of an Intelligent Designer.

My proposal is that we understand the biological function of the heart in terms of the historical explanation of why people and other organisms have hearts. The reason hearts evolved is that they provided a benefit to the organisms possessing them. The benefit was that hearts pumped blood. As a side effect of the evolution of such blood pumps, it turned out that organisms had noise makers in their chests. But the heart didn't evolve because it made noise. Making noise provided no advantage for survival and reproduction.

Here, then, is a naturalistic account of what it is for an object (or a characteristic) to have a function. We don't need to imagine that the object is present because of Intelligent Design. Natural selection (discussed in Chapter 6) is a perfectly satisfactory mechanism. My proposal is that "the function of o is to do F" means that o is present because o's do F. The function of the heart is to pump blood (rather than make noise), since individuals have hearts because hearts pump blood (not because they make noise). (For elaboration of this way of understanding the concept of function, see Larry Wright, "Functions," *Philosophical Review*, Vol. 85, 1973, pp. 70–86.)

The Function of the Desire-Generating Device

Why do individuals have desires? More specifically, why do individuals have devices (DGDs) that construct desires? What use could this faculty have had in our evolutionary past? The suggestion I want to consider is that the DGD has the function of representing what would be good for the organism. Consider the case of thirst. When an organism gets dehydrated, the organism would benefit from drinking some water. Organisms with minds seek out water when they are dehydrated because their DGD produces a desire for water. Like any device, the DGD might malfunction; if it fails to produce a desire for water when the organism is dehydrated, this could handicap the organism in its struggle to survive.

Bear in mind that there are other ways besides forming desires to get organisms to perform actions that satisfy their biological needs. Bacteria are capable of behaviors that satisfy their needs, but they don't have minds (or desires) to help them do this. The suggestion, then, is that the DGD has the function of representing what would be good for the organism; it isn't part of this suggestion that a DGD is the only way to get an organism to act so as to satisfy its needs.

Recall what this claim about the function of the DGD actually means. It means that we possess DGDs because, historically, such devices represented what was good for the organisms that possessed them; organisms with such devices did better at surviving and reproducing than organisms that lacked them (or had DGDs that were constructed differently). If this is right, we can understand why individuals who are in the grip of a compulsion aren't free. Their DGD is stuck; it is malfunctioning because it no longer can represent what would be good for the agent. Kleptomaniacs want to steal even though stealing isn't good for them; indeed, kleptomaniacs sometimes want to steal even when they *know* that it isn't good for them to have this want. Likewise, a compulsive handwasher has an overpowering desire to keep washing his hands even though there is ample evidence available that this is a harm, not a help.

A similar explanation can be given for why brainwashing is able to rob people of their freedom. When people are brainwashed, they are given beliefs and desires on which they subsequently act. These beliefs and desires are "implanted" by short-circuiting the normal function of the BGDs and DGDs. The process of brainwashing causes the BGD and the DGD to malfunction. This is why individuals who are brainwashed to perform an action don't perform that action of their own free will.

So my proposal about freedom is this: An agent freely performs an action if the agent's mind is functioning properly. This includes the idea that the agent's DGD is able to perform the function of representing what is good for the agent. In addition, the idea of well-functioning includes the idea that the agent can rationally deliberate, given the beliefs and desires he or she has.

Although the present proposal and Hume's idea are both compatibilist theories, they are different. Hume thought the crucial consideration was whether the agent's desires control the agent's behavior. The idea I've just described says that it is the entire psychological process—from belief and desire formation through the formation of an intention to act—that settles whether the agent's action is free.

I now want to consider how the present theory of freedom allows us to reply to the arguments described in Chapter 24. Each of these arguments, recall, aimed to show that we can't be free because of some fact about how our beliefs, desires, and actions are caused.

Reply to the Distant Causation Argument

I first turn to the Distant Causation Argument, which I represent as follows:

(1) If an agent freely performs an action, then the agent is responsible for the action.
(2) Agents are not responsible for actions that are caused by factors outside their control.
(3) Every action an agent performs is caused by factors (genes and early childhood environments) over which the agent had no control.

———————————

No action is performed freely.

The compatibilist theory of freedom advanced in this chapter (the "Weather Vane Theory") must reject this argument. But how? The argument is deductively valid. (Identify its logical form.) Therefore, if the conclusion is false, one or more of the premises must be false.

What Does Responsibility Mean?

To reply to this argument, I need to examine the concept of *responsibility*. Consider what it means to say that a storm was responsible for some crop damage. Here "responsible for" simply means "causes."

If we use this understanding of the concept of responsibility to clarify premise (2) of the Distant Causation Argument, we can see that premise (2) is false. A storm can cause crop damage even though there were causes of the crop damage that the storm didn't control. Consider the following causal chain:

$$X \rightarrow \text{Storm} \rightarrow \text{Crop damage}$$

The storm was caused by earlier events X, which existed before the storm occurred. If causation is transitive (see the box on transitivity in Chapter 24), X caused the crop damage. The storm didn't exercise any influence over X, since X happened before the storm even existed. But this does not entail that the storm didn't cause the crop damage.

So the fact that the crop damage had "distant causes" doesn't mean that the storm wasn't responsible for the crop damage. By the same token, I conclude that premise (2) in the Distant Causation Argument is false.

Moral Responsibility

It might be replied, in defense of the Distant Causation Argument, that "responsibility" isn't the simple causal concept I've just described. After all, if Patty Hearst was brainwashed by her kidnappers, we might say that she wasn't responsible for robbing the bank. This doesn't mean, however, that she played no causal role in the robbery.

If the storm wasn't responsible for the crop damage, this means that the storm didn't cause the damage. But if Patty Hearst wasn't responsible for what she did, this doesn't mean that she didn't do what she did. What, then, is the difference? We sometimes say that we don't "hold" people responsible for some of the things they do. In contrast, it sounds funny to say that we don't hold the storm responsible for what it did. Holding X responsible, and deciding not to hold X responsible, implies that we regard X as a moral agent.

When we say that we don't hold Patty Hearst responsible for what she did, I think we mean that we don't *blame* her for her action. We don't think she deserves moral criticism for the robbery if she did it while brainwashed. If an agent is *morally responsible* for an event (a bank robbery, say), this means (1) that the agent caused the event and (2) that the occurrence of the event reflects on the agent's moral character. Moral responsibility differs from the simpler idea of causal responsibility; it is this latter concept that we apply to storms, there being no implication of moral praise and blame in such cases.

Suppose we interpret the Distant Causation Argument to be talking about moral responsibility in the sense just described. Understood in this way, premise (2) is still false. We are morally responsible for many (if not all) of the actions we perform, though the beliefs and desires that cause those actions are themselves results of factors outside our control. The reason is that much of what we do shows what sort of moral character we have.

To say that someone is morally responsible for doing something wrong doesn't automatically mean that he or she should be punished. Unfortunately, the law often seems to connect these two issues. If members of the jury think that Patty Hearst shouldn't be punished for robbing the bank, they must find that she wasn't responsible for what she did. There is a question here that needs to be faced head on, however, one that shouldn't be allowed to slip by. Suppose someone does something wrong, and we take this to indicate a defect in the person's moral character. Maybe the rather minor lies that people tell have this feature. But surely we don't want to pass laws that say that anyone who lies will go to jail or pay a fine. The reason might be that this legal apparatus would intrude into private life so much that society would be worse rather than better as a result. We hold people responsible when they do such things, but this doesn't mean we think they should be punished.

The Distant Causation Argument tries to make it look as if agents have nothing to do with the actions they perform—as if it is people's genes and environments that cause their actions, *rather than the agents themselves*. But this is absurd—*we* cause things to happen and these actions reflect on our characters, even though there are causal explanations for why we are the way we are.

Reply to the Could-Not-Have-Done-Otherwise Argument

A second argument was presented in Chapter 24 that attempts to show that we lack free will. This is the Could-Not-Have-Done-Otherwise Argument, which can be represented as follows:

(1) If an agent freely performs some action A, then the agent could have done otherwise (that is, the agent could have performed some action other than A).
(2) People can't perform actions other than the ones they do, in fact, perform.

Agents never act freely.

Since I believe that the conclusion of this argument is false, I must reject one or both of the premises.

Actually I think that both are defective. Premise (1) is mistaken for reasons that Locke brought out in his discussion of the man who decides of his own free will to remain in a room to talk to a friend; unbeknownst to him, the door was locked. This was discussed in the previous chapter. Premise (2) also should be examined carefully. In Chapter 14, I formulated an idea that I called the thesis of the ambiguity of necessity. Statements about necessity and possibility often are ambiguous. The example I discussed there was the statement "Joe can't tie his shoes." Interpreted one way, the statement is true (Joe is holding two bags of groceries). Interpreted in another way, the statement is false (if Joe puts down the groceries, he could tie his shoes).

I think premise (2) in the above argument is ambiguous. It could mean either of the following:

(2a) Given the very beliefs and desires the agent had, and given that the agent rationally deliberated, he could not have performed a different action from the one he did.
(2b) Even if the agent had had a different set of beliefs and desires, the agent still could not have produced an action different from the one he did.

Proposition (2a) basically says that rational deliberation is a deterministic process—beliefs and desires determine a unique choice of action, if those beliefs and desires are rationally evaluated. Since I don't think that determinism is true, I doubt that (2a) is correct. Even if it were correct, however, I don't see why that would show that we are never free. Even if weather vanes were deterministic systems, that wouldn't show that they are never free. I believe the same holds true of the human mind.

Proposition (2b) denies that the agent's beliefs and desires make a difference; (2b) says that the agent would have done the same thing even if the agent had had different beliefs and desires. I think that this statement is false—it is basically the doctrine of fatalism, which I discussed and set aside in Chapter 24.

In summary, proposition (2) is ambiguous. If it is clarified to mean proposition (2a), then it fails to show that we are unfree. If it is clarified to mean proposition (2b), then it is false. I conclude that the Could-Not-Have-Done-Otherwise Argument fails to show that freedom is an illusion.

Are Coerced Actions Unfree?

The Distant Causation Argument and the Could-Not-Have-Done-Otherwise Argument don't refute compatibilism in general or the Weather Vane Theory in particular. I now want to consider an objection that is aimed specifically at the Weather Vane Theory. It criticizes the theory for what the theory says about coerced action.

It seems natural to say that coerced acts aren't performed freely. However, when the robber coerces you into surrendering your wallet, it doesn't seem to be true that your mind has malfunctioned. You correctly realize it is in your best interest to hand over your wallet, and that is what you do. Action under coercion is often no different from other, less dramatic, actions produced by rational deliberation, at least as far as the inner workings of the mind are concerned. So if coerced actions are always unfree, the Weather Vane Theory is in trouble, since the theory says that we act freely when our minds are functioning properly.

My reply is that coercion doesn't rob an individual of his or her free will. I think that when you hand your wallet to the robber because you want to stay alive, your will is functioning perfectly well. Your situation here is different from that of a kleptomaniac or compulsive handwasher, whose DGDs have malfunctioned.

Maybe there are *some* cases of coercion that rob people of their free will. Suppose that the robber's threat frightens you so much that you totally lose your capacity to think clearly. You are so overcome by fear that you hand over your wallet, but not for any good reason. In this case, perhaps the coerced action is unfree. However, I think that many (perhaps most) cases of coercion aren't like this. People in such situations rarely "lose their heads"; often they show a considerable degree of care and self-control (you gingerly hand over your wallet, all the while assuring the robber that you have no intention of resisting). I conclude that a coerced action doesn't have to involve the will's being unfree.

---

24 What is Coercion?

The robber says, "Your money or your life." You would prefer to stay alive without forfeiting your money, but that option isn't available. The choice is clear, and so you hand over the money.

You are in a grocery store and want a loaf of bread. The grocer will let you have the loaf only if you pay $3. You would prefer to have the loaf without handing over the money, but that option isn't available. The choice is clear, and so you hand over the money.

The robber has coerced you; the grocer has not. What is the difference?

There is a moral difference: What the robber did was wrong, but the grocer did nothing wrong. However, this doesn't seem to define what coercion is. You can coerce people for morally impeccable reasons. Suppose you are using a life preserver for a pillow and I need to throw the preserver to someone who is drowning. If you refuse to hand it over willingly, I may have to coerce you, but in doing so I've done nothing wrong.

There is a difference in magnitude: In the robbery example, you want to stay alive far more than you want to hold onto your wallet. In the grocer case, you would rather get the loaf than keep the $3, but the difference between these outcomes is far less momentous.

Does this mean that coercion means putting people in situations in which it makes a great deal of difference to them what they do? Suppose I offer you $1,000 if you smile. Have I coerced you into smiling? You would much rather have the money and smile than forego the money and not smile. That doesn't make my offer coercive, however.

Some years ago, there was a program of testing new drugs in prisons. Prisoners would receive time off their sentences if they agreed to run the risk of being guinea pigs. The program was discontinued, partly because the offer was thought to be coercive. Do you agree that this offer would be coercive?

Let's return to the original question: What distinguishes the grocer from the robber? What, in short, is coercion?

An Objection to the Weather Vane Theory: Freely Chosen, Rational Self-Sacrifice

Although the three objections I've just discussed don't undermine the Weather Vane Theory of Freedom, the one I'll discuss now poses a serious challenge. According to the Weather Vane Theory, the function of the DGD is to produce desires that represent what is good for the agent. I want to argue that this thesis is either too vague or is mistaken, if we consider the case of *rational self-sacrifice*.

Consider people who calmly and rationally decide to sacrifice their own interests to help others (perhaps their family or friends or nation). A soldier, for example, decides to throw himself on a grenade in order to save the lives of his comrades. Is it possible for a soldier to do this of his own free will?

I would say *yes*, but what does the Weather Vane Theory say? We have to ask whether the soldier's DGD is functioning properly here. Does the desire that it produces—the desire to sacrifice the agent's life to save the lives of his comrades—really represent what is good for the agent? Interpreted in one way, the answer seems to be *no*. The self-sacrifice would be good for others, but not for the soldier himself. If the DGD has the function of representing what is good for the agent, then it seems to have malfunctioned in this instance.

The other alternative is to interpret the account given of the function of the DGD so that the soldier's DGD is not malfunctioning in this case. We might say that the soldier's DGD *is* representing what is good for him to do, since he believes a moral principle that says that this sort of self-sacrifice is morally required. But now "representing what is good for the agent" is being interpreted to mean "representing what the agent *thinks* is good." The problem with this way of understanding the function of the DGD is that the kleptomaniac who thinks that stealing is the best thing in the world also will be said to have a well-functioning DGD.

This suggests, I think, that the description I've been using of the DGD needs to be modified. I don't think rational self-sacrifice indicates that the individual's will is unfree. According to the Weather Vane Theory, for an action to be unfree, the individual's DGD must have malfunctioned. To be able to say this, however, we need to revise the description of what the function of the DGD is.

This is all I'll say about the problem of freedom of the will. I hope you now understand what a compatibilist theory of freedom would be like. Even though the Weather Vane Theory isn't satisfactory as it stands, this theory, I think, suggests that there may be some merit in the compatibilist position. There does seem to be a difference between people engaged in normal rational deliberation and people who are caught in the grip of a compulsion. The Weather Vane Theory seeks to characterize what this difference is. It remains an open question in philosophy how the concept of freedom of the will should be understood.

Review Questions

1   In this chapter, I sketched a common-sense picture of what it means to say that a weather vane is "free." What is this common-sense idea? Why say that it is compatibilist in character?

2   A weather vane has a function because it was designed by people to do something. What could it mean to say that the heart functions to pump blood, if the heart isn't the product of Intelligent Design?

3   What is the difference between saying that X is causally responsible for Y (as in "The storm was responsible for the crop damage") and saying that X is morally responsible for Y?

4   What is mistaken in the Distant Causation Argument and in the Could-Not-Have-Done-Otherwise Argument?

5   Are coerced actions performed freely? What consequence does the answer to this question have for the Weather Vane Theory?

6   What problem does the existence of rational self-sacrifice pose for the Weather Vane Theory?

7   According to the Weather Vane Theory, what does it mean to say that a human being possesses "freedom of the will"? What conditions must be met in order for a human being to act freely? Why is this conception of freedom correctly characterized as "compatibilist"?

8   What function have I suggested we ascribe to a DGD (or "desire-generating device")? Why? In what cases might a DGD be said to malfunction?

9   How does the conception of human freedom suggested by the Weather Vane Theory differ from Hume's view of freedom?

10   Does the Weather Vane Theory suggest that people are not free when they act on the basis of misguided or foolish desires? Suppose that I desire to eat fast food for every meal, and act on the basis of this desire. Does this mean that my actions are not free?

Problems for Further Thought

1   In Chapter 5 on the Argument from Design, I said that Aristotle's teleological conception of the universe has been rejected by modern science. People, tools, and nonhuman organisms are goal-directed systems, but it seems implausible to think of a mountain or the solar system in this way. In the present chapter, I presented an account of what it means to ascribe a function to something. How does this account help explain why it is mistaken, for example, to say that the function of rain is to provide farm crops with water?

2   Can the Weather Vane Theory of Freedom be revised so that it avoids the counter-example presented here of freely chosen, rational self-sacrifice? How might this be done?

Recommended Readings, Video, and Audio

Visit the companion website at www.routledge.com/cw/sober for suggestions of readings, video, and audio, for this chapter.

Chapter 27

Psychological Egoism

In earlier chapters, I've used a standard and common-sense model of what rational deliberation is. This model was employed in the discussion of Pascal's Wager (Chapter 10) and in the three chapters (Chapters 24–26) on the free will problem. The idea is that rational deliberators decide what to do by taking account of their beliefs and desires. This common-sense idea has been made precise by the science called decision theory; rational agents are said to "maximize expected utility." This conception of what rationality is seems to lead to the conclusion that people, if they are rational, are fundamentally selfish: They act so as to achieve the goals they have—they act to get what they want. Not only is this true of a person we would ordinarily call selfish—for example, a business executive whose only goal is to make as much money as possible; in addition, the idea seems to apply to everybody. Even a person who devotes her life to alleviating suffering, and lives at the poverty level so as to devote all her resources to this cause, counts as selfish. She aims at satisfying her own goals. She gains satisfaction from her work, just as business executives gain satisfaction from theirs. If a person who devotes her life to alleviating suffering had done something else with her life, she would have felt guilty. The idea is that both the "selfish" business executive and the "selfless" helper of others act on the basis of their own wants; both do what they do in order to gain a feeling of satisfaction (and to avoid negative feelings like guilt). Both are selfish at heart.

The previous paragraph expresses in an imprecise way the idea that I'll call psychological egoism. In this chapter, I clarify what psychological egoism says and argue that in some important ways it is false. I won't reject the model of decision making used so far—that rational agents act on the basis of the beliefs and desires they have. However, I'll argue that psychological egoism does not follow from this model.

Two Truisms

I want to formulate what psychological egoism says more precisely. Let's begin by identifying two propositions that are not in dispute. The debate over whether psychological egoism is true is *not* settled by the following facts:

(1) Rational agents decide which action to perform by consulting their beliefs and desires.
(2) At times, rational agents are guided by desires that are other-directed.

Proposition (1) describes the model of rational deliberation I've been assuming. It says nothing about what the *content* is of people's desires; it doesn't say *what* people want. Statement (1) says that whatever it is that a rational agent wants, that agent's behavior will be aimed at achieving those goals. Proposition (1) is a "truism" to which defenders and critics of psychological egoism can agree. Proposition (2) is also a truism. It says that people often have desires that concern the situations of others. A benevolent person may want others to suffer less. A sadist may want others to suffer more. Both of these individuals have what I'll call *other-directed preferences*. It makes a difference to them what the situations of other people are like. This too is a thesis that friends and foes of psychological egoism both accept.

I'll use the term "other-directed preference" to refer to preferences that people have about the situations of others, preferences that don't mention their own situation. If I prefer that *others suffer less rather than more*, this is an other-directed preference that I have; note that the italicized words, which specify the content of the preference, refer to others, but not to me. Similarly, a *self-directed preference* is any preference I have that refers to my own well-being, but does not say anything about the situation of others. If I prefer that *I have more money rather than less*, this is a self-directed preference that I have. Some preferences are neither purely self-directed nor purely other-directed. They are *mixed*. If I want to be the best chess player in the world, this is a preference whose content refers both to me and to others.

Proposition (2) does not refute psychological egoism. I might genuinely desire that your back gets scratched, but I would be an egoist if my only reason for wanting this is that I see it as a way to have my back get scratched as well. Psychological egoism does not deny the existence of other-directed preferences. Rather, psychological egoism asserts that when we want others to do well (or ill), we don't care about others for their own sakes; the only reason we care about what happens to them is that we think that their welfare will affect our own welfare. Psychological egoism maintains that concern for others is *purely instrumental, never ultimate*.

Goals and Side Effects of an Act

The philosopher/psychologist William James (1842–1910), whose ideas about "the will to believe" were examined in Chapter 10 on Pascal's Wager, discusses psychological egoism in his influential book *The Principles of Psychology* (Henry Holt, 1890). He notes a fact about psychological egoism that we should consider. James points out (as did Aristotle) that an action may bring a feeling of satisfaction to an agent without the action's having been done in order to obtain the feeling. James thought that many altruistic acts are of this sort. We help people because we genuinely care about their situations. It happens that our helping others is accompanied by our receiving a glow of satisfaction. But, according to James, obtaining the glow is not the goal; it is an unintended side effect. James thinks that the glow of satisfaction we get when we see others benefit from our help is no more the goal of our action than is burning coal the goal of sailing steamships across the Atlantic.

If James were right, psychological egoism would be false. A defender of psychological egoism, however, would deny part of what James is saying. A defender of psychological egoism might say that James has the story precisely backward. It is true that an action can produce an effect that isn't the real goal of the action. But a psychological egoist might say that when we help others, what we are really after is the glow of satisfaction; the fact that others receive a benefit is merely a side effect of our trying to make ourselves feel good.

There is a point of agreement between James and this defender of psychological egoism. Although they disagree over which effect of the helping behavior is the goal and which is the mere side effect, they agree that there is a difference between the two. So let's identify a third proposition on which the two sides concur:

(3) That an action has a particular effect does not necessarily mean that it was performed in order to produce that effect.

It is easy to see why (3) is correct, quite apart from the issue of whether psychological egoism is true.

A Simple Example

In order to clarify what psychological egoism asserts, I want to focus on a simple example. You see an advertisement in a magazine. It asks you to send a check for $20 to help starving children. You are fairly well-off. You could find enjoyable things to do with the $20, but the picture in the ad is pathetic. You believe that a $20 contribution will make a real difference for the people involved (it won't solve the whole problem, of course). You think for a moment and then put a $20 check in the mail to the charity.

In this case, were you an altruist or an egoist? On the surface, it may appear that you were altruistically motivated. After all, it seems that you wrote the check because you felt a genuine concern for the starving children. An advocate of psychological egoism, however, would maintain that your real motives, of which you perhaps aren't fully conscious, were purely selfish. You derived a glow of satisfaction—a nice feeling about yourself—from the donation. You also avoided feeling guilty. These psychological benefits were the *real* motives for your behavior, or so psychological egoism asserts.

To decide what your motivation was in this situation, I want to describe four kinds of people. Three of them have altruistic motives; one of them has only egoistic motives. After I've explained these four possibilities, I'll consider how we might go about deciding which of the four categories you occupy.

Four Preference Structures

The first type of individual I'll call the Pure Egoist. This individual cares nothing for the welfare of others; the only thing that matters to a Pure Egoist is his or her own situation.

The following two-by-two table illustrates the preferences of the Pure Egoist. The table answers two questions about this individual. What preference does he have as to whether he will receive a benefit? What preference does he have as to whether the children do better rather than worse? The first question has to do with his self-directed preferences; the second concerns his other-directed preferences.

The Pure Egoist

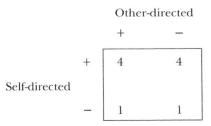

The Pure Egoist cares only that he himself receive more (+) rather than less (−) of whatever the benefit is. It is a matter of indifference to this person whether the children do better (+) or worse (−). This individual isn't benevolent; he also isn't malevolent. He simply does not care one way or the other about others.

The numbers in this table represent the order of the agent's preferences. The absolute values have no meaning; I could just as easily have used "9" and "5" instead of "4" and "1."

If you were a Pure Egoist, would you give $20 to charity? Donating the money would have two effects. You would receive a glow of satisfaction; and the children would be made better off. On the other hand, not donating the money also would have two effects. You would feel guilty about yourself and the children would be worse off. (For simplicity, I'm ignoring how you feel about retaining $20 or giving it away.) In this situation, there are two possible actions, whose consequences are represented in the table by the upper-left entry (+ to self and + to other) and the entry in the lower-right (− to self and − to other). In this situation, the Pure Egoist will choose the first action; he will donate the $20 to charity. He therefore chooses an action that benefits others. This benefit to others, however, is not the goal of his action, but rather is a mere side effect. If you were a Pure Egoist, you would help the starving children, but your real motive would be to make yourself feel good.

The second personality type is the mirror image of the Pure Egoist. It is the Pure Altruist:

The Pure Altruist

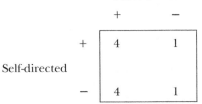

This individual cares nothing about his own situation, but only wants the other person to be better off. What would a Pure Altruist do if he had to choose between the actions represented by the entries in the upper-left and lower-right cells of the table? He either must benefit both self and other, or benefit neither. Notice that the Pure Altruist will choose the action that benefits both himself and the other person. If you were a Pure Altruist, you would donate the money to charity. A consequence of doing this would be that you would feel good about yourself. However, in this case, the benefit to self would be a side effect of the act, not the act's real motive.

In a choice between the upper-left and lower-right cells, the Pure Altruist will do the same thing that the Pure Egoist will do. Their actions will be the same, but their motives will differ.

The Pure Egoist acts solely in order to benefit himself; benefits to others are just side effects. The Pure Altruist acts solely to benefit others; benefits to self are just side effects.

People Are Rarely Pure Altruists or Pure Egoists

Which of these preference structures describes real people? I think that in the vast majority of cases, the answer is *neither*. In most choice situations, most of us care about both self *and* others. We don't like to feel guilty; we also enjoy the glow of satisfaction that comes from thinking well of ourselves. Most of us have preferences about having other goods (like money) as well. But besides these self-directed preferences, we also have other-directed preferences. We are often either benevolent or malevolent in what we want concerning the situation of others.

Both the Pure Egoist and the Pure Altruist have only one kind of preference. Real people usually have both. So we must complicate our representation.

I now introduce a third character—the S-over-O Pluralist.

The S-over-O Pluralist

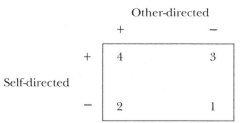

This individual prefers that he be better off rather than worse off (since 4 > 2 and 3 > 1). He also prefers that other people be better off rather than worse off (since 4 > 3 and 2 > 1). So this individual has both self-directed and other-directed preferences. This is why I call him a Pluralist. I've called this person an S-over-O Pluralist because of what he does when self interest *conflicts* with the interests of others. Suppose the choice is between two actions. The first action provides him with a benefit while the other individual goes without; this is the outcome in the upper-right box. The second action provides the other person with a benefit while he himself goes without; this is the lower-left outcome. When self-interest and the welfare of others conflict, the S-over-O Pluralist gives priority to himself (3 > 2). His self-directed preference is *stronger* than his other-directed preference.

What's the difference between the S-over-O Pluralist and the Pure Egoist? The Pure Egoist doesn't care at *all* about the situation of others. The S-over-O Pluralist *does* prefer that others be better off rather than worse. Both, however, say "me first" when self-interest conflicts with the welfare of others.

The last character I want to describe is the O-over-S Pluralist:

The O-over-S Pluralist

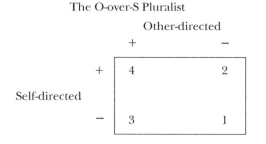

The O-over-S Pluralist cares about others and about himself as well; this is why he is a pluralist. I call him an O-over-S Pluralist to describe what he does when self-interest and the interests of others conflict. If an O-over-S Pluralist has to choose between the upper-right and lower-left cells, he will choose the lower left (3 > 2). He will sacrifice his own wellbeing so that the interests of the other person will be satisfied.

Notice that, of the four motivational structures I have described, only one of them completely lacks an altruistic motive. Psychological egoism says that people are Pure Egoists; it denies that people are ever motivational pluralists.

It should not be assumed that all of a person's motives, throughout his or her life, correspond to just one of these four motivational structures. For example, a person might be a Pure Egoist in one situation and an S-over-O Pluralist in another. These motivational structures are not intended to describe stable traits of people, but the traits that a person might have in a given situation in which there is a choice between actions that have consequences both for self and for someone else.

I noted before that when a Pure Altruist and a Pure Egoist face a choice between the upper-left and lower-right cells, they behave in the same way—both choose the action that benefits both self and other. The same is true of the S-over-O Pluralist and the O-over-S Pluralist. The four characters behave identically when self-interest *coincides* with the welfare of others. This means that how people behave in such situations is completely uninformative; the behavior does not help you figure out which of the four motivational structures they have. This is precisely what is going on in the example in which you donate $20 to charity. You would have donated the money no matter which of these four preference structures you possessed. How, then, are we to tell whether you are an altruist or an egoist?

The difference between Pure Egoists and S-over-O Pluralists, on the one hand, and O-over-S Pluralists and Pure Altruists, on the other, shows up when there is a *conflict* between helping one's self and having others be better-off. In a situation of this sort, the agent must choose between being in the upper-right box (+ to self, − to other) and the lower-left box (− to self, + to other). People who choose to help others at a cost to themselves in such conflict situations can't be Pure Egoists. However, people who help themselves and ignore the needs of others may be Pure Egoists, or they may be S-over-O Pluralists. To help figure out what your motives were when you gave $20 to the charity, let's put you in this sort of conflict situation.

When you contemplated sending $20 to the charity, there was no conflict between self-interest and the welfare of the starving children; the action that made you feel good also made the starving children better off. Because self-interest and the welfare of others *coincided*, it was impossible to tell what your motivation for helping was. To gain insight into your motives, we must ask what you would have done if there had been a conflict between self-interest and the welfare of the starving children.

An Experimental Test

To visualize what such a conflict situation would be like, suppose I had made you the following promise as you sat at your desk deliberating about whether to write a check to the charity that would feed the starving children:

> Once you decide whether to write the check, I'll give you a pill that will cause you to *misremember* what you did. Thus, if you write the check, the pill will cause you to believe that you didn't, and so you will end up feeling guilty. And if you decide not

to write the check, the pill will cause you to believe that you did do so, in which case you will end up feeling good about yourself.

Suppose you trust me to do what I say I'll do. Will you write the check or not? If you are in this hypothetical situation, self-interest and the welfare of others conflict. You can *either* feel good about yourself *or* help the starving children. You can't do both. What you choose shows what matters more to you.

My prediction is that you might well choose to write the check. If so, you have altruistic motives. It is false that the only thing you care about is feeling good about yourself. If, on the other hand, you decide not to write the check, how should this behavior be interpreted? I suggest that it is ambiguous. It is consistent with your being a Pure Egoist, but the behavior is also consistent with your being an S-over-O Pluralist.

When people send checks to charity in the real world, it may not be entirely clear why they do so. We can determine what their preference structures are if we consider what they would have done if self-interest and the interests of others had conflicted. The experiment described here is a way to think about that kind of situation. My guess is that many people who give money to charity have altruistic motives in the sense defined here.

If so, psychological egoism is false as a generality. At least sometimes, people care about others, not just out of self-interest, but because the welfare of others is one of their ultimate concerns. This doesn't mean that they don't care about themselves. It also doesn't mean that people don't value the glow of satisfaction and the freedom from guilt feelings they receive from helping others. Altruistically motivated people don't have to be Pure Altruists.

---

25 Apportioning Causal Responsibility

Events usually have more than one cause. A fatal car crash may be due to a slippery road surface, to the driver's carelessness, to the condition of the car's tires, to the position of a concrete wall, and so on. It is a mistake to think that precisely one of these was the "real" cause; each factor played a causal role.

Once we recognize that an event has many causes, we may wish to say which was "more important." The following situation provides an example of how the issue of apportioning causal responsibility may be addressed.

Suppose that you are a farmer who grows two fields of corn. The corn in the first field is shorter than the corn in the second. Upon investigation, you find that the corn in the first field has received less water and less fertilizer than the corn in the second. You suspect that the extra fertilizer going to the second field might have helped the corn there to grow taller; you also think that the additional water going to the second field might have helped as well. Your question is, did these factors really make a difference? And if so, which was more important, the extra fertilizer or the extra water?

This problem can be represented by a two-by-two table. The corn in the first field received one unit of fertilizer and one unit of water; the corn in the second field received two units of each. The entries in the table represent the average height of the corn in each field:

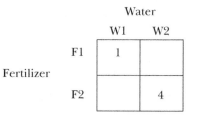

What experiment would you perform to find out whether an increase in fertilizer makes a difference? How would you find out whether an increase in water makes a difference? What would it mean to say that each makes a difference, but that one makes more of a difference than the other?

How is this problem related to the issue of egoism and altruism discussed in this chapter?

A Second Experimental Test

Here's a second experiment that may help clarify whether you had any altruistic motives when you sent the $20 check to the charity. As you are thinking about whether to do so, I tell you the following:

> As soon as you write the check or decide not to do so, I will give you a drug that will erase your memory of what you did, but will leave the rest of your mind intact. It isn't up to you whether you take this drug; my assistants will administer it to you regardless of whether you want it, and regardless of whether you decide to write the check to the charity.

This drug is an amnesiac. If you were a Pure Egoist, would you write the check to the charity?

If you are a Pure Egoist, you have no reason to write the check; you'll feel the same about yourself whether you write the check, or not.

If you write the check anyway, this is evidence that you are not a Pure Egoist. And if other people would write the check anyway, that would show that they are not Pure Egoists.

Conclusion

My thesis is not that people *always* have altruistic ultimate motives. Nor am I claiming that people have *only* altruistic motives. Rather, my claim is that some people some of the time have altruistic motives, even if they also have self-directed motives as well. This is enough to show that psychological egoism is false as a general theory of human motivation.

Review Questions

1   Give an example of an action that has two consequences, one of which was the goal of the action, the other of which was an unintended consequence.
2   What are self-directed and other-directed preferences? Give examples of each. Are there preferences that fall into neither category?
3   Represent each of the following preference structures by drawing a two-by-two table: (I) a *radical egalitarian* (someone who cares only that self and other receive the same degree of benefit); (II) a *utilitarian* (someone whose one concern is that more people benefit rather than fewer); (III) someone who is purely *malevolent* (who doesn't care about himself, but wants only that others be worse off rather than better).
4   What is the difference between the Pure Egoist and the Pure Altruist? There is a kind of choice situation in which these two individuals will behave in the same way. Describe a case of this kind.
5   What is the difference between the O-over-S Pluralist and the Pure Altruist? What is the difference between the S-over-O Pluralist and the Pure Egoist?
6   There is a kind of choice situation in which people who have altruistic motives will behave differently from people who do not. Describe a case of this kind.

7 When you help someone and this makes you feel good, how can you tell whether your motivation was altruistic or egoistic (or both)?

8 Does the thesis of psychological egoism deny the existence of other-directed preferences? If not, how does it reconcile such preferences with the view that all human beings are primarily motivated by concerns for their own benefit?

9 Why doesn't the fact that a Pure Egoist and a Pure Altruist will sometimes make the very same choices lend support to psychological egoism? What more would we have to show in order to vindicate the view that Pure Altruists are always motivated by egoistic concerns?

10 Can you think of any objections to the thought experiments I've proposed in this chapter? If so, how do you think that proponents of Psychological Egoism could use these (or similar) objections to defend their position?

Problems for Further Thought

1 In both the experiments I described, there is a *time lag* between my describing the pill to you and your deciding what you will do. Suppose you decide to send the check to charity. I claimed this behavior shows you have an altruistic motive. Could a defender of psychological egoism reply that you felt good about yourself in the time between my describing the pill to you and your deciding whether to write the check, and that your behavior was therefore selfishly motivated?

2 Suppose people with altruistic preference structures have them because their parents rewarded them with love and approval for helping others. Would this show that people are really egoists—that what really motivates them is parental approval?

3 In this chapter, I tried to clarify what it means to ask *whether* someone is altruistically motivated. Two quantitative issues remain. How would you measure *how* altruistic someone is? And what would it mean to say that one person is *more altruistic* than another?

4 (Suggested by Roy Sorensen) In the experiments described in this chapter, I assumed that the only egoistic motive that you might have is your wanting to feel good about yourself. This assumption allowed me to claim that if you donate to charity in the experiment, your motives are not exclusively egoistic. However, perhaps psychological egoism can be saved as a theory if we expand the list of what Pure Egoists care about. Why can't egoism maintain that people who donate to charity have the ultimate goal of being generous people. This goal is self-directed—the claim is that people want to have a certain type of personality. Evaluate this suggestion.

5 It is sometimes suggested that people donate money to charity only because this leads others to admire and respect them. The pill-taking experiment described in this chapter provides a way of testing this. Can you think of another way to test this hypothesis, one that is less science-fictiony?

6 The excerpt from Plato's *Republic* on the companion website describes an argument that Glaucon makes for psychological egoism. He claims that people never seek justice for its own sake, but do so only because it is a means to some selfish end. Use the material in this chapter to analyze Glaucon's argument.

Recommended Readings, Video, and Audio

Visit the companion website at www.routledge.com/cw/sober for suggestions of readings, video, and audio, for this chapter.

Part V

Ethics

Ethics—Normative and Meta

The philosophical study of ethics (morality) concerns the nature of good and bad, right and wrong, justice and injustice. In the section of this book on the theory of knowledge, I addressed the question of what a person should *believe*. Ethics focuses on the question of *action*—what actions should a person perform? Ethics deals with what may be the most fundamental personal question of all—how should you lead your life?

Ethics and Religion

People often think that ethical questions are inseparable from religious ones. During childhood, many of us had our moral training and our religious training mixed together. We were taught basic ethical principles (such as the Golden Rule) by being told how God wants us to act. In adulthood, disagreements about some ethical questions (for example, the permissibility of contraception or abortion) sometimes reflect differences over religious doctrine.

If you think that ethics and religion are tightly bound together, it may well puzzle you how an atheist or an agnostic could have strong moral convictions. Maybe you suspect that such people are being inconsistent. If someone doesn't believe that God exists, how can he or she hold that there is a difference between right and wrong? A character in Fyodor Dostoyevsky's novel *The Brothers Karamazov* expresses this idea when he says, "If God is dead, then everything is permitted."

If you tend to connect God and morality in this way, it may surprise you that a very central tradition in Western philosophy has sought to separate questions of ethics from the issue of what God wants us to do. This tradition goes back to Plato in fourth-century B.C.E. Greece. The philosophers in this tradition usually were not atheists. They believed in God (or in the gods), but thought that ethical questions should be addressed independently of assumptions about whether there is a God and what God commands. I'll discuss this idea in Chapter 31.

Metaethics and Normative Ethics

The study of ethics is usually divided into two large areas. These are *metaethics* and *normative ethics*. The prefix *meta* suggests the idea of "aboutness." For example, metamathematics is a part of mathematics in which the objects studied are mathematical axioms and proofs; meta-linguistic statements are statements about language. In metaethics, we consider general questions about the nature of morality and about the meaning of moral concepts. In metaethics, we don't ask whether murder is wrong rather than right. Rather, we ask whether there is really a difference between right and wrong, and we try to clarify what it means to classify an action as "wrong" or "right." In normative ethics, on the other hand, the usual procedure is to assume that there is a difference between right and wrong and then to ask which actions fall into the one category and which into the other. For example, utilitarians say that whether an action should be performed depends on whether it promotes the greatest happiness for the greatest number of individuals. An alternative position is that actions should not be performed if they are unjust, where the dictates of justice may not always coincide with what makes people happy. This dispute assumes that there is a correct answer to the question of what principles people should use to guide their actions. The problem in normative ethics is to determine what those principles are.

Truth and Opinion

Way back in Chapters 1 and 2, I drew a distinction between truth and opinion. It is one thing to say that the Rockies are more than ten thousand feet tall. It is something else to say that many people believe that the Rockies are more than ten thousand feet tall. The first of these propositions is true independently of anyone's believing it or saying that it is so. The second, obviously, depends for its truth on what people believe. There are objective facts about geology over and above the subjective opinions that people happen to have about geology.

Does this distinction apply to ethics? There is variation in ethical opinions; people sometimes disagree about whether a given action is right or wrong. But is there, in addition, a fact of the matter as to whether the action really *is* right or wrong? That is, are there objective facts in ethics that exist above and beyond the subjective opinions that people happen to have? This is the main metaethical question I'll consider in this chapter.

After surveying a range of possible answers to this question, I'll move on to normative ethics in Chapter 32. When I do this, I'll simply assume that there is a real difference between right and wrong. Given this assumption, I'll ask what makes some actions right and others wrong.

Alternative Metaethical Positions

To get started on the metaethical question of whether there are objective facts in ethics, I'm going to provide a road map to the different positions I'll consider. These positions divide up according to how they answer the following two questions:

(1) Are there any ethical truths?
(2) If so, what makes the ethical truths true?

Subjectivism

What would it mean to answer "no" to the first question? The idea here is that there are various ethical *opinions* that people have about right and wrong. But no statement that says that an action *is* right (or wrong) is, in fact, *true*. Opinions occupy what I've called *the subjective realm*. So the theory that says there is opinion but no truth in ethics is called *ethical subjectivism*.

One way to describe this position is to use a distinction David Hume made famous. It is the distinction between *is* and *ought*. Science aims to discover what *is* the case; ethics tries to describe the way things *ought* to be. A negative answer to question (1) might be understood to mean that all true propositions are *is*-propositions; there are no true *ought*-propositions. I'll consider in the next two chapters several arguments that have been given for saying that "no" is the correct answer to question (1).

Realism

Consider next what the options are if you answer "yes" to question (1). That is, suppose that some ethical statements are true. Question (2) then becomes relevant: what makes those statements true? One possibility is that they are true independently of anyone's say-so. Ethical truths are true whether or not anyone thinks they are. This position is called *ethical realism*.

When philosophers talk about ethical realism, the term "realism" does not mean what it means in politics—as when we say that someone is a political realist. We sometimes call people "political realists" when they are "practical"—they don't try too hard to do the right thing because they think that justice is unattainable anyway. (Humphrey Bogart is a realist of this sort at the beginning of the movie *Casablanca*, though he changes at the end.) Rather, ethical realism is the view that there are objective ethical facts that exist independently of anyone's say-so. If murder is wrong, this isn't because you, I, or anyone says (or thinks) it is wrong. Hamlet says that nothing is right or wrong, unless thinking makes it so. This bit of poetry rejects ethical realism.

Conventionalism

The remaining option in metaethics asserts that there are ethical truths, but maintains that these truths are true because of someone's say-so. I'll use the term *conventionalism* to label this metaethical position. Conventionalists differ from subjectivists in the way they answer question (1); they differ from realists in the way they answer question (2).

In the United States, people drive on the right side of the road. In England, they drive on the left. There is nothing inherently better about one procedure (let's suppose). They are equally workable. The key idea about conventions is that they embody *arbitrary decisions*. The reason you should drive on the right in the United States is simply that the people there have agreed that that is the rule to follow. In this case, a fact (you should drive on the right) is brought into being by people's saying that things shall be one way rather than the other.

In Chapter 2, I made a general remark about how we should avoid "wishful thinking." For the vast majority of propositions we could consider, thinking (or saying) that they are true does not, all by itself, make them true. Saying or thinking that the Rocky Mountains are more than ten thousand feet high does not make them so. Descartes (Chapter 13) thought he had found an exception to this pattern; he thought that the proposition "I am thinking" is made true by my thinking that it is true. Conventionalism in ethics holds that the same goes for right and wrong. Someone's saying (or believing) that murder is wrong makes murder wrong. Conventionalists disagree among themselves as to whose say-so does the job.

Three Varieties of Conventionalism

The first conventionalist theory I'll consider is called the *Divine Command Theory*. It says that an act is right or wrong because and only because God says that it is. It isn't that murder (or whatever) is inherently bad. Rather, murder has the moral status it does only because God commanded that we behave in a certain way.

The second conventionalist theory is called *ethical relativism*. This view says that what is right or wrong is determined by the society you inhabit. If your society adopts norms that prohibit murder, then it is wrong for you to murder. If some other society adopts different standards, then it may be permissible for someone in that society to murder. Ethical truths are relative, not absolute. Murder isn't wrong absolutely; it is wrong relative to the norms of one society but may be right relative to the norms of another. According to ethical relativism, it isn't God's say-so that makes the ethical truths true, but society's.

The third and last conventionalist theory I'll consider asserts that each individual constructs his or her own morality. It isn't just that each of us must decide for ourselves how we should live. Rather, the idea is that we make our actions right or wrong by deciding which standards to adopt. This idea is part of one version of the philosophy called *existentialism*. In his book *Existentialism*, the French philosopher Jean-Paul Sartre (1905–1980) describes a young Frenchman during World War II who must decide between joining the Resistance to fight the Nazis or staying home to care for his ailing mother. Sartre says that there is no standard of conduct that determines what the young man ought to do. *He* must choose whether he wants to be one sort of person or another. Once this choice is made, his subsequent action thereby counts as good or bad. For Sartre's existentialism, it is the individual's say-so that makes an action right or wrong.

This menu of options in metaethics is summarized in the following flow chart. At the bottom of the chart are the names of the positions described above them:

In the next two chapters, I'll consider various arguments that have been made for subjectivism. After that, I'll discuss various conventionalist theories in metaethics, beginning with the Divine Command Theory and Plato's famous criticism of it. The position I'll reach by the end of my discussion of metaethics is that there is no good argument against ethical realism. I don't claim that I can prove that realism is true, but I do think the attempts to refute it by conventionalists and subjectivists have not worked.

Review Questions

1   What is subjectivism? What does it mean to distinguish objective fact from subjective opinion in science? In ethics?
2   What does it mean to say that ethical truths are "conventional?"
3   What does it mean to say that ethical truths are "relative," as ethical relativism asserts? Relative to what?
4   What is ethical realism? How is it similar to conventionalism? How is it different? What is the difference between metaethics and normative ethics? Is it possible to consider metaethical questions in isolation from questions about normative ethics? Why or why not?
5   How does Hume's distinction between "is" and "ought" relate to ethical subjectivism? Do you find this distinction plausible? If not, why not?
6   Can conventionalists disagree about what makes actions right or wrong? If so, why are advocates of such distinct metaethical views classed together as "conventionalists"?

A Problem for Further Thought

The study of ethics often involves discussion of principles that tell people that they should have acted in a way different from the way they did act; for example, sometimes these principles require people to be less selfish and more altruistic. In the previous section of the book, I argued that people have free will and that the thesis of psychological egoism is false. If either of these claims were mistaken, would there still be a point to discussing ethical principles? Defend your answer.

Recommended Readings, Video, and Audio

Visit the companion website at www.routledge.com/cw/sober for suggestions of readings, video, and audio, for this chapter.

Chapter 29

The Is/Ought Gap and the Naturalistic Fallacy

Based on the previous chapter, you now should have a preliminary grasp of what ethical subjectivism is and of how it differs from ethical realism and ethical conventionalism. In this chapter and the next, I'll consider several arguments for thinking that subjectivism is true, and I'll suggest that none of them is convincing.

Subjectivism: Ethical Statements Are neither True nor False

In the previous chapter, I said that subjectivism is the view that no ethical statement is true. Often the view is given a slightly different formulation: subjectivism says that ethical statements are *neither true nor false*. I think this representation of the doctrine is less apt to mislead, and so I'll use it from now on. This is a small change, since if a statement is neither true nor false, it isn't true.

Subjectivism says that ethical statements have a particular characteristic. But what is an ethical statement? Examples include any statement of the form "X is morally wrong," "X is morally permissible," "X is unfair," or "X is unjust." The X may be filled in by a description of an action. So *both* the following statements are ethical statements:

(1) Murder is always morally wrong.
(2) Murder is sometimes morally permissible.

Ethical subjectivism claims that the first of these statements is not true. According to subjectivism, it isn't true that murder is always wrong. But the reason (1) isn't true is not that it is sometimes morally permissible to murder. Remember, (1) and (2) are *both* ethical statements, and subjectivism claims that no ethical statement is true.

---

26   Emotivism

Subjectivism says that there are no ethical facts. If subjectivism is true, why do we have ethical sentences in our language? What function do they perform if there are no ethical facts for them to describe? The emotive theory of ethics (emotivism) attempts to provide an answer.

"Ouch!" I exclaim when I hit my thumb with a hammer. "Whoopee!" I exclaim when a birthday cake is placed before me. In both cases, I've used language, but not to make an assertion. It would be a mistake to ask whether my utterances were true or false. They were neither. "Ouch!" and "whoopee!" *express* how I feel. Emotivism claims that ethical sentences allow speakers to express their feelings and attitudes. To say "Murder is wrong" is not to make an assertion that is either true or false; it is to express a certain sort of attitude toward murder.

There is no doubt that ethical language is sometimes used in this expressive way. The question is whether there is anything more to ethical discourse than this. When someone puts his face close to yours and yells "You are an ignorant pig!" the sentence is used to express the speaker's attitudes or feelings. However, that does not show that the sentence is neither true nor false. Besides having an expressive function, the sentence makes an assertion, which is either true or false depending on the characteristics you happen to have.

At first glance, it might seem that (1) and (2) have the following characteristic: one of them must be true. Ethical subjectivism denies this because it holds that there are no ethical facts about murder. The formulation of ethical subjectivism that I'm using—that ethical statements are *neither true nor false*—should alert you to the fact that subjectivism says that (1) and (2) are *both* untrue.

Does the Existence of Ethical Disagreement Show that Subjectivism Is True?

What arguments might be presented to support subjectivism? Sometimes it is suggested that there can't be any ethical facts on the grounds that people disagree over what's right and what's wrong. In our own society, there are moral controversies. Some people hold that abortion is sometimes permissible, others that it never is. And even when you find actions about which there is broad consensus in our society, you often can find other times and places at which there was no such consensus. For example, most people in our society would now agree that slavery is wrong; however, if you go back 150 years (or even less), there was no such broad consensus.

Is the fact that ethical opinions vary (in space and time) a reason to accept subjectivism? I don't think so. Science also contains controversies. And what now is accepted often was controversial in the past. To use an example discussed in Chapters 5 and 6, scientists now accept the idea that all life on earth is genealogically related—all the organisms on our planet trace back to one or a few common ancestors. This scientific consensus, however, didn't always exist. And even now, there are people—creationists—who deny this idea of common ancestry. Even though there is and has been variation in opinion about this question, all parties in the dispute believe there is a fact of the matter about whether common ancestry is true. No one denies that there are facts about the history of life on Earth. So lack of consensus about what the answer is to a question does not show that there is no objective answer to the question.

It is important to remember that ethical subjectivism is *not* the view that some ethical statements are controversial or are hard to prove or disprove. It says that each and every ethical statement is untrue. This includes "slavery is wrong" and "torturing babies for fun is wrong," just as much as it includes presently controversial claims about the moral status of abortion or capital punishment. If you are prepared to say that even one moral statement is true, you are rejecting subjectivism.

The Genetic Fallacy

Another argument for subjectivism focuses on the explanation of why we hold the ethical beliefs we do. To formulate this argument, consider the fact that most people think it is wrong for parents to totally neglect their children. What might account for why we think this? Two kinds of explanation come to mind. First, society teaches us to think this way. Second, evolution may have led us to think this way; people who totally neglected their children would have been less reproductively successful than people who didn't, and so the less fit trait of total child neglect would gradually have disappeared from the population. (The basics on how a selection process works were outlined in Chapter 6.)

Suppose there is a social or an evolutionary explanation for why people now think it is wrong to totally neglect their children. Does it follow that the ethical statement "it is wrong to totally neglect your children" is untrue? I don't think so. A belief is not shown to be untrue by the mere fact that you can explain why people hold the belief.

Consider arithmetic. How do you explain the fact that most of us think that $2 + 3 = 5$? Society has taught us to think this, and I suppose that evolution has somehow contributed to our capacity to have opinions about mathematics. However, this does not show that there is no fact of the matter about whether $2 + 3 = 5$.

Philosophers call the mistake I'm discussing here "the Genetic Fallacy." The word *genetic* means "cause" (as in the genesis of a belief). The Genetic Fallacy has nothing to do with chromosomes. The mistake is to think that a fact about how you come to believe something by itself settles whether the belief is true. In the next chapter, I consider a slightly different and more subtle version of this argument. For now, the point is that you can't prove that subjectivism is true just by pointing out that there is a social or an evolutionary explanation for why we have the ethical beliefs we do.

So much for these two arguments for subjectivism. I now turn to two others. The first focuses on Hume's distinction between is-statements and ought-statements; the second involves G. E. Moore's idea of a "naturalistic fallacy."

Hume: The Is/Ought Gap

Hume claimed that an ethical statement (describing what *ought* to be the case) can't be validly deduced from a premises that describes only what *is* the case. Consider the following argument:

Torturing babies for fun causes great suffering.

Hence, torturing babies for fun is wrong.

The single premise of this argument describes what is the case, not what ought to be the case. The conclusion concerns what ought to be the case. Hume said you can't deduce an ought-conclusion from exclusively is-premises. The above argument, he claimed, is not deductively valid.

Of course, this argument can be turned into a deductively valid argument by adding another premise. The following argument *is* deductively valid:

> Torturing babies for fun causes great suffering.
> Causing great suffering is wrong.
> _____
> Hence, torturing babies for fun is wrong.

Remember what it means to say that an argument is deductively valid (Chapter 2). In a deductively valid argument, *IF* the premises are true, then the conclusion can't fail to be true. In saying that an argument is valid, I'm not saying that the premises are true (remember the *IF!*).

The last argument displayed does not deduce an ought-conclusion from exclusively is-premises. The second premise in the argument is an ought-statement. So Hume's point might be put like this: If a deductively valid argument has an ethical conclusion, at least one of the premises must be ethical in character as well.

Hume's point is sometimes characterized by saying that you can't infer an ethical conclusion from purely nonethical premises. This is an acceptable rendition of Hume's thesis, if "infer" is taken to mean *validly deduce*. However, if nondeductive inference (Chapter 3) is involved, I don't accept the formulation just given. It seems to me that the fact that torturing babies causes great suffering is an excellent reason for thinking that the action is wrong. *X* can be a reason for *Y* even though *Y* doesn't deductively follow from *X*.

(S₁): An Argument for Subjectivism with Hume's Thesis as a Premise

Hume's thesis concerns a fact about deductive implication. Does this thesis lead to subjectivism? Again, I think the answer is *no*. To see why, consider the following argument for subjectivism:

> You can't validly deduce an ethical statement from purely is-premises (Hume's thesis).
> _____
> Hence, ethical statements are neither true nor false.

This argument is not deductively valid. A premise can be added, however, so that the resulting argument is valid:

> You can't deduce an ethical statement from purely is-premises (Hume's thesis).
> If ethical statements are not deducible from purely is-premises, then ethical statements are neither true nor false (reductionist premise).
>
> (S₁) _____
> Hence, ethical statements are neither true nor false.

(S₁) is a deductively valid argument for subjectivism. I find the second premise highly dubious, however. Why not adopt an antireductionist view of the status of ethical statements? That is, why not hold that some ethical statements are true, even though they aren't reducible to (deducible from) purely is-statements?

Here's an analogy. It is pretty clear that astronomy and anthropology describe different sorts of facts. Astronomers are interested in planets, stars, and other such objects. Anthropologists, on the other hand, study similarities and differences among human cultures. What does it mean to say that these are different subjects? One implication is that you can't deduce anthropological statements from purely astronomical ones. Describing the orbits and masses of the planets in the solar system does not allow you to deduce which customs are followed in which human cultures. Would it be plausible to conclude from this that there are no anthropological facts, simply because anthropological statements can't be deduced from astronomical statements? Presumably not. That is, the following argument is not deductively valid:

You can't deduce anthropological statements from purely astronomical premises.

Hence, anthropological statements are neither true nor false.

The following argument, though deductively valid, has a dubious reductionist second premise:

You can't deduce anthropological statements from purely astronomical premises.
If a statement isn't deducible from purely astronomical premises, then the statement is neither true nor false (reductionist premise).

Hence, anthropological statements are neither true nor false.

We should reject this argument. A perfectly sensible position is that there are facts in anthropology and facts in astronomy, even though neither reduces to (is deducible from) the other. The facts coexist as separate aspects of reality.

The Naturalistic Fallacy

The idea of a "naturalistic fallacy" is due to the English philosopher G. E. Moore (1873–1958). In his book *Principia Ethica* (1903), Moore criticized the idea that the ethical properties of an action—for example, its rightness or wrongness—might be identical with some "natural" property of that action. An example of such a naturalistic theory is provided by one form of utilitarianism, which I'll call hedonistic utilitarianism. This theory says that for an action to be ethically right is for it to maximize pleasure and minimize pain for those affected by it.

I'm not suggesting this theory is correct. My point is that it is an example of a moral theory that says that an ethical property is identical with some natural property. This theory says that the rightness of an action is one and the same property as the action's maximizing pleasure and minimizing pain. A natural scientist—a psychologist—could inquire whether one action produces more pleasure and less pain than another. According to hedonistic utilitarianism, this scientist would be investigating whether the first action is ethically preferable to the second. Utilitarianism proposes an "identity thesis," which bears a logical similarity to the Mind/Brain Identity Theory discussed in Chapter 22. An ethical property is said to be identical with a natural property. By natural property, I mean a property that the natural sciences (including psychology) might investigate.

Moore thought that hedonistic utilitarianism and theories like it make a mistake, which he called the Naturalistic Fallacy. Moore thought it is always a mistake to say that an ethical property of an action is the same property as one of its natural properties. Why is it a fallacy to do this? According to Moore, we can see this by considering the meanings of the terms involved. The phrase "morally right" doesn't mean the same thing as the phrase "maximizes pleasure and minimizes pain." From this, Moore thought it followed that hedonistic utilitarianism is mistaken. Moore's argument goes like this:

> The expression "x is morally preferable to y" does not mean the same thing as the expression "x produces more pleasure and less pain than y."
>
> (NFA) ——————
>
> Hence, the property named by the first expression is not identical with the property named by the second.

Moore thought that any ethical theory that equates an ethical property with a natural property could be refuted by this type of argument. Any such theory, he said, commits the Naturalistic Fallacy. Let's call this argument of Moore's the Naturalistic Fallacy Argument (NFA).

I claim that Moore is mistaken. For two terms to refer to the same property, it isn't essential that they mean the same thing—they need not be synonymous. Chemistry tells us that the temperature of a gas is one and the same property as the gas's mean molecular kinetic energy. This claim is not refuted by the fact that "temperature" and "mean kinetic energy" are not synonymous expressions. Consider the following argument:

> The expression "temperature" differs in meaning from the expression "mean kinetic energy."
>
> ——————
>
> Hence, the property named by the first expression is not identical with the property named by the second.

This argument is a fallacy. So is Moore's. That is, I think Moore's argument concerning the Naturalistic Fallacy is itself a fallacy. He commits what I'll call (following John Searle) the Naturalistic Fallacy Fallacy.

Moore failed to establish the thesis that ethical properties are not identical with naturalistic properties. Call this "Moore's thesis." I now want to consider a separate question. Suppose, just for the sake of argument, that Moore's thesis is correct. Would subjectivism follow from this? Moore didn't think so. Moore was no subjectivist. He believed that there are ethical facts and that these ethical facts exist quite apart from the naturalistic facts investigated by science. For Moore, there are two kinds of truths—ethical truths and naturalistic ones. Others have gone in the opposite direction. They have thought that Moore's thesis leads to ethical subjectivism; they have claimed that if ethics fails to reduce to naturalistic facts, then there are no ethical facts at all.

(S_2): An Argument for Subjectivism with Moore's Thesis as a Premise

Moore's thesis does not, all by itself, imply subjectivism. Rather, Moore's thesis, combined with a second idea, leads to subjectivism. Here's the argument we need to consider:

> Ethical properties are not identical with naturalistic properties (Moore's thesis).
> If ethical properties are not identical with naturalistic properties, then ethical statements are neither true nor false (reductionist thesis).
>
> (S_2) ——————
>
> Hence, ethical statements are neither true nor false.

I'll call this argument (S_2).

I've suggested that Moore's argument for the first premise in (S_2) doesn't work. What I want you to see now is that the first premise, even if it were true, would not be enough to establish subjectivism. To reach the conclusion that subjectivism is true, (S_2) requires the reductionist thesis as well as Moore's thesis. I call the second premise "reductionist" because it says that a property must reduce to (be identical with) a naturalistic (scientific) property if there are to be any ethical facts.

Is the second premise in (S_2) plausible? Why not reject it and adopt, instead, an *antireductionist* position, according to which ethical statements are sometimes true, even though ethical properties are not identical with naturalistic properties? We agree that anthropological statements are sometimes true even though anthropological properties aren't identical with astronomical properties. Why not take the same view with respect to the relation of ethics and natural science?

Summary

Hume correctly noted that you can't deduce an ought-conclusion from purely is-premises. This thesis of Hume's is true. Subjectivism does not follow just from this point, however. Rather, to get subjectivism from Hume's insight, you've got to make a reductionist assumption. I see no compelling reason to be a reductionist about ethical statements. I conclude that (S_1) isn't a convincing argument for ethical subjectivism.

Moore correctly claimed that ethical expressions are not synonymous with naturalistic expressions. Moore, however, went on to claim that ethical properties are not identical with naturalistic properties. This thesis of Moore's doesn't follow. Even if Moore were right that ethical properties are irreducibly different from natural properties, subjectivism wouldn't follow from that. So I reject argument (S_2).

Although (S_1) and (S_2) are different arguments for subjectivism, they have something in common. Both assume that if there are ethical truths, these truths must be connected in an especially intimate way with naturalistic truths; ethical statements must somehow "boil down to" the facts described by is-propositions if ethical statements are to be true. Can this assumption that the two arguments share be defended or refuted?

Review Questions

1   How do subjectivists view the statement "lying is always wrong"? Do subjectivists reject this statement because they think that lying is sometimes morally legitimate?
2   Does the fact that people disagree about ethical issues show that subjectivism is true?
3   Suppose there is a social or a biological explanation for why people have the ethical beliefs they do. Does this show that those beliefs are untrue?
4   Hume saw that there is a "gap" between *is* and *ought*. What does this mean? Does Hume's insight show that subjectivism is true?
5   What does Moore mean by the *naturalistic fallacy*? If Moore were right about the naturalistic fallacy, would subjectivism follow?
6   What is an ethical expression? Is the statement "there is nothing wrong with committing genocide" an ethical expression? Is the statement "some people think that there is nothing wrong with committing genocide" an ethical expression? Explain your answers.
7   Why might one think that Moore's argument is misguided, or even fallacious? Try to construct and evaluate a counter-argument.
8   What does reductionism about ethical statements entail? Why, and on what grounds, might we want to reject such reductionism?

Problems for Further Thought

1   In Chapter 19, I explained Frege's distinction between *sense* and *reference*. How can this distinction be used to clarify the mistake Moore makes in his Naturalistic Fallacy Argument (NFA)?

2   In discussing the Genetic Fallacy, I argued that you can't prove that a sentence is untrue just by showing that there is a causal explanation for why people believe the sentence. Can you construct an example in which the explanation for why people believe a sentence makes it highly improbable that the sentence is true? If such an example can be constructed, does this show that the so-called genetic fallacy isn't a fallacy at all?

Recommended Readings, Video, and Audio

Visit the companion website at www.routledge.com/cw/sober for suggestions of readings, video, and audio, for this chapter.

Chapter 30

Observation and Explanation in Ethics

Some people find ethical subjectivism an attractive philosophical position because they think ethics and science are fundamentally different. For them, it seems reasonable to talk about scientific facts. It strikes them, however, that ethics is very different—different enough that it is a mistake to think there are any ethical facts at all. The problem for subjectivism is to make precise the gut feeling that there is a difference here: can it be stated in such a way that a convincing argument in favor of ethical subjectivism emerges?

Reasoning about Ethical Issues

All too often the idea that there is an important difference between science and ethics rests on a misconception of one, the other, or both. One such misconception is the idea that reasoning can play no role in ethics—that ethics is nothing more than the irrational outpouring of feelings about what we think and do.

It is true that people often are strongly moved by feelings when they talk about right and wrong. However, people sometimes care passionately about scientific matters and about nonethical matters that arise in everyday life. In addition, it is important to see that reasoning *can* play a role in ethics—that ethical statements can be subjected to rational criticism. An example of how this can occur is provided by Gilbert Harman (in his book *The Nature of Morality*, Oxford University Press, 1977). He asks us to consider the following principle:

"If you have a choice between five people alive and one dead, or one alive and five dead, you should always choose the first option over the second." This principle is a generalization. Should we accept it?

One way to decide is to see what the generalization implies about specific examples—about concrete situations that people might sometimes confront. Harman asks us to consider the following example, which is one test case for the principle:

> You are a doctor in a hospital's emergency room when six accident victims are brought in. All six are in danger of dying but one is much worse off than the others. You can just barely save that person if you devote all your resources to him and let the others die. Alternatively you can save the other five if you are willing to ignore the most seriously injured person.

Harman says that in this case, the doctor should save the five and let the sixth person die. This is Harman's moral judgment about the example. I agree with Harman about this, and I'll assume that you do too. So in this case, what we are prepared to say about the example is consistent with the dictates of the principle we are considering. Harman concludes that this example is *evidence in favor* of the general principle.

Harman next considers a very different situation that a doctor might face:

> You have five patients in the hospital who are dying, each in need of a separate organ. One needs a kidney, another a lung, a third a heart, and so forth. You can save all five if you take a single healthy person and remove his heart, lungs, kidneys, and so forth, to distribute to these five patients. Just such a healthy person is in Room 306. He is in the hospital for routine tests. Having seen his test results, you know that he is perfectly healthy and of the right tissue compatibility. If you do nothing, he will survive without incident; however, the other five patients will die. These five patients can be saved only if the person in Room 306 is cut up and his organs distributed (and you can kill him painlessly). In that case, there would be one dead but five saved.

Harman's judgment about this case, with which I also agree, is that it would be wrong for the doctor to save the five by killing the sixth and harvesting his organs. This example, then, is evidence that the general principle stated before is false.

Testing General Principles by Applying Them to Specific Examples

As Harman's example illustrates, we can reason about the correctness of a general principle by seeing what it implies about concrete cases. We reject the principle because of an ethical judgment we are prepared to make about a concrete case (the second example situation mentioned above). Alternatively, if you disagree with Harman about his judgment on this second case, you might conclude that the general principle is plausible after all. The point is that we can run a *consistency check* on the various ethical opinions we have, making sure that our general principles do not contradict what we believe about specific cases.

This kind of procedure is very important in ethics. Philosophers frequently evaluate a general moral theory by seeing what it implies about specific examples. For this procedure to be possible, we must be prepared to make ethical judgments about the cases considered. This is what Harman did when he used his moral judgment about the example of organ harvesting to argue that the general principle is false.

Let's compare this specimen of ethical reasoning to what scientists do when they want to test a theory. Scientists also test general theories, and they do so by seeing what they imply about particular cases. For example, a general theory about electrons might predict that a laboratory instrument in a certain experiment will register "7.6" at a certain time. The scientist then can look at the instrument and see if it says what the theory predicts. If the reading differs from what is predicted, this may count against the theory.

Thought Experiments versus Empirical Experiments

In science, one figures out what a theory implies about what can be observed; then one makes the required observations. In the ethical case just discussed, however, no observation was required. We figured out what the general principle implies about the hypothetical case of the doctor contemplating the transplant operations, decided that this implication is unacceptable, and thereby rejected the general principle. The ethics case involved what is sometimes called a *thought experiment*.

Thought experiments differ from empirical experiments in that thought experiments don't involve *actually* making observations. So we now face this question: Does ethics differ from science in that science involves observation, whereas ethics does not? Harman poses the question as follows:

> You can observe someone do something, but can you ever perceive the rightness or wrongness of what he does? If you round a corner and see a group of young hoodlums pour gasoline on a cat and ignite it, you do not need to *conclude* that what they are doing is wrong; you do not need to figure anything out; you can see that it is wrong. But is your reaction due to the actual wrongness of what you see or is it simply a reflection of your moral "sense," a "sense" that you have acquired perhaps as a result of your moral upbringing?

Observations Are "Theory Laden"

Harman argues that there are no "pure" observations—that all observation is "theory laden." What does this mean? For you to see *that the children have poured gasoline on a cat and have ignited it*, you have to understand the concepts involved. If you don't know what a child is, or what a cat is, or what gasoline is, then you won't see that this is what is going on.

To make this more precise, let's distinguish two aspects of the process we call *seeing*. We talk about seeing objects ("*S* sees the cat"), and we talk about seeing that this or that proposition is true ("*S* sees that the cat is on fire"). I'll call these *objectual seeing* and *propositional seeing*. Notice that the expression following the verb in objectual seeing names an object (the cat), whereas the expression following the verb in propositional seeing expresses a proposition (that the cat is on fire). The distinction between these two kinds of seeing is somewhat similar to that drawn in Chapter 12 between objectual and propositional knowledge.

Can you see a cat without knowing what a cat is? I would say *yes*. Young children can see a nuclear power plant without knowing what they're looking at. Propositional seeing, however, is different. To see that it is a cat that is on fire, you must understand the concepts that are found in the proposition. So propositional seeing is "theory laden" in this sense: you must have information of various sorts if you are to see that a particular proposition is true.

Now let's go back to the comparison between ethics and science. When you round the corner and see what the children are doing, do you see *that they are doing something wrong*? I agree with Harman that the answer is yes. You make use of your background information —in this case, information about right and wrong. In just the same way, when you round the corner, you are able to see *that the children are setting a cat on fire*; you do this by making use of your background information (concerning what a cat looks like, etc.). So Harman concludes (and I agree) that we make ethical observations every day, just as we make observations that concern nonethical matters. We are able to do this by using background information to interpret the visual, auditory, and other sensory signals we receive.

Of course, a person who had no beliefs at all about right and wrong wouldn't be able to see that what the children are doing is wrong. It is also true, however, that the child who has no information about what a nuclear power plant is would be unable to see that there is a nuclear power plant on the hill. The child's incapacity does not show that there are no objective facts about whether the hill has a nuclear power plant on it. I claim that we should say the same thing about the moral ignoramus. This person is unable to see that what the children are doing is wrong, but that does not refute the thesis that what the children are doing is objectively wrong. You don't prove that subjectivism is true just by describing the incapacities of a moral ignoramus.

Observation Does Not Imply Objectivity

Saying that people make ethical observations does not imply that ethical facts exist. Consider aesthetic judgments—judgments about the beauty of a painting, for example. Suppose you are looking at a painting by Monet and judge that it is a beautiful example of French Impressionism. You wouldn't be able to do this without a certain fund of background information. In addition, you need to use your visual system to make this judgment. So perhaps it is true that you see that the painting is beautiful. We may conclude that observations occur in aesthetics. This, however, is not enough to show that there are "aesthetic facts"—that there is an objective fact about whether a given painting is beautiful. Someone might concede that people make aesthetic observations and still insist that beauty is in the eye of the beholder.

So far I've criticized two ideas—that ethics does not involve reasoning and that there is no such thing as observation in ethics. Both may seem to mark a difference between ethics and science, but neither really does, or so I have argued. At the same time, I have to admit that the fact that ethics involves both reasoning and observation does not prove there are ethical facts.

Insoluble Disagreements

I'll now consider a third possible difference between science and ethics. It sometimes seems that there isn't much possibility of rational persuasion in ethics. Two people may quite sincerely hold the views they do, and no matter how much they discuss their differences, neither will budge. In science, disagreements are common, but often they can be solved by bringing in new evidence that neither party initially has available. In ethics, it seems that people sometimes stick to their convictions no matter how much new information is imported. If so, there are *insoluble* disagreements about ethics. Perhaps this marks a difference between ethics and science.

I won't argue that there is no difference here (though we should not forget that people can be pigheaded about nonethical matters as well). I do want to claim, however, that the alleged difference is not enough to establish ethical subjectivism.

Think of a slave owner and an abolitionist in the United States in the 1850s arguing at length over the morality of slavery. The slave owner has shut his eyes to the humanity of slaves and to the suffering they endure. Imagine that the slave owner was made to take these facts to heart. Maybe some slave owners would have changed their minds if they had had to confront the full implications of slavery. But probably there were some slave owners whose hearts were sufficiently hardened (at least partly out of economic self-interest) that even full information would not have made a difference to them. Let's imagine that the slave owner and the abolitionist are caught in an insoluble disagreement of this kind. Does it follow that there are no ethical facts?

Ethical facts, if they exist, often will be very hard for people to grasp. The reason is that our apprehension of them often will be clouded over by self-interest and self-deception. As difficult as scientific questions about atoms and cells sometimes are, ethics is in this respect even harder. Maybe ethics will be the last frontier of human knowledge; even after we have unlocked the secrets of the atom and of life itself, the problem of discovering the truths of ethics may remain unsolved.

So *IF* ethical facts exist, it wouldn't be surprising that there are ethical disagreements, even insoluble ones. And of course, *IF* subjectivism were true, it likewise wouldn't be surprising that there are ethical disagreements. So both hypotheses—that there are ethical facts and that there are not—can account for the observation that insoluble ethical disputes sometimes occur.

27 Values in Science

Hume's distinction between is-statements and ought-statements often leads people to think that science is value-free. This seems to follow from the idea that science aims to establish what is the case and takes no stand on any ethical issue.

It is important not to confuse a distinction between different kinds of *statements* with a distinction between different sorts of *activities*. Hume's distinction concerned the former; it does not follow from Hume's distinction that science is an activity that is value-free. In fact, the practice of science is saturated with values. Some of these are more or less internal to the practice of research; others have to do with how science affects the rest of society.

A scientist's decision to pursue one research problem rather than another is a decision about what is of value. Sometimes a problem is worth pursuing because it promises to yield practical benefits. Research in medicine and engineering provides obvious examples. At other times, a scientist will pursue a problem because it is thought to be theoretically important. This too is a judgment of value; in sciences that are more theoretical than practical (more "pure" than "applied"), a problem may be judged important because scientists believe that its solution would advance our understanding of the world.

Judging the value of pursuing a research problem, whether practical or theoretical, becomes especially important when the research would impose significant costs. Research is often expensive, and the expense is often supported by government money. Another cost arises when the research is done on organisms that may suffer and die in the course of the investigation. Responsible science requires that these considerations be taken into account.

After the scientist chooses a problem, value issues continue to be important. When scientists judge that the available evidence counts strongly against some theory, they will conclude that they *ought not to believe* the theory. Judgments about plausibility and evidence are *normative*; they concern what we should and should not believe.

Once the scientist has reached some judgment about what the solution is to the problem under investigation, another value issue arises. Should the results be published? If so, in what forum should they be aired? It is sometimes suggested that scientists should keep their results to themselves if publishing would be harmful. Others hold that society is better-off in the long run if even the most unpleasant scientific results are made public. Notice that both of these opposing positions take a stand on an issue of value: when should a scientist publicize the carefully tested results of inquiry?

Is Subjectivism Preferable to Realism on Grounds of Parsimony?

We are considering two competing hypotheses—subjectivism, which denies that there are ethical truths, and realism, which asserts that there are ethical truths that are true independently of anyone's say-so. Is there any way to choose between these two hypotheses? Perhaps subjectivism has the advantage of being more *parsimonious* (an idea discussed in Chapter 22 on the Mind/Brain Identity Theory). If subjectivism can explain everything we observe just as well as the hypothesis that says there are ethical facts, then perhaps we should prefer the former hypothesis.

Harman advances an argument of this sort. He thinks that in spite of the similarities between science and ethics just described, there is nevertheless one big difference. It concerns the problem of explanation. In abductive arguments (Chapter 3), you produce a reason for thinking that something exists by showing that the existence of the thing is needed to explain some observation. Recall that Mendel never saw a gene, but he had a good abductive reason to think that genes exist. Harman argues that we don't need to postulate the existence of ethical facts to explain any observations. Adding to this a principle of parsimony (which tells you that you should assume that something does not exist if it isn't needed to explain anything), Harman concludes that subjectivism is correct.

Harman describes a physicist who is looking at the screen of a cloud chamber (a device for observing particle interactions). He sees a vapor trail on the screen and says, "There goes a proton." How should we explain why the scientist believes that a proton is present? The answer, according to Harman, involves a fact about what is going on inside the cloud chamber—namely, there really is a proton in there. The proton produces the vapor trail; the scientist sees the vapor trail and comes to believe that a proton is present in the chamber. Part of the explanation of why the scientist has the belief is that what he believes is, in fact, true. The causal chain that explains the scientist's belief goes like this:

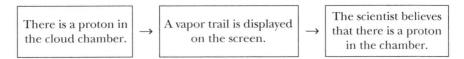

Notice that the causal chain traces something in the subjective realm (a belief) back to something in the objective realm (a proton).

Our common-sense beliefs often have a similar explanation. Suppose you want to explain why Jane believes there is a tiger in the cage. You might do this by citing the fact that her visual system is in good working order, that she knows what a tiger looks like, and that, indeed, there *is* a tiger in the cage that Jane is looking at. We explain a person's perceptual beliefs (apart from their hallucinations) by describing the ways things are outside the mind. In this case, the causal chain looks like this:

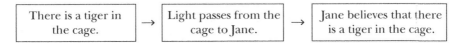

Part of the explanation of why Jane believes the proposition is that the proposition, in fact, is true.

Let's compare Harman's example from science and the similar example about Jane to the moral judgment we made when we saw the hoodlums set fire to the cat. How are we to explain the fact that we hold this ethical belief? Harman says that we don't need to postulate the existence of an ethical fact to explain this. All we need to do is show how our moral beliefs were shaped by our upbringing—by the society in which we live (and perhaps by the genes we possess).

According to Harman, there is a striking difference between ethics and science. Scientific facts *are* needed to explain why people have the scientific beliefs they do, but ethical facts are *not* needed to explain why people have the ethical beliefs they do. Harman concludes that this is why we have a good abductive reason to think that there are protons, genes, and so on, but no good abductive reason to think that there are ethical facts.

Harman concedes that we will cite moral principles when we are asked to explain why it is wrong for the children to have acted as they did. If asked why the children were wrong to have set the cat on fire, we might appeal to some general ethical principle (for example, its being wrong to impose gratuitous suffering). Here we cite a general ethical principle to explain some more specific ethical conclusion. Harman's point, however, is that you don't need to postulate ethical facts to explain why we *believe* that the children were wrong in what they did. Ethical facts aren't needed to explain why people have *beliefs* about right and wrong (though scientific facts *are* needed to explain why scientists have some of the scientific beliefs they do).

Harman's picture of the explanatory relationships is as follows:

Causing gratuitous suffering is wrong.   Our upbringing
$$\downarrow$$ $$\downarrow$$
What the children did was wrong. $\longrightarrow\!\!\!/$ We believe that the
                                                          children acted wrongly.
            ETHICS   PSYCHOLOGY

I'm not going to contest Harman's claim that this diagram is correct. My question is …

Does Subjectivism Follow?

The Principle of Parsimony says that we should not postulate the existence of something, if the something isn't needed to explain *anything*. If postulating the existence of ethical facts served no explanatory purpose whatever, the Principle of Parsimony would conclude that there are no ethical facts. But Harman has not shown that ethical facts aren't needed to explain *anything*. Rather, he has shown something more modest—simply that you don't need to postulate ethical facts to explain why people have the ethical beliefs they do. Ethical facts aren't needed to explain this fact about our *psychology*.

Harman grants that we sometimes make ethical observations. We look at the children and say, "What they are doing is wrong." Harman also grants that the ethical properties of specific actions may be explained by general ethical principles. As just noted, a general principle might help explain why what the children did was wrong. Putting these two points together, we may conclude that *general ethical principles can help explain the ethical properties of specific actions*.

The point I want to make here is similar to what I said about Hume's distinction between is-statements and ought-statements in the previous chapter. The argument for subjectivism I called (S_1) says that since ought-conclusions aren't deducible from is-statements, there are no ethical facts. I pointed out that this argument requires a reductionist premise. To reach the subjectivist conclusion, you need to assume that if ethical facts exist, they must be deducible from is-statements. Harman's argument is abductive, not deductive.

I grant that ethical facts aren't needed to explain why we have the beliefs we do. Nevertheless, for subjectivism to follow from this, an additional assumption is needed. Harman needs to assume that we should not postulate the existence of ethical facts if they aren't needed to explain why we have the beliefs we do. I find this assumption implausible. Why should the reality of ethical facts stand or fall on their role in psychological explanation?

An Explanatory Role for Ethical Principles

The previous diagram *does* accord an explanatory role to some ethical facts. If you think that what the children did was wrong, then there is at least one ethical truth that requires explanation. General ethical theories may be evaluated by their ability to explain this and other specific ethical facts about particular situations. If one theory does a better job of explaining such ethical facts than another, it is plausible to hold that the former is more likely to be true.

Thus, if you concede that there are at least *some* ethical facts, then postulating *other* ethical facts can be justified on abductive grounds. On the other hand, if you demand that ethical facts be judged by their ability to explain facts in psychology, you'll end up with subjectivism. I conclude that Harman's argument does not justify subjectivism. He has not shown that there are no ethical facts. Nor has he shown that postulating ethical facts isn't needed to explain *anything*. Rather, the more limited conclusion he has established (I grant) is that postulating ethical facts isn't needed to explain certain facts about psychology (that is, about why we believe what we do).

What Is the Point of Ethics?

Harman claims that ethical statements should be regarded as true only if they are needed to explain why we have the beliefs we do. However, the point of ethics isn't to explain or describe what we think. Ethics isn't psychology. The point of an ethical statement is to *guide* behavior—to say how we *ought* to think and act, not to describe how we actually think and act. Ethics is in a normative, not a descriptive, line of work. But that does not show that there are no ethical facts.

Review Questions

1   Why does Harman think that reasoning from general principles to claims about specific cases occurs in both science and ethics? Why does he think that observation is something we do in both science and ethics?
2   Does the occurrence of reasoning and observation in ethics show that there are ethical facts?
3   Suppose there is someone who can't be convinced that slavery is wrong. Does this show that subjectivism is true?
4   What does the Principle of Parsimony have to do with the question of whether there are ethical facts?
5   Harman says that an abductive argument can be found for thinking that protons exist, but none for thinking that ethical facts exist. Why does he think this? Is his argument convincing? If we don't need to appeal to ethical facts to explain why we have the ethical beliefs we do, is there any reason to appeal to ethical facts at all? What could such reason(s) be?
6   I have argued that ethics, like science, involves both reasoning and observation. Does this suggest that ethical facts exist? Why or why not?

7   I have argued that cases of persistent (or even insoluble) ethical disagreement do not show that ethical facts do not exist. But does persistent ethical disagreement suggest that ethical reasoning is impossible? Explain your answer.

8   Almost all of us make ethical observations on a daily basis; but it seems that some of us—namely, the morally ignorant—do not. Is this a reason to think that subjectivism is true? If so, why? If not, why not?

Problems for Further Thought

1   If parsimony is a good reason to prefer a materialistic theory like the Mind/Brain Identity Theory or for preferring functionalism over dualism, why isn't it also a good reason to favor ethical subjectivism over ethical realism?

2   Consider the following passage from Hume's *Treatise of Human Nature* (1739; III, 1, 1):

> Morality [does not consist] in any matter of fact, which can be discover'd by the understanding.... Take any action allow'd to be vicious: Wilful murder, for instance. Examine it in all lights, and see if you can find that matter of fact, or real existence, which you call vice. In whichever way you take it, you find only certain passions, motives, volitions, and thoughts. There is no other matter of fact in the case. The vice entirely escapes you, as long as you consider the object. You never can find it, till you turn your reflexion into your own breast, and find a sentiment of disapprobation, which arises in you, toward this action. It lies in yourself, not in the object. So that *when you pronounce any action or character to be vicious, you mean nothing but that from the constitution of your nature you have a feeling or sentiment of blame from the contemplation of it.* Vice or virtue, therefore, may be compar'd to sounds, colours, heat and cold, which according to modern philosophy, are not qualities in objects, but perceptions in the mind: And this discovery in morals, like that other in physics, is to be regarded as a considerable advancement of the speculative sciences; tho', like that too, it has little or no influence on practice. Nothing can be more real, or concern us more, than our own sentiments of pleasure or uneasiness; and if these be favourable to virtue, and unfavourable to vice, no more can be requisite to the regulation of our conduct and behavior.

What analogy is Hume drawing between moral properties and colors? Is Hume right to think they are similar? Does Hume's analogy justify ethical subjectivism?

3   Is it question-begging to claim, as I do in this chapter, that ethical facts are needed to explain other ethical facts?

Recommended Readings, Video, and Audio

Visit the companion website at www.routledge.com/cw/sober for suggestions of readings, video, and audio, for this chapter.

Conventionalist Theories

In philosophical writing about ethics, it is not customary to lump together under one heading the three theories I'll discuss in this chapter. Nor is it especially standard to label any of these theories "conventionalist." So let me explain why I'm lumping and labeling in this way.

The Divine Command Theory holds that an action is right or wrong solely because God says that it is; ethical relativism maintains that an action is made right or wrong in a society by the norms the society adopts; and the existentialism of Jean-Paul Sartre says that individuals freely create the ethical standards that determine whether their lives are good ones or bad ones. Existentialist writers often begin with the idea that there is no God and argue that people therefore must create their own ethical facts. This is obviously very different from the Divine Command Theory, which sees ethical truth as flowing from God. Both these positions differ from ethical relativism, which views ethics as neither divinely given nor individually chosen, but as socially constructed.

What Makes a View Conventionalist?

In spite of these differences, the three views have two things in common. First, they agree that there are ethical truths. Second, they agree that those truths are made true by someone's say-so. Third all three theories reject ethical subjectivism on the one hand and ethical realism on the other. The disagreement among them arises when these theories are asked to specify *whose* say-so does the trick—are ethical propositions made true by God's, society's, or each individual's decision?

Why say that these theories are forms of "conventionalism"? Each claims there is nothing inherent in an action (torture, for example) that makes it right or wrong. The action, considered all by itself, could easily be right or wrong. Rather, something outside of the action (extrinsic to it) makes the action right or wrong. It is God, society, or an individual who makes a pronouncement on the action and thereby endows it with one ethical property rather than another. In Chapter 28, I gave an example of something that I think is really conventional. It is a conventional matter which side of the road people should drive their cars on. The essential ingredients in a convention are *arbitrariness* and *decision*. Let me give another example that illustrates what this means.

Trivial Semantic Conventionalism

Consider the fact that we use the word "dog" to refer to dogs. Things didn't have to be this way. Other words would have worked just fine. We could have called dogs by the name "cat" and cats by the name "dog." So how did dogs come to have the one name rather than the other? Dogs have the name they do because of a *decision*. *We* make it true that, in our language community, dogs are called "dogs." The rules of our language are something we control; they aren't forced on us from the outside. I'll call this kind of conventionalism *trivial semantic conventionalism*. I call it trivial because it describes a fairly boring and unimportant fact. I call it *semantic* because it describes how pieces of language come to refer to things in the world.

A philosophically interesting conventionalist theory must say something beyond what trivial semantic conventionalism says. The ethical views I'll consider here don't make the trivial point that the words "right" and "good" might have been used to mean something different from what they mean in present-day English. If we used the word "right" to mean *morally wrong*, then most of us would treat the sentence "torturing babies for fun is right" as expressing a truth. But this is trivial.

Substantive versus Trivial Conventionalism

To see how substantive conventionalism (SC) differs from trivial semantic conventionalism (TSC), we need to distinguish a proposition from the sentence that expresses it (a distinction drawn in Chapter 4). The first of the following claims is true, whereas the second is false:

(TSC) If we used language differently, the word "dog" might not name a four-legged animal.

(SC)   If we used language differently, dogs might not be four-legged animals.

The sentence "dogs are four-legged animals" would not express a truth if we used the word "dog" to refer to fish. But changing the way we talk would not affect the proposition that the sentence expresses; talking differently wouldn't turn dogs into fish!

Conventionalism in ethics isn't a thesis about language. It does not assert that ethical *language* is under the control of someone's say-so; it says that the ethical *facts* are determined by someone's say-so. It says that ethical *propositions* are made true or false by someone's decision. Ethical conventionalism asserts a substantive thesis, not to be confused with trivial semantic conventionalism. Ethical conventionalism holds that ethical propositions are very different from most other propositions. Consider the fact that the Rocky Mountains are more than ten thousand feet high. This proposition isn't made true by someone's believing it or saying it; rather, its truth is *independent* of anyone's say-so. Conventionalism in ethics rejects the idea that ethical propositions have the same status as geological propositions like this one.

Plato's Critique of the Divine Command Theory

One of the earliest discussions of the Divine Command Theory is in Plato's dialogue *The Euthyphro*. This is a dialogue between Socrates, who was Plato's teacher, and Euthyphro. They meet outside a law court where Euthyphro has just made a charge of murder against his own father. A servant of his father's had killed a slave. Euthyphro's father had the servant chained up and thrown in a ditch while someone went to the priest to ask what should be done. In the meantime, the servant died. Euthyphro is confident that indicting his father is the pious thing to do, though Euthyphro's relatives are angry at him for prosecuting his father for murdering a murderer. Socrates and Euthyphro discuss what piety is. Euthyphro claims to have a clear view of this, but Socrates shows that Euthyphro is very confused.

The Divine Command Theory comes up in this dialogue when Socrates asks if an action is pious because it is loved by the gods, or is it loved by the gods because it is pious? We might substitute any moral term we wish (like "obligatory," "right," "good," or "just") for "pious." And also, if we wish, we may substitute monotheism for the polytheism of the ancient Greeks. With these substitutions, we can reformulate Socrates' question as follows: Is an action morally obligatory because God commands us to do it, or does God command us to do it because the action is morally obligatory? Socrates' question has to do with which item is the cause and which the effect in the following diagram:

The Divine Command Theory says that the arrow goes from left to right. Ethical realism, on the other hand, holds that an action is right or wrong independent of anyone's say-so (even God's). So if you are a realist and think that God exists and makes true pronouncements on ethical matters, you'll think that the arrow goes from right to left. Your view will be that God knows a fact that exists independently of him and correctly describes what that fact is.

Notice that both the options depicted in the preceding diagram assume there is a God. So rejecting the Divine Command Theory isn't the same as embracing atheism. A number of philosophers, beginning with Plato himself, were theists and ethical realists at the same time. Since the problem that Socrates poses assumes that the gods exist (in our reformulation, that there is a God), I'll go along with this assumption. We now want to ask what determines what in the diagram. Which way does the causal arrow point?

One point that Socrates emphasizes is that the gods sometimes disagree with each other. (In many of the Greek myths, one god approves of an action, while another disapproves.) This allows Socrates to convict the Divine Command Theory of being contradictory. Socrates does this by supposing that the Divine Command Theory says that an action is right (or wrong) if at least one god says that it is. So, if the gods disagree about an action, the theory entails that the action is both right and wrong at the same time. Socrates sees that it is easy to reformulate the theory so that it avoids this problem. Suppose the theory says that an action is right (or wrong) if *all* the gods say it is. The theory then says nothing about those actions on which the gods disagree. If we assume that there is just one god, what happens to this problem? There is no longer a question of what the theory says when the gods disagree. However, two further problems have been posed for monotheistic versions of the Divine Command Theory.

Two Objections to the Divine Command Theory

Although monotheists hold that there is just one God, they recognize that there are many *religions*. If different religions disagree about what God commands, how are we to tell what God wants us to do? Even if all religions agree about how God regards some action, there is still the question of whether they correctly report what God commands. Although this point is often offered as an objection to the Divine Command Theory, I do not think that it shows that the theory is false. The theory doesn't claim to describe how we can find out which actions are right or wrong; the theory describes only what makes one action right or wrong. This epistemological criticism of the theory is, therefore, off the mark.

The second difficulty is deeper; it is separate from this problem about knowledge. To pinpoint this further problem, let's suppose not just that there is a God, but that we know what God wants us to do. For example, let's suppose that God wants us to follow the Ten Commandments. We can now ask Socrates' question: does God say that we should not murder (for example) because it is wrong to murder, or is it wrong to murder because God says so?

If the Divine Command Theory were true, then *anything at all* would be right (even torturing babies for fun), if God said that it were. Likewise, *anything at all* would be wrong (even reducing the suffering of sick children), if God said that it were. The idea that God might order us to torture babies for fun probably strikes you as quite horrible. "Surely, God wouldn't order us to do this," you'll say, "since God is good." Let's analyze this reaction more carefully. The point to notice is that this reaction is actually *inconsistent* with the Divine Command Theory. For this reaction to make sense, there would have to be such a thing as goodness, which exists independently of God's say-so. To say that "God would not do X, since X is wrong" is to say that the arrow points from right to left, not from left to right, in the diagram. Remember, the Divine Command Theory says that there is nothing inherent in an action that makes it good or bad; the action has its moral status simply because God chooses to label it good or bad.

I'm not doubting here that God has the power to make us the kinds of creatures we are. Let's assume that God has given us bodies that make us capable of feeling pain. It follows that God is partly responsible for why the following ethical truth is true: *stabbing someone for fun is wrong*. God helps make this ethical proposition true because God is responsible for the fact that stabbing people causes them pain (if he had made our bodies otherwise, that might not be so). However, the Divine Command Theory says much more than this. It claims that the following ethical proposition is true only because God says it is: *inflicting pain for fun is wrong*. I think that this last proposition is true, independent of anyone's say-so, even God's.

This is the most famous of Plato's objections to the Divine Command Theory. If the *only* thing that makes an action right or wrong is God's say-so, then God has no *reason* to decide one way or the other. According to the theory, God makes an *arbitrary* decision about what to say, but his say-so somehow creates an ethical fact. Before the pronouncement, there is no ethical fact; afterward, there is. Frankly, I find it baffling how facts can be brought into being by someone's say-so. If God makes an arbitrary decision when he issues his decree, what binds us to think that what he says is true? To be sure, God can punish us if we disobey his orders. This, however, only makes it *prudent* for us to go along with what he says; it does not show that what he says is true. (Recall the distinction between prudential and evidential reasons discussed in Chapter 10 in connection with Pascal's Wager.) If God's decision to say that X is wrong is arbitrary, then the proposition that X is wrong seems to be arbitrary as well—there is no reason to think that it is true.

It may be replied that the ways of God are mysterious—God can bring ethical facts into being just by issuing a decree, even though we can't understand how this is possible. To this reply I say that if the matter *is* mysterious, then we should decline to endorse the Divine Command Theory. If we can't understand the process postulated by a theory, that is hardly a reason to accept what the theory says.

Ethical Relativism

I now want to consider ethical relativism. This theory holds that the rightness or wrongness of an action is settled by the say-so of the society to which the actor belongs. For example, in traditional Eskimo culture, it was customary for people to put their aging ailing parents outside to die in winter; according to ethical relativism, an Eskimo who did this would have been doing the right thing. In contemporary American society, this isn't the social norm; so relativism asserts that in our society, it would be wrong for us to act in this way. Ethical relativism says that what it is right or wrong to do depends on (is relative to) the society in which you live.

Ethical Relativism Is Normative, Not Descriptive

Let's make this theory more precise. First, we need to be clear that ethical relativism is a normative thesis, not a descriptive one. It makes a claim about how people *should* act. There is a quite separate descriptive thesis, which says that customs and norms *in fact* vary from society to society. Having already absorbed Hume's point about the is/ought gap (Chapter 29), you should be able to see that descriptive relativism (an is-proposition) does not deductively imply normative relativism (an ought-proposition).

A comment on the descriptive claim: it is fairly obvious that societies do vary in their customs and values. It is less obvious, however, that they do so with respect to the values that are most fundamental. For example, someone might grant that traditional Eskimos practiced euthanasia (mercy killing) in contexts that we do not, but still maintain that deep down Eskimo culture and our own have the same fundamental values. Perhaps both societies adopt norms that aim to promote the general welfare, but because of different conditions of life, we and they end up choosing more specific norms that are different. I don't maintain that there are such "fundamental universals." I merely point out that descriptive relativism might be granted for some "superficial" customs but denied for some more "fundamental" ones. Anthropology is the subject that can assess whether this is correct.

A Further Clarification of Ethical Relativism

The second point of clarification is that there is an obvious sense in which what we ought to do depends on (is relative to) the situation we are in. I think that in most situations, it is wrong to steal. Suppose, however, that your family is starving and you have no money to buy food for them. Suppose you have the opportunity to steal a loaf of bread from a prosperous baker (this is the situation that Jean Valjean faced in Victor Hugo's novel *Les Miserables*). In this case, I think you would be doing the right thing to steal the loaf. Whether it is right or wrong to steal the bread depends on your circumstances.

People in different societies often live in different circumstances. People in one society may face situations in which it is wrong for them to steal, while those in another may face situations in which stealing is the right thing to do. Ethical relativism, however, says more than this. It goes beyond the uncontroversial fact that what you ought to do depends on the situation you are in.

Ethical Relativism Is a Version of Conventionalism

To see what this extra ingredient is, we must remind ourselves that normative ethical relativism is a conventionalist theory. It doesn't just say that what someone should do varies from society to society. It says that an action is right or wrong *solely because* of society's say-so. An ethical realist can grant that people in one society shouldn't steal, whereas those in another should do so; a realist, however, will reject the relativist's explanation of why this is so. For, according to ethical relativism, ethical facts are brought into being simply by a society's adopting various norms of behavior.

So far, I've presented two clarifications of ethical relativism. First, it is a normative theory, not a descriptive one. Second, it is a conventionalist theory. Having said this, let's see whether there is any reason to think that the theory is true.

If Imperialism Is Wrong, Does That Justify Ethical Relativism?

Ethical relativism enjoyed a fair amount of popularity in the social sciences (in anthropology, especially) during the twentieth century. As Western social scientists improved their understanding of other cultures, they often came to feel considerable respect for those cultures. The idea took hold that it is wrong for Western nations to impose their own standards on other cultures. From the sixteenth century down to the present, many Western nations created and extended empires by conquest and commercial domination. Often this was said to be justified in the name of bringing Christianity to the conquered peoples; Europeans sometimes talked of a "white man's burden"—of a responsibility to bring Western civilization to the rest of the world.

Maybe you'll find ethical relativism an attractive moral theory if this sort of imperialism strikes you as wrong. If you think that the idea of a "white man's burden" was simply a rationalization for exploitation, what better way to express this than by saying that each society determines its own ethical values? Europe and the United States don't get to decide what's right and wrong for the rest of the world. Rather each society decides this matter for itself. Partly for this reason, ethical relativism became popular among those who defended a kind of *noninterventionism* (this is the idea that one society should not meddle in the affairs of another).

Let's assume, for the sake of argument, that there have been many cases in history in which one society was wrong to impose its will on another. Does this view make ethical relativism plausible? I think not. Are we prepared to say that a society can do anything it pleases to the individuals in it, as long as most of the people in the society believe that this is the right thing to do? It could become "customary" in a society that a certain group of people is oppressed (like the lower castes in India), even systematically murdered (like Jews, Gypsies, and homosexuals in Nazi Germany). Would this be made right if most people in the society thought it was right? I find this highly dubious.

Don't confuse the question of rightness with the question of whether some other country should intervene militarily to put a stop to the objectionable practice. These are separate issues. There might be cases in which foreign intervention would be wrong, even though some practices going on inside the country are wrong. For a practice to be wrong is one thing; what steps should be taken to end the wrong is a separate matter.

In addition, it is important to see that ethical relativism does not prohibit the kind of interventionism that its supporters tend to condemn. Should members of my society engage in colonial conquest? According to ethical relativism, I should answer this question by seeing whether the norms of my society permit people to engage in colonial conquest. Far from condemning interventionism, this consideration will have the consequence of justifying it. If you asked in nineteenth-century Britain whether it was "customary" for individuals to help extend and maintain the British Empire, the answer would have been *yes*. Paradoxically, ethical relativism does not imply that societies ought to respect each other.

Finally, it is worth noticing that the kinds of objections I made against the Divine Command Theory also apply to ethical relativism. A conventionalist view of this kind says that an action is made right in a society simply because it is the norm. This, however, has such bizarre consequences as the following:

> If our society considered it ethically permissible to torture babies for fun, then it would be ethically permissible for us to do this.

Ethical relativism doesn't say that our society *will* ever be like this. It does, however, endorse the above if/then statement. My view is that the above if/then statement is false. If our society were to adopt this norm, then our society would have become morally abhorrent. To say this is to talk like an ethical realist. What is morally right and wrong isn't settled by society's say-so.

Ethical relativism has the consequence that *conformism* is always right. It entails that a person should *always* conform to the norms laid down by his or her society. If you think that the norms in a society can be wrong, you are rejecting ethical relativism. Consider what ethical relativism says about a society that changes its norms. Some two hundred years ago, most of the people living in the United States probably believed that slavery was ethically permissible. Later the majority opinion changed. According to relativism, slavery was right until a certain date, but then it suddenly became wrong, *simply because the number of people who endorsed slavery dropped below 50 percent*. Just as in the case of the Divine Command Theory, I find it baffling how ethical truths can flip–flop simply because of someone's say-so. It seems to me that if slavery was wrong after 1865, it was wrong before that date as well.

---

28 Two Views of Democracy

Why is it right for a society to decide certain issues by majority vote? We can reformulate this question by mimicking the question that Plato posed in *The Euthyphro*. Is X wrong simply because the majority thinks that it is, or is the rightness and wrongness of X not settled by the majority say-so?

Believing that democratic procedures are the best way to decide what a society ought to do does not require one to endorse ethical conventionalism. One can be an ethical realist and still maintain that democracy is often the best practical procedure a society can use for discovering what it should do. According to this position, the opinion of the majority is fallible, but majority rule is *less* fallible than other procedures (dictatorship, for example) that might be adopted.

Sartre's Existentialism

I now turn to the third conventionalist theory—existentialism. There is a lot more to existentialism than I can discuss here. It is important to realize that existentialist writers differ a great deal among themselves. Here I'm focusing on a single strand in the thinking of some important existentialists; this is the idea (expressed by Sartre) that individual human beings must freely create their own moral values.

Sartre holds that the scope of human freedom is far wider than most of us suspect. People often believe that only a small range of options is open to them—that the large-scale features of their lives are forced upon them from the outside. Sartre thinks this is an illusion; people stumble without reflection into stereotyped and conventional ways of life without realizing that they in fact are making a choice. Freedom is a frightening burden that we must shoulder without kidding ourselves. Sartre goes so far as to say that we are responsible for every feature of the lives we live. Although I think that this last idea is a piece of rhetorical overstatement, Sartre's general stress on the responsibility of individuals to shape their own lives is important. There is a lot to be said for really reflecting about what you think and do—for regarding options critically and not falling into a pattern out of unreflective habit. However, Sartre says something more than this; this something more is the conventionalist element in his existentialism that I want to identify and criticize.

In Chapter 28, I mentioned that Sartre (in his book *Existentialism*) describes a young Frenchman during World War II who has to decide whether to join the Resistance or stay at home to care for his ailing mother. Let's distinguish two claims that might be made about this young man:

(1) He should think the choice over carefully and not do what he does out of unreflective habit.
(2) There is no moral fact of the matter about what he should do until he makes a decision. If he decides that he wants above all to be a good son, he should stay home; if he decides that he wants above all to be a good Frenchman, he should join the Resistance. But there is no standard that exists independently of his choice that determines what he should want most of all.

Sartre claims that both (1) *and* (2) are true. He thinks that this story about the young Frenchman exhibits a very general pattern. In *every* choice we make, we create moral facts. It is (2) that embodies the conventionalist element in Sartre's existentialism.

Sartre chose this example because he thought it poses a difficult moral problem. But even if the problem were one that we might see as clear-cut, Sartre would view it as calling for an arbitrary decision. Consider a third option that the young man has. He could leave home and volunteer to torture prisoners for the Gestapo. The young man has to decide whether he wants to be a good son, a good Frenchman, or a good Nazi. Sartre's position is that there is no fact of the matter about what the young man should do until he makes a decision about what he wants most. Just like the other conventionalist theories discussed in this chapter, Sartre's existentialism implies the following if/then statement:

If the young man decides that he wants above all to be a good X, then it is morally permissible for him to do what it takes to be a good X.

I've already noted why I find this claim implausible. Sartre thinks this conventionalist thesis follows from the fact that there is no God. He thinks that if there is no God to lay down the moral law, then each of us must lay down the law for ourselves. An ethical realist would disagree. Why can't moral facts exist independently of anyone's (God's, society's, or the individual's) say-so? Sartre has no very good argument against this realist alternative.

In this and the previous few chapters, I have not provided any strong argument in favor of ethical realism. Rather, I have criticized the subjectivist and conventionalist alternatives to realism. In what follows, I'll assume that there are ethical truths that are true independently of anyone's say-so. The goal will be to consider some theories that try to say what those truths are.

Review Questions

1 What is the difference between trivial semantic conventionalism and substantive conventionalism?
2 Consider this statement: "We should do what God says we should do." Can an ethical realist and a defender of the Divine Command Theory agree on this? If so, what do they disagree about?
3 Consider this statement: "What may be right for a person in one culture to do may not be right for a person in another culture to do." Can an ethical realist and a defender of ethical relativism agree on this? If so, what do they disagree about?
4 Does ethical relativism entail that people in one culture should respect the standards of conduct obeyed in another culture?
5 Consider this statement: "People must figure out for themselves what they should do." Can an ethical realist and a defender of Sartre's existentialism agree on this? If so, what do they disagree about?
6 There is a Yiddish story about the wise men of Chelm. The town council met to discuss what could be done about the shortage of sour cream. They decided to solve the problem by calling water "sour cream." (They put aside the problem of what they would do about the resulting water shortage for future deliberation.) How does this story illustrate the difference between trivial semantic conventionalism and substantive conventionalism?
7 What three features do all the theories dubbed here as "conventionalist" have in common?
8 How does ethical relativism differ from ethical subjectivism? Can one be an ethical subjectivist and an ethical relativist? Why or why not?
9 Does rejecting Divine Command Theory necessitate the denial of (a) God's existence, or (b) the relevance of religious teachings to the discovery of what's right and wrong? Explain your answers.
10 What objection can be raised against all three conventionalist theories I've discussed above? (Hint: What are the essential "ingredients" of conventionalism? Why might these ingredients be a problematic basis for an ethical theory?)
11 Different societies and cultures have often been committed to widely diverging values. Is this evidence for the truth of ethical relativism? Why or why not?

Problems for Further Thought

1 Is there a third coherent option for the theist who rejects both the Divine Command Theory and ethical realism? Defend your answer.
2 Do facts about evolution suggest that there may be fundamental norms that are cultural universals despite the numerous ways in which human cultures differ from each other?

3   In this chapter, I said that it is "baffling" how an ethical truth can be made true simply because someone says that it is. But there are lots of mundane situations in which statements are made true solely because of someone's say-so. For example, when the baseball umpire says "you're out," you are therefore out. It isn't baffling that this is the way things work. So why should it be baffling that ethical truths are made true by God's or anyone else's say-so?

Recommended Readings, Video, and Audio

Visit the companion website at www.routledge.com/cw/sober for suggestions of readings, video, and audio, for this chapter.

Chapter 32

Utilitarianism

Utilitarianism is an ethical theory whose central idea is "the greatest good for the greatest number." The idea is that ethically correct actions are ones that promote the greatest happiness of the individuals affected by it. We will soon see that this formulation of the theory requires fine-tuning.

Utilitarianism is a philosophical idea that has exercised considerable influence on the world of practical affairs. Jeremy Bentham (1748–1832) and John Stuart Mill (1806–1873) were deeply involved in the political controversies of their age. Both defended utilitarianism in publications that the educated classes in England read with great attention. Utilitarianism wasn't an abstract "ivory tower" theory that only professors found worth discussing. It stirred the interest of great numbers of people who cared about the institutions of their society.

Bentham and Mill thought that many of these institutions needed reform because they failed to promote human welfare. A central political agenda at this time was extending the vote to men who didn't own property. Mill also wrote in favor of women's suffrage, although women didn't receive the right to vote until much later. The abolition of slavery was another political struggle in which utilitarians participated. In these and other cases, utilitarians argued that institutions had to be changed because they advanced the interests of the few to the detriment of the many. Utilitarians attacked the idea that the rich and powerful had some special "right" to arrange society as they saw fit. On the contrary, the point of utilitarianism is that each individual must be taken into account because each individual is capable of experiencing happiness.

In this chapter, I'll discuss the general ethical theory, not the specific political issues that at were and are the focus of utilitarian concern, though on the companion website , there is an article about famine and affluence by Peter Singer—a problem to which utilitarian ideas apply.

By now (as we near the end of this book), it should be abundantly clear that the following is not a valid deduction:

> If utilitarianism is true, then slavery is morally wrong.
> Slavery is morally wrong.
> ———————————————
> Utilitarianism is true.

I don't doubt the premises, but I'll try to show that there are some serious questions to be raised about the conclusion.

Mill's Defense of the Greatest Happiness Principle

Before describing in more detail what utilitarianism says, I want to discuss how someone might go about evaluating whether the most basic principle in utilitarianism is true. Mill calls this basic idea the Greatest Happiness Principle. It says that the action we ought to perform in a given situation is the one that promotes the greatest happiness.

In his essay "Utilitarianism," Mill attempted to prove that the Greatest Happiness Principle is correct. Mill's argument begins with an analogy between desirability and visibility. He says that just as the only proof that something is visible is that someone sees it, so the only proof that something is desirable is that someone desires it. He then claims that what people ultimately want is their own happiness. Mill concludes from this that the most desirable action is the one that produces the most happiness overall.

Let's reconstruct Mill's argument as follows:

(1) Seeing something proves that it is visible.
———————————————
(2) Hence, desiring something proves that it is desirable.
(3) The only thing that each person ultimately desires is his or her own happiness.
———————————————
(4) The only thing that is ultimately desirable for a person is his or her own happiness.
———————————————
Hence, each person should perform those actions that promote the greatest happiness.

I've drawn three horizontal lines in this argument to indicate that (2) is supposed to follow from (1), (4) is supposed to follow from (2) and (3), and the final conclusion is supposed to follow from (4).

There are several problems with this reasoning. First, (1) doesn't provide much of a reason for accepting (2). Visibility and desirability are different. If something is visible, this means that it is possible to see it. However, if something is desirable, this doesn't just mean that it is *possible* to desire it; if something is desirable, this means that it *should* be desired. Visibility is a descriptive concept, while desirability is a normative one. So although "*x* is visible" does follow from "*x* is seen," "*x* is desirable" does *not* follow from "*x* is desired."

What does the word *ultimately* mean in step (3)? It means that everything else people want they want only as a means to the end of securing their own happiness. If I desire that the starving receive food, Mill is saying that I want this only as a means to securing a certain end—namely, my own happiness. I argued against this thesis in Chapter 27; it simply asserts a form of psychological egoism. Three of the four preference structures discussed there (all except Pure Egoism) entail that people care about the welfare of others in addition to caring about their own well-being. If Psychological Egoism is false (as I think it is), then premise (3) of Mill's argument is false.

Does (4) follow from (3)? No—for the same reason that (2) doesn't follow from (1). Even if a person ultimately desires his or her own happiness, it doesn't follow that the most desirable thing is for the person to have his or her desires satisfied. What people ultimately desire is a *descriptive* question, but what is desirable is a *normative* question. Hume was right that ought-statements do not follow from exclusively is-premises.

Finally, even if (4) were true, the conclusion of the argument would not follow. The fact that your own happiness is the most desirable thing *for you* does not imply that you should try to maximize *everyone's* happiness. The conclusion of this argument sometimes requires you to act unselfishly—to sacrifice your own happiness if doing so brings with it a more than compensating increase in the happiness of others. This does not follow from (4).

Reciprocal Illumination

Mill had another idea about how utilitarianism could be rationally justified. Instead of trying to deduce the Greatest Happiness Principle from premises that would be plausible even to a nonutilitarian, we can evaluate the principle by seeing how it measures up against the moral judgments we are prepared to make about concrete cases. This was the method I described Harman as using in Chapter 30. A general principle has implications about what it is wrong or right to do in specific situations. If we are prepared to make ethical judgments about these situations, we can use these judgments to evaluate the general theory (recall Harman's example about the transplant operation). If a theory implies that an action is right in a given situation and we believe that the action would clearly be wrong, we might take this as evidence that the theory is false.

So judgments about specific cases can lead us to reject a general theory. The reverse can happen as well. If we think that a theory is very plausible and then find that it implies that a given action is wrong (which, before thinking about it much, we thought was right), we might decide to allow the theory to guide us—to lead us to revise our opinions about the ethical problem posed by the particular case. We see here a two-way influence—a process of *reciprocal illumination*—by which our judgments about specific cases can influence how we regard a theory, and our views about a theory can affect our judgments about specific cases. A utilitarian who does not think that slavery is wrong might come to see that one or the other of these ideas must be abandoned. Which idea should be abandoned depends on which is overall more plausible (the general theory or the judgment about the specific institution), given the other beliefs that he or she has. I now want to use this technique of evaluation to fine-tune utilitarianism and then to suggest that it faces some serious difficulties.

What Is Happiness?

I'll begin by focusing on the idea of happiness. What is happiness? I'm not asking for *examples* of activities that make us happy. Rather, I want to know what happiness itself is. Compare: If I ask you what bankruptcy is, I'm not asking you what activities cause bankruptcy. Bankruptcy isn't the same as reckless investment; neither is happiness the same thing as a warm puppy. A partial answer might be that happiness is a feeling. This is only partial, of course, because there are many other feelings besides happiness. If, however, happiness is something in the mind (something purely subjective), we can formulate a problem that utilitarianism must address.

The Problem of the Experience Machine

In Chapter 13, I discussed how Descartes grappled with the problem of refuting the hypothesis that he was systematically misled by an evil demon. Contemporary philosophers sometimes give Descartes' problem a modern twist by asking how we know that we aren't brains in vats. According to the brain-in-the-vat hypothesis, your brain now rests in a vat filled with a liquid that keeps it alive. It is hooked up to a giant computer, whose electrical impulses furnish you with a rich stream of experiences. These impulses generate the illusion that you have a body and that you are having sensory contact (via sight, smell, hearing, touch, etc.) with the external world. According to the brain-in-the-vat hypothesis, almost everything you believe about your present and past is false. You don't really have a face; you're not really looking at a philosophy book right now, and so on.

The point of this bizarre hypothesis is that it poses a philosophical challenge. The challenge is to show how you know that the brain-in-the-vat hypothesis is false. None of us believes this hypothesis about ourselves. Can this conviction be rationally justified, or is it just a groundless prejudice?

As just formulated, the brain-in-the-vat problem falls within the theory of knowledge; it is a part of epistemology. I now will reformulate the problem so as to turn it into an ethical issue, one that tells us something about utilitarianism. The computer described in the brain-in-the-vat problem is an *experience machine*. Suppose that the machine could be set up so it would provide you with whatever experiences would make you the happiest, and that it is up to you to decide whether you wish to be plugged into the machine. If being a great concert violinist would give you maximal pleasure, plugging into the machine will give you a rich, complex sequence of experiences of this sort. If you would be happiest being a political leader loved and admired by millions of people, the experience machine can furnish the feelings that would derive from being loved and admired by millions. Of course, the experience machine does not make you into a concert violinist or a political leader. Rather, the machine gives you the precise set of experiences you would get from having those sorts of lives.

If utilitarianism were true (where utilitarianism is understood in terms of maximizing happiness, a subjective state), it would be preferable for people to plug into experience machines rather than lead real lives that provide a lesser degree of happiness. But, contrary to what utilitarianism says about this kind of choice, I for one (and I bet you feel the same way) put considerable value on leading a real life. If you're plugged into the experience machine, virtually all your beliefs are false. You are proud of yourself because you think you are a great violinist and you take pleasure in your skill. If the machine leads you to think that you are a great political leader, you may think you have created world peace and so you feel good about doing so. However, in both cases, your pride and your pleasure rest on an illusion. Most of us value something beyond the feeling of happiness that comes from doing certain things. We also place a value on the reality of the doing. However, to think this way is to say that something matters beyond the subjective feeling of happiness. This goes contrary to the form of utilitarianism we're considering. (The example of the experience machine comes from Robert Nozick's *Anarchy, State, and Utopia*, New York, Basic Books, 1974.)

There are a number of science fiction novels and movies that make this same point. Aldous Huxley's *Brave New World* and Woody Allen's *Sleeper* are examples. These works of fiction describe a future in which people are drugged by their governments into being docile, happy citizens. People are contented, but the novel or movie usually takes the point of view that there is something deeply wrong with a society like this. Usually what's wrong is that people lack *autonomy*. Their own beliefs and desires have been distorted or altogether destroyed; what they do and feel is the result of the drugs they take. If you agree that there is something wrong with a society of this sort, you may have to say that there is something over and above "happiness" (a state of mind) that is ethically important.

Mill on "Higher" and "Lower" Pleasures

Mill himself grappled with a problem of this kind. He asked why it is better to be "Socrates dissatisfied" rather than a satisfied fool. Socrates was acutely aware of the imperfections of the world around him; it isn't true that each of his daily experiences filled him with pleasure. But a "satisfied fool," Mill says, would be delighted by every detail of life. If the latter individual is happier, utilitarianism seems to recommend that we become more like the fool and less like Socrates.

Mill denied that utilitarianism has this implication. He thought that Socrates was capable of enjoying "higher" pleasures, whereas the fool could only experience "lower" pleasures. Higher pleasures derive from exercising higher mental abilities (such as abstract reasoning); lower pleasures come from using mental abilities that are lower (such as sensation). Mill claimed that higher pleasures provide more happiness than lower ones. To see that this is true, Mill recommends that you ask individuals who have experienced both sorts of pleasures which they enjoyed more. Mill was confident that these "competent judges" would say that higher pleasures bring more happiness than lower ones.

There are some higher and lower pleasures for which Mill's prediction might be true. For example, someone who does nothing but drink beer and watch television might find that "higher" pleasures are better, once he or she is exposed to them. There are other cases, however, in which Mill's prediction seems mistaken. Imagine someone who has been leading a real life and then is plugged into an experience machine. Once he is unplugged, we could ask him which life made him happier. I think most people would have to admit that their life while plugged in provided more happiness than the real life they led before. This doesn't mean that people *prefer* to live the phony life that results from being plugged into the experience machine; it just means that life in the experience machine provides more happiness.

The same may be true of the people in the science fiction works mentioned earlier. Maybe drugs provide them with more happiness than they would receive if they were autonomous. Again this doesn't mean that they *prefer* being drugged by their governments, but that they receive a greater quantity of happiness in that state. To move closer to real life, consider a drug like heroin. Suppose someone could live a life as a heroin addict without facing dangers like AIDS and being killed by drug dealers. Maybe in that case the drug would be so intensely pleasurable that people who had experienced life with it and life without it would have to concede that life is happier with it. This doesn't mean that they would *prefer* to have such a life. Rather, what it shows is that our preferences are influenced by factors other than the quantity of happiness we receive.

Objection to Hedonistic Utilitarianism

My conclusion is that Mill's argument about higher and lower pleasures does not work. Mill believed that Socrates dissatisfied had a better life than a satisfied fool, but I don't see that Mill has a way of explaining why this is so. So we have here an objection to the first form of utilitarianism I want to distinguish. It is *hedonistic utilitarianism*, which says that the right action is the one that maximizes pleasure and minimizes pain (not just for the agent, but for all individuals who are affected). According to this form of utilitarianism, we should plug into the experience machine; we should become more like the fool and less like Socrates. Both these ought-statements strike me as false. If they are false, then hedonistic utilitarianism should be rejected.

Preference Utilitarianism

There is another form of utilitarianism, one that is not undermined by these problems. I call it *preference utilitarianism*. The idea of this kind of utilitarianism is not to maximize pleasure, but to maximize the degree to which people get their preferences satisfied. If people generally prefer to lead real lives rather than to plug into experience machines, then a preference utilitarian will have no problem explaining why it would be wrong to plug people into experience machines. And if people prefer to live their lives drug-free, then preference utilitarianism can easily explain why it would be wrong for the government to surreptitiously give people a diet of pleasure-producing drugs. So preference utilitarianism avoids a problem that is fatal to hedonistic utilitarianism. But preference utilitarianism has problems of its own. The first of these becomes clear when we try to apply the view to specific cases.

The Apples and Oranges Problem

The problem is that it is often difficult to know how to compare one person's preferences with those of another. This is something that a preference utilitarian must do if those preferences conflict. Consider a state government that has to decide whether a tract of land should be opened to commercial use or reserved for recreational use. There are the profits and jobs that some people will receive on the one hand, and the enjoyment from camping and swimming that other people will receive on the other. How are these two interests to be compared? For preference utilitarians to answer this question, they need to measure how intensely each person prefers one option over the other. Then they need to sum over this totality of individual preferences to decide which action maximizes the satisfaction of preferences collectively. Suppose that the economic losses from not going the commercial route were "small," whereas the recreational (and aesthetic) losses from going the commercial route were "large." What conclusion would preference utilitarians extract from this? The problem is that it is often obscure what "small" and "large" mean in such cases. Let's call this the *Apples and Oranges Problem:* How can you compare the intensity of one person's gain with the intensity of another person's loss?

Sometimes this kind of question is settled by using money as a mode of comparison. If you want to know how intensely the developers want to develop the land commercially, you can find out how much they are prepared to pay to do so; to ascertain how intensely other people want the land to be preserved for recreational use, you can see how much they are prepared to pay to attain this goal. Then see how much money stacks up on the one side and how much on the other—which option has attracted the higher bid? The problem with this procedure is that how much money people are willing to spend is often influenced by factors other than the intensity of their desires. A rich person may be prepared to pay more for a loaf of bread than a poor one, but that doesn't mean that the rich person wants it more.

Sometimes the Apples and Oranges Problem is addressed by taking a vote among the individuals affected; let a referendum be held, with each person having a single vote. The problem with using voting as a way of solving this problem (which economists call the problem of interpersonal utility comparison) is that voting does not represent the *intensities* of people's desires. If I mildly prefer the commercial option to the recreational one, I'll vote for the commercial option; if you strongly prefer the recreational use to the commercial one, you will vote for the recreational use. Your vote and mine count equally, but this fails to represent something that is important to the calculation that a preference utilitarian must make.

In practical politics, voting is often a reasonable procedure (whether it *always* is reasonable will be discussed in what follows). However, I'm not talking about choosing a workable (if imperfect) procedure. I'm talking about the problem of making sense of what preference utilitarianism actually says. The problem is that it is often unclear what it means to say that a given action has a higher utility for one person than the opposite action has for another person. Although this is a serious problem for preference utilitarianism, I'm going to assume in what follows that the Apples and Oranges Problem can be solved—that the intensity of people's preferences can be compared. I make this assumption in order to explore some additional criticisms that have been made of preference utilitarianism.

Utilitarianism and Justice: The Case of the Lonesome Stranger

I'll begin with a problem that can be illustrated by an example. A gruesome murder has occurred in a town. The sheriff has discovered that the murderer himself is dead; however, the sheriff knows that no one will believe him if he says this, even if he lays out all the evidence he has. Meanwhile, the townspeople are becoming more and more agitated. The sheriff realizes that if a suspect isn't put on trial very soon, there will be a riot and it is quite probable that many innocent people will be injured and a few killed. As the sheriff is mulling this over in his office, in strolls a lonesome stranger. This fellow tells the sheriff that he has no friends or relations in the world and that he is feeling depressed and has no particular desire to continue living. The sheriff then gets an idea: why not frame the lonesome stranger? There is capital punishment in this locale, so the sheriff can arrange that the stranger be tried, convicted, and executed. Suppose the sheriff can arrange it so that the framing will always remain a secret. Should the sheriff frame the stranger?

What would a utilitarian say here? For a hedonistic utilitarian, the answer is easy. If you frame the stranger (and keep the facts secret), one person dies, but the peace of mind of the townspeople is restored; if you don't frame him, a bloody riot will ensue and more than one person will die. The way to maximize happiness is for the sheriff to frame the stranger and always keep this secret. For a preference utilitarian, the question is more complicated. If the people in the town have strong preferences that innocent people should not be punished, then the sheriff should not frame the stranger. Suppose, however, the people don't care about this; let's suppose they care only about their own safety and peace of mind. In this case, preference utilitarianism will tell the sheriff that he ought to frame the stranger. The problem here is that utilitarian considerations seem to conflict with considerations of *justice*. It is unjust to punish people for crimes they did not commit. If you think this moral requirement overrides considerations that reflect the utility of punishing the lonesome stranger, then you will interpret this example as an objection to utilitarianism. [Notice that this problem resembles the one described in Chapter 30 concerning a physician who must decide whether to kill a patient so that the patient's organs can be harvested and then transplanted to save the lives of five people who would otherwise die.]

Punishment

Before considering how a utilitarian might reply to this objection, I want to say a little more about punishment. A utilitarian will answer the question of whether someone should be punished by asking whether punishing would have good consequences. If punishment does not deter people from similar wrongdoing and does not reform the character of the person punished, then a utilitarian may say that there is no point in punishing people who are guilty of even the most awful crimes. For a utilitarian, the distinction between guilt and innocence does not have to coincide with the distinction between those who should be punished and those who should not be.

A nonutilitarian view of punishment (there is more than one) will see things differently. The principle of an eye for an eye—of retribution for wrongdoing—is not a utilitarian idea. Retributivists want the punishment to fit the crime; they will say that someone should be punished if and only if they deserve to be punished. People who are innocent of any wrongdoing must never be punished and people who are guilty of some wrongdoing must be punished. For retributivists (people who think that punishment is justified because it is retribution for wrongdoing), it doesn't matter whether punishing improves anything after the crime is committed. For utilitarians, it is precisely the consequences of punishment (not the crime committed) that is relevant to deciding whether someone should be punished.

Utilitarian discussion of punishment usually focuses on the question of why *the guilty* should be punished. But, as the case of the lonesome stranger illustrates, the question can also be posed of why the innocent should not be punished. According to utilitarianism, there is no absolute requirement that the guilty must be punished nor is there a requirement that the innocent must not be punished. What should be done depends entirely on which course of action will maximize the collective happiness.

A Reply: Distinguish Rule and Act Utilitarianism

I've argued that the lonesome stranger example provides an objection to utilitarianism (whether of the hedonistic or the preference variety). It illustrates how considerations of justice can conflict with utilitarianism. Recall that this assessment of utilitarianism depends on making a moral judgment about the example situation. Without this, there is no way to use specific cases to evaluate the general principle.

There is a standard reply that utilitarians often make to this and similar objections. Their strategy is to distinguish two kinds of utilitarian theory and to claim that one of them is perfectly consistent with the idea that the sheriff should not frame the lonesome stranger. I described utilitarianism as saying that an action should be performed only if it promotes the greatest happiness or the greatest preference satisfaction. However, there is an ambiguity here. Are we evaluating *kinds* of actions, or individual actions, one by one? That is, are we to use utilitarian considerations to decide what general rules to follow, or should we apply these considerations each time a specific act is at issue? Here I'm drawing the type/token distinction discussed in Chapter 23 and applying it to the question of how utilitarianism should be formulated.

That is, utilitarianism (regardless of whether it says to maximize happiness or preference satisfaction) can take the form of *rule utilitarianism* or *act utilitarianism*. How does this choice affect the way we understand the lonesome stranger example? According to the rule utilitarian, the sheriff's decision making should have two parts. First, he must decide what general rule to adopt. Second, he must determine how that general rule applies to the concrete case he confronts.

The first problem involves deciding which of the following two general rules has better consequences:

(R1) Punish the innocent when it is convenient.
(R2) Never punish the innocent.

A rule utilitarian will argue that (R2) has better consequences for people's welfare, and so it is (R2) that the sheriff should use. Note that once (R2) is applied to the specific situation the sheriff confronts, he will decide *not* to frame the stranger. Why think that (R2) has better consequences than (R1)? Part of the reason is that rules that are used again and again become generally known. If people generally believe that (R1) is the policy the government follows, this will produce a great deal of unhappiness. An act utilitarian, on the other hand, will not focus on general rules, but will focus instead on the specific choice at hand. The act utilitarian's procedure has one step, not two. In the unique, concrete situation that the sheriff faces, he will maximize utility by framing the lonesome stranger. Which general rule has the best overall consequences is not relevant to the sheriff's deliberation, according to the act utilitarian.

Thus, the defender of utilitarianism is suggesting the following: the claim is that the example of the lonesome stranger constitutes an objection to *act* utilitarianism, not to *rule* utilitarianism. The idea is that rule utilitarianism recommends that the sheriff not frame the stranger, and this recommendation coincides with what most people find plausible.

In reply, I want to argue that adopting a rule utilitarian formulation won't save utilitarianism from the difficulty posed by the example of the lonesome stranger. I agree that (R2) has better consequences as a general policy than (R1) does. However, I think that a utilitarian must concede that (R2) is inferior to the following rule:

(R3) Don't punish the innocent, unless doing so will maximize utility.

I think a utilitarian must agree that (R3) is preferable on utilitarian grounds to (R2). And the sheriff, acting on (R3), will frame the lonesome stranger. I conclude that rule utilitarianism and act utilitarianism are equally subject to the objection posed by the example of the lonesome stranger.

Utilitarianism and Tolerance: The Problem of the Fanatical Majority

I now turn to a different objection to utilitarianism. An important fact about preference utilitarianism is that it does not allow you to ignore people's preferences on the grounds that you morally disapprove of them. People's preferences, whether we approve of them or not, must be taken into account when we decide what laws our society should adopt or what actions each of us should perform. The problem for utilitarianism is that we sometimes think it is our moral duty to *ignore* people's preferences because we think those preferences are morally objectionable. If it is ever morally legitimate to do this, preference utilitarianism is in trouble.

Consider what happens to nonconformists in a society of fanatics. Here we might be talking about people in a minority religion, who live in a society in which the majority is made of religious fanatics. Or consider a society in which a minority of people are homosexual and the heterosexual majority is very intolerant. Another case concerns political nonconformity—a minority with one set of political beliefs living with a majority that not only disagrees with them, but is extremely hostile toward them. How would a utilitarian view the idea that people should be free to live as they see fit?

A utilitarian will decide this question by calculating how policies of repression or toleration would satisfy people's preferences. If the intolerant majority is fanatical enough, the utilitarian scales may tip in favor of prohibiting nonconformity. If a fanatical majority gets upset enough at the presence of nonconformists, then there will be a utilitarian justification for banning nonconformity. Of course, this sort of policy will not be the one that the nonconformists prefer. However, since they are in the minority, their strong preferences may be outweighed by the strong preferences of the fanatical majority.

Many of us would want to say that people have certain rights—to freely pursue the religion of their choice (or no religion at all), to engage in the sexual practices they prefer (or none at all), to discuss and promulgate their favored political opinions (or to be apolitical)—as long as doing so does not endanger the life and property of others. The fact that these practices might enrage an intolerant majority, many of us would want to say, simply does not count against a person's being entitled to do what he or she wants. To think this way is *not* to think like a utilitarian.

We have here an objection to utilitarianism. I'll call it the *Problem of the Fanatical Majority*. John Stuart Mill considered this issue in his famous essay "On Liberty." Mill was a liberal in the sense of that word used in the nineteenth century. Liberals believe in liberty. An imprecise slogan embodying liberalism is that "people should be free to do what they want, as long as doing so does not hurt others." One reason this is imprecise is that fanatics might claim to be "hurt" (offended, distressed, outraged, etc.) simply by knowing that there are people who live their lives differently from the way they do.

Mill was a utilitarian who believed in the kinds of personal liberties I just mentioned. His problem was to reconcile utilitarianism with the idea that people have a right to the kinds of freedoms I've just enumerated. Mill sought to effect this reconciliation by distinguishing *public* and *private* actions. A public action affects individuals in addition to the actor; a private action, on the other hand, does not affect others. Mill argued that people are entitled to live lives of nonconformity, if they wish, since the activities involved here are private, not public.

29 Liberalism and Conservatism

Mill believed that the right to personal nonconformity flows from utilitarian considerations. He also thought that economic activity is public and therefore might have to be limited for utilitarian reasons. A corporation's activities (even a single person's buying and selling) affects others. A regulated economy (as opposed to an absolutely free market) therefore is preferable, Mill thought, on utilitarian grounds. Mill was a *liberal*, in the nineteenth-century meaning of that term. Liberals believed in liberty—that each person should have the maximum amount of freedom, consistent with not compromising the freedom of others.

The terms "liberal" and "conservative" have different meanings in the United States today. To understand what each involves, let's distinguish two "markets" in which each of us participates: the marketplace of *ideas* and the *economic* marketplace (of goods and services that we buy and sell).

Liberals in the United States now often oppose censorship and think that the government should not promote religion (or promote one religion over any other). They believe that the government should not interfere in the marketplace of ideas. Yet they tend to believe, on utilitarian grounds, that the government should regulate the economy. So-called "conservatives," on the other hand, tend to take the opposite view. They often favor some sorts of censorship and want the government to promote religion (by encouraging prayer in the public schools, for example). Yet, when it comes to the economic marketplace, they tend to favor more freedom and less regulation.

Although both political positions are influenced by utilitarian considerations, each makes use of nonutilitarian ideas as well. Liberals often talk about "rights" of free speech, which people are said to have even if some forms of free speech make lots of people very unhappy. And conservatives sometimes argue that pornography should be censored on religious grounds or on other grounds that are not utilitarian.

Liberalism and conservatism are not the only political options available. In the United States, both hold that capitalism is the best form of economic organization, and both have favored military interventions of various kinds (in Korea, Vietnam, Iraq, and Afghanistan, for example). Some critics on the left—socialists and communists, for example—doubt the viability of capitalism and have opposed military interventions such as the ones mentioned. Some critics on the right (libertarians, for example) reject the government's entitlement to intervene in people's lives without their consent—for example, to collect taxes, to censor pornography, and to regulate the economy.

Mill defended a totally free (*laissez-faire*) marketplace of ideas. He described ideas as being in competition. Everyone benefits from unrestrained competition, Mill said, because competition tends to select the best ideas. Ideas compete in the way organisms do in the process of Darwinian natural selection (Chapter 6).

Defenders of a free economic marketplace have often put forward a similar argument. In *The Wealth of Nations*, the eighteenth-century economist Adam Smith argued that when everyone freely pursues his or her selfish economic interests, everyone benefits. The nation as a whole becomes richer, and so prosperity "trickles down" to even the worst-off people in the society. Liberals have criticized this trickle down defense of a perfectly free market economy. They claim that an unregulated economy produces catastrophic swings ("boom and bust cycles," like the one that produced the Crash of 1929 and the ensuing Great Depression). An unfettered market, they argue, can make everyone worse off than they would be if the market were regulated. This liberal argument against a perfectly free market is utilitarian in character.

Does this argument secure the kinds of freedoms I have been discussing? Not entirely. In a society in which most people are intolerant fanatics, the most that a nonconforming minority can hope for is the right to be *secret* nonconformists. It is only when such practices are performed in secret that they can count as private in Mill's sense. However, I think most of us believe in liberties that are more extensive than ones that are kept in the closet. Whether it be in the religious, sexual, or political arenas, most of us think there are practices affecting others (because they are not kept secret) that a minority is entitled to engage in, even if this distresses fanatics.

Utilitarianism and Personal Integrity: The Problem of Dirty Hands

The next objection to utilitarianism that I want to discuss I'll call the *Dirty Hands Objection*. Consider an individual contemplating a choice between an action that is clearly right and one that is clearly wrong. Suppose, however, that the morally wrong action has this characteristic: if the individual does not perform this bad action himself or herself, someone else will. An example of this kind of situation is provided by a case I discussed in connection with Sartre's existentialism in Chapter 31. Imagine someone who is considering whether he should become a torturer for the Nazis. Suppose that if he doesn't do this, someone else will. Examples less horrible than this are common in everyday life. Maybe if you are studying to be an engineer, you will get a job offer to work on developing a new weapon for the government. Perhaps you will feel that it is wrong to have this weapon developed—that it will provide new ways to harm people without making our country or any other more secure. Of course, your participation in the development of this weapon is not *necessary* for the weapon to get produced. If you don't do the job, someone else will.

What will a utilitarian say about such cases? If you decline the job offer, the bad consequences (the torturing, the development of the weapon) occur nonetheless, but without your participation. If you accept, the same bad consequences occur, this time with your participation. A utilitarian will have to conclude that *it makes no difference*, morally speaking, whether you accept the job offer or decline it. The net consequences are the same. I think that in many cases like this, it *does* make a moral difference what you decide to do. For example, it is wrong to be a torturer for the Nazis. If you become a torturer, you have done something wrong; if you don't become a torturer, you have avoided doing something evil. There is a moral difference here that should guide your conduct. The moral issue of what sort of a person you ought to be is not something that utilitarianism takes into account. According to utilitarianism, what you should do in such cases is to look at the net consequences that would occur under different circumstances; this is different from considering what kind of a person you ought to be.

Sometimes utilitarians reply to this objection in the same way I described them replying to the lonesome stranger example. They propose a distinction between rule and act utilitarianism and claim that rule utilitarianism has the plausible consequence that it *does* make a moral difference whether you become a torturer or not. Utilitarians who make this reply reason as follows. To decide what you ought to do in this specific situation, you first must decide which general rule should be followed by you and others. The two rules you might consider are as follows:

(S$_1$) If the government offers someone a job as a torturer, the offer should be accepted.
(S$_2$) If the government offers someone a job as a torturer, the offer should be rejected.

The rule utilitarian then points out that the consequences would be better if everyone adopted (S$_2$) than if everyone adopted (S$_1$). The conclusion about this pair of rules is then applied to the specific choice you confront. You should apply (S$_2$) to decide what to do; hence, you should decline the offer from the Nazis.

I hope you see how this pattern of argument parallels what rule utilitarians have said in reply to the objection based on the lonesome stranger example. My view is that this reply to the problem of dirty hands is no more successful than the previous reply to the lonesome stranger problem. I grant that (S$_2$) has better consequences than (S$_1$). However, it seems to me that a utilitarian can't explain why (S$_2$) is superior to the following rule:

(S₃) If the government offers someone a job as a torturer, the offer should be rejected, unless it makes no difference to the collective utility whether it is accepted or rejected.

A utilitarian can't explain why (S₂) is a better rule than (S₃). For this reason, the dirty hands problem is, I think, a telling objection to utilitarianism.

Utilitarianism and Personal Loyalties

The last problem for utilitarianism that I want to consider concerns the role that personal loyalties play in our judgments about morality. Imagine that a boating accident occurs and you have to choose which of two people you are going to save from drowning. One of them is your own daughter. The other is another child. What should you do? If you think it makes a moral difference what you do, how can this be explained? It may be true that the consequences for the collective welfare are the same, whether your child lives and the other child dies, or yours dies and the other lives. If so, utilitarianism can't explain the special obligations we have to our own family.

By now, the rule utilitarian reply to this objection should be something you can anticipate. Compare the general consequences of obeying each of the following general rules:

(T₁) People should not make an effort to preserve the lives of their own children.
(T₂) People should make an effort to preserve the lives of their own children.

Of course, general adherence to (T₂) has better consequences than general adherence to (T₁). But that isn't enough to get utilitarianism out of trouble, since it is hard to see how a utilitarian can argue that (T₂) is superior to (T₃).

(T₃) People should make an effort to preserve the lives of their own children, except when no additional utility comes from doing so.

A Psychological Objection to My Criticisms of Utilitarianism

There is a different sort of reply that utilitarians sometimes make to examples like this one. They say that in a situation of crisis, people don't have time to calculate what they ought to do. They merely act on impulse. What they do in such cases is more a consequence of the habits of character they have developed than of reasoning from general principles.

I grant this psychological point, but it seems to me to be irrelevant. Utilitarianism makes a claim about which actions are right and which are wrong. It doesn't demand that people take the time and energy to reason abstractly about what the Greatest Happiness Principle entails. Nor does utilitarianism say that people in fact engage in dispassionate calculation in situations of crisis. My criticisms of utilitarianism have to do with what the theory says people *ought* to do; in each of the cases I surveyed, I argued that the theory errs in its moral recommendations.

Summary

I've raised several objections to utilitarianism. The lonesome stranger objection is supposed to show how utilitarianism can conflict with the value of justice. The problem of the fanatical majority shows how utilitarianism can conflict with the value of liberty. Finally, the problem of dirty hands and the problem of loyalty both show that utilitarianism can fail to detect moral differences between alternative actions that really do differ morally. In each of these cases, utilitarianism was judged by seeing what it implies about a concrete example situation. The arguments all proceeded by advancing a moral judgment about the examples and then showing that this judgment conflicts with the dictates of utilitarianism. I grant that someone who is not prepared to endorse the moral claims I've made about the examples will not find this discussion a conclusive refutation of utilitarianism. However, if you agree with what I've said about one or more of these examples, then this should be enough to make you doubt that utilitarianism is correct.

Review Questions

1 Mill presents an argument for the Greatest Happiness Principle and also says that the principle can be defended by what I've called "reciprocal illumination." Explain what the argument is and what reciprocal illumination is.
2 What is the difference between hedonistic utilitarianism and preference utilitarianism? How does the example of the experience machine bear on each of these theories?
3 What is the Apples and Oranges Problem?
4 How does the case of the lonesome stranger pose a problem for utilitarianism?
5 How does the Problem of the Fanatical Majority present a difficulty for utilitarianism?
6 How does the Dirty Hands Objection present a difficulty for utilitarianism?
7 How might a utilitarian use the distinction between act utilitarianism and rule utilitarianism to reply to the objections involved in questions 4–6? How do utilitarians typically propose to explain the special obligations we have towards our family? Do you think this proposal is successful? Why or why not?
8 How does act utilitarianism differ from rule utilitarianism? Can you think of an example, in addition to those already considered in this chapter, in which the moral recommendations of an act-utilitarian and a rule-utilitarian would significantly differ?
9 Why does Mill distinguish between "higher" and "lower" forms of pleasure? What problem does he intend this distinction to solve? Is his solution successful? Why or why not?
10 What does it mean to say that "desirability" is a normative concept? How does it differ from a descriptive concept, like "visibility"? What implications does this difference have for Mill's defense of the Greatest Happiness Principle?
11 How do utilitarians typically justify punishment? Does utilitarianism recommend that we always punish the guilty and refrain from punishing the innocent? If not, why not?

Problems for Further Thought

1 In defending the Greatest Happiness Principle, Mill says that the only proof that something is visible is that someone sees it. Is this a correct claim to make about dispositional properties (discussed in Chapter 20) like visibility? Is it true that the only proof that something is soluble is that someone dissolves it? If not, can Mill's argument be repaired so as to avoid this problem?
2 In discussing the Apples and Oranges Problem, I argued that the problem would not be solved by having a referendum in which each person casts a single vote. Would it be a solution to give each person ten votes, and to ask people to cast the number of votes that reflects the intensity of their preferences?

3   When I discussed preference utilitarianism, I interpreted that theory to mean that what should be maximized is the satisfaction of the preferences that people *actually* have. However, there is another form of utilitarianism that is important to consider. Let's say that a person's *revealed preferences* are the preferences he or she would have if provided with full factual information about the situation at hand. A person's actual preferences and his or her revealed preferences may differ if the actual preferences are based on incomplete or incorrect assumptions. Can some of the objections to preference utilitarianism discussed in this chapter be met if we shift our formulation of utilitarianism from actual to revealed preferences?

4   Hedonistic utilitarianism says that the pleasure and pain of *all beings* affected by an act must be taken into account in deciding whether that act should be performed. Preference utilitarianism says that the preferences of *all beings* affected by an act must be taken into account in deciding whether that act should be performed. Some utilitarians (for example, Peter Singer, in *Animal Liberation*, New York, Random House, 1975) have drawn the conclusion that the way human beings treat animals is morally outrageous. They argue that the pleasure and nutrition people obtain from eating meat does not outweigh the suffering and death of the animals that are eaten. Is there any way to avoid this conclusion while still remaining true to utilitarian principles?

5   If utilitarianism requires us to maximize the amount of happiness there is in the world, won't it require us to have as many children as possible? Even if overpopulation lowers the *average* (per person) quality of life, won't this be outweighed by the total number of individuals who obtain some amount of happiness from the lives they lead? How could a utilitarian argue for the desirability of zero population growth?

6   In this chapter, I used Nozick's example of the experience machine to argue that hedonistic utilitarianism is false. My claim was that when people refuse to lead their whole lives plugged into this machine, this shows that they value something other than states of their own consciousness. Is my objection refuted by the Arnold Schwarzenegger movie "Total Recall," in which people in a future society choose to take "vacations" by plugging into an experience machines for a few days?

Recommended Readings, Video, and Audio

Visit the companion website at www.routledge.com/cw/sober for suggestions of readings, video, and audio, for this chapter.

Chapter 33

Kant's Moral Theory

To understand the basic approach that Immanuel Kant (1724–1804) developed in his moral theory, it is useful to begin with a somewhat common-sensical idea—an idea that Kant rejects. This is the idea that reason can play only an instrumental role in guiding people's actions. Reason does not tell you what your ultimate goals should be; rather, it tells you what you should do, given the goals you happen to have. To say that reason is purely instrumental is to say that it is merely a tool (an instrument) that helps you achieve your goals, your goals having been determined by something other than reason.

This simple idea can be elaborated by viewing actions as the joint products of beliefs and desires. Reason can tell you what to believe, given the evidence at hand. However, reason cannot tell you what to want. Desires must have some other, nonrational, source:

Hume on Reason's Role

David Hume articulated this idea about the contribution that reason makes to the actions we perform. In *A Treatise of Human Nature* (1738), he says that "reason is and ought to be the slave of the passions." Hume expresses the same idea in the following passage:

'Tis not contrary to reason to prefer the destruction of the whole world to the scratching of my finger….

'Tis as little contrary to reason to prefer even my own acknowledg'd lesser good to my greater, and have a more ardent affection for the former than the latter.

The main point about Hume's idea is that actions *never derive from reason alone; they must always have a nonrational source.*

Kant Rejects the Idea that Reason Is Purely Instrumental

Kant's theory of morality rejects this Humean doctrine. According to Kant, it is only sometimes true that actions are produced by the agent's beliefs and (nonrationally generated) desires. This is the way things work when we act out of "inclination." However, when we act out of duty—when our actions are guided by moral considerations rather than by our inclinations—matters are entirely different. When we act, there is a goal we have in mind—an end in view—and also a means we use to try to achieve that goal. Hume thought that reason determines the means we choose, but not the end we have in mind. Kant agreed that this is correct when we act out of inclination. But when morality drives our actions, reason determines the end as well as the means. Kant thought that morality derives its authority from reason alone. Reason alone determines whether an action is right or wrong, regardless of the desires that people happen to have. According to Kant, when we act morally, our actions are guided by reason in a way that Hume's theory says is impossible.

Kant: Moral Rules Are Categorical Imperatives

It is clear, as Hume said, that reason can show us which means to use, given the ends we already have. If I want to be healthy, reason may tell me that I should stop smoking. Here reason provides an imperative that is *hypothetical* in form: it says that I should stop smoking *if* I want to protect my health. Hume thought that reason can do no more than this. Kant, however, held that moral rules are *categorical*, not hypothetical, in form. An act that is wrong is wrong—period. Moral rules say "Don't do X." They do not say "Don't do X if your goal is G." Kant tried to show that these moral rules—these *categorical* imperatives—are derived from reason just as surely as hypothetical imperatives are. Moral rules, which take the form of categorical imperatives, describe what we must do whether we want to or not. They have an authority that is separate from the inclinations we happen to have. So, when we act morally, Kant thought, we are guided by reason, not by inclination. In this case, reason plays more than an instrumental role.

The Moral Law

Another important ingredient in Kant's moral philosophy is his idea that moral laws and scientific laws have something deep in common. A scientific law is a generalization that says what *must* be true in a specified kind of situation. For example, Newton's universal law of gravitation says that the magnitude of the gravitational force F_g between two objects is proportional to the products of their masses (m_1 and m_2) and inversely proportional to the square of the distance (r) between them:

$$F_g = Gm_1m_2/r^2$$

That is, the law says that if the masses are m_1 and m_2 and if the distance is r, then the gravitational force *must* take the value Gm_1m_2/r^2, where G is the gravitational constant.

There is clearly a difference between scientific laws and moral rules (like "Don't cause gratuitous suffering"). Newton's law doesn't say what the planets ought to do; it says what they do, of necessity. If a scientific law is true, then nothing in the universe disobeys it. On the other hand, people sometimes violate moral laws. Moral laws say how people ought to behave; they don't say what people in fact will do. To use vocabulary introduced earlier, moral laws are normative, while scientific laws are descriptive.

In spite of this difference, Kant thought that there is a deeper similarity between them. Scientific laws are *universal*—they involve *all* phenomena of a specified kind. They are not limited to certain places or certain times. Furthermore, a proposition that states a law does not mention any particular person, place, or thing. "All of Napoleon's friends spoke French" may be a true generalization, but it can't be a law, since it mentions a specific individual, Napoleon. I'll mark this feature of scientific laws by saying that they are "impersonal." Moral laws, Kant thought, also must be universal and impersonal. If it is right for me to do something, then it is right for anyone in similar circumstances to do the same thing. It isn't possible that Napoleon should have the right to do something simply because he is Napoleon. Moral laws, like scientific laws, don't mention specific people.

One more element in Kant's moral philosophy must be mentioned before I can describe why Kant thought that reason alone dictates what our moral principles should be. Recall from the previous chapter that utilitarianism asserts that the moral characteristics of an action are settled by the consequences the action would have for people's happiness or preference satisfaction. Utilitarianism is therefore said to be a "consequentialist" ethical theory. Kant's theory is not consequentialist. Kant rejected the idea that the consequences an action settle whether the action is morally obligatory. This may come as a surprise to you—what else, besides the consequences the action would have if it were performed, could be relevant to deciding whether the action is right?

Kant: The Moral Value of an Act Derives from Its Maxim, Not from Its Consequences

Each action can be described as an action of a certain kind. If you help someone, you may think of this as an act of charity. In this case, you may be acting on the maxim that you should help others. Alternatively, when you provide the help, you perhaps are thinking of this as a way of making the recipient feel indebted to you. Here the maxim of your action might be that you should place others in your debt. To see what moral value your action has, look at the maxim you had in mind that led you to do what you did.

The reason we need to look at the agent's motives, and not at the action's consequences, is not hard to grasp. Kant describes a shopkeeper who never cheats his customers. The reason is that he's afraid that if he cheats them, they will stop patronizing his store. Kant says that the shopkeeper does the right thing, but not for the right reason. He acts *in accordance with* morality, but not *from* morality. To discover the moral value of an action, Kant says we must see *why* the actor performs it; the consequences the action happens to have do not reveal this.

If the shopkeeper acts by applying the maxim "Always be honest," his action has moral value. If, however, his action is a result of the maxim "Don't cheat people if it is likely to harm you financially," his action is merely prudent. Moral value comes from motives, and the motives are given by the maxim that the agent applies in deciding what to do.

Kant Rejected Consequentialism

Kant is undoubtedly correct in saying that knowing an individual's motives is important in assessing *some* moral properties of an action. For example, if we wish to evaluate an agent's moral character, knowing the agent's motives is important; the consequences the action has may be an imperfect guide. After all, a good person can unintentionally cause harm to others and a malevolent person can unintentionally provide others with a benefit. However, it is important to see that this point does not imply that an action's consequences are irrelevant to deciding whether to do it. Kant maintains this further thesis: What makes an action right or wrong is not whether the consequences are harmful or beneficial. Kant rejects *consequentialism* in ethics.

The Universalizability Criterion

I now can describe Kant's idea that reason determines what it is right and wrong to do. Recall that a moral law (like a scientific law) must be universal. This means that a moral action must embody a maxim that is *universalizable*. To decide whether it would be right to perform a particular action, Kant says you should ask whether you can intend that the maxim of your act should be a universal law. Universalizability is the basis of all categorical imperatives—that is, of all unconditional moral injunctions. Moral acts can be universalized; immoral acts cannot be.

It is important to grasp what Kant's proposed test involves. Kant is *not* saying that you should ask whether it would be a good thing or a bad thing if everyone did the act you are contemplating. The point about immoral actions is not that it would be *bad* if everyone did them; rather, the point is that it is *impossible* for everyone to do them (or, more accurately, Kant thinks it is impossible for you to will that everyone do them). As Kant's examples illustrate, Kant is proposing a logical test for whether an action is moral.

Four Examples

In his book *The Groundwork of the Metaphysics of Morals* (1785), Kant applies the universalizability criterion to four examples. He first describes a man who is tired of life and is contemplating suicide. Kant says that the maxim the man is considering is to end one's life if continuing to live would produce more pain than pleasure. Kant says that it is

> questionable whether this principle of self-love could become a universal law of nature. One immediately sees a contradiction in a system of nature whose law would be to destroy life by the feeling whose special office is to impel the improvement of life. In this case, it would not exist as nature; hence that maxim cannot obtain as a law of nature, and thus it wholly contradicts the supreme principle of all duty.

Kant is suggesting that it is impossible for there to exist a world in which all rational living things rationally decide to commit suicide when their lives promise more pain than pleasure.

Since there could be no such world, it is wrong for the individual in Kant's example to commit suicide. The act is wrong because it cannot be universalized.

Kant's second example concerns promise keeping. You need money and are deciding whether to borrow. The question is whether it would be permissible for you to promise to pay back the money even though you have no intention of doing so. Kant argues that morality requires you to keep your promise (and therefore not borrow it under false pretenses):

> For the universality of a law which says that anyone who believes himself to be in need could promise what he pleased with the intention of not fulfilling it would make the promise itself and the end to be accomplished by it impossible; no one would believe what was promised to him but would only laugh at any such assertion as vain pretense.

Kant is saying that promise keeping could not exist as an institution if everyone who made promises did so with the intention of breaking them whenever they felt like doing so. That is, the institution can exist only because people are usually trustworthy. Again, the reason we are obliged to keep our promises is that it is impossible to have a world in which everyone made promises with the intention of breaking them at will. Universalizability is the acid test.

Kant's third example is intended to show that each of us has an obligation to develop our talents. Why should we work hard at "broadening and improving our natural gifts"? Why not, instead, choose a life of "idleness, indulgence, and propagation"? Each person must choose the former, Kant says, "for, as a rational being, he necessarily wills that all his faculties should be developed, inasmuch as they are given to him for all sorts of possible purposes."

Kant's fourth example concerns a man whose life is going well, but who sees that others live lives of great hardship. Is he obliged to help others? Kant grants that the human race could exist in a state in which some do well while others suffer, but he claims that no rational agent could intend (will) that the world be that way:

> Now although it is possible that a universal law of nature according to that maxim could exist, it is nevertheless impossible to will that such a principle should hold everywhere as a law of nature. For a will which resolved this would conflict with itself, since instances can often arise in which he would need the love and sympathy of others, and in which he would have robbed himself, by such a law of nature springing from his own will, of all hope of the aid he desires.

Kant's point is not that the pattern cannot be universal, but that no rational agent could will that it be universal.

Evaluation of Kant's Examples

Of these examples, the first is perhaps the weakest. It is not impossible for there to be a world in which all terminally ill people who are the victims of great suffering commit suicide. Moreover, it seems perfectly possible for a rational agent to will that all people spare themselves an agonizing death.

The second example is somewhat more plausible. The institution of promise keeping does seem to rely on the fact that people usually believe the promises made to them. If people intended to break their promises whenever they felt like doing so, could the institution persist? Kant says no. However, perhaps circumstances can be contrived in which this conclusion is evaded. For example, couldn't the institution of making and keeping promises persist if people intend to try hard to keep their promises while recognizing that they may break them if sufficiently weighty considerations of utility present themselves? Kant seems to be exaggerating—what the institution of promise making and promise keeping requires if it is to persist is just that people keep their promises often enough, so that it makes sense for people to believe many or most of the promises that are made to them. We know full well that when people promise us the world, they probably won't do what they say, but that doesn't lead society to abandon the institution of promise making and promise keeping. Perhaps there is something to be said for Kant's argument about our duty to help others. Each of us needs some sort of help at some time in our lives. Each of us therefore would wish to avoid a situation in which no one would give us the help we need. We therefore can't will that no one should ever provide help. This means it would be wrong for us to lead a life in which we totally refuse to help others. Again the reason it would be wrong is that we cannot will that the pattern be universal.

What is Kant's argument in his third example concerning the duty each of us has to develop our talents? The thought here seems to be similar to the one Kant deploys in his discussion of the duty to help others. I want others to develop talents that would be beneficial to me; for example, I want physicians to perfect their skills, since one day I'll need them. This means, however, that I can't will that everyone should neglect to develop their talents. It is supposed to follow that I have a duty to develop my own talents.

I emphasized earlier that the universalizability criterion does not ask whether it would be a good thing if everyone performed the action the agent is contemplating. Kant is not asking a consequentialist question. Rather, Kant's question is whether it would be *possible* for everyone to do so, or whether it would be *possible for a rational person to will* that everyone should do so. If we keep this point clearly in mind, it is doubtful whether Kant can reach the conclusions he wants concerning his last two examples without taking consequences into account. Clearly, it *is* possible that the world be a place in which no one helps others and no one develops his or her talents. This is a sorry state of affairs, not an impossible one. What about Kant's second formulation of his universalizability criterion—could a rational agent *will* that people never help others or develop their talents? That depends on what one means by "rational." If rational means *instrumentally* rational, then there seems to be no impossibility here. As Hume says, I might be perfectly clear in my means/end reasoning (and so be instrumentally rational) and still have the most bizarre desires you can imagine. On the other hand, there is a sense of "rational" according to which a rational agent would not want the world to be a place in which people never help others or develop their talents. A rational agent would not want this *because of the consequences such behaviors would have.* There would be a great deal of suffering, alienation, and despair; life would be bleak. I conclude that it is unclear how Kant can analyze his last two examples as he does without considering the consequences that would follow from making the actions universal.

A Problem for the Universalizability Criterion

There is a general problem that pertains to all of Kant's examples—indeed, to the whole idea of the universalizability criterion. Recall a simple point from the chapter on functionalism (Chapter 23): *A token exemplifies many types.* This means that a given (token) action can be described as embodying many different properties. Kant seems to assume that there is just one maxim that each action embodies, so we can test the morality of the token act by looking at the universalizability of this maxim. But there are many maxims that might lead to a given token action; some of these may universalize whereas others do not.

Let's see how this problem arises in the context of Kant's example about promise keeping. A man has to decide whether to borrow money by promising to repay it, though he has no intention of keeping his promise. What would it mean for everyone to behave like this? One way to describe this action is to say that it flows from the maxim "Make a promise even though you intend to break it." Kant claims universalizing this is impossible because the following proposition is a contradiction: "Everyone makes promises, even though no one intends to keep the promises he makes." However, we can also describe the man's action as flowing from a rather different maxim: "Don't make a promise unless you intend to keep it, except when you are in a life and death situation and your intention to break your promise would not be evident to others." Universalizing *this* maxim does not lead to contradiction, since the following is a perfectly possible way the world might be:

> Everyone makes promises, and people generally expect to keep their promises. Exceptions arise when there is an enormous personal advantage to making a promise without intending to keep it, and the intention to break the promise is not evident to others.

Far from being impossible, the above generalization seems to describe fairly accurately the world we actually inhabit.

The same point holds if we focus on the formulation of the universalizability criterion that is stated in terms of its being rational to will that the maxim of one's act be universal. Would it be rational for someone to will that everyone should obey the following maxim?

> Keep your promises except when you obtain new information that shows that lots of people would be harmed if you kept your promise, whereas lots of people would be helped if you broke your promise.

I see nothing irrational about willing that everyone should follow this conditional policy. I don't know if it exactly captures what the best moral policy on promise keeping would be, but it certainly is better than the unconditional promise keeping that Kant thinks is a requirement of rationality.

You should notice a similarity between the problem that Kant faces and a problem that rule utilitarianism encountered in the previous chapter. "What would happen if everyone did it?" is a question that the rule utilitarian thinks is important in assessing the moral properties of an action. Kant's question is a different one; he asks, "Could everyone do it?" or "Could a rational agent will that everyone does it?" Though the questions differ, similar problems derive from the fact that there are multiple ways of describing any action.

The universalizability criterion may seem plausible if one takes seriously the analogy between moral laws and scientific laws. Both must be universal and impersonal. However, another comparison of these two ideas may diminish the plausibility that anything like Kant's universalizability criterion can be made to work. Scientific laws must be universal, but no one thinks the true explanation of a specific phenomenon can be derived *a priori*. Reason alone can't tell me what the laws of physics are; this is why physicists make observations of what happens out there in nature and do experiments in their laboratories. Yet, Kant held that what it is right to do in a specific situation is dictated by the rational requirement of universalizability.

It is an important fact about morality that if it is right for me to do a particular action, then it is right for anyone similarly situated to perform the same action. This is the idea that moral laws—the general principles that dictate what it is right to do—are universal and impersonal. The problem is that this requirement is not *sufficient* to reveal which moral generalizations are true. The analogy between scientific laws and moral laws has implications different from the ones Kant tried to develop.

Kant: People Are Ends in Themselves

Kant believed that an important consequence of his universalizability test is that we should treat people as ends in themselves, and not as mere means. By this, Kant meant that we should not treat people as means to ends to which they could not rationally consent. Kant believed that slavery is prohibited by this principle. The same may be true for punishing people for crimes they did not commit, even if doing so would placate a dangerous mob. Kantian theory seems to provide firmer grounds than utilitarianism does for the idea that individuals have rights that can't be overridden by considerations of utility. It isn't the maximization of happiness that matters in Kant's theory. Reason alone is supposed to dictate principles of fairness, impartiality, and justice.

Even though Kant predates the utilitarians, his theory seems designed to correct the defects present in utilitarianism. The idea of rights is a plausible corrective to the idea that every aspect of an individual's life has to pass the test of maximizing the happiness of all. Even so, there are major logical difficulties in Kant's theory. And the absoluteness of some of his pronouncements seems to be wildly at odds with strongly held common-sense moral convictions. Surely it is extremely implausible to think that promises must *always* be kept—that we must *never* tell a lie—no matter what the consequences are. Besides noting the defects in the arguments that Kant gave to justify such injunctions, we should also note that these moral requirements should not receive an unconditional justification in the first place.

If the universalizability criterion fails to provide a procedure for deciding which actions are right, and if Kant's moral judgments about promise keeping, suicide, and other actions are implausible, what is of value in his ethical theory? Many philosophers find Kant's description of *the moral point of view* to be one of his enduring contributions. Desires and preferences can move us to action, and these actions can produce different mixtures of pleasure and pain. This sequence of events, however, occurs among creatures—cows and dogs, perhaps—who by no stretch of the imagination have a morality. What, then, distinguishes action motivated by morality from action driven by inclination, whether benevolent or malevolent?

Kant's answer was that moral action is driven by principles that have a special sort of rational justification. Ordinary language is perhaps a little misleading here, since we can talk about the desire to act morally as if it were on the same footing with the desire for pleasure or profit. But Kant did not think of the determination to do what morality requires as one inclination among many. He saw morality and inclination as existing in entirely different realms. To identify the moral thing to do, one must *set aside* one's inclinations. By fixing our attention on universal and impersonal laws, we can hope to diminish the degree to which self-interest distorts our judgment concerning what we ought to do.

The Rabbit and the Hat

Kant thought that morality rests on rationality. As I have emphasized, his universalizability criterion is not the idea that you should perform an action if and only if the world would be morally better than it is now if everyone performed that type of action. Rather, the idea is that you should perform an action precisely when it is logically possible for a rational agent to will that everyone should perform that type of action. As you can see, whether Kant's ethical theory is correct depends on what it means to be a rational agent.

To pull a rabbit out of a hat, you first have to put the rabbit into the hat. My suspicion is that Kant is putting morality into his notion of rationality; this is why he thinks it is possible to derive morality from rationality. There is narrow notion of rationality that does not permit this derivation to be carried out. This is the austere notion of instrumental rationality. This is the notion of rationality that Hume has in mind when he says that "reason is and ought to be the slave of the passions." According to this conception, rationality doesn't give you goals. Rather, it merely allows you to identify the best means of achieving the goals you antecedently have. You can't derive morality from *instrumental* rationality. Is there a richer notion of rationality that permits the Kantian project to go forward, where this richer notion does not beg the question?

Review Questions

1   What does it mean to say, as Hume did, that every action has a cause that is "nonrational"? Why did Kant reject this thesis?
2   Kant believed there are important similarities between scientific laws and moral laws. What are these?
3   What does Kant's universalizability criterion assert? Does it say that you shouldn't perform an action if the world would be a worse place if everyone did the same? What does it mean to say that the universalizability criterion is non consequentialist?
4   How does Kant try to show that the obligation of promise keeping follows from the universalizability criterion? Is he successful?
5   You are in a boat that is tipping dangerously to one side because all the passengers are on the right. You are considering whether it would be a good idea to move to the left. You ask yourself, "What would happen if everyone did this?" This question has an ambiguity in it. What is it? How is this ambiguity relevant to assessing Kant's universalizability criterion?

Problems for Further Thought

1   Kant believes that the duty to treat others as ends in themselves, not as means, follows from the universalizability criterion. Try to construct an argument that shows how this might be true. Is Kant correct in thinking these two principles are closely related?
2   Kant thought of the moral law as constraining what one's life should be like, but not as determining each and every detail of it. That is, for Kant, one is free to pursue one's private goals and projects as long as they do not violate any categorical imperatives. These particular projects are morally permissible, not morally obligatory.

   Utilitarianism, by contrast, sees morality as determining each and every aspect of one's life. Each action one performs must be evaluated in terms of the Greatest Happiness Principle. A private project is permissible only if it promotes the greatest good for the greatest number of people. Such acts aren't just permissible; they are obligatory.

   Construct a concrete example in which these features of the two theories lead them to make opposite judgments about whether an act is morally permissible. Which theory strikes you as more plausible in what it says about your example?
3   Kant's ethics had a powerful influence on the political philosophy of John Rawls. In *A Theory of Justice* (Harvard University Press, 1971), Rawls argues that the correct rules of justice for a society are the ones that all persons would choose if (1) they were self-interested, and (2) they didn't know various details about themselves (like their talents,

sex, race, and what projects they will want to pursue). The only facts that people know in this hypothetical situation are general facts about human psychology and human life. Rawl's idea is partially an attempt to capture Kant's idea that personal inclinations must be set aside if you want to see what your moral obligations are. What principles of conduct do you think people would choose in this hypothetical situation?

Recommended Readings, Video, and Audio

Visit the companion website at www.routledge.com/cw/sober for suggestions of readings, video, and audio, for this chapter.

Chapter 34

Aristotle on the Good Life

How Far Do Obligations Extend?

Some ethical theories hold that each and every aspect of a person's life is to be decided by ethical principles that describe obligations. Utilitarianism, for example, says that it is wrong to do some action if an alternative action could be performed that would better promote people's happiness or preference satisfaction. Other ethical theories hold that considerations of obligation don't answer every question about how people should lead their lives. Kant's ethical theory is often thought to be of this type. According to Kant, you must treat others with justice and accord them dignity and respect. However, this seems to leave open a large number of issues concerning what sort of plan for your life you ought to pursue.

The same would be true of an ethical theory that held that all obligations flow from the principle that people have the right to structure their own lives, as long as doing so doesn't infringe on the rights of others. If you accepted an ethics of this sort, many questions concerning how you should live your life would remain to be answered. The reason these questions are left open is that the ethical principle just mentioned is largely *negative* in its implications. It mainly tells you what you should *not* do. In consequence, questions such as the following are left unanswered: What sort of work should you take up? Should you get married? Should you have children? What sorts of friendships should you try to nurture? Should you try to develop talents you have other than those that figure in the work you do? Should you participate in the political affairs of your community? Nation? The Earth? What importance should you assign to these various activities? The ethical principle of *do no harm* provides little or no guidance on these matters.

The Theory of the Right and the Theory of the Good

Philosophers sometimes distinguish the *theory of the right* from the *theory of the good*. In doing so, they are indicating that principles of obligation and prohibition fail to address questions like the ones listed in the previous paragraph. The theory of the good attempts to describe what the good life would be like.

According to this distinction, living a good life is not limited to fulfilling your obligations. It is easy to miss this point, since "be good" may sound like the same advice as "do the right thing." One way to see that there is a difference here is to imagine someone who breaks no moral prohibitions, but still fails to lead a good life. An example might be someone who breaks no laws, but shuns all human contact, has a dull and repetitive job, and spends all his or her time outside work reading comic books. This person may do no harm, but it would be implausible to say of him, "he really led a good life."

Are There General Principles about the Good Life?

It seems plausible that the theory of the right will include principles of some generality. "Do not murder" is a rule that covers you, me, and everyone else. Are there comparable principles to be found in the theory of the good? That is, are there principles that describe what a good life would be like that cover all human beings? Or is the issue of the good life more personal and individual? Even if we all are subject to the same obligations and prohibitions (described in the theory of the right), perhaps there is nothing interesting in common between what would be a good life for you and what would be a good life for me.

In his ethical theory (as developed primarily in *The Nicomachean Ethics*), Aristotle (384–322 B.C.E.) attempts to describe what a good life would be like. In fact, his goal is to describe what *the* good life for human beings amounts to. As I'll soon explain, he maintains that since we're all members of the same biological species, general principles can be described that specify what a good life would be for any human being. For Aristotle, the good life is to be understood by way of the concept of human nature.

What Is a Good X?

A good person lives a good life. But what makes a person good? Aristotle proposes to understand the idea of a *good human being* by first considering what it means to say that something is good. What is a good hammer? Here we aren't talking about ethical issues, of course. A hammer is a tool. A hammer is a good hammer when it is able to perform the tasks that are specific to hammers. Hammers have the function of driving nails into wood. A good hammer optimally performs that function. Consider another example, this one having to do with the roles that human beings play. What is a good father? To answer this question, we have to ask what the function of a father is. Plausibly, a father's function is to help his children grow into loving, responsible, and independent adults. If so, a good father is one who optimally performs that function. Human beings perform other functions. What is a good nurse? Evidently, the function of a nurse is to help sick patients return to full health as much as possible. If this is right, we can tell from the function of a nurse what a good nurse would be.

---

30 Good versus green

A green apple and a green shirt must have something in common. However, according to Aristotle a good hammer and a good violinist need have nothing in common. What is the difference between greenness and goodness that accounts for this?

To be a green apple is to be green *and* an apple. To be a green shirt is to be green *and* a shirt. Being a green apple is a conjunctive property ("conjunction" means *and*). Being a green apple involves having two properties; the same is true of being a green shirt. This explains why there is something that green apples and green shirts have in common; there is a property—greenness—that they share.

To be a good hammer is not the same as being good *and* a hammer. To be a good violinist is not the same as being good *and* a violinist. The property of being a good hammer and the property of being a good violinist aren't conjunctive properties in which *being good* is one of the conjuncts. This is why good hammers and good violinists need have no property in common.

Consider other adjectives. We use terms such as "big," "soft," and "old." Are these more like "green" or more like "good"?

These examples—the hammer, the father, the nurse—tell us something about the concept of goodness. The first lesson is that we can decide what it is to be a good *X* by seeing what the function is of *X*s. The concept of goodness is intimately connected with concepts of goal, function, and purpose. The second lesson is that what it takes to be a good *X* depends on the choice of *X*. For example, the character traits required for being a good father may be very different from the ones required for being a good harpist or a good baseball player. Aristotle emphasizes both these points about the concept of goodness.

It is no mystery what a good hammer is, and it isn't that difficult to say what it means to be a good father or a good nurse. Perhaps the same strategy will work when we ask what a good person is. Aristotle thought that once we figure out what the function is of human life, we'll thereby know what a good human being is. This, in turn, will tell us what the good life amounts to.

Human Beings Are Goal-Directed Systems

In Chapter 5, I briefly explained how Aristotle's biology and physics are *teleological* in character. Aristotle thought that living things as well as inanimate objects are goal-directed systems. The goal of a living thing is to grow and reproduce. The goal of a rock is to reach the place where the center of the earth now is. Of course, not all living things grow and reproduce, and not all rocks find their way to the earth's center. But each has a *natural tendency* to do those things. *Interfering forces* may prevent an object from reaching its natural state.

We human beings are goal-directed systems. What is the end state that we seek? Aristotle's answer is that human beings seek *happiness*. A good life is a life of happiness—a life in which the goal of human life has been achieved.

Before saying how Aristotle understood happiness, it is important to note a difference between human beings and other goal-directed systems. Human beings seek happiness; trees aim to grow and reproduce. One difference between us and other living things comes from *how* we pursue the goals we have. Other living things pursue the goals of growth and reproduction *innately* and *mindlessly*. A tree doesn't have to be taught to send its roots deep into the soil or to send its leaves where they can absorb sunlight. In fact, trees don't need to have beliefs and desires to engage in these activities. Trees do these things *by nature*. In contrast, we human beings are better or worse at seeking happiness according to the upbringing we receive. Some people seek their happiness in wealth or fame or power. Others seek it in love. According to Aristotle, *how* we seek our happiness is not determined by our nature, but by our upbringing; a good upbringing is one that helps us develop habits and character traits that are conducive to the good life.

In Chapter 21, on methodological behaviorism, I briefly discussed the nature/nurture controversy. We now understand that dispute in terms of the task of explaining variation in some characteristic (like height or intelligence). Human beings have different heights. How much of that variation is explained by genetic differences, and how much by differences in environment (like nutrition)? Aristotle also drew the nature/nurture distinction, but in a rather different way. First, he didn't have the idea of genes. Second, the fact of variation within a species was much less important to him than it is in present-day biology. For Aristotle, what is biologically significant about human beings is that human beings have something in common; this is what *human nature* is. When Aristotle thought about "nature" (as opposed to nurture), he thought about characteristics that all members of a species *share;* current biology thinks about "nature" (as opposed to nurture) in terms of genetic *differences* among members of the same species. For Aristotle, human beings have a common nature that sets them apart from the rest of the living world. It is part of human nature to seek happiness. How human beings go about doing this varies from person to person. The explanation for this variation, Aristotle held, is environmental. It is differences in nurture—in our upbringing—that explain why human beings live their lives in different ways.

The Capacity to Reason

The function of a hammer is something that distinguishes hammers from other tools. A hammer that is able to perform that function well is a good hammer. By the same line of thinking, we can approach the question of what function human beings have by asking what distinguishes human beings from other beings. A human being who is able to perform that function well will count as a good human being.

Human beings are organisms, and so survival, growth, and reproduction are goals that human beings try to achieve. However, in addition, there is a characteristic that distinguishes human beings from other organisms. This is the development of rationality—the capacity for abstract thinking. The basic contours of Aristotle's theory of happiness can now be stated. Human beings, unique among living things, possess the capacity of rationality. The good life for human beings is one in which rational capacities are developed and exercised to a high degree. In doing this, human beings find the best sort of happiness that is possible for them.

Aristotle draws a distinction between theoretical and practical reasoning. Practical reasoning involves the kind of means/ends reasoning so familiar in everyday life. The conclusion you draw in practical reasoning is a decision to do something—to perform some action. For example, you want an article of clothing that will keep you warm in winter. You realize that a cloak will perform this task. So you decide to buy a cloak. Note that this bit of reasoning concludes with the intention to buy a cloak, not with a prediction that you will do so. In contrast, the conclusion you draw in theoretical reasoning is that some proposition is true. Theoretical reasoning is reasoning given over to the disinterested search for knowledge. It is "pure" inquiry, not "applied." In theoretical inquiry, you seek understanding for its own sake. The life of contemplation is devoted to the sort of intellectual activity that occurs in science, philosophy, and the arts. The best life, for Aristotle, is the life of theoretical reason.

Aristotle: Happiness Is Not a Subjective State

When Aristotle asked what happiness is, he wanted to know what sorts of activities make for a happy life. The word "activity" is important here; a happy life is a life of *doing*. The good life is one in which those traits that are specifically human are brought to a high level of cultivation. The happy life is one of flourishing—of doing well. Happiness, for Aristotle, is emphatically not the same as pleasure. The sensation of pleasure is possible for a brain in a vat, but a brain in a vat is not a flourishing human being, even if it has the illusion of leading an ideal life. Real happiness, then, is not a sensation (compare this with the discussion of happiness in Chapter 32, on utilitarianism). People can believe themselves to be happy and still not be. Whether you are flourishing is not settled by the mere fact that you think you are.

Although pleasure is not the goal of human life, pleasure naturally accompanies the good life. For Aristotle, the good life involves exercising the faculty of reason. It is natural for people to take pleasure in exercising this ability, just as people take pleasure in the vigorous functioning of a healthy body, as in athletics.

Aristotle thought that human beings have godlike as well as animal characteristics. Our nature as animals decrees that we must eat, grow, breathe, and reproduce. In addition, we are social beings by nature, and so the good life includes participation in politics. But the divine spark is also present, and this means that we're directed toward the divine activity of contemplation. When Aristotle says that the good life consists in contemplation (intellectual activity), he is not denying that the activities we share with animals are important to us; nor did he mean that involvement in practical political affairs is unimportant. But the life of contemplation was for him a life that emphasized what was best (= highest) in us. It is an expression of what we have in common with the gods.

Why the Life of Rational Activity Is Best: Two More Reasons

I've already mentioned Aristotle's main reason for thinking that the human goal of happiness is best achieved by the life of rational activity; our capacity to be rational is unique in the living world. However, Aristotle had two other arguments in favor of this conclusion.

The first is specifically tied to his conception of how the human mind works. Aristotle thought that activities that call for fine and multifaceted discriminations make people happier than activities that call for fewer and more one-dimensional discriminations. Chess is superior to checkers, and checkers is superior to tic-tac-toe. Sports that require a variety of skills are better than ones that require fewer, and sports that require fine discriminations are better than sports that require only coarse discriminations. Aristotle saw this as a basic feature of the human mind. Its highest happiness is to be found in activities of these sorts. Aristotle thought that theoretical reasoning—the kind that artists, scientists, and philosophers pursue—involves mental activities in which the finest and most multifaceted discriminations are drawn.

A further consideration led Aristotle to this conclusion. In choosing a life for ourselves, we must decide which of our capacities we wish to develop. For example, this might involve trying to become a great athlete or a great politician. Aristotle thinks it is highly significant that success in sports or politics depends on a number of factors that are outside the individual's control. Athletes of great talent can suffer injuries. Politicians can be deprived of power if others oppose them. In contrast, the life of rational activity is much less dependent on factors outside the agent's control. Contemplation can last a lifetime. It does not require a youthful body, wealth, power, or the admiration of others. Of course, it isn't wholly independent of external circumstance, but given the perils that can subvert other plans for a life, the life of contemplation makes the most sense, according to Aristotle.

Although Aristotle holds that the good life is devoted to theoretical reasoning, he has a great deal to say about the character traits that good people will display in dealing with other human beings. For example, Aristotle discusses friendship, justice, liberality (generosity), and courage. These virtues, he believes, can be understood within a single theoretical framework, provided by his Doctrine of the Mean.

The Doctrine of the Mean

The Doctrine of the Mean says that many (if not all) virtues are located on a continuum, their perfection consisting in the fact that they avoid the extremes; they avoid both excess and deficiency. For example, courage is a virtue; Aristotle claims that it is in between foolhardiness and cowardice. Similarly, liberality is a virtue; people who are liberal with their money are neither misers nor spendthrifts.

Aristotle didn't think that the mean had to be an arithmetic average. If 10 units of food is too much and 2 units is too little, the correct amount is somewhere in between; it needn't be 6. Furthermore, Aristotle emphasized that the right amount for one person might not be the right amount for another. The wrestler Milo requires more food than other people do. The mean for him may differ from the mean for others.

Although the Doctrine of the Mean is sometimes represented by the slogan "moderation in all things," this is a rather misleading summary of Aristotle's idea. Aristotle says that spitefulness and envy are bad, as are adultery, theft, and murder. They are wrong in themselves; virtue doesn't consist in doing them a little but not too much.

Once these clarifications are noted, however, it is unclear how much of a theory the Doctrine of the Mean actually provides. To apply it in a given case, we first must decide what the continuum is on which the activity or virtue is located. Generosity is fairly easy; the scale on which it is located is the amount of money you give away. But what is the scale on which justice is located? And if abstaining from murder is a mean, what is the scale on which it is to be represented?

A second problem arises after one has identified the scale on which the activity or character trait is to be represented. Let's grant that being liberal with money is a mean between being a miser and being a spendthrift. The question is why the intermediacy of the trait should be what makes it a virtue. Is being courageous better than being cowardly or foolhardy *because* courage falls between cowardice and foolhardiness? Aristotle thought that this is so, but it is by no means clear that he was correct.

A Second Criticism of Aristotle's Theory—Defining What a Good *X* Is Differs from Saying What Is Good for an *X*

Recall the overall strategy of Aristotle's argument. He begins by asking what the good life is for human beings. This question, he believes, would be answered if we knew what a good human being is. He then proposes to say what a good human being is by determining what function human beings have. It is the first step in this reasoning that I want to question. Aristotle assumes that if a good human being is rational, then rationality is good for human beings. The general principle Aristotle uses here is this:

If a good X is F, then F is good for Xs.

To say that someone is a good X is often just to say that they are good at X-ing: a good teacher is good at teaching, a good parent is good at parenting, a good butcher is good at butchering, and a good thief is good at stealing.

As the last example suggests, to say that you are a good X is not to say that it is a good thing for you to be an X. You might be a good shoplifter, even though shoplifting is bad for you. This is why I reject the principle just displayed.

---

31 "Natural" and "Normal"

The term *natural* is used in two very different ways. Sometimes it has a normative meaning, as when "natural" and "unnatural" are used as code words for *good* and *bad*. Sometimes it has a purely descriptive meaning, as when "natural" is used to mean *found in nature*.

The same is true of the term *normal*. Usually, when we say that something is "abnormal," we mean that there is something wrong with it. But there is a purely descriptive meaning that the term also has. Sometimes saying that an activity is "normal" just means that it often occurs.

It is clear that there are some unusual characteristics that are undesirable. More people have healthy blood than cancerous blood, and so when we say that leukemia is an abnormal condition, we mean both that it is uncommon and that something has gone wrong when a person has leukemia.

In other cases, matters are just the reverse. Most adults in the United States are overweight. Given this, how should you interpret the doctor's comment that your weight is "normal"? If this means that it is common, you might decide that there is something wrong. If the comment means that your weight is healthy, then you may be pleased.

These two examples—of leukemia and weight—illustrate that there is no simple connection between what's common and what's good. Given this, you should be skeptical of any argument that attempts to show that some activity is wrong or bad simply by pointing out that the activity is rare. And the claim that something is "natural" or "normal" also should not be taken as providing an automatic justification.

What bearing do these observations have on Aristotle's attempt to explain what the good life is by developing a theory of human nature?

A good human being, Aristotle holds, is someone who is good at characteristically human activities. Aristotle singles out the use of reason as the characteristic activity; he concludes that good human beings devote themselves to lives of contemplation, developing their rational faculties to the utmost.

My criticism suggests that it is not always correct to think about the concept of a good X in the functional way that Aristotle proposes. It is plausible to think of a good hammer and a good harpist in the way Aristotle suggests, but the concept of a good human being seems to require a different treatment.

A Third Criticism—Why Single Out Contemplation as the Best Life?

My last criticism of Aristotle's theory has to do with his exclusive focus on rationality. He notes that human beings share with other animals the tendency to grow and reproduce. He then asks which characteristic is uniquely human, and he comes up with rationality as his answer. But surely there are many behaviors and capacities that are unique to human beings. Collecting money for charity is one of them; engaging in genocide is another. If the good life consists in developing those capacities that are uniquely human, why should contemplation constitute the good life? There are many ways to be uniquely human.

Aristotle provides a second reason for singling out the life of theoretical reason as best. As noted earlier, Aristotle thinks human beings find happiness in drawing fine discriminations and in mastering complex tasks. The life of contemplation provides the greatest opportunity for these activities. Even if we accept this as a basic fact about the human mind, it is unclear why this shows that the life of contemplation is best. Human beings find happiness in other activities as well. Why think of mastering complexity as *the best* activity? Aristotle's answer seems to be the one just discussed: What's best for human beings is the development of traits that are uniquely human. I've already noted why I find this answer unsatisfactory.

Aristotle gives a third reason for thinking that the life of contemplation is best. This life is least dependent on others. However, here again it is hard to see that this characteristic is unique to the life devoted to theoretical reason. It also is hard to see why this characteristic should make the life of contemplation the one most worth living.

Aristotle thinks that loving others, including your children, is part of the good life. He goes so far as to say that you can't be happy—lead a good life—if your children suffer or hate you. Notice that in saying this, Aristotle is granting that the good life involves dependency on others. Given this, it is unclear why the life of contemplation is best *because* it is relatively independent of others.

In summary, Aristotle offers three arguments for thinking that the life of theoretical reason provides the best form of happiness. The first and most important argument appeals to the fact that the capacity to reason is uniquely human. The second claims that human beings find happiness in drawing fine discriminations and in mastering complex tasks. The third sees the contemplative life as supremely good because it is the life in which one is most independent of others. I've suggested that none of these arguments is very persuasive.

In each of them, Aristotle attempts to show why the contemplative life is the best one for human beings without assuming a fully developed theory of value. For example, in the first argument, it is a fact about human biology that is said to justify his conclusion. In suggesting these arguments, Aristotle is following the analogy with other goal-directed systems. We can say what a good hammer is, or a good father, or a good nurse, without assuming anything about whether it is a good thing or a bad thing to be a hammer, a father, or a nurse. Perhaps the reason that Aristotle's various arguments run into trouble is that there is a *disanalogy* between these cases and the problem of describing what the good life is. The good life must be a life that is worth living. A good life must be a life that would be good to have. You can approach questions about what a good teacher is (or a good general, or a good nurse, or a good shoplifter) with a certain detachment. You can say what these roles require without committing yourself to taking up any of them for yourself. The problem of the good life, however, admits no such detachment. If you grant that the life of contemplation is the good life for human beings, you commit yourself to the desirability of living such a life.

This may help explain why Aristotle's strategy for solving this important problem was unsuccessful. Another reason may be that Aristotle thought that there is a single form of life that is *the* best one for everyone. His arguments pay scant attention to the differences that distinguish each of us from other human beings. As noted before, the good life for human beings is to be discovered by investigating human nature, and human nature is what all human beings have in common.

Aristotle had the idea that the good life involves actualizing the best capacities we possess. We must find what is best in ourselves and build a whole life on that foundation. Perhaps we should accept this idea, even if we reject Aristotle's suggestion that the good life for every human being consists in actualizing a characteristic that is uniquely human. Perhaps there is no such thing as *the* good life for human beings; rather, there may be many good lives, each uniquely fitted to the unique constellation of traits that each of us possesses.

Review Questions

1   What is the difference between the theory of the right and the theory of the good?
2   What do a good pizza and a good dancer have in common? What does "good" mean?
3   Why did Aristotle think that the good life for human beings would be a life of contemplation?
4   What is the Doctrine of the Mean? Does it say that we should pursue each activity a little but not too much?
5   What connection did Aristotle see between the concept of a *good human being* and the idea that certain activities would be *good for human beings*? Was he right in connecting these ideas in the way he did?
6   How, on Aristotle's view, is "happiness" to be distinguished from "pleasure"? How does the happy life relate to the good life, and why? (Hint: Why did Aristotle think that happiness could not be a subjective state?)
7   Why does Aristotle pay little attention to the unique differences between particular human beings? How does he explain the variability between different people's manners of conceiving of and pursuing happiness?
8   Suppose that Aristotle is right, and human beings are happier when they are engaged in making fine distinctions and mastering complex tasks than they are while performing less complex activities. Does it follow that the best life will be primarily devoted to the former activities? Can you reconstruct Aristotle's argument such that this conclusion doesn't follow?
9   Aristotle argued that, because rationality is a uniquely human capacity, the best human life is one of contemplation. I have suggested that the capacities for genocide or collecting charity are also uniquely human. How do you think Aristotle might respond to this line of criticism? Are some "uniquely human" capacities or characteristics more fundamental or fundamentally human than others? If so, why?

Problems for Further Thought

1   Aristotle says that the function of human beings is to reason well. This is what human beings are *for*. In Chapter 26, on the Weather Vane Theory of Freedom, I defined what it means to say that *the function of the heart is to pump blood*. The definition I offered involves the modern idea of natural selection; the theory of natural selection, of course, was unknown to Aristotle. Apply this definition of function to the statement *the function*

of human beings is to be rational. Is what Aristotle says plausible if his claim about function is understood in this modern way? Explain your answer.

2   There is an interpretation of what Aristotle thinks the good life is that differs from the one I've offered. Instead of seeing the good life as given over to contemplation, this interpretation has Aristotle saying that a good life is one in which reason suffuses all human activities, both theoretical and practical. This interpretation relies on the fact that human beings are *not* the only things capable of rationality—there are the gods as well. What's unique to human beings is the *mixture* of animal nature and the capacity to reason. Gods can engage in pure contemplation; human beings must lead less mono-lithic lives.

According to this interpretation, Aristotle is saying that good human beings judi-ciously apply reason to the activities they take up. If Aristotle is interpreted in this way, two problems remain for his view. The first is that we need to provide a list of the activities that comprise the good life. The second is that a principle needs to be pro-vided that says how these various activities are to be integrated and balanced against each other. For example, if the good life includes a family, participation in politics, and contemplation, how are the demands each activity places on your time and energy to be judged?

Without answering these questions, the advice to use reason in all your activities seems to be pretty empty. Do passages from Aristotle's *Nicomachean Ethics* help provide any answers?

Recommended Readings, Video, and Audio

Visit the companion website at www.routledge.com/cw/sober for suggestions of readings, video, and audio, for this chapter.

Glossary

abduction A form of nondeductive inference, also known as inference to the best explanation. The Surprise Principle and the Only Game in Town Fallacy are relevant to deciding how strong an abductive inference is.

altruism An ultimate desire (a desire that one wants to come true for its own sake, not because it instrumentally contributes to attaining some other goal) is altruistic if it seeks the well-being of some other person. If there are ultimate altruistic desires, then psychological egoism is false. *See* psychological egoism.

analogy argument A nondeductive inference in which one infers that a target object *T* has some characteristic on the ground that *T* is similar to some other object *A* (the analog), and *A* is known to possess that characteristic. Example: "Other galaxies probably contain life, since they are quite similar to our own galaxy and our own galaxy contains life." The strength of analogy arguments is an issue relevant to the Argument from Design and to the problem of other minds.

analytic An analytic sentence is one whose truth or falsehood is deductively entailed by definitions. Many philosophers have held that mathematical statements are analytic. If a sentence isn't analytic, it is synthetic.

a posteriori A proposition that can be known or justified only by sense experience. An *a posteriori* argument is an argument in which at least one premise is an *a posteriori* proposition. See *a priori*.

a priori A proposition that can be known or justified independent of sense experience. An *a priori* proposition can be known or justified by reason alone (once you grasp the constituent concepts). Truths of mathematics and definitions are often thought to be *a priori*. An *a priori* argument is an argument in which all the premises are *a priori* propositions. The Ontological Argument for the existence of God is supposed to be an *a priori* argument. See *a posteriori*.

Argument from Design An *a posteriori* argument that God exists, advanced by Aquinas and Paley, criticized by Hume. The argument claims that some feature of the world (like the simplicity of its laws or the fact that organisms are intricate and well adapted) should be explained by postulating the existence of an intelligent designer, namely God.

Argument from Evil An argument that claims that the existence of evil shows either that there is no God, or that God can't be all-powerful, all-knowing, and all-good.

axiom In mathematics, a starting assumption from which conclusions (theorems) are deduced.

begging the question An argument begs the question when you wouldn't accept the premises unless you already believed the conclusion.

behaviorism *See* logical behaviorism and methodological behaviorism.

bias *See* sample bias.

Birthday Fallacy   The error in reasoning that one would make in thinking that "everyone has a birthday" deductively implies that "there is a single day on which everyone was born."

categorical imperative   An imperative (a command) that is unconditional (it contains no *if's*). In contrast, a hypothetical imperative is a command of the form, "If you have goal *G*, then perform action *A*." Kant thought that moral rules (like "don't lie") take the form of categorical imperatives. In contrast, rules of prudence (like "stop smoking if you want to be healthy") are hypothetical.

causal argument for the existence of God   An argument that Descartes gives in the *Meditations* for the claim that God exists and is no deceiver: Since (1) I have an idea of a perfect being, and (2) there must be at least as much perfection in the cause as there is in the effect, it is said to follow that the cause of the idea of God that I have must be a perfect being, namely, God himself.

circularity   *See* begging the question.

clarity and distinctness criterion   Descartes maintained that if a belief is clear and distinct, then it can't fail to be true. The reason clear and distinct ideas must be true is that God exists and is no deceiver.

compatibilism   The thesis that free will and determinism are compatible. Soft determinism is a version of compatibilism. Hard determinism and libertarianism are incompatibilist theories.

compatibility   Two propositions are compatible if the truth of one wouldn't rule out the truth of the other. Example: (1) this shirt is blue; (2) this shirt is torn. Propositions (1) and (2) are compatible. This doesn't mean that either is true.

conditional   An if/then statement. The if-clause is called the antecedent; the then-clause is called the consequent.

consequentialism   A kind of ethical theory that holds that the ethical properties of an action (its rightness or wrongness, its justness or unjustness, etc.) can be determined by seeing what consequences the action would have if it were performed. Utilitarianism is a consequentialist theory. Kant's theory isn't.

conservation law   A law in physics that says that some quantity (like matter or mass/energy) can neither increase nor decrease in a closed system.

contingent   A being is contingent if it exists in some but not all possible worlds; a proposition is contingent if it is true in some but not all possible worlds. You are an example of a contingent thing; though you exist in the actual world, you could have failed to exist.

conventionalism   Trivial semantic conventionalism holds that a true sentence might have been false if we had defined our terms differently. For example, the sentence "dogs have four legs" might have been false if we had used the word "dog" to refer to fish. A philosophically interesting conventionalism must go beyond this unsurprising point. Substantive conventionalism holds that a particular proposition is true only because of someone's say-so. For example, the following is a substantive conventionalist claim (and a false one): Dogs would have lacked four legs if we had used the word "dog" to refer to fish. *See* ethical conventionalism and proposition.

cosmological argument   An argument for the existence of God that cites some large-scale feature of the universe as a whole—for example that things are in motion, that events are related by cause and effect, or that contingent beings exist. Aquinas's first three ways are instances of this type of argument.

counterexample   A counterexample to a generalization is an object that refutes the generalization. A rotten apple in the barrel is a counterexample to the claim "All the apples in this barrel are unspoiled."

deductive validity   An argument is deductively valid because of the logical form it has. A deductively valid argument is one in which the conclusion must be true if the premises are true.

descriptive/normative distinction   A descriptive claim says what is the case, without commenting on whether that is good or bad. A normative claim says whether something should be the case, or whether it is good or bad. "Drunk drivers kill thousands of people every year" is a descriptive claim; "drunk driving shouldn't be so lightly punished" is a normative claim.

design argument   An argument for the existence of God that begins with the observation that features of the universe show evidence of design. The inference is then drawn that an intelligent designer brought these features into being. The most familiar form of this argument cites the complex adaptive features of organisms. Creationists endorse the argument from design and reject evolutionary theory.

determinism   The thesis that a complete description of the causal facts at one time uniquely determines what must happen next. There is only one possible future, given a complete description of the present. Newtonian physics says that the behavior of physical objects is deterministic. *See* indeterminism.

Divine Command Theory   The theory that ethical statements are made true or false by God's decreeing how we should act.

dualism   The thesis that the mind and the body are two distinct entities. Dualists claim that a person's mind is made of a nonphysical substance. Dualism rejects materialism.

Duhem's thesis   The thesis that theories in physics typically do not, by themselves, make predictions about observations, but do so only when supplemented with auxiliary information. See box in Chapter 9 ("Neptune and Vulcan") for an example. Pierre Duhem states this in his 1914 book *La Théorie Physique—Son Object, Sa Structure* (translated as *The Aim and Structure of Physical Theory*, Princeton University Press, 1954). The thesis is generally thought to apply to science in general, not just to physics.

egoism   *See* psychological egoism.

emotivism   A theory about ethical statements. Such statements are never true or false; rather, they merely allow the speaker to express feelings and attitudes. Emotivism is a form of ethical subjectivism.

empirical   For a proposition to be empirical is for it to be *a posteriori*. See *a posteriori*.

epistemology   The branch of philosophy concerned with concepts like knowledge and rational justification.

equivocation, fallacy of   An argument commits this fallacy when it uses a term with one meaning for part of the argument and then shifts to another meaning for the rest of the argument. Example: "I put my money in the bank. A bank is a side of a river. Hence, I put my money in the side of a river." Arguments that commit this fallacy should be clarified so that the terms in them are used with a single meaning throughout.

ethical conventionalism   The thesis that ethical statements are made true by someone's say-so. The divine command theory, ethical relativism, and Sartre's version of existentialism are conventionalist theories. *See* conventionalism.

ethical realism   The thesis that some ethical statements are true, and are true independently of anyone's thinking or saying that they are.

ethical relativism   The thesis that an ethical statement is true or false in a society because of the norms adopted in that society. Ethical relativism is a normative, not a descriptive, thesis. It is not the claim that different societies have different views of right and wrong.

ethical subjectivism   The thesis that there are no ethical facts, only ethical opinions. Ethical statements are neither true nor false.

evil   *See* Argument from Evil and theodicy.

existentialism   A twentieth-century philosophical movement that places great weight on the fact that individuals are free and so must take responsibility for how they live their lives. In Sartre's version of existentialism, each person creates ethical facts for himself or herself by making a free decision.

fallacy   An error in reasoning.

falsifiability   A hypothesis is falsifiable if it deductively implies an observation sentence. If hypothesis H deductively implies that observation statement O is true, and if O is observed to be false, then this refutes H. Hypotheses that are falsifiable have this property—if they are false, you can find out by observation that they are false. A true statement can be falsifiable; "falsifiable" doesn't mean false.

fatalism   The theory loosely expressed by the slogan "whatever will be, will be" (*que sera, sera*). According to this theory, what happens to us doesn't depend on what we think or want or try to do. Example: Oedipus, the myth says, was fated to kill his father and marry his mother. Fatalism and determinism are different.

foundationalism   The view that all the propositions we know to be true can be divided into two categories. First, there are the foundational propositions, which have some special property (like indubitability) that explains why we know them to be true. Second, there are the superstructural propositions, which we know because they bear some special relationship (like deductive implication) to the foundational propositions. Sometimes foundationalism is understood as a thesis about justified belief, not knowledge.

functionalism   The theory in the mind/body problem that says that psychological properties (types) aren't identical with physical properties, because psychological properties are multiply realizable. In addition, functionalism maintains that psychological properties are to be understood in terms of their causal roles.

genetic fallacy   The mistake of thinking a statement can't be true simply because there's a causal explanation for why people believe that it's true.

hard determinism   The incompatibilist doctrine that holds that human actions are unfree because they are causally determined.

identity theory   The thesis that the mind and the brain are identical and that psychological properties are identical with physical properties.

if and only if   "X is true if and only if Y is true" means that the truth of X is both necessary and sufficient for the truth of Y. "X if and only if Y" means that X and Y are either both true or both false.

incompatibilism   *See* compatibilism.

incorrigibility of the mental, thesis of the   This thesis claims that we can't be mistaken in the beliefs we have about the contents of our own minds. If you believe that you believe P and want Q to be true, then it must be true that you believe P and want Q to be true.

independent   Two propositions are logically independent of each other if the truth or falsity of one doesn't deductively imply the truth or falsity of the other. Example: It was discovered in the eighteenth and nineteenth centuries that Euclid's parallel postulate is independent of the other axioms and postulates of his system of geometry.

indeterminism   The thesis that even a complete description of the present doesn't uniquely determine what will happen next. There's more than one possible future, each with its own probability of coming true, given a complete description of the present.

induction   A nondeductive argument in which characteristics of individuals not in a sample are inferred from the characteristics of the individuals in the sample. The strength of an inductive inference is influenced by sample size and sample bias.

is/ought gap   Hume argued that ethical statements concerning what ought to be the case can't be deduced from statements that describe only what is the case. See descriptive/normative distinction.

JTB theory   The theory that knowledge is justified true belief. In other words, the theory advances the following proposal: For any person S and any proposition p, S knows that p if and only if (1) S believes that p; (2) p is true; and (3) S is justified in believing that p.

KK-principle   This principle says that if S knows that p, then S knows that S knows that p The principle is rejected by the reliability theory of knowledge.

law   A scientific law is a proposition that is general (it concerns all objects of a certain kind), that doesn't refer to any individual, place, or time, and that has a kind of necessity called nomological necessity. The term is often reserved for *a posteriori* propositions satisfying these conditions.

Leibniz's Law   If a and b are identical, then they must have all the same properties. Mind/body dualists defend their view by attempting to find some property that the mind has but the body lacks; they thereby appeal to Leibniz's Law.

libertarianism   The incompatibilist doctrine that holds that some human actions aren't causally determined, since they are free.

logical behaviorism   The thesis that the meanings of mentalistic terms can be given in exclusively behavioral terms. For example, logical behaviorists maintain that it is possible to define what it means for someone to be in pain strictly in terms of the person's behavior.

logical form   The logical form of an argument is what makes it deductively valid or deductively invalid. *See* deductive validity.

materialism   The thesis that every object is a physical object. The Mind/Brain Identity Theory and functionalism are materialistic theories about the mind. Both reject the dualist claim that minds are made of an immaterial substance.

mentalism   The view that mental states are inner causes of outward behavior. Beliefs and desires are "inside" the subject; they cause behavior, which is more directly observable by others.

metaphysics   The branch of philosophy concerned with specifying the basic kinds of things that exist. Whether electrons exist is a problem for physics, not metaphysics, but whether physical objects exist is a metaphysical question. Other metaphysical questions include the following: Do numbers exist? Does God exist? What is the nature of the relationship between minds and bodies?

method of doubt   The method Descartes used to determine which propositions are foundational. If it's possible to doubt the proposition, then it fails the test. To see if it's possible to doubt a proposition, see if you can construct a story in which the proposition is false even though you believe that it's true.

methodological behaviorism   The view that science shouldn't talk about the inner states of organisms when it attempts to explain behavior.

mind/brain identity theory   *See* identity theory.

multiple realizability   A property (type) is multiply realizable if the tokens that fall under the type need have nothing in common physically. The property of being a mousetrap is multiply realizable. Functionalism claims that psychological properties are multiply realizable.

mutually exclusive   Two characteristics are mutually exclusive when nothing can have both of them. Being a triangle and being a circle are mutually exclusive properties.

naturalistic fallacy   G. E. Moore argued that the ethical properties of an action (for example, its being morally obligatory) aren't identical with any of the "naturalistic" properties that the action has. To deny this, Moore held, is to commit the naturalistic fallacy. A naturalistic property is a property that might be studied in a natural science.

necessary Necessary beings exist in all possible worlds; a necessary proposition is true in all possible worlds. It is customary to distinguish three kinds of necessary propositions: ones that are logically necessary (like "bachelors are bachelors"), ones that are nomologically necessary (like "nothing moves faster than the speed of light"), and ones that are circumstantially necessary (like "this bomb will explode in five minutes").

necessary condition "X is a necessary condition for Y" means that if Y is true, then so is X. That is, it's necessary for X to be true in order for Y to be true. *See* sufficient condition.

normative claim *See* descriptive/normative distinction.

objective A proposition describes an objective matter if the proposition is true (or false) independently of whether anyone believes that the proposition is true (or false).

observation An observational proposition is one you come to believe via the "direct" testimony of sense experience (sight, hearing, taste, touch, smell). One philosophical question about observation concerns what "direct" means in this definition.

Ockham's Razor *See* Principle of Parsimony.

Only Game in Town Fallacy The error of thinking that you are obliged to believe a proposed explanation of an observation just because it's the only explanation that has been proposed.

Ontological Argument An *a priori* argument for the existence of God, proposed by Anselm. It attempts to show that the definition of the concept of God entails that God exists, necessarily.

other minds, problem of This is the problem of explaining how we know that other individuals have minds and how we know what the contents of those minds are.

physicalism *See* materialism.

positivism The philosophical view that sentences about God, morality, aesthetics, and metaphysics are meaningless and are shown to be so by the testability theory of meaning. *See* testability theory of meaning.

possible *See* necessary and contingent.

pragmatism In this book, the philosophical theory that claims that the usefulness of believing a proposition is what makes it reasonable to believe that the proposition is true. Pragmatists also proposed a theory about what truth is.

Principle of Parsimony Otherwise known as Ockham's Razor. This principle says that an explanation that postulates fewer entities or processes is preferable to one that postulates more.

Principle of Sufficient Reason The thesis that everything that happens in nature has an explanation. This idea is part of Aquinas's and Clarke's different versions of the cosmological argument (Lectures 4 and 7).

Principle of the Common Cause A principle governing abductive inference. It asserts that when two or more objects exhibit an intricate set of similarities, the similarities should be explained by postulating a common cause; this is preferable to a separate cause explanation, according to which each object obtained its characteristics independently. Example: Two students hand in identical essays in a philosophy class. It is more plausible to explain this as the result of plagiarism than to think that each student worked independently. The Common Cause Principle is an application of the Surprise Principle.

Principle of the Uniformity of Nature (PUN) The thesis that the future will resemble the past. Hume believed that all inductive arguments presuppose that this principle is true.

proposition   That which is expressed by a true or false declarative sentence. Though the sentence "Lemons are yellow" is part of the English language, the proposition that this sentence expresses is no more a part of English than it is a part of any other human language. A variety of philosophical theories maintain that some declarative sentences don't express propositions (though they may seem to). For example, ethical subjectivism says that ethical statements are neither true nor false. Logical positivism maintains that the statement "God exists" is neither true nor false.

propositional attitudes   Consider the following statements: "*S* believes that lemons are yellow"; "*S* wants to drink a cup of coffee"; "*S* doubts that it will rain." In each of these, a subject, *S*, is said to have an attitude—believing, desiring, or doubting—toward a proposition.

psychological egoism   The doctrine that people's ultimate desires are always self-directed; whenever a person has a desire concerning the situation of others, this desire is purely instrumental—you care about what happens to others only because you think that this will benefit yourself. Psychological egoism denies that people ever have altruistic ultimate motives. Psychological egoism is a descriptive, not a normative, theory.

random   A sampling process is random when each object in the population from which the sample is drawn has the same probability of being drawn.

realism   *See* ethical realism.

reductio ad absurdum   A deductively valid form of argument in which one proves that *P* is true by showing that (1) if *P* were false, *A* would have to be true, and (2) *A* is false.

Redundancy Theory of Truth   This theory claims that to say that a statement is true is to do nothing more than assert the statement: "It's true that snow is white" is just a long-winded way of saying that snow is white.

reference   *See* sense and reference.

relativism   *See* ethical relativism.

relativity   The truth or falsity of a proposition *p* is a relative matter, if *p*'s truth or falsehood depends on an arbitrary choice. Example: Sue and Mary are walking side by side. Is Sue to the left of Mary? That depends on (is relative to) a choice of point of view. There are several equally correct such choices. Whether it's true or false that Sue is to the left of Mary depends on that (arbitrary) choice.

Reliability Theory of Knowledge   A theory that exploits the analogy between a thermometer's reliably representing the temperature and a subject's knowing a proposition to be true. The theory says that *S* knows that *p* if and only if (1) *S* believes that *p;* (2) *p* is true; and (3) in the circumstances that *S* occupies, *S* wouldn't have believed that *p* unless *p* were true.

sample bias   An inductive inference is weakened by its being based on a biased sample. If you want to know what percentage of Americans believe in God, don't conduct your survey by using church membership lists. To do so would probably bias your estimate.

sample size   An inductive inference is made stronger by increasing its sample size. In telephone surveys, your conclusion about the population sampled is on firmer ground if you call more people than if you call fewer.

sense and reference   Two terms in a language may refer to a single object, even though they have different meanings (senses). For example, "The inventor of bifocals" and "the first U.S. ambassador to France" have different senses, though both refer to the same person, namely, Benjamin Franklin. Frege held that terms with the same sense must have the same reference.

skepticism   The thesis that knowledge (or rational justification) is unobtainable. Descartes tried to refute skepticism about knowledge; Hume was a skeptic about the rational justifiability of induction.

soft determinism   The compatibilist thesis that human actions are both free and causally determined.

solipsism   The thesis that the only thing that exists is my mind and its contents.

subjective   A proposition is subjective if its truth or falsehood depends on what occurs in the mind of some subject. *See* objective.

subjectivism   *See* ethical subjectivism.

sufficient condition   "X is a sufficient condition for Y" means that if X is true, so is Y. That is, for Y to be true, it's sufficient for X to be true. *See* necessary condition.

Surprise Principle   A principle governing abductive inference. An observation O strongly favors one hypothesis H_1 over another H_2 when the following two conditions are satisfied, but not otherwise: (1) If H_1 were true, we would expect O to be true; (2) if H_2 were true, we would expect O to be false.

synthetic   *See* analytic.

teleology   An object is described in a teleological fashion when it is described in terms of its goals or purposes.

testability theory of meaning   A positivist doctrine which says that a meaningful sentence must either be analytic or empirical. Statements whose truth or falsity cannot be decided either by reasoning or by observation are meaningless. Some positivists proposed to understand what it means to be empirical in terms of falsifiability. *See* falsifiability.

theodicy   The attempt to reconcile the existence of evil in the world with the idea that God exists and is all-powerful, all-knowing, and all-good.

theorem   *See* axiom.

type/token distinction   A type is a property or characteristic. The individual items that populate the world are called tokens. A given token falls under many types. So, for example, you are a token of the type human being and a token of the type object on the surface of the earth. The type/token distinction is important to functionalism's critique of the Mind/Brain Identity Theory.

universalizability criterion   Kant thought that the ethical permissibility of an action could be determined by seeing if it passes the universalizability test: See if it is possible for the action to be universal (performed by everyone) or if it is possible for a rational agent to will (intend) that the action be universal.

utilitarianism   The ethical theory that the action you should perform in a given situation is the one that would promote the greatest good for the greatest number of individuals. Hedonistic utilitarianism equates goodness with the feeling of pleasure and the absence of the feeling of pain. Preference utilitarianism says that the good to be maximized is the satisfaction of preferences. Utilitarian theories also are distinguished by whether they are act or rule utilitarian. An act utilitarian says that it's the consequences of the token action under consideration that need to be considered. A rule utilitarian says that it's the long-term effects of the type of action that are relevant to deciding whether to perform a token act of that type.

validity   *See* deductive validity.

verifiability   *See* testability theory of meaning.

vitalism   The theory that living things differ from nonliving things because they possess a special immaterial substance—an *élan vital*—that animates them with life. Vitalism and dualism both reject materialism.

Index

Made in the USA
Columbia, SC
18 January 2021